Bashar Hikmet Malkawi

Jordan and the World Trading System

D1806324

Bashar Hikmet Malkawi

Jordan and the World Trading System

A Case Study for Arab Countries

VDM Verlag Dr. Müller

Impressum/Imprint (nur für Deutschland/ only for Germany)
Bibliografische Information der Deutschen Nationalbibliothek: Die Deutsche Nationalbibliothek
verzeichnet diese Publikation in der Deutschen Nationalbibliografie; detaillierte bibliografische
Daten sind im Internet über http://dnb.d-nb.de abrufbar.
Alle in diesem Buch genannten Marken und Produktnamen unterliegen warenzeichen-, marken-
oder patentrechtlichem Schutz bzw. sind Warenzeichen oder eingetragene Warenzeichen der
jeweiligen Inhaber. Die Wiedergabe von Marken, Produktnamen, Gebrauchsnamen,
Handelsnamen, Warenbezeichnungen u.s.w. in diesem Werk berechtigt auch ohne besondere
Kennzeichnung nicht zu der Annahme, dass solche Namen im Sinne der Warenzeichen- und
Markenschutzgesetzgebung als frei zu betrachten wären und daher von jedermann benutzt
werden dürften.

Coverbild: www.ingimage.com

Verlag: VDM Verlag Dr. Müller GmbH & Co. KG
Dudweiler Landstr. 99, 66123 Saarbrücken, Deutschland
Telefon +49 681 9100-698, Telefax +49 681 9100-988
Email: info@vdm-verlag.de
Zugl.: Washington, American University, Law, Diss., 2005

Herstellung in Deutschland:
Schaltungsdienst Lange o.H.G., Berlin
Books on Demand GmbH, Norderstedt
Reha GmbH, Saarbrücken
Amazon Distribution GmbH, Leipzig
ISBN: 978-3-8364-9256-0

Imprint (only for USA, GB)
Bibliographic information published by the Deutsche Nationalbibliothek: The Deutsche
Nationalbibliothek lists this publication in the Deutsche Nationalbibliografie; detailed
bibliographic data are available in the Internet at http://dnb.d-nb.de.
Any brand names and product names mentioned in this book are subject to trademark, brand
or patent protection and are trademarks or registered trademarks of their respective holders. The
use of brand names, product names, common names, trade names, product descriptions etc.
even without a particular marking in this works is in no way to be construed to mean that such
names may be regarded as unrestricted in respect of trademark and brand protection legislation
and could thus be used by anyone.

Cover image: www.ingimage.com

Publisher: VDM Verlag Dr. Müller GmbH & Co. KG
Dudweiler Landstr. 99, 66123 Saarbrücken, Germany
Phone +49 681 9100-698, Fax +49 681 9100-988
Email: info@vdm-publishing.com

Printed in the U.S.A.
Printed in the U.K. by (see last page)
ISBN: 978-3-8364-9256-0

Jordan and the World Trading System

A Case Study for Arab Countries

By

Bashar Hikmet Malkawi

To my mother, my father, and my sister. All my joy and love

ACKNOWLEDGEMENTS

This work would not have been achieved without Allah's guidance to give me the will and health to pursue this endeavor. Although I believe in "the Bicycle Theory" of international trade, meaning the trading system should move forward without stopping as trade negotiations proceed, otherwise, risk standstill and falling; I would like to thank some people where the bicycle that I ride made major stops before launching a new stage. For those whose names are not mentioned in these stops, minor or major, I ask your forgiveness for not mentioning yours at this time.

In the final stop, my deepest and sincere gratitude goes to Professor Padideh Ala'i, my mentor, in Washington D.C for devoting hours of her time to discuss my work. Many thanks for her critical comments, encouragement, and advice. Believing also in the most-favored-nation rule, meaning any advantage or privilege extended to one party must be extended to other parties, my same deepest and sincere gratitude goes to Professor David A. Gantz in Arizona for giving me the chance to be here from the outset, and for his constructive guidance. My first exposure to the world of international trade law was by his hand that left upon me a lifetime impression. I also thank Professors Jerry Levinson, Christine Farley, and Mohammad Mattar, American University Washington College of Law for their comments. I am also indebted to Donna B. Butler of American University Law School and Deborah Beaumont, library specialist at the University of Arizona College of Law for their comments on earlier drafts of this work. I also would like to thank Eleazar Jimenez Esq. of Sonora, Mexico and Cristos Velasco Esq. of Mexico City, Mexico for their input on NAFTA. My thanks also go to Dr. Yasser K. Hamed of Minnesota, and Betty R. Thomas of Michigan for their unforgettable assistance. My appreciation is due to Robert and Martha Ludwig in Colorado, Ronald and Roemae Canfield in Utah, Charles and Dorothy Sutherland in California, Bill and Kay Trowbridge in Idaho, and the bicycle will keep pedaling.

TABLE OF CONTENTS

CHAPTER I. ISLAMIC LAW AND INTERNATIONAL TRADE

CHAPTER II. ARAB COUNTRIES AND THE WORLD TRADING ORGANIZATION

CHAPTER III. JORDAN BID FOR ACCESSION TO THE WTO

TABLES

INTRODUCTION

The purpose of this book is to examine the implications of the international trading system to Arab countries. Given Jordan accession to the WTO and its free trade agreement with the United States (U.S.), the country is an ideal candidate to serve as a case study for other Arab countries. Jordan applied for WTO membership in 1994. After a lengthy and costly process of negotiations, Jordan became a WTO member in 2000. Furthermore, in 2000, the U.S. and Jordan concluded a bilateral trade agreement.

My claim is that acceding to the WTO and signing a bilateral trade agreement with the U.S. is like choosing between Scylla and Charybdis, because onerous trade liberalization commitments ensue from such actions. The WTO system as an institution may not be perfect. There are deficiencies in the system. However, membership in the WTO could afford better chances compared with bilateral trade agreements like the one between the U.S. and Jordan. Membership in the WTO could help Jordan, in cooperation with other Arab countries, preserve its rights. In current bilateral trade agreements, economic hegemonies such as the U.S. dictate the rules and weave them to their advantage. In sum, I make the point that the alternative to the WTO system is bilateral trade agreements with the U.S., and they are trade agreements in which Arab countries are bound to be disadvantaged.

Historically, the study of international trade (law) in Arab countries was an obscure subject for a handful of economics specialists. This book will help pinpoint the lacunae in this kind of scholarship by cutting across many subjects, using multiple methodologies and interdisciplinary approaches, such as religion, naked economics, and law-international as well as domestic. The book will pave the way for a new scholarship that involves international trade legal economists in addition to agricultural economists, industrial economists, political economists, or econometricians.[1] Therefore, it is hoped that this book will contribute to an understanding of the under-studied international trade law in Arab countries.

ROADMAP

The book will proceed in five chapters. Chapter I analyzes Islamic law and economics and their relevance to international trade. It discusses Islamic thought on matters such as reciprocity, taxes, subsidies, price mechanisms, and role of the state. Chapter I concludes by proving that Islamic law is inclined toward free trade. However, Islamic law sets out limitations on free trade. International trade in Islamic law is trade with what might be termed as Islamic purifier.

---

[1] No graphs, equations, or complex diagrams will be used, just plain English. See Richard C. Wydick, *Plain English for Lawyers* (4th ed., Academic Press 1998). Most economics texts rely far too much on algebra manipulation, complex diagrams, equations, excessive use of mathematics, and inaccessible jargon. For more see Charles Wheelan, *Naked Economics: Undressing the Dismal Science* X, XVII (Norton & Company 2002).

Chapter II explores trade patterns of Arab countries. It addresses some of the obstacles Arab countries face in acceding to the WTO. Chapter II also examines the effects of accession to the WTO on selected sectors such as agriculture and oil for Arab countries. Chapter II concludes that Arab countries are not active participants in the WTO work. Arab countries also lack effective missions in Geneva solely dedicated to the work of the WTO. Moreover, the dream of Arab regional trade agreement or common market has not come true, despite the fact that free trade once profoundly reigned in the region, and despite the fact that many Arab countries are bound together by ties of common culture, ethnicity, and language.

Chapter III addresses the status of international trade agreements into the domestic law of Jordan. It also tackles the relationship between the National Assembly, the executive branch, and the judiciary in respect of international trade, and the bodies in Jordan that have the power to enter into international agreements. It touches on the legal effects of international agreements, and the cases where international agreements prevail over domestic law. Chapter III also offers insights into Jordan's accession to the WTO. Further, it uncovers commitments Jordan undertook in its accession to the WTO as a case study for other Arab countries. Chapter III concludes that government agency conflict in Jordan appears in the overlapping jurisdictions of the different executive authorities rather than between the executive and the National Assembly. In its accession, Jordan undertook onerous terms and conditions as a price for accession to the WTO. Jordan did not benefit from any transitional period in its accession to the WTO except in implementation of commitments on tariff reduction. Jordan met some of its WTO commitments at the time it entered the WTO. However, Jordan was committed to meet other requirements after accession over time. Many areas of implementation of the WTO agreements require heavy administrative and financial investment.

Chapter IV scrutinizes U.S.-Jordan Free Trade Agreement including its environmental and labor provisions. Chapter IV concludes that the bilateral trade agreement between the U.S. and Jordan will lead to trade dependency on the U.S. market. The approach adopted in drafting the bilateral trade agreement is a cut and paste approach in which U.S. laws were incorporated into the agreement with few changes in article, numbers or words. The entire bilateral trade agreement was an adhesion or unconscionable contract submitted by the U.S. as a *fait accompli*. Jordan was a "rule-taker" rather than a "rule-maker". The parties in the trade agreement entered into asymmetrical commitments in areas such as services and intellectual property.

Chapter IV concludes that the free trade agreement between the U.S. and Jordan would have been of little value, giving the volume of trade between the parties, except for including environment and labor within the text of the agreement. The U.S. acted as demander for including labor and environment within the free trade agreement. The environmental and labor provisions of the free trade agreement represent material steps in advancing the environmental and labor agenda by linking the free trade agreement with non-trade provisions. However, these articles fall short of expectations. The trade agreement does not prohibit the parties from encouraging trade by relaxing domestic environmental and labor laws. Instead, the free trade agreement simply urges the parties not to relax their laws. Free trade agreement does not define the relationship between the trade agreement and the multilateral environmental agreements. The free trade agreement includes a scapegoat clause that allows each party not to effectively enforce its environment or labor laws on the basis of reasonable exercise of discretion or *bona fide* decision to allocate resources. Chapter IV concludes that environment and labor will be, as they have traditionally been viewed, secondary to trade agreements. The U.S. should not use Jordan as a pawn to advance its own agenda on environment and labor. In Islamic jurisprudence,   there   are   historical   links   to   trade.

CHAPTER I

ISLAMIC LAW AND INTERNATIONAL TRADE

I. Links to the Past[2]

As for the sea, we hold it is as the way of dry land. Allah said:
Allah it is who subdued to ye the sea that vessels may sail thereon by his
command and that ye may seek of his bounty. Therefore, he has given
permission that he who wills may trade thereon and I hold that no
obstacle shall be placed between it and any of the people. For the dry land
and sea alike belong to Allah. He has subdued them for his servants
to seek of his bounty in both of them. How then should we intervene
between Allah's servants and their means of livelihood?[3]

Muslims believe that Islam is the last religion. Islam is called the seal of religions.
Islam, unlike the Talmud for Orthodox Judaism or Bible in Christianity, not only covers
moral or spiritual teachings, but also it covers every aspect of life such as trade. Islamic
shari'a places religion as well as economics in the consciousness of Muslims. Therefore,
Islam is comprehensive in coverage. Some rules in Islam may be stretched out to meet

---

[2] The perspective presented in this chapter is neither perfect nor an oversimplification of a complicated
topic. The researcher is not a scholar of Islam and certainly learns about Islamic teachings on a daily basis.
The whole history of trade in Islam will not be discussed in this chapter. This chapter will not involve a
process whereby selective ideas are extracted from Islamic law to claim that Islam and free trade are the
same. This chapter is suitable for Westerners who may not have heard about Islam and free trade until
recently, but not Arabs who may know it well. This chapter also serves to endear the topic to the ears of
Arabs because they do need to look back in order to move forward. Moreover, the purpose is to write a
chapter that would invigorate the reader to explore, beyond the scope of the chapter, the question of trade
and Islam.
[3] Sermon delivered by the Caliph *'Umar Ibn 'Abd Al-'Az̄iz*. See *Al-Khal̄ifah Al-'ꟼadil 'Umar Ibn 'Abd
Al-'Az̄iz, Kh̄amis Al- Khulaf̄a' A R̄ashid̄in [The Fifth Rightly-Guided Caliph 'Umar Ibn 'Abd Al-\
'Az̄iz], Li-Ab̄i Muhammad 'Abd All̄ah Ibn 'Abd Al-Hakam; Riw̄ayat Ibnihi Ab̄I 'Abd All̄Ah
Muhammad, Mur̄aja'ah Wa-ta'l̄iq Ahmad 'Abd Al-Taww̄ab 'Awad* 101 (D̄ar al-Fad̄ilah 1994).

10

current issues while maintaining certain core principles as static.[4] Indeed, Islam is a durable living force.

Free trade is about people selling and buying as they want without barriers or obstacles. Free trade has links in Islam. This proposition is to refute any doubt that free trade is alien to Arab countries and a response to the myth that Islamic law is passé or just is not applicable to modern trade law. This proposition is also an opportunity to discuss matters beyond interest, the centerpiece of Islamic economics.[5] However, Islamic law and economics do not adopt free trade as the single theorem *per se* or economic code of Islam. There are limitations on free trade in Islam such as prohibition of trade in pork and alcohol. International trade in Islam is trade with an Islamic "purifier". This is an Islamic market economy.

According to the teachings of the Prophet Muhammad (s.a.w), the pursuit of trade and profit are not inferior but honorable.[6] Allah's choice of prophet, who was a trader by profession from a trading society, highlights the importance of trade.[7] The dominant tribe in Mecca, *Quraysh*, earned its livelihood for decades selling commodities for a profit.[8] Camel caravans, originating in the Middle East, are well known in history for travel along major trade routes.

---

[4] These core principles are stated in the discussion of sources of law in Islam, p. 15.

[5] See Timur Kuran, *The Discontents of Islamic Economic Morality*, 86 Am. Econ. Rev. 438, 439 (1996) (Islamic economics is dedicated to restructuring economic thought and practice on the basis of fundamental Islamic teachings. Its founders were Indian Muslims in the 1940s. Sayyid Abu 'l-A'la Maududi coined the term "Islamic economics" around the time of India's partition. Afterward, Pakistanis have made the largest contribution to the literature. The blanket prohibition against interest became the centerpiece of Islamic economics. Attention then turned to issues such as rules of barter, rights of slaves, and transactions. The intended effect of Islamic economics is to reform human nature. The goal of Islamic economics is to transform selfish and acquisitive Homo economicus into a paragon of virtue, Homo Islamicus). Although interest and Islamic banking is the first and perhaps the most interesting application of Islamic economics relevant to modern times, interest and Islamic banking has been written about to death.

[6] S.A.W letters are abbreviations for the Arabic words "*Salla Allahu 'Alaihi Wa Sallam*". It is an Islamic term of respect typically following a reference to the name of the Prophet Muhammad. "Peace be Upon Him" is used by English speaking Muslims. However, "Peace be Upon Him" does not give full meaning to "*Salla Allahu 'Alaihi Wa Sallam*" words. Therefore, the words "*Salla Allahu 'Alaihi Wa Sallam*" should be used. See *Glossary of Islamic Religious, Banking & Financial Terms*, 6 J. Islamic L. & Culture 135, 148, 150 (2001). To determine if profit is profiteering, there must be an analysis of prevalent market prices and trading practices among similar merchants.

[7] See Chibli Mallat, *Commercial Law in the Middle East: Between Classical Transactions and Modern Business*, 48 Am. J. Comp. L. 81, 92 (2000) (a long-standing tradition of Islamic civilization is its association with and the centrality of trade. The tradition relating to the other great monotheistic epigones in the figures of Abraham and Jesus does not acknowledge the centrality of trade and commerce in any similar way. In the case of Jesus, the episode of the Temple merchants even points in the opposite direction, with the mercantile pursuit of wealth depicted in a derogatory manner. Neither classical Christianity or Judaism seems to have extolled the virtues of commerce in such a detailed or enthusiastic argument for the commercial professions as did *Dimashqi* in his *Mahasin al-tijara*, The Virtues of Commerce).

[8] See Gene W. Heck, *The Economic Dynamic of the Early Islamic State* 43-44 (1995).

11

The holy Qur'an is filled with numerous verses using the language of trade. For instance, it states, "O ye who believe! Eat not up your property among yourselves in vanities; But let there be amongst you traffic and trade by mutual good will".[9] This verse signifies trade on the basis of mutual consent free from undue interference. The Qur'an also states, "For the covenants (Of security and safeguard Enjoyed) by the Quraysh, Their covenants (covering) journeys by winter and summer- Let them adore the Lord of this House, Who provides them With food against hunger, And with security Against fear (of danger)".[10]

Discussion of international trade and its relevance will be limited to Islamic law.[11] However, before discussing Islamic law and its relation to international trade it would be helpful to provide a background of Islamic law, one of the world's major legal systems along with Jewish law (Halacha), civil law, and common law. The Discussion of Islamic law and its sources is essential to understanding the importance of these sources on the relationship between free trade and Islam.

A. Sources of Law in Islam

The law or *shari'a* in Islam may be thought of as being composed of at least two parts: revealed and non-revealed.[12] The revealed form of *shari'a* has two proper sources: the Qur'an (the holy book) and the *sunna* (traditions based on the *hadith*, sayings and actions of the prophet).[13] Non-revealed sources of *shari'a*, developed by Muslim jurists after the revelation of the Qur'an and the *sunna*, include *ijma* (consensus of Muslim scholars on a point of law) and *qiyas* (a sub-*ijtihad* species of strict analogical reasoning). These are the authoritative sources of jurisprudence (*usul al-fiqh*).[14] *Usul al-fiqh*

---

[9] See Qur'an 4:29. See also Qur'an 2:282, 17:66, 24:37, 35:28, and 62:11.

[10] *Id.* 106:1-4. The historical background of these verses is that the *Quraysh*, the dominant tribe in Mecca, conducted international trade by setting out two caravan journeys, one from Mecca to the warmth of Syria in summer and the other to the cooler Yemen in winter, to sell cheaper leather and clothing than those made in Syria and Yemen. Thus, trade provided them with a living. However, for the safety of these caravans, trade agreements were concluded with the tribes on the routes. In return, the *Quraysh*, agreed to collect these tribes' goods to sell, and on the way back hand them over other goods See Patricia Crone, *Meccan Trade and the Rise of Islam* 109, 205-209 (Princeton U. Press 1987).

[11] For a Christian biblical and theological themes on international trade see Daniel Rush Finn, *Just Trading: On the Ethics and Economics of International Trade* 47-87 (Abingdon Press 1996) (stating that it would be a serious mistake to expect to find in the biblical sources a neatly transferable ethic of international trade for Christians today. At the same time, however, it would be a mistake to presume that international trade is a purely modern phenomenon).

[12] *Shari'a* is an Arabic word meaning way. The *shari'a* was compiled during the first three centuries after Muhammad's (s.a.w) death. See Ahmed Zaki Yamani, *The Eternal Shari'a*, 12 N.Y.U. J. Intl. L. & Pol. 205, 205-06 (1979).

[13] The Qur'an is divided into 114 chapters, known as *surahs*. Each *surah* is divided into verses, called "*ayas*" which mean "signs", referring to signs from and of Allah. There are roughly 6000 verses. See Bhala, *infra* n. 21, at 680.

[14] See William M. Ballantyne & Howard L. Stovall, *Arab Commercial Law: Principles and Perspectives* 28-30 (ABA 2002). See also John Walbridge, *Logic in the Islamic Intellectual Tradition: The Recent Centuries*, Vol. 39 No. 1 Islamic Stud. 55, 68 (2000) (Islamic law is divided into two disciplines: *fiqh*, which the content of the sacred law, and *usul al-fiqh*, the principles by which it is deduced. *Usul* is a system of rules by which new law is derived from a fixed body of source materials. It deals with such problems as

incorporates both deductive (from broad general principles in the law to a particular case) and inductive (from a particular case to general principles) methods of reasoning. Other sources of non-revealed *shari'a* include *ijtihad* (individual intellectual effort and wider independent reasoning), *istihsan* (equity or juristic preference), *istishab* (presumption of continuity), *istislah* or *maslaha* (opinion based on public interest), *darura* (necessity), *urf* (custom), and *fatwa* giving *(responsa)* of *muftis* (jurisconsults) such as the Egyptian grand *mufti* Muhammad 'Abduh.[15]

To establish direct support for a legal proposition a Muslim legal scholar should be able to pinpoint to a verse of the Qur'an, or at least a tradition or *hadith* of the Prophet Muhammad (s.a.w). While the Qur'an provides the written law, the *sunna* supplies a sort of case law, consistent with the Qur'anic text. The *sunna* embodies the application of the Qur'an's written law to concrete disputes and hypothetical questions that arose during the prophet's life. Some *sunna* cases simply explain the Qur'anic principles and rules. Some cases interpret the Qur'anic text by providing new insights into the written law. Some provide new principles and rules, supplementing the Qur'an's protected knowledge.

If direct support of a legal proposition in the Qur'an and *sunna* is not possible, then a Muslim legal scholar seeks an instance when all legal scholars or jurists agree on a particular point of law or interpretation. Consensus may be relied upon as a valid source of law. Use of analogical reasoning, *qiyas*, is quite strict. First, one must find a verse in the Qur'an, a *sunna* of the prophet, or a rule on which consensus was achieved as the point of departure. Then the direct cause, purpose or rationale, narrowly conceived, must be determined, and the relationship between the two concerns, the one in which there is a rule and the one to which one is considering extending the rule, must be elucidated in such a way as to demonstrate that the rule should be extended. For example, the Qur'anic prohibition of drinking wine extends to other alcoholic beverages without concern about gray areas. On the other hand, the relaxation of the duty to fast in cases of illness and

---

how to derive a general rule from a known particular case, how words can legitimately be interpreted, and so on).

[15] See Hasbullah Haji Abdul Rahman, *The Origin and Development of Ijtihad to Solve Modern Complex Legal Problems*, Vol. 43 The Islamic Q. 73, 75-76 (No. 2, 1999) (*ijtihad* must not be exercised as to the existence of Allah, the truism of the prophets of Allah, and the authenticity of the Qur'an. To exercise *ijtihad* a Muslim has to be knowledgeable of the Qur'an, *sunna*, and *usul al-fiqh*. A Muslim also must be a good Muslim, pious and law-abiding, and not influenced by heresy, just, and reliable). See also *Islamic Legal Interpretation: Muftis and their Fatwas* 4-32, 286-296 (Muhammad Khalid Masud et al. eds., Harvard U. Press 1996) (a *fatwa* is a nonbinding advisory opinion to an individual questioner (*mustafti*) in connection with ongoing human affairs. A *fatwa* may cover issues concerning mosques, intergenerational transmission of property, and marriage of children, and banking operations and interest. *Fatwa* began as a private activity that was independent of any state control before being transformed into a mechanism of religious legitimization. The formulation of *fatwa* is patterned after a question-answer model. Important *muftis* in the pre-modern era were *Mu'adh b. Jabal*, *Ibn 'Abbas*, and *Ibn Rushd*. Modern era muftis include *Muhammad Sayyed Tantawi*, grand *mufti* of the Egyptian Republic and head of *Dar al-ifta'*, *Makhluf* (*Fatwa* Office), *al-Qaradawi*, and 'Abd al-'Aziz b. 'Abd Allah Ibn Baz.). An example of the use of *fatwa* as a mechanism of religious legitimization is the plan of Egypt's Ministry of Religious Affairs in 2004 to connect all 5,000 of Cairo's mosques to a city-wide wireless network, so that five times a day the Muslim call to prayer [*adhan*] could be broadcast in a single voice, in the same instant. To counter criticism for the idea as *bid'a* (irreligious innovation), the Ministry obtained several *fatwas*.

traveling cannot be extended so easily.[16] Applying the concept of hardship to the deliberation is not helpful because travelers would not always find fasting a hardship. Moreover, *hardship* is a very broad and fuzzy concept. The divine purpose or cause of the rule is not mere hardship, and so extension of the relaxation would not be discrete or defined.

All Muslim scholars agree that the Qur'an is the core of Islamic law. However, there is disagreement among them about the rank of other sources of Islamic law. Consequently, there have arisen four main schools of law in *Sunni*: the Hanafi, Maliki, Shafi'i, and Hanbali.[17] Hanafi scholars rely on reason and opinion, using analogy and equity as sources of law. The Maliki school requires strict application of the *sunna* of the Prophet and minimizes the role of opinion. The Shafi'i school has tried to reconcile the Maliki and Hanafi principles.[18] The Hanbali school is well known for its strict adherence to the text of the Qur'an and the *sunna*. Analogy is recognized as a source of Hanbali law.

The *shari'a* tries to describe all possible human acts, classify it as obligatory, recommended, neutral, objectionable, or forbidden by Allah (s.w.t), the supreme legislator.[19] Islamic law addresses matters ranging from the timing of daily prayers and prohibitions against eating certain foods to marriage, inheritance, and commerce. The Qur'an speaks much more explicitly and completely about personal status (marriage and inheritance), morality, and an individual's relationship with Allah (s.w.t) than it does about commerce.[20]

---

[16] See Gamal M. Badr, *Islamic Law: Its Reaction to Other Legal Systems*, 26 Am. J.Comp.L. 187, 189 (1978).

[17] Islam embraces two principal branches: Sunnism, the majority faith, and Shi'ism. The most important group in Shi'ism is the Twelvers. Other Shi'ism schools include Ismailism and Zeydism. See Yann Richard, *Shi'ite Islam: polity, ideology, and creed* 1, 5-9 (Antonia Nevill trans., Blackwell 1995) (Shi'ites are Muslims, like the Sunnis, but there are differences between them. Unlike Sunnism which insists on the arbitrary will of Allah, Shi'ism proclaims that Allah can only act within the bounds of justice. The Imam in Shi'ism plays a fundamental role in the relations between Allah and man. Moreover, Shi'ite doctrines are based on collections of traditions quite distinct from those of the Sunnis. Shi'ite doctrine varies noticeably from Sunni as regards inheritance and marriage). See David Bonderman, *Modernization and Changing Perception of Islamic Law*, 81 Harv. L. Rev. 1169, 1174 (1968) (schools of law in *Sunni* appeared in the first and second centuries of Islam. They developed initially due to geographical separation-one at Medina, one at Kufa in Iraq, one in Syria- for example. After a few centuries, each school became personalized and took the name of its leading scholar. Each school developed its own body of legal doctrine, but they were similar in broad precepts. They disagreed as to particular points of law).

[18] Al Shafi'i, the founder of al- Shafi'i law school, has been known as the founder of Islamic jurisprudence. He was the first jurist to compile and systematize Islamic sources of law.

[19] S.W.T letters are abbreviations of the words *"Subhanahu Wa Ta'ala"* which means that *Allah is* purified of having partners or sons. When the name of Almighty Allah is pronounced, a Muslim is to show his respect to him by reciting these words. See *Glossary of Islamic Religious, Banking & Financial Terms, supra* n. 6, at 153.

[20] For an interesting discussion of Islamic law see M. Cherif Bassiouni & Gamal M. Badr, The *Shari'ah: Sources, Interpretation, and Rule-Making*, 1 UCLA J. Islamic & Near E. L. 135, 149 (2002) (the Qur'an and the *sunna* contain the greater number of norms applicable to the areas of criminal law, family law, contracts and obligations, procedure, and inheritance law as compared to other subjects within the *mu'amalat* category (societal relations and individual interactions). Being a book [Qur'an] of spiritual guidance and not a legal code, it is not surprising to find only 500 verses with legal content).

With respect to the daily, private lives of all Muslims, Islam has five pillars that are the essential obligations. These are: (1) the profession of faith (the *Shahada* which affirms monotheism in its first part, and the authenticity of Prophet Muhammad (s.a.w) in its second part as it states that "There is no God but Allah; Muhammad is the messenger of Allah"), (2) regular prayer (called *salat* which is performed five times a day), (3) compulsory charity (called *zakat*), (4) fasting during the month of Ramadan (called *sawm*), and (5) pilgrimage (the *Hajj*).[21]

II. The Role of Islamic State

Medina, known previously as *T̄abah*, was much poorer than Mecca because its people were not merchants. *Medina* had no pilgrimage destination like the Ka'ba. *Medina* also experienced deep-rooted enmity between groups of its citizens.[22] After his arrival in *Medina*, Prophet Muhammad (s.a.w) established a Mosque (*Masjid*) for worship and education. His next act was to create a new set of trade regulations. These were based on the principles of no restrictions.[23] Neither did Prophet Muhammad (s.a.w) nor did the four Rightly-Guided Caliphs (*Al-Rashidin*) who succeeded him, directly engaged in trade and competition.[24] They regulated trade so as to prevent unfair trade, deception or fraud.[25] However, later Islamic governments tempted by profitability, competed with enterprises to the detriment of their societies.

---

[21] See Raj Bhala, *Theological Categories for Special and Differential Treatment*, 50 U. Kan. L. Rev. 635, 677 (2002). Muslims, both Sunnis and Shi'ites, are under the ritual obligation to accomplish *hajj* to the holiest sites in Mecca at least once in their lifetime. Shi'ites give importance to visiting the tombs of saints. The great centers of Shi'ite pilgrimage in Iraq are Karbala, Najaf, Samarra, and Kazemeyn. The great center of Shi'ite pilgrimage in Iran is Mashhad. See Richard, *supra* n. 17, at 8-9.

[22] See Muhammad Al-Ghazali, *Understanding the Life of the Prophet Mohammad* 155 (Intl. Islamic Fedn. Student Org. 1997). Due to the sanctuary of Mecca, trade created an environment where rivalry was foregone even among enemies. Qur'an states, "Nor wickedness, Nor wrangling In the Hajj. It is no crime in you If ye seek of the bounty Of your Lord (during pilgrimage)". See Qur'an 2:197-198.

[23] After the persecution of the newly Muslims at the hand of the people of Mecca became unbearable, Allah ordained the Muslims to migrate, *Hijra*, to *Medina*. See Abd Assamii Al-Misry, *Al-Masrif Al-isl̄Am̄i 'Ilm̄iyan Wa-'Amal̄iyan* [Islamic Bank in Theory and Practice] 7 (Maktabat Wahbah 1988) (ranking free trade as the first characteristic of the new regulations in *Medina* followed by justice, avoidance of cheating, and monopolies).

[24] Caliph *Umar* said that the ruler should not trade because when he involves himself in trade he has it entirely for himself and to the detriment of others, even if he does not like to do so. See 'Ubayd, *supra* note 3, at 103.

[25] Prophet Muhammad (s.a.w) objected to some cases of deception, known in Islam as *Najsh*, when one raises the prices of goods, in an auction, without the intention of buying. He considered the practice improper. See KHAN, *infra* n. 42, at 198. Other example of objections involved alteration of measure and weight in goods. The Qur'an commands that full measure and weight be given fairly in trade. The Qur'an states, "Woe to those who when they have to give by measure or weight to men, give less than due". See Qur'an 83:1-3. Prophet Muhammad (s.a.w) acted in determining the measures upon verse 83:3. A special institution was established in Islam, known as *al-hisba*, to regulate standards and measures of goods to prevent deception for consumers. Additionally, Islamic jurisprudence prohibits selling below market price. For example, Caliph *Umar bin al-khttab* directed another person, who sold goods below the price available in the market, and demanded him either to raise the price or to leave the market. See Munazzmat Al-Mu'tamar Al-Isl̄am̄i, *infra* n. 48, at 118, 163.

In Islamic society, like in most others, some have more resources than others and some are gifted with more abilities than others.[26] In other words, people are not equal in terms of resources and abilities. The role is for the individual himself to make an effort in the direction of increasing his share.[27] Many Muslim jurists agree that a Muslim must do his utmost to earn a livelihood.[28] They assert the negative effects of subsidies. Muslim jurists tend not to support the arguments made for subsidies that they alleviate poverty and increase equality and efficiency.[29] By the same token, infant industries should not depend on state subsidies. Subsidies should be temporary. Nevertheless, the Islamic state has the role of addressing social injustice through available mechanisms such as *Zakat*, Islamic rules of inheritance, and taxes. These mechanisms can be used to redistribute wealth.

The role of the early Islamic state was confined to provide necessities such as public services and law enforcement.[30] The state should be a minimal state in terms of being involved in trade.[31] The state should not be in the business of making profit. When the Islamic state relaxes its grip on trade, prosperity may flourish for society.

A. The Administration of Tariffs in the Early Islamic State

The most visible barrier to trade is a tariff, a tax imposed on imported products at the border.[32] Islam recognizes a number of taxes. These taxes fall into four main categories.

---

[26] The Qur'an states, "It is He Who hath made You (His) agents, inheritors of the earth: He hath raised You in ranks some, above others". See Qur'an 6:165. The Qur'an also states, "Allah has bestowed His gifts Of sustenance more freely on some Of you than others". See Qur'an 16:71, 4:32. See also Sayyid Abu 'L-A'la Maududi, *Towards Understanding the Qur'an*, VOL.IV 344, 345 (Zafar Ishaq Ansari Trans., Islamic Found. 1988).

[27] See Qur'an 62:10

[28] The Qur'an stresses "Will Allah change the condition Of a people until they Change their own inner selves". *Id.* 13:11. Caliph *Umar* emphasized that no one should refrain from seeking a livelihood and say, O Allah! Give me sustenance, for the sky will certainly not rain gold and silver. For more on opinions of jurists see M.Umer Chapra, *Islam and the Economic Challenge* 232 (Islamic Found. 1992).

[29] *Id.* 292.

[30] Government may need to deliver public services because of free-rider problems, otherwise these services would not be produced.

[31] For discussion on the role of the government see Muhammad Akram Khan, *Public Finance in Islam*, 40.2 Islamic Stud. 227, 231, 251 (2001) (public expenditure in Islamic economy will follow hierarchy of needs giving priority to essentials, followed by complementaries, and desirables. The government should refrain from performing all the functions that the private sector can perform. On the whole, *shari'a* is tilted toward free trade).

[32] *Ibn Khaldun* explained that tariffs, *maks* in Arabic, seem to come from custom or habit. Tariffs are imposed by the state degree by degree to the extent that they exceed the just limit and they become a custom. See Ibn Khaldun, *Muqaddimat Ibn Khaldun [Introduction of Ibn Khaldun], Mahhada Lah¯a Wa-Nashar Al-Fus¯ul Wa-Al-Faqar¯at Al-N¯aqisah Min Tab¯ath¯a, Wa-Haqqaqah¯A Wa-Dabat Kalim¯atah¯a Wa-Sharahah¯a Wa-'Allaqa 'Alayh¯a Wa-'Amilafah¯arisah¯A 'Al¯i 'Abd Al-W¯ahid W¯af¯i*, VOL. II, 668-669 (Lajnat al-Bay¯an al-'Arab¯i 1957). For an English translation in three volumes of *Ibn Khaldun*'s *Muqaddimah* see Ibn Khaldun, *The Muqaddimah: An Introduction to History* LIV (Franz Rosenthal trans., Princeton U. Press 1958) (*Ibn Khaldun* wrote his masterpiece, *Muqaddimah*, in 1377. Ibn Khaldun's *Muqaddimah* is the first volume of seven volumes which comprise his book "*Kitab al-'Ibar*". In

The first is *Zakat*, an obligatory religious tax, calculated annually on a minimum of possessions at a fixed rate paid to assist the poor as commanded by the scripture.[33] The second is *Sadaqa*, a voluntary tax on every Muslim.[34] Each Muslim, if he agrees to pay *Sadaqa*, pays from his own money according to his capacity and for the benefit of the eligible, such as the poor.[35] The third is *Ghanima* which is the share of the Islamic government from the proceeds of war.[36] In modern times, where war may be rare, *Ghanima* is inapplicable. The last tax is known as *Jizya*, a tax imposed on the people of religions other than Islam for their protection.[37] Beyond these four main religious taxes, no other taxes formed any source of public revenue for the early Islamic state.

The question that comes to mind next is, if *Zakat, Sadaqa, Ghanima,* and *Jizya* were the only taxes imposed in the early Islamic state, then how were the subsequent expenditures of the Islamic state financed, especially after its enlargement? An Islamic state has the right to impose other taxes according to Prophet Muhammad (s.a.w) *Hadith* "in your money, there are taxes besides *Zakat*".[38] However, a tax system ought to be based on equity, efficiency, and simplicity.[39]

The Prophet Muhammad (s.a.w) condemned the imposition of tariffs in the strongest words. He said in a *Hadith*; "One who wrongfully takes an extra tax (*Sahib Maks*) will not enter Paradise".[40] The *Hadith* addresses customs duties specifically as well as *Zakat* taken by the tax collector on above what is due. Moreover, the *Hadith* places a blanket prohibition on tariffs regardless of the citizenship, or religion of a trader, or local content of Muslim goods.

The *Hadith* of Prophet Muhammad (s.a.w) regarding tariffs not only set out the doctrine, it was also practiced. Trade in *Medina* remained duty-free for nearly seventy years until customs duties were levied during the reign of Caliph *Mu'awiyah Bin Abi Sufyan*. Customs duties were abolished in the reign of Caliph *Umar Abd Al-Aziz*. However, later in time, when it came to his knowledge that Muslim goods were subject to duty in other states, Caliph *Umar Abd Al-Aziz* imposed *ushur*, 10 percent duty on their

---

Kitab al-'Ibar, Ibn Khaldun discussed events of the pre-Islamic world and Arab and Eastern Muslim history. He also discussed the history of the Muslim West).

[33] See Qur'an 2:43, 83, 110, 177, 277, 4:77, 9:5, 11, 18, 60, 71, 73:20, and 98:5.

[34] *Id.* 2:263. 264, 271, 280, and 57:18.

[35] *Id.* 2:267, 65:7, and 9:60. Those eligible for *Sadaqa* are the poor, the needy, workers of charity, newly converts, slaves, debtors, warriors, and travelers. In some instances, *Sadaqa* is mandatory for example, in the case of non-fulfillment of an oath. *Id.* 5:89.

[36] *Id.* 8:41

[37] *Id.* 2:29.

[38] Taxes are not the only source of revenue for the government. The government can impose user fees for delivering its service, fines for violations, and charges for renting its buildings. Moreover, the government can raise money through borrowing, domestically or internationally.

[39] Toward the end of the *Umayyad* ruling of the Islamic world (661-750 C.E), rulers overburdened Muslims through taxes. See S. M. Hasanuz Zaman, *Economic Functions of an Islamic State: The Early Islamic Experience* 115 (2n ed., The Islamic Found. 1991).

[40] See Ahmad Hasan, *Sunan Abu Dawud*, Vol. II, Chapter 1095, 830 (Sh. M. Ashraf 1984). *Maks*, an Arabic word, is defined as toll or customs duty. See H.A.R.Gibb & J.H.Kramers, Concise Encyclopedia of Islam 317 (4th ed., Brill Academic Publishers 2001).

imports.[41] Today, by way of analogy, if other countries impose tariffs on trade of Muslims, Muslims may impose tariffs on them. The early Islamic state tariff policy was one based on reciprocity.

B. Market Agents and Forces in Islam

After the expansion of the Islamic state beyond *Medina*, vast lands came into the hands of Muslims. Prophet Muhammad (s.a.w) and his followers recognized individual entrepreneurship, the basic premise of free trade. They encouraged the maximum utility of barren land.[42]

Islam also cherishes the inviolability of private property.[43] Private property is limited only by the realization of others' rights and public interest. Some argue, correctly, that economics of Islam is based on mixed ownership.[44] Since Allah (s.w.t) owns all natural resources, the Islamic state can exercise control over *anfal* such as land, water, and mineral deposits.[45] Thus, Islamic economics embraces a dual ownership concept. In other words, even though private ownership is guaranteed, the owner of such property acts as a trustee or agent for Allah (s.w.t), the ultimate owner.

Interestingly, Islamic law lacks clear substantive rules on the protection of intellectual property.[46] Perhaps because of the nature of ideas as incorporeal objects, there

---

[41] See Al-Manhaj al-iqtis¯ad¯i f¯i al-Isl¯am : bayna al-fikr wa-al-tatb¯iq / al-Mu'tamar al-Ilm¯I al-Sanaw¯i al-Th¯alith, al-Q¯ahirah 9-12 Ibr¯il 1983. [The Islamic Economic System between Theory and Practice]. 436 (J¯ami'at al- Mans¯urah, Kull¯iyat al-Tij¯arah 1983). Verse 2:193 of the Qur'an authorizes retaliation, in kind, if Muslims are subject to actions. Some old books treat the term *Ushur* the same as *Maks*, though, *Maks* is more indicative as a customs duty. *Ushur* is defined as the tenth or tithe levied for public assistance, frequently used in the sense of *Zakat* and *Sadaqa*. See Gibb & Kramers, *supra* note 40, at 611.
[42] Prophet Muhammad (s.a.w) is reported to have said, "Who revives dead land, it is for him". See ZAMAN, *supra* note 39, at 33. Caliph *Umar Al-Khattab* is quoted saying, "He who restores dead land, owns it". See also Heck, *supra* note 8, at 122. Prophet Muhammad (s.a.w) said, "There is none amongst the Muslims who plants a tree or sows seeds and then a bird, or a person or an animal eats from it, but is regarded as a charitable gift for him". See Muhammad Muhsin Khan, *Sah¯ih Al-Bukh¯ar¯i*, vol. 3, 295 (4th ed., D¯ar al-'Arab¯iyat li-i- Tib¯a'at wa al-Nashr wa al-Tawz¯ir 1985).
[43] The Qur'an states, "And do not eat up Your property among yourselves For vanities, nor use it As bait for the judges, With intent that ye may Eat up wrongfully and knowingly A little of (other) people's property". See Qur'an 2:188. Prophet Muhammad (s.a.w) in his farewell pilgrimage said, "No property of a Muslim is lawful to his brother except what he gives him from the goodness of his heart, so do not wrong yourselves". See AL-Ghazali, *supra* n. 22, at 457.
[44] See Sohrab Behdad, *Islamization of Economics in Iran Universities*, 27 Intl. J. Middle East Stud. 193, 201 (1995). The Qur'an states, "Unto Allah belongeth whatsoever is in the heavens and whatsoever is in the earth". See also Qur'an 3:129.
[45] See Behdad, at 202.
[46] See Steven D. Jamar, *The Protection of Intellectual Property Under Islamic Law*, 21 Cap. U. L. Rev 1079, 1082, 1093 (1992) (protection of intellectual property in Islamic law is neither mandated nor prohibited. There is lack of any express statements about it). See Amir H. Khoury, *Ancient and Islamic Sources of Intellectual Property Protection in the Middle East: A Focus on Trademarks*, 43 IDEA 151, 187-202 (2003) (Islamic law does not directly address the issues pertaining to intellectual property rights. The possible hurdles to intellectual property protection within Islamic law appear to emerge from a moral and ethical basis in Islam. Intellectual property rights grant a monopolistic benefit to their owners while the "Maslaha" (public good or interest) doctrine in Islam calls for distributive justice. The prevailing

18

can, according to Islamic law be no absolute legal rights to intellectual property. The Islamic state is not obliged to protect intellectual property. Protection of intellectual property would fall into the category of permitted action. The Islamic state, based on its discretion, can "honor" intellectual property.[47] Islamic law concentrates first and foremost on material objects as property, thus reducing incorporeal objects to second or third degrees of importance.

Prices in Islam should be determined solely on the basis of the market, the law of supply and demand. The cheapness or dearness of prices is in the hand of Allah (s.w.t), who fixes the prices. Prices should not be fixed, but left to divine guidance.[48] In an anecdote, Prophet Muhammad (s.a.w) refused to interfere in market prices, which had risen abnormally in *Medina*, even though the people asked him to. However, the available Islamic literature reveals some cases in which Prophet Muhammad (s.a.w) exercised his authority as head of the Islamic state and interfered. In one case, Prophet Mohammad (s.a.w) knew that people met the caravans away from the market to buy the goods and then sold them at a higher price in the market.[49] This case was considered at the time a kind of deception or illegal trading practice.[50] The obligation not to interfere in setting prices is not unfettered. There are situations in which government involvement is needed to remedy market failures when the market does not operate efficiently because of informational deficiencies.

Islamic approach to copyright has been that there should be no obstruction to the duplication of original materials since the most widespread dissemination of knowledge is for the good of all). See also Ali Khan, *Islam as Intellectual Property "My Lord! Increase me in Knowledge,"* 31 Cumb. L. Rev. 631, 632-635, 649-650 (2001) (Islam itself as protected knowledge is a unique form of intellectual property. The Qur'an, the *Sunna*, and the unique marks and symbols of faith such as mosque and the greeting of *assalam-u-alaikam* (peace be upon you), together constitute the protected knowledge of Islam. However, there are differences between the well-known kinds of secular intellectual property rights such as copyrights, patents, and trademarks, and knowledge-based Islam. The former is the product of human intellect, innovation, and effort. In contrast, Islamic assets cannot be created by human. Intellectual property is often commercial in nature and protected for a short duration. Unlike intellectual property, the protected knowledge of Islam is not for sale or commercial exploitation and it is timeless. The protected knowledge of Islam is universal free for the benefit of all. Copies of the Qur'an may be freely made and published without any prior permission and without paying royalties to any person, family, or nation. It has been copyrighted in perpetuity as Allah's authentic work. No individual, no family, and no nation can claim proprietorship of these assets. In fact, no concept of ownership applies to the knowledge-based assets of Islam, as it does to intellectual property).

[47] The state can protect intellectual property under its powers to regulate human activity in a manner consistent with Islamic law. See Jamar, at 1083.

[48] See Munazzmat Al-Mu'tamar Al-Isl̄ami, Isl̄am Wa Al-Niz̄am Al-Iqtis̄adi Al-Dawli Al-Jad̄id [Islam and the New International Economic System] 118, 161 (D̄ar Sir̄as li-i- Nashr 1982).

[49] Prophet Muhammad (s.a.w) said "Do not go ahead to meet the caravan (for buying the goods) (but wait) till it reaches the market". See Khan, *supra* n. 42, at vol. 3, 207.

[50] *Al-Majallah* (The Book of Rules of Justice) introduced the concept of deception in several of its articles. See AL-MAJALLAH, arts. 18, 30, 165, 286 (1879). The *Majalla* was part of the reform movement in the Ottoman Empire that started in 1839. The *Majalla* is based, in part, on the *Hanafi* school of law. The *Majalla* codified, rather than modified, the Islamic rules which served as the civil law of the Ottoman Empire. It consists of an introductory section and sixteen books each treating a different subject: sale, hire, guarantee, transfer of debt, pledges, trust and trusteeship, gifts, wrongful appropriation and destruction, interdiction, constraint and preemption, joint ownership, agency, settlement and release, admissions, actions, evidence, and administration of oath and administration of justice by the court.

III. Limitations on Free Trade in Islamic Law

Freedom of trade in Islam is not absolute. There are some moral or religious strictures. The first limitation in Islam is the prohibition of illegitimate goods, those that are *haram* (forbidden), such as pork and alcohol.[51] In other words, the source of goods in Islam must be legally permissible and not harmful or corrupt.

The other limitation to free trade in Islam is *riba*. *Riba* is translated into English as usury.[52] It involves unjust profit or advantage.[53] Islamic law and modern trade come into conflict when addressing *riba*.[54] Islamic theory holds that money should be used in a financial system only to facilitate the purchase or sale of goods and services, but should not for example be "commoditized" by depositing money with banks for a guaranteed return over time. In other words, Islamic law encourages enterprise rather than the hoarding of money.

The debate is squared on the issue of whether Islamic law should assign quantity value or time value for money. An example of the quantity value would be when one person lends $100 in singles to another person for three months. On the one hand, when the money is due, then the second person ought to return the $100 in singles without regard to its value. On the other, according to time value or pure time preference theory, the second person ought to return the $100 in singles as well as a bit more. Charging a "bit more" could be justified on the basis that if the first person did not lend money he could have invested the money elsewhere in something profitable. Alternatively, during the three month period, the currency may be devalued. Therefore, $100 three months ago may worth $50 three months later after indexation.[55]

---

[51] See Qur'an 5:3, 90, 2:219.

[52] The Qur'an states, "Allah has made buying and selling lawful and usury unlawful". See Qur'an 2: 275-278. From a comparative viewpoint, Judaism and Christianity have prohibited *riba* as well. See Jean-François Seznec, *Ethics, Islamic Banking and the Global Financial Market*, 23-SPG Fletcher World Aff. 161, 165 (1999) (interest and usury are discussed in the Bible in Ezekiel 18:8 and Deuteronomy 23:19. These paragraphs, which apply to Jews and Christians, clearly forbid the use of usury in dealing with people. For centuries, Christians had a very strong prejudice against interest, which they used however reluctantly. The Catholic Church only lifted the ban on interest in the mid-nineteenth century. Today, there are banks in Israel that cater to Jews who refuse to take or pay interest). There is an exception to the prohibition of usury in Judaism which permits Jews to charge and pay interest to non-Jews.

[53] *Riba* is of two kinds: *riba al-fadl*, in which a person acquires an unlawful, excessive profit, and *riba al-nasi'a*, in which a person gains an unlawful advantage by speculating on uncontrollable risks. *Riba al-nasi'a* is form of *gharar*.

[54] Great amount of literature is devoted to *riba* as to its definition and impact. The core of the debate is what constitutes *riba*. Some classical Muslim jurists define *riba* broadly to include any interest or increase. Other modest jurists define it narrowly to include excessive interest or doubling beyond the real value of money if the borrower defaults during specific time. In the latter view, excessive interest should be prohibited and not any mere increase. Prohibition of *riba* is applied variably in Muslim countries such as Iran, Pakistan, Saudi Arabia, and Sudan. For more see Barbara L. Seniawski, *Riba Today: Social Equity, the Economy, and Doing Business under Islamic Law*, 39 Colum. J. Transnatl. L. 701, 707-720 (2001).

[55] The "bit more" presumes devaluation of currency. However, there could be a scenario where the price of the currency increases. As such, the lender would perhaps receive double the amount he gave. In this case, the terms of the agreement between the parties ought to be adjusted to ensure fairness.

To avoid the issue of *riba*, new alternatives have been developed to make trade and to finance international trade possible. These alternatives are *mudaraba, musharaka,* and *murabaha.* All these alternatives include the concept of sharing profit and loss.[56]

Mudaraba (trust finance) is a business undertaking in which a person participates with his money and another with his effort and skill.[57] The owner of the capital is known as *rab 'ilmal* and the other partner is known as *mudarib.* In other words, it is a contract in which an investor (Islamic bank) entrusts his money to another party called an entrepreneur for making profit.[58] Therefore, it is a form of a business association.

Musharaka can be defined as a partnership between two or more persons. It can be divided into two forms: contractual partnership and non-contractual partnership. On the one hand, non-contractual partnership comes into existence when two or more persons get joint ownership of some asset without entering into a formal relationship, when two persons receive an inheritance for example. On the other, in a contractual partnership parties enter willingly into a partnership. Contractual partnership includes four kinds. First, a contractual partnership could be a partnership whereby two persons pool their physical and/or mental labor without sharing capital investment. Any profits will be shared according to their agreement.[59] Second, contractual partnership could also involve partners who use their reputation and goodwill rather than capital. The third kind of contractual partnership enjoys equality in the areas of capital, management, and right of settlement.[60] All profits and losses are shared equally among the partners. The fourth kind of contractual partnership involves partners that need not be equals in their contribution of capital or management. However, an additional share of the profit will be granted to the partner who manages the enterprise.[61] In this kind of partnership, there is no set formula for profit sharing and each case is dealt with on its own merit. The amount of liability is limited to the percentage of his share in the enterprise. Again, *musharaka* is a form of a business association.

---

[56] Islamic finance is based on the concept of profit and loss sharing with Islamic banks being willing to take on risks associated with title and to participate in the financial structures established for their clients. It is not based on the concept of guaranteed return without any notion of risk or participation. Ahmed A.M.S. Al-Suwaidi, *Finance of International Trade in the Gulf* 42-43 (Graham & Trotman 1994) (trade finance represents the majority of Islamic banking transactions. More specifically, *murabaha* (cost-plus financing) accounts for 70 percent of Islamic finance transactions). Some Muslims believe that these alternatives are interest-based devices but under different names.

[57] *Mudaraba* is a pre-Islamic custom used to finance the caravan trade in Arabia. It is an example of a commercial arrangement identical to the economic and legal institution which became known in Europe as the Commenda. *Id.* 73.

[58] The investor will have his capital and a predetermined profit between himself and the entrepreneur. The profits, if any, are shared upon in advance, but not as a guaranteed return. Thus, the profits are uncertain in this case. The loss, if any, is borne only by the investor and must not exceed the amount of capital, unless the loss is due to negligence by the *mudarib*. If the loss is equivalent to the capital, the Islamic bank will receive nothing. *Id.* 75.

[59] *Id.* 79.

[60] *Id.* 80.

[61] *Id.* 81.

Murabaha can be defined as the purchase price of goods plus a fixed profit.[62] It is a kind of sale contract in which the final price includes the cost plus profit, which is known to the parties in advance without any deception. An example of this type of Islamic finance is a form of auto finance. If a person wants to buy a car, he can request an Islamic bank to purchase it from a supplier and resell it to him at the original purchase price plus a negotiated profit on agreed terms. The negotiated profit, or mark-up, would compensate the bank for its time and effort spent for communication, currency exchange, etc. One downside for *murabaha* is if the bank ends up with the car because the person defaults on payment or refuses to accept the car. The Islamic bank, as a title holder, will bear any risk to the goods during the time of its ownership up to the time the person examines and accepts it.

Murabaha is the main product of Islamic finance compared with *mudaraba* and *musharaka* instruments. The reason for this is that in conventional lending a bank is concerned with the creditworthiness of a borrower. In contrast, in *mudaraba* type of lending, an Islamic bank would be concerned with more than creditworthiness. It would be concerned with profitability since the Islamic bank would enter into profit/loss sharing arrangement. An Islamic bank would be careful to double-check the profitability of an enterprise before putting its capital in. Therefore, it would be difficult for an Islamic bank to check bookkeeping of an enterprise or for an entrepreneur to declare himself as less profitable which might be true as a matter of fact.

Another limitation to trade in Islamic law is *gharar* (uncertainty or speculation).[63] *Gharar* involves future contracts in which goods are not determined at the time of contracting, such as the sale of fish in the sea before being caught, day trading, or life insurance. To give an example, suppose that a person purchases life insurance to secure his family's well-being in case of an unexpected event. In Islamic law, some would argue that life insurance is a kind of betting on that person's life.[64] Allah (s.w.t) has the control over and knowledge of that person's life.[65] From time immemorial, Allah (s.w.t) pre-determined each person's fate and destiny. On the other hand, other Muslim scholars would argue that modern life in society is complex and unpredictable, which makes life insurance important to individuals.

To secure a person's family in case of an unexpected event, alternatives to life insurance there exist in Islamic society such as laws of inheritance, *Zakat*, and social security. Moreover, Islamic insurance, known in Arabic as *takaful*, as opposed to

---

[62] *Id.* 98.

[63] See AL-Manhaj Al-Iqtis⁻ad⁻i F⁻i Al-Isl⁻am: Bayna Al-Fikr Wa-Al-Tatb⁻iq, *supra* n. 41, at 616.

[64] See Samir Mankabady, *Insurance and Islamic Law: The Islamic Insurance Company*, 4 Arab L. Q. 199 (1989) (some Muslim scholars differ on the legality of insurance. *Abu Zhra*, a *Hanafi* scholar, believed that cooperative insurance is legal. Other types of insurance could not be placed under the groups of contracts known in Islamic law: sale, donation, and hire). See Mohd. Masum Billah, *Life Insurance? An Islamic View*, 8 Arab L. Q. 315-319 (1993) (other grounds against the validity of life insurance include *riba* since the beneficiaries of the assured will gain more than the assured has paid to the insurer. This additional gain is *riba*). See also Ahmad A. Al-Ghadyan, *Insurance: The Islamic Perspective and its Development in Saudi Arabia*, Arab L. Q. 332-335 (1999).

[65] See Qur'an 31:34.

conventional insurance, can operate in line with Islamic concepts.[66] Aside from the life insurance debate, if the theory of *gharar* were applied narrowly, it would make economic life impossible.[67] After all, there is an element of speculation and uncertainty in everything. It would be appropriate to develop a benchmark against which "excessive" speculation is considered *gharar*.

IV. Ibn Khaldun and the Theory of Commercial Policy

The wealth of nations, according to Adam Smith, is derived from specialization and trade. Nations can gain economically from specializing in production and trading the surplus produce. Specialization and trading in surplus produce would generate multiplier effects, known as the doctrine of mutual gains from trade in the form of increased national income, higher consumption, and an improved standard of living. British political economist David Ricardo expounded, in his 1817 publication of Principles of Political Economy and Taxation, by stating that specialization and trade were based on comparative advantage (relative costs) rather than primarily on absolute advantage (production costs) as had been thought earlier.[68]

Similarly, it is a source of pride that *Ibn Khaldun* (1332-1406 C.E), Adam Smith of the Arabs and the great Islamic sociologist-cum-economist, was among the pioneers who analyzed the economic problem scientifically and tried to resolve it.[69] However, if he had discussed his economic ideas in a separate treatise rather than in a scattered manner, among many other subjects in his masterpiece *Al-Ibar*, he could have been recognized as

---

[66] Islamic insurance functions like conventional cooperative insurance. In cooperative insurance, resources in insurance companies are pooled whereby policyholders are considered shareholders sharing in profits. However, in a *takaful* company, policyholders and shareholders are distinct in which both own capital and share in annual profits. *Retakaful* insurance also functions like conventional reinsurance.

[67] For more on this matter see Sajjad M. Jasimuddin, *The Stock Exchange and Islamic Finance: Some Thoughts for a Reconsideration*, Vol. 14 The Islamic Q. 105, 108 (No. 2, 2001) (some Islamic scholars found stock exchange objectionable because Islamic law does not permit the sale of an article until one has the physical possession of it. Trading in stocks is usually done without their physical possession and there is an element of chance. Therefore, trading in shares, bonds, and debentures is objectionable. Stock exchange is further objectionable for its elements of speculation. On the other hand, other Islamic scholars argue that speculation in the stock exchange is a process that involves the intelligent forecasting of future prices. This is not the same as tossing dice).

[68] See Jagdish Bhagwati, *Political Economy and International Economics* 3-34 (Douglas A. Irwin ed., MIT Press 1991) (classical free trade theory rested on a number of crucial but questionable assumptions. These include there being perfect competition, perfect information, labor and capital are not mobile internationally, production process exhibits constant returns, market prices will accurately reflect relative real costs, and absence externalities. Over the years, the traditional model of international trade has been supplemented and to some extent supplanted by new models. These models include neo-classical theory [Pareto superiority and optimality and its follow-up criterion of Kaldor-Hicks compensatory principles], Hecksher-Ohlin model, endogenous growth theory, factor price equalization theorem, and Stopler-Samuelson theorem. Free traders acknowledge some divergence from free trade such as optimal tariff, infant industry, second best, and externalities arguments).

[69] The researcher uses the terms Adam Smith of the Arabs and sociologist-cum-economist in referring to *Ibn Khaldun* to highlight the contributions made by *Ibn Khaldun*.The economic problem consists of man-against-nature struggle, scarcity of resources, and the inability of individual in his limited capacity to satisfy all of his needs.

the father of free trade.[70] *Ibn Khaldun*, nevertheless, deserves to be listed as one of the great economists of all time along with Adam Smith, David Ricardo, and other great thinkers.

Ibn Khaldun stated that Allah (s.w.t) created man in a form that can live only by food. Allah (s.w.t) guided man to a natural desire for food and enabled him to obtain it.[71] *Ibn Khaldun* also called for specialization. For example, if a tailor has the skill necessary for his job, he has, neither, the necessary skills, nor, the time to be a carpenter or builder. Even assuming that he could be skilled in crafts, he would not be efficient in both of them at the same level.[72] Specialization and social organization of labor would allocate resources to their most efficient uses.

Specialization and division of labor would lead to a surplus of production which can be used for trade. Therefore, international division of labor can also be applied to trade among countries. The basis of trade is to make a profit by producing goods at a lower price and selling them at a higher price. Profits could be accrued by supplying goods to other countries where demand for these goods is greater than in the home country.[73]

There is disagreement among Muslim scholars on the role of state. *Ibn Khaldun* was suspicious of the state.[74] He maintains that commercial activity on the part of the ruler is

---

[70] One of the differences between *Ibn Khaldun* and Adam Smith is that *Ibn Khaldun* discussed different topics in his *Muqaddimah* such as the rise and fall of state, dynasty, and Bedouins while Adam Smith focused on economics in his book, The Wealth of Nations of 1776. When Ibn Khaldun discussed division of labor he did so in chapter one (titled human civilization in general) of *Muqaddimah* not in chapter five (titled on the various aspects of making a living such as profit and the crafts) which deals with economics. The other difference between *Ibn Khaldun* and Adam Smith is the concept of human nature. For Adam Smith, harnessing human nature means every man working for his own selfish interest will be led by an invisible hand or spontaneous order to promote the public good. See Abdol Soofi, *Economics of Ibn Khaldun Revisited*, 27:2 Hist. Pol. Econ. 387, 391-400 (1995) (discussing the coherent Khaldunian economics theory of production based on human labor, theory of value based on labor input, theory of distribution based on optimum of salary, profit, and taxes, and theory of population and public finances cycles). Although Adam Smith is considered the father of free trade, his work did not escape criticism. See also Robert A. Blecker, *The "Unnatural and Retrograde Order": Adam Smith' Theories of Trade and Development Reconsidered*, 64 Economica 527, 529 (1997) (stating that Adam Smith for nearly two centuries has been considered a poor trade theorist for failing to discover the law of comparative advantage. He had some interesting but disconnected ideas about the benefits of free trade. Adam Smith has three separate theories of trade based on absolute advantage, market-widening, and vent-for-surplus).
[71] *Ibn Khaldun* stated that the power of the individual human being is not sufficient for him to obtain the food he needs, and does not provide him with as much food as he requires to live. Even if we assume an absolute minimum, that is food enough for one day, for example a little of wheat, that amount of food could be obtained only after much preparation, such as grinding, baking, and cooking. Each of these three operations requires utensils and tools than can be provided only with the help of several crafts such as blacksmith, carpenter, and potter...Through cooperation, the needs of a number of persons, many times greater than their own number, can be satisfied. IBN KHALDUN, *supra* n. 32, at VOL. I, 272, VOL. III, 859.
[72] *Id.* VOL. III, 884, 930.
[73] *Id.* VOL. III, 915.
[74] See Syed Farid Alatas, *Introduction to the Political Economy of Ibn Khaldun*, Vol. 45 The Islamic Q. 307, 320 (No. 4, 2001) (*Ibn Khaldun* theory is founded on the assumption that the state is a problematic entity that acts in a way that creates the very conditions for economic misfortune).

harmful to his subjects and ruinous to the tax revenue. The ruler has the job of protecting citizens from aggression of other nations.[75] In contrast to *Ibn Khaldun*'s "government hand-off" approach, *Ibn Hazm*, a Muslim scholar, has called for government intervention.[76]

The economic ideas of Islamic jurists may seem not to have a systematic methodology. However, one can argue that each of these Islamic jurists had a different approach to the economic problem of the Islamic state in their respective eras. Second, they approached their solutions within the parameters of the Islamic *shari'a*. Hence, there could be no difference in the substance of their positions, but a difference in the form. Therefore, it is possible for Muslim jurists to develop different views of the same rule within the overall framework. Even assuming that each Islamic jurist lived at the same time, it would not obscure the fact that their ideas are neither completely right nor completely wrong. The issue is not to allow one approach (state control of means of production) to encroach aggressively on the other (free trade). At the present time, countries adopt elements of both approaches. Therefore, there is no such thing as pure free trade.

Islamic economics have called for avoidance of *israf* (waste or extravagance). Indeed, the term *iqtisad* (economics) implies the concept of moderation. Islamic economics is not against materialism *per se*; rather, it is "excessive" materialism that Islamic economics shun. *Ibn Khaldun* also warned of the "obsession" of excessive materialism. Excessive materialism breeds a culture in which the typical individual becomes materialistic and luxury-oriented.[77] In this kind of culture, the animalistic side of the human being takes precedence. Based on materialism, a growing individualistic egoism is bound to be born with the society's social solidarity undermined.[78] In other words, individualism, characterized through actions of autonomous and separate persons within a state, undermines collectivity in which an individual is positioned within a social context of family or community.

---

[75] See IBN KHALDUN, *supra* n. 32, at VOL. I, 273. Some Muslim scholars could argue on the basis of *Ibn Khaldun*'s statement in which he declares that the ruler has to protect his citizens from aggression of other nations, and that the ruler could also exercise unlimited authority in regulating trade. However, *Ibn Khaldun* statement must not be interpreted because it is used in referring to military rather than economic affairs.

[76] See Al-Manhaj Al-Iqtis̄ ad̄ i F ̄ i Al-Isl̄ am: Bayna Al-Fikr Wa-Al-Tatbiq, *supra* n. 41, at 104.

[77] See Mahmoud Dhaouadi, *An Interpretation of the Implications of Human Nature for Ibn Khaldun's Thinking*, Vol. 32 The Islamic Q. 10, 20 (No. 1, 1988) (*Ibn Khaldun*'s position seems to be in line with the outlook on development in the third world. The emphasis is on human development instead of only on economic development).

[78] *Id.*

Conclusion

Not only does Islam cover morality and individual's relationship with Allah (s.w.t), but also does cover trade. Islam regulates every aspect of life including trade. The fact that the Prophet Muhammad (s.a.w) started his career as a merchant is unique to the Islamic Prophecy.

Islamic law is inclined toward free trade. Islamic law condemned imposing tariffs on trade with other states. Even when tariffs were imposed, they were imposed based on reciprocity. Moreover, Islamic law provided thought on free trade in areas such as price mechanism. In general, prices in Islam should be determined on the basis of market forces. Islam also protects private property. Early Islamic governments did not directly engage in trade because they understood profitability and competition as self-serving. The role of early Islamic governments was limited to prevent unfair trade, deception or fraud. Additionally, the role of the early Islamic states was confined to providing necessities such as public services and law enforcement.

Although Islamic law is inclined toward free trade, there are certain limitations. These limitations include the prohibition of trade in illegitimate goods such as pork and alcohol. In other words, goods that are in conformity with Islamic teachings are acceptable. Otherwise, these goods and services are prohibited. The other limitation to free trade in Islam is *riba*. To avoid the issue of *riba* and finance trade, new alternatives have been developed. These alternatives are *mudaraba*, *musharaka*, and *murabaha*. All these alternatives include the concept of sharing profit and loss. Islamic law also sets out limitation to trade concerning *gharar* (uncertainty or speculation). In sum, international trade in Islam is trade with an Islamic "purifier". Islamic law embraces Islamic market economy.

Ibn Khaldun, considered to be the Adam Smith of the Arabs, examined and explored specialization and social organization of labor. *Ibn Khaldun* explained that man in his individual capacity could not satisfy all his needs. However, through division of labor man can maximize his satisfaction. Division of labor can also be applied to trade among countries. Specialization and division of labor would lead to increase in production. Goods could be traded with other countries where demand for these goods is greater than in the home country. As *Ibn Khaldun* phrased it, commercial activity on the part of the ruler is harmful to his subjects and ruinous to the tax revenue. The role of the ruler is to protect citizens from aggression of other states. In addition, *Ibn Khaldun* warned of excessive materialism, whereby the individual becomes materialistic and luxury-oriented. Excessive materialism leads to individualism which weakens the social solidarity of society.

Enough resources exist in Islamic jurisprudence that can help Arab countries integrate into the modern multilateral trading system while abiding by Islamic teachings. The dimensions of the multilateral trading system must be recognized as an opportunity and challenge. Arab countries will not steer away from the multilateral trading system as represented by the WTO.

CHAPTER II

ARAB COUNTRIES AND THE WORLD TRADE ORGANIZATION

Chapter I discussed how trade was an integral part of the early Islamic state. The founder of Islam, Prophet Muhammad (s.a.w) was himself a merchant. Islamic law and economics have rich intellectual heritage as they relate to international trade. While Islamic law and economics covered areas such as reciprocity, trade finance, taxes, subsidies, price mechanism, and full measure and weight, they also set limitations on free trade such as prohibition against trade in alcohol and *riba*. Arab countries can become integrated in the WTO while abiding by Islamic doctrines.[79]

The proposition in Chapter II is that the WTO is not a perfect institution. However, the WTO could and must integrate Arab countries in the work of the organization through accepting membership of Arab countries into the WTO at an accelerated rate, hiring more staff from Arab countries at the WTO Secretariat, and using Arabic, a language spoken by 280 million people as a working language along with the other three working languages (English, Spanish, and French) in the trade body. Additionally, Arab countries could use the WTO dispute settlement mechanism to guard their rights. In light of the proliferation of regional trade agreements worldwide, it is time for the unfinished common Arab economic project to be revisited seriously. A critical examination of current, bilateral or regional Arab trade agreements must be pursued to identify different forms of effective economic integration. Current Arab trade agreements are flawed in part because they exclude sectors or products from their coverage, adopt weak institutions, and incorporate sloppy enforcement mechanisms.

I. History of International Trade in Arab Countries

Although trade plays a unique role in the history of Islam, it has existed in all civilizations dating back to ancient times. Trade agreements have come alongside with trade. For example, Egypt and Babylonia entered into an agreement on payment of tariffs.[80] The current international trading system is based on the principle of free trade which dates back to the works of Adam Smith, David Ricardo, and others. The watershed event in the history of international trade occurred by the repeal of British Corn Laws of 1846 and the conclusion of Cobden-Chevalier trade agreement between Britain and France in 1860.[81] Other European countries concluded a series of free trade agreements.

---

[79] For purposes of this book, Arab countries as existing today will be defined as: Algeria, Bahrain, Comoros, Djibouti, Egypt, Iraq, Jordan, Kuwait, Lebanon, Libya, Morocco, Mauritania, Oman, Gaza Strip and West Bank, Qatar, Saudi Arabia, Sudan, Syria, Somalia, Tunisia, United Arab Emirates, and Yemen. Wherever the term "Greater Syria" is used indicates current Syria, Jordan, Palestine, Lebanon, and Iraq. Whenever the term "Transjordan" is used indicates the Hashemite Kingdom of Jordan. Whenever relevant, reference will be made to Iran and Afghanistan.
[80] Gilbert R. Winham, *The Evolution of International Trade Agreements* 16 (U. Toronto Press 1992).
[81] British Corn Laws were complex speculative regulations on exports and imports of corn which controlled the entry of corn depending on annual harvest. At the center of the British Corn Laws was the debate between liberalism and mercantilism which materialized, for the first time, as theories with specific agenda and membership. Cheryl Schonhardt-Bailey, *Free Trade: The Repeal of the Corn Laws* XIV (Thoemmes

However, the ascendancy of free trade did not last long since by the late nineteenth century European powers engaged in tariff wars.[82]

At the same time when free trade was in ascendancy in the West, Arab countries in the East, as a whole, fell under the rule of the Ottoman Empire for nearly four centuries. The Ottoman Empire adopted a semi-free trade policy by allowing imports into the Empire but letting nothing out. This policy created a persistent trade deficit. The Ottoman Empire adopted such a trade policy based on misinterpretation of religious and economic rules.[83] On the domestic side of trade policy, the Ottoman Empire formed a customs union, with the exception of Egypt, where all goods were traded duty free.[84] Had the Ottoman Empire allowed exports to flow freely outside the Empire, it would have formed a stronger customs union and trade negotiating power. Unfortunately, misinterpretation of religious and economic rules put Ottoman domestic industries at a disadvantage.

The Ottomans concluded trade agreements with the Persians and Europeans. The most important of those was the Anglo-Ottoman Convention of 1838 between Britain and the Ottoman Empire.[85] The Anglo-Ottoman Convention was followed by series of trade agreements with Iran and France.[86] The Ottoman emperors opened the door wide to foreign producers who enjoyed non-reciprocal access to the Ottoman Empire.[87]

Egypt rendered itself as a special case in the trade policy of the Ottoman Empire. In theory, Egypt, as part of the Ottoman Empire, was subject to any international trade

---

Press 1996). See also Andrew Marrison, *Free Trade and its Reception 1815-1960* , VOL. I, 37-43, 70-74, 173 (Routledge 1998).

[82] Shift of agricultural comparative advantage from Britain to the New World, increase foreign imports and competition, growing sentiment of nationalism, rise of interest groups, industrial downturn, and eruption of World War I led to Britain's abandonment of free trade and decline in international trade. See Marrison, at 254-255. All of these factors prove that free trade is susceptible to contraction.

[83] In pursuing semi-free trade policy, the Ottomans believed that exports impoverish the Empire, low prices of domestic goods creates favorable export balance, sale to the infidels is immoral, and pressure should be on the foreign consumer if he wishes to buy Ottoman goods. See Charles Issawi, *An Economic History of the Middle East and North Africa* 18 (Columbia U. Press 1982). One wonders if the Ottomans had not known that increased exports create favorable trade balances since foreign consumers would pay in their own currencies for imported goods which would ultimately find their way to Ottoman manufacturers, and Islam nowhere prohibited trade with people of other religions.

[84] Ahmad Al-Shirb¯in¯i, *T¯ar¯ikh al-tij¯arah al-Misr¯iyah f¯i `asr al-hurr¯iyah al-iqtis¯ad¯iyah, 1840-1914 [History of Egyptian Trade in the Age of Free Trade, 1840-1914]* 409 (Al-Hay'ah al-Misr¯iyah al-`¯Ammah lil-Kitab 1995).

[85] The Anglo-Ottoman Convention prohibited domestic restrictions in the Ottoman Empire. It also imposed 12 percent *ad valorem* tariff on exports and 5 percent *ad valorem* tariff on imports. Later on, tariffs on imports were raised to 8 percent and lowered on exports to 8 percent. See Issawi, *supra* n. 83, at 19.

[86] The trade agreement between the Ottoman Empire and France in 1861 imposed 8 percent *ad valorem* tariff on imports and exports of the Empire with 1 percent annual reduction until tariff reaches 1 percent. As for transit goods, the agreement imposed 1 percent *ad valorem* tariff. If a good in transit warehoused in the Empire for six months for re-export, 1 percent tariff was applied. If 8 percent tariff had been applied, good in transit was eligible for drawback in the amount of 7 percent. The trade agreement restricted trade in weapons and tobacco. The Ottoman Empire and France agreed that the trade agreement expires in 28 years. See Al-Shirb¯in¯i, *supra* n. 84, at 391.

[87] Initially, Ottoman emperors made such concessions in order for foreigner manufacturers to produce what the emperors needed of luxury goods. *Id.* at 257.

agreement signed by the Ottomans. However, Muhammad Ali adopted a mercantile policy.[88] He wanted to build up an independent military "Egyptian Empire" to secede from the Ottoman Empire. In pursuing such a political goal, Muhammad Ali created monopolies, restricted imports to protect domestic industry, used administrative measures to delay the application of the Anglo-Ottoman Convention in his region, controlled land distribution and crops plantation, controlled prices of raw materials, directed agricultural and industrial production to military–related activities such as cloth production for military personnel.[89] In sum, Muhammad Ali centralized the economy.

Muhammad Ali used trade policy to promote his drive of independence from the Ottoman Empire and then conquered new lands. During his reign, trade became an agent for the government aimed to amass money and ensure government supervision of national resources so that they could best be channeled to the army. The trade policy of Muhammad Ali brought him into conflict with the Ottoman sultan and Britain, since the latter needed markets in the Middle East for its goods and sought to destroy the regime in Egypt as a means of exerting influence on the region.[90]

In 1840, Britain pressed Muhammad Ali to conclude a trade agreement that extended gradually, through most-favored-nation rule, to Austria and other European countries. Foreign producers enjoyed concessions and unlimited access to the Egyptian market while Egyptian producers were hampered by all sorts of barriers.[91] Thus, local producers

---

[88] Muhammad Ali was an Albanian officer whom the Ottoman Porte named *pasha* (viceroy) of Egypt in 1805.

[89] *Id.* at 12-18.

[90] The conflict that emerged between Muhammad Ali and the Ottoman sultan was settled in 1841. As part of the settlement, Egypt was given a special status in concluding trade agreements. However, Egypt was still obligated by the agreements, including trade agreements, concluded by the Ottoman Empire. Thus, Egypt had the right to enter into trade agreements but within the jurisdiction of the Ottoman Empire. The special status of Egypt was rendered useless since the Ottomans obligated Egypt by trade agreements they concluded. Greece, after independence from the Ottoman Empire, concluded a trade agreement with Egypt in 1884. *Id.* at 21, 394-401.

[91] Concessions favored foreign manufacturers against nationals in laws and regulations. For example, foreign producers were exempted from domestic taxes. On the other hand, domestic producers were subject to all kinds of taxes that hampered their development. Local taxes were imposed on trade between a city and another city in Egypt which led to higher costs of production. Foreign nationals had their own courts which had the authority to impose very small fines in the amount of one Egyptian sterling and seven days in jail and only in cases of misdemeanor. Foreign producers controlled government procurement, especially in the supply of the army. Domestic factors such as prohibition on *riba*, limited investment in sectors other than agriculture, and government mismanagement and corruption contributed to the plight of the domestic industry. Some religious leaders would issue *fatwas* claiming that investing money in companies is *haram*. Banks in Egypt were controlled by foreigners as Egyptians believed that collecting interest is forbidden by Islamic law. In the absence of domestic banking, interest rate on loans given to cotton farmers in Egypt was sixty percent. Egyptian producers enjoyed growth in cotton production. As a result, Egyptian producers bought more land. They thought it was more secure to invest in land and agriculture, yet neglecting other important sectors of the economy. *Id.* at 31, 52-56, 66-69, 76-80, 94-101. Even though domestic taxes provided a source of revenue for the government, they also killed the domestic industry. If phase-out periods or preferential treatment were available in trade agreements of the Ottoman Empire, some domestic industries would have been more likely to survive. Prohibition on *riba* is not a sufficient excuse not to enroll in the banking sector and compete with foreign banks. Egyptian producers needed to diversify

were not afforded equal opportunities to compete with foreign capital and foreign manufacturers controlled the economy.

By dependence on foreign trade, Britain had transformed from an advocate of free trade to imperial power. In 1882, Britain occupied Egypt.[92] Egypt specialized in the production of cotton as a raw material.[93] On the other hand, domestic producers of manufactured cotton in Egypt faced tariff restrictions when exporting to Britain.[94] Complaints arose in such trade environment created by Britain.[95]

It is interesting to note that how quickly the icons of free trade, Britain in the nineteenth century transformed into colonial powers once they no longer enjoyed to the fullest their earlier comparative advantage. Trade policy of colonial powers was to find new land from which raw materials can be obtained and exploited that land's cheap labor. These raw materials would be manufactured in the imperialist countries and then re-exported to the colonies.

By early twentieth century, trade was pursued on a bilateral basis in the absence of international agreements or institutions. The U.S., one of the biggest trade policymakers of that time, passed the Smoot-Hawley Act of 1930 which increased tariffs significantly and encouraged retaliation from other trade powers in Europe. Subsequently, many conferences were held to restore the world's confidence in the trading system, but with little success.[96]

---

production and export. One would have imagined a scenario if a pest attacked cotton crops in Egypt. It would have been on the brink of famine akin to the Irish potato famine in the nineteenth century.

[92] In 1878, Gladstone condemned the concept of occupation as immoral and unnecessary. Additionally, Cobden, a Manchester industrialist and leading member of the anti-corn league, believed that free trade should not lead to imperialism.

[93] In 1849, cotton exports from Egypt were 31 percent of total exports. After the British occupation, cotton exports were 81 percent of total exports. In terms of trade volume, in the nineteenth century Britain received 43 percent of Egypt exports. From 1885-1889, Egypt received 63 percent of its imports from Britain. *Id.* at 25, 51, 247, 282, 342, 384.

[94] Britain has lost its title as "workhouse of the world" as a result of growing competition, increased imports, and high percentages of unemployment. Therefore, Britain focused on its colonies as markets for its production. In order to achieve this, Britain had to restrict the development of the colonies' native industries so as not to compete with the mother country. The U.S. emerged from the civil war with an industrial revolution in its perspective. It closed its market to foreign goods. See Marrison, *supra* note 81, at 190-191. In the 1890s, Britain along with France applied their protectionist policy toward their colonies in Yemen, Algeria, Morocco, and Tunisia.

[95] One Egyptian pamphlet said, "who among you can trade in Britain. . . . who among you works in Paris Customs service . . . as we have here. . . . even if you trade in Paris you see a French man who buys from you even if the goods are not available in his country". *Al-Ahram* newspaper wrote that domestic consumers, the rich, followed the taste and the clothing of the Europeans. *Al-Ahali* newspaper also wrote, "Egyptians were affected by the customs of the west . . . this killed the eastern Egyptian industry . . . before that Egyptian was Egyptian in his clothing, food, and drink . . . .". See Al-Shirbīnī, *supra* n. 84, at 56, 257, 403.

[96] Some of the conferences were the International Financial Conference in 1920, the Genoa Conference in 1922, and the World Monetary Conference in 1933. See Rondo Cameron, *A Concise Economic History of the World* 358-359 (3rd ed., Oxford U. Press 1997).

During the 1930s, Arab countries applied high tariffs. Arab countries also introduced new mechanisms such as quotas, exchange controls, and import and export licensing.[97] From the 1930s and onwards, each Arab country followed its own trade policy in seeking to achieve the take-off stage of economic development.

Recognizing the devastation created by protectionist trade policies, the Allies held the Bretton Woods conference.[98] The Bretton Woods institutions initially envisioned to include the International Monetary Fund (IMF), the International Bank for Reconstruction and Development (World Bank), and the International Trade Organization (ITO). The ultimate goal for the Bretton Woods institutions was to abandon protectionist trade policies, rebuild the deteriorating world economy, and regulate the economic relationship especially among the major economic powers at that time.[99]

In October 1945, the United Nations (U.N.) was established.[100] The Bretton Woods institutions are part of the U.N system.[101] In 1947, representatives of fifty-seven countries met in Havana, Cuba to negotiate the Havana Charter which was intended to create the ITO.[102] The Havana Charter would have complemented the roadmap of the international economic order.[103] However, the U.S. Congress never ratified the Havana Charter.[104] The ITO was pronounced dead in 1951.

---

[97] See Issawi, *supra* n. 83, at 22.

[98] On July 1-22, 1944, the Bretton Woods Conference was held in the resort town of Bretton Woods, New Hampshire. Some 700 delegates from 44 states participated in the Conference. The participants held a preparatory process for the Bretton Woods Conference in U.S. in cities such as Atlantic City, New Jersey. See Raymond F. Mikesell, *The Bretton Woods Debates: A Memoir* 30 (Princeton U. 1994).

[99] Harry D. White, a leading U.S. economist of that era, envisioned the IMF as an institution designed chiefly to prevent the disruption of foreign exchange, strengthen monetary and credit systems, and help in the restoration of foreign trade, whereas the World Bank was designed chiefly to supply huge volume of capital to the United Nations and associated nations needed for reconstruction, relief, and economic recovery. *Id.* at 30.

[100] The charter of the U.N determined, among other goals, the establishment of international relations based on principles of equality among nations and cooperation to resolve the economic and social problems. Moreover, the charter established the Economic and Social council. The purpose of the Economic and Social council is to achieve prosperity, stability, and justice. See U.N Charter arts. 1, para. 3, art. 2, para. 1, 55, 60. The first meeting of the Economic and Social Council of the U.N was in 1946. The meeting called for an international conference on trade and employment, establishment of preparatory committee for a convention on promoting free trade, and the establishment of the ITO. See U. N. ESCOR, 1st Sess., Plenary Meeting, U.N. Doc. E/22 (1946).

[101] However, in practice, the Bretton Woods institutions operated separately from the U.N.

[102] The process of drafting a charter for the ITO passed through four stages: 1) the original American draft of Sept. 1946, 2) draft charter revised at the London meeting of the preparatory committee of the international conference for trade and employment between Oct.-Nov. 1946 (the London Draft), 3) further revised draft in Geneva in Apr.-Aug. 1947 (the Geneva Draft), and 4) the charter revised in Havana in Nov. 1947-Mar. 1948 (the Havana Charter). See Jonathan Reuvid, *A Handbook of World Trade: A Strategic Guide to Trading Internationally* 5 (Kogan Page 2001).

[103] See U.S. Dept. State, *Havana Charter for an International Trade Organization* arts. 73 & 74 (Off. Pub. Affairs 1948). The Havana Charter provided commitments on Tariffs, Preferences, Internal Taxation and Regulation (arts. 16-19), Quantitative Restrictions and Related Exchange Matters (arts. 20-24), Subsidies (arts. 25-28), State Trading and Related Matters (arts. 29-32), General Commercial Provisions on Freedom of Transit, Anti-Dumping and Countervailing Duties (arts. 33-39), Special Provisions for Free Trade Areas and Customs Unions and Consultation (arts. 40-45), Restrictive Business Practices (arts. 46-54), and Inter-Governmental Commodity Agreements (arts. 55-70).

Signatories of the Havana Charter included some Arab countries such as Egypt, Iraq, Lebanon, Morocco, Syria, Transjordan, and Tunisia. Had the U.S. Congress ratified the ITO Charter at its birth, those Arab countries would have become members of the ITO. Arab countries would have become integrated in the world economic system.

In 1947, the General Agreement on Tariffs and Trade (GATT) was concluded in Geneva as an interim agreement until the creation of the ITO.[105] Many articles of Havana Charter 1948 and GATT 1947 duplicated each other, though the Charter was more comprehensive.[106] Since the ITO never came into existence from its inception, the GATT had to operate as an agreement and as a *de facto* organization for decades.[107]

---

[104] The U.S. President submitted the ITO draft charter to Congress in 1948 but it did not move beyond a vote in the Senate. In 1951, the President announced that he would no longer seek approval. The death of the ITO was attributed to the domestic political situation in the U.S. The Truman administration confronted a new protectionist and isolationist Republican Congress. The U.S. refused to join the ITO because of perceived threats to national sovereignty and the danger of too much ITO intervention in markets. Congress feared that the ITO would be too much supranational. It was feared that there would be double delegation of power from Congress to the U.S. President and from the President to an international organization, thereby usurping the functions of Congress. In other words, an international organization would establish a World Government. Also, the U.S. Congressional support for the ITO was conditioned on dismantling of the British Imperial Preference system (Commonwealth system) devised at the Ottawa Conference in 1932; a system which was enacted partly in response to the U.S. Smoot-Hawley Act, because, as the U.S. contended, it contravened the most-favored-nation rule. Because of the British Commonwealth system, U.S. economic interests were excluded from the British market and its satellite countries or dominions, such as South Africa, Canada, and India. The British refused to yield their position unless they received assurances from Congress to lower American tariffs. However, the U.S. administration did not lower its tariffs and stood for its pledge to Congress by dismantling the British Commonwealth system [despite an earlier agreement between the U.S. and Britain, the Lend-Lease Agreement in Mar. 1941, which mandated dismantling trade barriers]. The linkage between the most-favored-nation rule and the Commonwealth system was a factor for loss of support for the ITO. Moreover, the U.S. constitution authorizes congress to regulate commerce with foreign nations. See U.S. Const. art.1, δ 2. Therefore, the U.S. Congress considered the Executive had exceeded its mandate under the constitution. In the 1950s, there had been an agreement for the establishment of the Organization for Trade Co-operation (OTC) that would take over the GATT and police world trade. See George Bronz, *An International Trade Organization: The Second Attempt*, 69 Harv. L. Rev. 440, 447-449, 473-476 (1956). President Eisenhower asked Congress to allow the U.S. to become a member of the OTC. However, again, there was difficulty shepherding the OTC bill through Congress.

[105] See General Agreement on Tariffs and Trade, opened for signature Oct. 30, 1947, 61 Stat. pts. 5,6, T.I.A.S. No. 1700, 55 U.N.T.S. 187. The GATT has no formal relationship to the U.N. The GATT is not a U.N agency. However, GATT maintains close relation with the U.N. For example, the Geneva-based International Trade Center is run jointly by GATT and UNCTAD.

[106] If the ITO came into existence, GATT 1947 would have been incorporated in the ITO. Drafters of the GATT contemplated that once the Havana Charter entered into force, and with it the ITO, Part II of the GATT, which contains the bulk of the international legal commitments (other than the most-favored-nation obligation and tariff commitments), would be suspended. Countries in the ITO are referred to as "members" while under the GATT 1947 they are referred to as "contracting parties". If an article denotes to all parties of the GATT, then contracting parties is written in capital letters "CONTRACTING PARTIES". If, however, an article denotes to one party to the GATT, then contracting party is written in lowercase "contracting party". See *id.* art. XXV.1. U.S. negotiators, under the mandate of domestic law, invented the term "contracting party" in GATT 1947 to avoid the suggestion of an organization.

[107] When Congress failed to ratify the ITO Charter, the GATT was renewed every three years until it was made a permanent organization in 1955.

GATT 1947 was negotiated by twenty three countries. As an agreement, it never itself came into force. GATT was always applied provisionally through the Protocol of Provisional Application.[108] GATT 1947 was a code under which countries will conduct their mutual commercial relations. The purpose of the GATT was to establish an open system of world trade between the contracting parties.

The non-discriminatory provisions of article I (MFN Treatment) and article III (National Treatment on Internal Taxation and Regulation), article II (Schedule of Concessions), and article XI (General Elimination of Quantitative Restrictions) in GATT 1947 are the "key" provisions which express its basic structure.[109] GATT 1947 includes articles that support and extend articles I and III.[110] GATT 1947 includes other articles

---

[108] In order to enter into force, article XXVI.6 of GATT 1947 requires governments with a minimum share of world trade to deposit their instruments of acceptance. However, only a few countries did so. Therefore, the GATT was applied through the Protocol of Provisional Application. See Protocol of Provisional Application to the General Agreement on Tariffs and Trade, signed Oct. 30, 1947, 61 Stat. A2051, 55 U.N.T.S. 308.

[109] Article I of GATT requires each contracting party to extend, immediately and unconditionally, any advantage, favor, privilege, and immunity given to a product of a contracting party to the "like product" of all other contracting parties. The GATT includes seventeen provisions using the words like product, like commodity, and like merchandise. Decisions on what constitutes like product are made on a case-by-case basis after applying a variety of criteria that GATT panels have found to be relevant, including product characteristics, consumer tastes and habits, and product end-uses in a particular market. In general, like product has a broader interpretation when it is used in GATT 1947 basic obligations, such as the MFN treatment, and a narrower interpretation in GATT 1947 exceptions, such as article VI regarding anti-dumping and countervailing duties. See Rex J. Zedalis, *A Theory of the GATT "Like Product" Common Language Cases*, 27 Vand. J. Transnatl. L. 33, 45-51, 78-83 (1994). Article II requires each contracting party to apply to products of other contracting parties tariff concessions stated in its schedule. Tariffs concessions could be easily nullified if a contracting party was allowed to impose internal taxes, regulations, or laws on imported products different from those imposed on domestic products once imported products pass the borders of the importing country. Article III protects the "competitive opportunities" enjoyed by imports vis-à-vis like domestic products in the importing country. For illustrative cases under article III of GATT 1947 see Kevin C. Kennedy, *The GATT-WTO System at Fifty*, 16 Wis. Intl. L.J. 421, 432, 433 (1998). Article XI of GATT 1947 provides for tariffication of non-tariff trade barriers, except under specific conditions.

[110] Articles IV (Special Provisions Relating to Cinematograph Films), V (Freedom of Transit), VIII (Fees and Formalities Connected with Importation and Exportation), XIII (Non-Discriminatory Administration of Quantitative Restrictions), and XVII (State Trading Enterprises) support the non-discriminatory provisions of GATT 1947.

that qualify articles I and III.[111] There are other articles concerned with special cases.[112] GATT 1947 includes procedural articles that govern the application of the GATT.[113]

II. Lebanon and Syria in GATT 1947

Of the twenty-three original contracting parties to the GATT 1947, only two, Lebanon and Syria, were from the Arab Middle East.[114] However, Lebanon withdrew from GATT four years later. Six months after Lebanon's withdrawal from the GATT, Syria followed suit.[115] Today, neither are members of the WTO because they withdrew from the GATT in 1951. Lebanon and Syria did not attempt to join the GATT/WTO until 1999 and 2001 respectively.[116]

In 1950, Lebanon notified the CONTRACTING PARTIES of its intention to withdraw from the GATT.[117] The only hint for withdrawal was the need for "readapting". A contracting party under the provisions of GATT 1947 is not obligated to clarify its reasons for withdrawal from the GATT.[118] Moreover, since GATT was applied through the Protocol of Provisional Application, any contracting party can withdraw from the Protocol on sixty days' notice rather than the six months' notice required by article XXXI of the GATT.

---

[111] Articles VI (Anti-Dumping and Countervailing Duties), XII (Restrictions to Safeguard the Balance of Payments), XVIII (Government Assistance to Economic Development), XIX (Emergency Action on Imports of Particular products), XX (General Exceptions), XXI (Security Exceptions), XXIV (Customs Unions and Free-Trade Areas), and XXVIII (Modification of Schedules) qualify the operation of the non-discriminatory provisions of GATT 1947.

[112] Articles VII (Valuation for Customs Purposes), IX (Marks of Origin), X (Publication and Administration of Trade Regulations), XXIII (Nullification or Impairment), and part IV (Trade and Development) address special circumstances. Part IV of GATT 1947 was added in the Kennedy Round to meet the interests of developing countries, See Raj Bhala, *International Trade Law: Cases and Materials* 104 (Michie 1996).

[113] Articles XXV (Joint Action by the Contracting Parties), XXVI (Acceptance, Entry into Force and Registration), XXX (Amendments), XXXI (Withdrawal), XXXIII (Accession), and XXXV (Non-Application of the Agreement between Particular Contracting Parties) govern procedurals matters in GATT 1947.

[114] In addition to Lebanon and Syria, there were eight other developing countries as follows: Burma, Ceylon, Republic of Chile, Republic of China, Republic of Cuba, India, Pakistan, and Southern Rhodesia.

[115] See Notification of Withdrawal of the Government of Syria from the General Agreement on Tariffs and Trade (June 7, 1951), 90 U.N.T.S. 324.

[116] The Working Party on accession of Lebanon was established in Apr. 1999. A formal request for accession under Article XII of the WTO was sent to the Director-General of the WTO by Syria on Oct. 10, 2001 and was circulated to WTO members on Oct. 30, 2001.

[117] Then Lebanese Foreign Minister Philippe Takal communicated his government intention to withdraw from GATT 1947 without further elaboration for the reasons of withdrawal. In his communication he said, "I have the honor to inform you that owing to the necessity of readapting decided to denounce the General Agreement on Tariffs and Trade signed in Geneva on 30 Oct. 1947, and this is in conformity with Paragraph 5 of the Protocol of Provisional Application signed on the same date. Lebanon wishes nevertheless to remain a member of the General Conference of the ITO". See *Notification of Withdrawal of the Government of Lebanon from the General Agreement on Tariffs and Trade* (Dec. 27, 1950), 77 U.N.T.S. 367.

[118] See GATT, *supra* n. 105, art. XXXI.

One may suspect that the reason for Lebanese withdrawal was the consideration by Israel to join the GATT.[119] In 1947, the government of the United Kingdom, acting as a mandatory power for Palestine, opened negotiations for the accession of Palestine to the GATT. Negotiations for Palestine's accession resulted in Schedule XIX that contained concessions granted by the government of the United Kingdom. However, after the United Kingdom ceased to be a contracting party to the GATT with respect to the customs territory formerly included in the Palestine mandate, Israel made no declaration indicating its willingness to be bound by the GATT.[120] Therefore, Israel (the successor state) was not bound by the concessions negotiated by the United Kingdom (the predecessor state). It was not until 1962 when Israel assumed full status in the GATT.[121]

Lebanon had at its disposal an alternative option that it could have invoked rather than an outright withdrawal. The non-application clause of article XXXV of the GATT clearly stipulates that the GATT will not apply between a contracting party (Lebanon in that case) and an acceding country (Israel) if either one of them does not agree to its application of the other party "at the time of accession".[122] Resorting to article XXXV is more convincing especially as article XXXV was added at the first session of the Contracting Parties in 1948, well before Lebanon's withdrawal.[123] Therefore, Lebanon could have employed article XXXV if Israel was to accede to the GATT.

---

[119] Israel was established as an independent state on May 14, 1948. See *Israel's Present Position in Relation to G.A.T.T.*, 2 Econ. News 75, 76-78 (No. 2, Dec. 1949) (The advantages of Israel's adherence to the GATT would mean that, within the framework of the MFN doctrine, it would find itself in possession of rights similar to those of other GATT states. The main disadvantage of acceding to the GATT is the restriction of freedom to enter into bilateral agreements affecting trade policy. Since Israel was only at the first stages of developing its economy, it might be premature to give up already now Israel's liberty to find out which principles it has to choose as definite).

[120] See The Position of Palestine in Relation to the Agreement: Item 8 of the Agenda to the Annecy GATT Conference, Apr. 29, 1949, GATT Doc. No. GATT/CP.3/17, page 1 (The doctrine of state succession in international law is not well defined, but generally speaking, the authorities agree that there is no automatic succession to obligations arising from commercial treaties such as the GATT. The fact that the obligations under the GATT are far-reaching and important reinforces the conclusion that there should be no succession).

[121] Israel was party to the GATT through the application of provisional accession in 1959. See GATT Analytial Index, *infra* n. 123, at 1046, 1051.

[122] India set a precedent when it became the first country to invoke article XXXV in 1948 with respect to South Africa. See *Id.* at 958. Egypt, Morocco, and Tunisia invoked article XXXV of GATT with respect to Israel upon their accession to the GATT. See Ariel M. Ezrahi, *Opting Out of Opt-Out Clauses: Removing Obstacles to International Trade and International Peace*, 31 L & Poly Intl. Bus. 123, 138 (1999).

[123] See *GATT Analytical Index: Guide to GATT Law and Practice* 961 (6th ed., Contracting Parties to the General Agreement on Tariffs and Trade 1994).

III. Arab Countries and UNCTAD and WTO

From the birth of the GATT in 1947 until 1993, few Arab countries have joined the GATT-type multilateral trading system.[124] Like many other developing countries, Arab countries, after the end of colonialism, called for a new world economic order that would take their development needs into account.[125] Thus, the United Nations Conference on Trade and Development (UNCTAD) was born. The UNCTAD was set up as a permanent organ of the U.N General Assembly in 1964, and it meets every four years.[126]

In UNCTAD, negotiations were conducted by the bloc approach, with "the Group of 77" representing the developing countries.[127] UNCTAD can be best described as the developing countries' GATT. Over the span of its life, UNCTAD's most cited achievement is the Generalized System of Preferences (GSP) whereby developed countries give preferential, non-reciprocal, and non-discriminatory treatment to developing countries trade.[128] Although the GSP has functioned with relative success, its limited coverage of beneficiary countries and products, coupled with conditions that beneficiary countries must meet before being eligible for such a preferential treatment led to disgruntling feelings on the part of the recipients. Moreover, many of UNCTAD tasks now fall within the contours of the WTO whose membership is essentially the same.

---

[124] Egypt, Kuwait, Morocco, Mauritania, and Tunisia were the only countries to join the GATT 1947. For example, Egypt and Tunisia first acceded to the GATT provisionally. Provisional accession means that the GATT contracting parties extend the GATT rights including tariff concession to acceding countries if the latter reciprocate. However, acceding countries did not have a direct right regarding tariff concessions negotiated prior to their accession to the GATT. In other words, acceding countries were not entitled to compensation in case tariff concessions were withdrawn.

[125] The main reason for not joining the GATT system was the doctrine of reciprocity embedded in the GATT. The doctrine of reciprocity obliges countries to reciprocate their concessions. See Adeoye Akinsanya & Arthur Davies, *Third World Quest for a New International Economic Order: An Overview*, 33 Intl. & Comp. L. Q. 208 (1984). See also *Declaration on the Establishment of a New International Economic Order*, G.A. Res. 3201, U.N. GAOR, 28th Sess., Supp. No. 1, at 3, U.N. Doc. A/9559 (1974) (the new international economic order should be founded on full respect for preferential and non-reciprocal treatment for developing countries, wherever feasible, in all fields of international economic cooperation whenever possible).

[126] UNCTAD held its first meeting in 1964 in Geneva, Switzerland. See Kele Onyejekwe, *International Law of Trade Preferences. Emanations from the European Union and the United States*, 26 St. Mary's L.J. 425, 447 (1995) (the foundation of the new international economic order movement was the theory of "structuralism" which called for a fundamental realignment of the international order to correct deep imbalances between developed and developing countries that would, if uncorrected, perpetuate underdevelopment).

[127] There were four lists. African countries, Asian countries, and Yugoslavia fell under List A. List B contained the developed capitalist countries. Latin American and Caribbean countries were under List C. List D included the socialist countries of Eastern Europe. Countries on Lists A and C formed the Group of 77. *Id*. In reality, the number of countries in the Group of 77 is more than 77.

[128] Other UNCTAD achievements included concluding codes of conduct such as code of conduct on transfer of technology, code of conduct on liner conferences, and code of conduct on restrictive business practices and commodity agreements for products such as sugar, copper, and coffee. Many of those codes and commodity agreements fell by the way side either due to objections from List B developed countries who were outvoted in the approval of those codes or disagreement among developed and developing countries over their share in commodity quotas.

However, UNCTAD still has a role to play even though the WTO made UNCTAD relatively anachronistic.[129]

Arab countries are believed to have little enthusiasm for the general free trade agenda that the WTO encourages.[130] In practice, the majority of Arab countries are protectionist and are likely to stay that way for the years to come.[131] Arab countries are interested in guarding their sovereignty and protecting domestic industry from flood of foreign imports. Arab countries do not acknowledge the benefits the WTO offers.[132] Trade liberalization is perceived as a threat to cultural traditions.[133]

The WTO created a new reality, and Arab countries cannot afford not to join.[134] One can pose the following question: can Arab countries imagine getting engaged in the multilateral trading system without being part of the WTO? With the world becoming more and more economically integrated, Arab countries will have the chance to be involved and their interests represented appropriately.[135] In an era of internationalizing the economy, any Arab country which does not join would be isolated.

---

[129] See Jagdish Bhagwati, *A Stream of Windows: Unsettling Reflections on Trade, Immigration,and Democracy* 29-35 (MIT Press 1998) (recalling the glory of UNCTAD under the leadership of Raul Prebisch, was an institution ahead of the curve. The memory of the institution has faded in OECD countries where it has become commonplace in some influential quarters to think of UNCTAD as if it was instead UNWASHED and UNKEMPT. It has been criticized that the institution focuses on politics rather than economics, and it is too partisan). The reasons for the OECD displeasure with UNCTAD may be the fact that it encompasses a majority of developing countries with strong voting power.

[130] See David R. Karasik, *Securing the Peace Dividend in the Middle East: Amending GATT Article XXIV to Allow Sectoral Preferences in Free Trade Areas*, 18 Mich. J. Intl. L. 527, 545 (1997).

[131] For example, Arab countries adopt fixed exchange rates, impose customs duties on manufactured goods, restrict access to service suppliers, and institute preferential government purchasing programs. Even if the idea of free trade has been accepted, the practical application of its principles might be highly unpopular among politically sensitive groups across Arab countries. *Id.*

[132] *Id.*

[133] Prince Bandar Bin Salman Bin Mohammad Al-Saud remarked that each country has its own experience and the way it deals with foreign investment, e-commerce, and WTO which corresponds with its system, culture, and belief. See *Strengthening Relations with Arab and Islamic Countries through International Law: E-Commerce, WTO Dispute Settlement Mechanism, and Foreign Investment* 4 (The International Bureau of the Permanent Court of Arbitration ed., Kluwer L. Intl. 2002).

[134] The following are the Arab countries that joined the WTO: Bahrain (Jan. 1, 1995), Djibouti (May 31, 1995), Oman (Nov. 9, 2000), Qatar (Jan. 13, 1996), United Arab Emirates (Apr. 10, 1996), and Jordan (Apr. 11, 2000). In addition there are seven other Arab countries in the process of joining: Algeria, Iraq, Lebanon, Libya, Saudi Arabia, Sudan, and Yemen.

[135] Developing countries had noticeable impact on developed countries in the WTO. For example, Guatemala and Ecuador, not satisfied with the settlement of the banana dispute, blocked the proposal of the EC to obtain a waiver for the Fiji Convention that gives preferential treatment for African, Caribbean, and Pacific (ACP) countries. Developing countries played an important role in the debate over the selection of Director General for the WTO to replace Renato Ruggeiro in 1999. Additionally, developing countries aired their concerns toward the green room negotiations module in Seattle Ministerial meeting. See *id.* at 182-183.

Adhering to the rules of the WTO may enhance global confidence in the Arab countries, and thus likely to increase foreign direct investment.[136] As for the individual Arabic citizen, one can imagine how consumers would be if all those goods not made in his home country became available at his fingertips. The loss of sovereignty is not specific to Arab countries but for all countries joining the WTO.[137] Membership in the WTO would ensure Arab countries a fair forum for settling their potential trade disputes with other members who may wield more trading power. Reviewing some of the WTO cases would reveal this fact.[138] WTO agreements have safety valves such as antidumping measures that can be used provisionally to counter imports.

IV. The Uruguay Round

The GATT 1947 was the beginning of a series of negotiations that ended up with the establishment of the WTO in 1994. Countries held eight rounds of negotiations which led ultimately to the birth of the WTO fifty years later with the successful conclusion of the Uruguay Round negotiations.[139] Over the span of eight rounds, there has been an increase in the number of the participating countries in those rounds, time lapsing between the starting of the negotiations and their conclusions, change of the venue of negotiations from developed countries to developing countries as the number of participating developing countries increased, and a variety of items discussed at the negotiations table.[140]

---

[136] Personal choice, voluntary exchange, freedom to compete, and security of privately-owned property are the cornerstones of economic freedom. In a study conducted on economic freedom in the world, Jordan ranked 36 in 2002, Bahrain ranked 31, Morocco ranked 83, and Egypt ranked 74 .See James Gwartney & Robert Lawson, *Economic Freedom of the World: Annual Report (2004)* 53, 81, 107, 120 (The Fraser Inst. 2004).

[137] The U.S. and other developed countries have much more to worry about in terms of sovereignty since they have many great issues at stake. For more on sovereignty see Jenik Radon, *Sovereignty: A Political Emotion, Not a Concept*, 40 Stan. J. Intl. L. 195, 203, 208 (2004) (despite the long history of the sovereignty concept, it has always been a term in search of a definition. The notion of sovereignty has always been problematic and ephemeral. The U.S. approach toward sovereignty is grounded on the legacy of American exceptionalism. For the U.S., joining the WTO met with opposition and suspicion. Joining the WTO amounted to the surrender of U.S. sovereignty. On the other hand, for small countries, accession to regional and global bodies gives them more sovereignty). Under the Uruguay Round Agreements Act, any member of Congress can offer a joint resolution every five years to have the U.S. withdraw from the WTO. This is an example of U.S. concern over ceding its sovereignty by joining the WTO.

[138] See Appellate Body Report, *United States-Import Prohibition of Certain Shrimp and Shrimp Products*, WT/DS58/AB/R (Oct. 12, 1996).

[139] For a list highlighting the eight rounds of negotiations see Table 1 in appendix 1, page 217. For more on the Doha Development Agenda see *Doha and Beyond: The Future of the Multilateral Trading System* 68, 115 (Mike Moore ed., Cambridge U. Press 2004) (the study, conducted by the WTO Advisory group set up by former WTO Director General Mike Moore, addresses the challenges facing the WTO and the development dimension of the multilateral trading system).

[140] Even though negotiations may first start in a developing country, subsequent negotiations are held in Geneva.

In earlier years, countries held negotiations on a product-by-product basis. In the Kennedy Round, countries adopted across-the-board method.[141] Countries shifted from negotiating tariffs reductions to negotiating non-tariff barriers as they are being erected such as voluntary exports restraints or orderly marketing agreements.[142]

Despite the obvious achievements of the GATT rounds, there were loopholes in the trading system.[143] The GATT operated as an agreement and a pragmatic institution. For example, although article XXV (3) & (4) call for one vote per nation and decisions to be taken by majority vote, in practice consensus was developed among parties. Consensus means that any party can block the adoption of a decision or an agreement. For example, any Arab country can prevent the adoption of a panel decision.

To avoid the "free rider" problem, countries adopted the code approach.[144] Under the code approach, countries in the Tokyo Round created two level trade regimes: the GATT 1947 and the codes themselves. Since codes were open to whoever accepted them, membership in these codes was at variance.[145] Therefore, codes were open only to those countries that were prepared to accept the rights and obligations contained in them. The code approach eroded one of the basic principles of the GATT, viz, the unconditional

---

[141] See G.J.Lanjouw, *International Trade Institutions* 10 (Open U. Netherlands 1995). In the Tokyo Round, participants adopted a mathematical tariff reduction formula applied on industrial tariffs, known as the Swiss formula. It works as follows:

$z = ax/x + a$ where z is post-Tokyo Round tariff rate, x is the pre-Tokyo Round tariff rate, and a is a constant. In other words, the Swiss formula means products with higher tariffs would be subject to deeper cuts, thus bringing them closer to lower-tariff products by incorporating a non-linear approach and forming the degree of cuts on the basis of a single agreed coefficient. Under the Swiss formula, the smaller the coefficient figure, the greater the cuts required.

[142] Voluntary exports restraints or orderly marketing agreements are classical examples of new protectionism. Those agreements are theoretically not barred by the GATT. Voluntary exports restraints or orderly marketing agreements are self-imposed restrictions on trade by an exporting country rather than discriminatory quantitative restrictions by an importing country, which would be prohibited. For an explanation on the reasons for the use of non-tariffs barriers and the shift in trade policy of the U.S. see Edward John Ray, *The Political Economy of International Trade Law and Policy: Changing Patterns of Protectionism: The Fall in Tariffs and the Rise in Non-Tariffs Barriers*, 8 Nw. J. Intl. & Bus. 285, 294-298, 303-305 (1987).

[143] The first Secretary-General of the GATT, Eric Wyndham White, referred to the GATT as "It is anything but neat and orderly". See Gardner. Patterson & Eliza. Patterson, *The Road from GATT to the MTO*, 3 Minn. J. Global Trade 35, 37 (1994). As the acronym of the GATT indicates, GATT scope was limited only to tariffs and trade in goods. It did not contain rules aimed at the liberalization of trade in services and other sectors.

[144] According to the MFN doctrine in GATT 1947, any concession agreed between two parties will extend automatically and unconditionally to a third contracting party without the latter's adherence to any obligation.

[145] See Paul Demart, *The Metamorphoses of the GATT: From the Havana Charter to the World Trade Organization*, 34 Colum. J. Transnatl. L. 123, 128-129 (1995). While most developed countries were signatories to the codes many countries, especially developing ones, remained outside. For example, the number of developing countries which signed on to the following codes were: Technical Barriers to Trade 14, Subsidies 13, Import Licensing 10, Customs Valuation 9, Antidumping 9, and Government Procurement 3. See Beverly M. Carl, *Trade and the Developing World in the 21ST Century* 85 (Transnatl. Publishers 2001).

MFN doctrine. The rights and obligations under those codes were not extended to all members of GATT, but only to those who accepted them.

The GATT gives special treatment to the developing countries.[146] However, in practice, developing countries' needs have not yet been met in the trading system.[147] Since justice demands that equals be treated equally, it also requires that unequals be treated unequally, at least, in proportion to the inequality to achieve equality among all in the end. Therefore, the GSP was created to meet the demands of developing countries.[148] However, as trade negotiations reduce tariffs further, the MFN rate will equal the GSP rate. Thus, benefits for developing countries would be eroded.[149]

GATT 1947 contained general provisions regarding how to settle disputes in articles XXII and XXIII. Formal legal actions in the GATT were seen as unfriendly. Therefore, the GATT developed the diplomacy rule.[150] The EC took the view that dispute settlement under the GATT should be a natural consequence of the negotiation process, known as

---

[146] For example, article XVIII authorizes a country to restrict imports for the establishment of a particular industry or for balance of payment purposes. Developed countries should not expect reciprocity in concessions from developing countries. Article XXVIII.a *bis* stipulates that the needs of less-developed countries for the use of tariffs to protect their economies and for revenue purposes must be taken into account. Moreover, an enabling clause was developed so as to give permanent preferential treatment to developing countries during the Tokyo Round. The so-called "Enabling clause" was developed through a decision taken by the contracting parties to the GATT. The text of the clause states that contracting parties "may" accord differential and more favorable treatment to developing countries. Abdulqawi A. Yusef, *Differential and More Favorable Treatment: The GATT Enabling Clause*, 14 J.W.T. 488 496-498, 506 (1980).

[147] Part VI, was qualified by many words that rendered it aspirations rather than legal binding commitments. For example, under article XXXVII.1, developed countries can apply preferential treatment to the "fullest extent possible". See *Developing Countries and the Multilateral Trade Agreements: Law and the promise of Development*, 108 Harv. L. Rev. 1715 (1995).

[148] The GSP was seen as an *ex gratia* favor on the part of the developed countries. For more on the views of the critics and proponents of the GSP see Ndiva Kofele-Kale, *The Principle of Preferential Treatment in the Law of GATT: Toward Achieving the Objective of an Equitable World Trading System*, 18 Cal. W. Intl. L. J. 302, 315, 322 (1987/88). Ten Arab countries are designated as beneficiaries of the U.S. GSP: Bahrain, Djibouti, Egypt, Jordan, Lebanon, Morocco, Oman, Sudan, Tunisia, and Yemen. See CARL, *supra* n. 145, at 522-523, 341. Country membership in OPEC would disqualify them from GSP benefits. On the other hand, U.S. GSP identifies as ineligible for GSP any country that belongs to a group of countries that "withholds supplies of vital commodity resources or to raise the price of such commodities to an unreasonable level, and to cause serious disruption of the world economy. This condition includes the implicit OPEC reference. As the list indicates the GSP system is not a general system. The GSP is established on the basis of pick and choose. The GSP list can be changed from time to time upon the occurrence of certain conditions.

[149] Although the assumption of erosion of preferences might have been true for GSP products, it did not hold true for non-GSP covered imports from developing countries that could have benefited from MFN tariff reduction at the end of the Tokyo Round. See Bela Balassa, *The Tokyo Round and the Developing Countries* 14 J.World Trade L. 98 (1980).

[150] For review of the legal action and diplomacy approaches and the drawbacks of the GATT 1947 dispute mechanism see Richerd G. Shell, *Trade Legalism and International Relations Theory: An Analysis of the World Trade Organization*, 44 Duke L.J. 829, 835-838, 840-848 (1995). See also Harold H. Koh, *The Legal Markets of International Trade: A Perspective on the Proposed Canada-United States Free Trade Agreement*, 12 Yale J. Intl. L. 193, 194-197 (1987). See Michael K. Young, *Dispute Resolution in the Uruguay Round: Lawyers Triumph Over Diplomats*, 29 Intl. L. 389, 392-405 (1995).

the pragmatic approach.[151] On the other hand, the U.S. viewed the dispute system under the GATT as a rule-based system in which violations are exposed and subject to sanctions, known as the adjudication approach.[152] The consensus approach applied practically by the GATT meant that any decision taken by the GATT Council could be blocked even by the challenged party at any level of the dispute.

Against this background, the GATT parties decided, at their 1986 Punta del Este Ministerial meeting, to launch the Uruguay Round. The agenda covered traditional GATT subjects such as tariffs, non-tariff barriers, subsidies, and safeguards. It also added intellectual property, services, and trade-related investment measures. It also specifically provided that the results of the Uruguay Round "shall be treated as parts of a single undertaking".[153] In other words, participants would accept all the results or nothing.[154]

Almost seven years later, the Uruguay Round came to an end. It brought with it legalization of world trade politics after the GATT was considered a geopolitical document created to contain the spread of non-market ideology to other countries.[155] In addition to all areas covered in the negotiations, the WTO institution was established. The functions of the WTO, as set out in Article III of the WTO Charter, are to provide the framework for the implementation of all the agreements that had been or might be negotiated. In addition, it provides the forum for future trade negotiations, and administer the dispute settlement system and the trade policy review mechanism.[156] The function of

---

[151] Countries advocating the pragmatic approach, highlighted the ambiguity of GATT rules, the political sensitivity of trade disputes, and the complex trade-offs of competing interests that go into the formulation of any trade rule. Thus, those countries argued that GATT dispute resolution should not be formal, legal, or adjudicatory. See David K. Tarullo, Logic, *Myth and International Economic Order*, 26 Harv. Intl. L.J. 533 (1985).

[152] The U.S. argued that the GATT rules will become more clear and predictable if the GATT dispute resolution is characterized by rule-based decisions rendered through an adjudicatory dispute resolution process. The adjudication approach will increase compliance with the GATT standards and will alleviate protectionist pressures. See John H. Jackson et al., *Legal Problems of International Economic Relations: Cases, Materials, and Text on the National and International Regulation of Transnational Economic Relations* 339 (3rd ed., W. Publg. Co 1995). Adjudication approach advocates could be called "trade litigators". One can imagine if the EC approach was followed how developing countries would be harmed otherwise in the adjudication approach. By and large, the most important achievement of the WTO 1994 is to have a panel and Appellate Body making no difference between small or big trading countries. All is equal. The cases decided so far by the WTO panels and Appellate Body bear witness that no bullying by big countries in the system is tolerated any more.

[153] Single undertaking is known also as the principle of globality or single roof policy. See Demart, *supra* note 145, at 134. See also generally Thomas J. Dillon, *The World Trade Organization: A New Legal Order for World Trade?* 16 Mich. J. Intl. L. 349 (1995).

[154] The Punta del Este Declaration recognized the need to establish legal basis for new dispute settlement procedures, new institutional framework for the Secretariat, and cooperation with other international organizations to the end of ensuring greater coherence in global economic policy-making.

[155] At some point, U.S. officials declared GATT a Western-type of document.

[156] The covered agreements of the Final Act of the Uruguay Round include, in addition to the WTO Charter, the Multilateral Trade Agreements. The Multilateral Trade Agreements are: the GATT 1994, which includes, with certain exceptions, GATT 1947, its subsequent agreements and many of its decisions and waivers, GATS Agreement, TRIPs Agreement, Dispute Settlement Understanding, and Trade Policy Review Mechanism (hereinafter the Multilateral Agreements). See *Marrakesh Agreement Establishing the World Trade Organization*, ann. 1A, 1B, 1C, 2 & 3 (Apr. 14, 1994), 1867 U.N.T.S. 3. Countries in the

the WTO as a forum for future trade negotiations allows for further evolution of the international trading system to include new multilateral agreements between its members.

The Uruguay Round results both clarified and extended existing GATT obligations in virtually every facet.[157] Many of the WTO Agreements establish specific treatment for developing and least developing countries. Special treatment for developing and least developing countries takes the form of a prolonged transitional period accompanied with lesser obligations normally imposed on countries participating in these agreements.[158]

In one of its most impressive successes, the WTO provides a unified dispute resolution regime in the Understanding on Rules and Procedures Governing the Settlement of Disputes (DSU).[159] The DSU expressly prohibits the "jungle rule" so a country does not take its rights into its own hands.[160] Perhaps, it is fair to say that the dispute settlement mechanism under the WTO is the only rule-based body in the system.[161]

When a dispute arises, parties first consult. Where consultation fails to bring about a mutually agreeable solution, a party to the dispute may call for the establishment of a

---

Uruguay Round concluded Plurilateral Trade Agreements. These were: Agreement on Trade in Civil Aircraft and the Agreement on Government Procurement (hereinafter Plurilateral Trade Agreements). *Id.* ann. 4. The Plurilateral Trade Agreements create neither rights nor obligations for those countries who have not accepted them.

[157] GATT 1994, which incorporates GATT 1947, excludes the Protocol of Provisional Application, which limited GATT's application in national law. *Id.* Final Act 1125, at 1154. For illustrations of changes and clarifications of the different agreements such as safeguard, antidumping, and countervailing see Demart, *supra* n. 145, at 138 -155.

[158] For example, under the Agreement on Subsidies and Countervailing Measures (SCM), export subsidy prohibition, as mentioned in article 3.1.a. of the Agreement, does not apply to least developing countries designated by the U.N as such and some developing countries having GNP per capita less than one thousand dollar annually such as Bolivia, Egypt, and Morocco at the time the WTO came into effect. According to article 27.4, other developing countries have to phase out their export subsidies progressively within eight years from the date the WTO enters into force upon fulfilling certain conditions.

[159] The Tokyo Round established separate dispute resolution procedures in some of the separate codes negotiated during the Tokyo Round such as the code on subsidy and anti-dumping. As such, the GATT has been described as the centerpiece of a solar system of independent agreements with their own dispute settlement mechanism. For an excellent historical review on the different approaches to the dispute resolution under GATT and the Tokyo Round see Miquel Montanai Mora, *A GATT with teeth: Law Wins over Politics in the Resolution of International Trade Disputes*, 31 Colum. J. Transnatl. L. 103, 107, 123-128, 129-136 (1993). See also John H. Jackson, *The Birth of the GATT-MTN System: A Constitutional Appraisal*, 12 Law & Policy Intl. Bus. 21 (1980). The DSU of the WTO applies to all the covered agreements. See Final Act, *supra* n. 156, ann.2. art.1.

[160] Article 23 of the DSU states, "When members seek the redress of a violation . . . they shall have recourse to, and abide by, the rules and procedures of this understanding". See Final Act, *supra* n. 156, art. 23.1, at 1241.

[161] The WTO covered agreements adopt many concepts and proposals advanced by the U.S. and EC during the Uruguay Round such as tariffication in agriculture. Moreover, WTO Ministerial Conferences are clouded by mini-meetings or group meetings where the real negotiations are held. At the WTO headquarters in Geneva, green room meetings are the norm.

WTO panel.[162] Panel reports may be appealed to the Appellate Body for review of legal issues. Establishment of panels and the Appellate Body and adoption of their decisions are to be achieved through inverted consensus.[163] In other words, panel decisions are adopted unless all WTO members present at the meeting of the DSB decide by consensus not to adopt panel decisions. Thus, establishment of panels and adoption of their decisions are assured in all cases. The remedies available to a complaining country are first conformity of the violating member's measures with the DSB adopted decision.[164] If conformity is not achieved within the time required by the decision, then the complaining party may request compensation.[165] If the parties do not agree on compensation, then the complaining party may request retaliation in the sector subject matter of the dispute, and if it believes that retaliation in that sector would be unsatisfactory, it may then request retaliation across sectors and/or agreements.

The enforcement of obligations under DSU proves elements of legal proceedings with a depoliticized nature. Over eight years of the DSU's existence, panels have issued almost 30,000 pages of decisions. Reviewing the myriad of these decided cases reveals a deeper legal quality of the system.

V. The League of Arab States and Boycott to Israel

The Arab League trade boycott of Israel has a profound impact on the relationship between Arab countries and the WTO.[166] Additionally, the question of concern is whether the Arab boycott of Israel is legitimate or not, and if so, whether it could be subject to a

---

[162] The DSU created the Dispute Settlement Body (DSB) to administer the rules and procedures of the Understanding. A respondent to a dispute may prevent the establishment of a panel in the DSB meeting. However, if a complaining party requests the establishment of a panel at the following DSB meeting, a panel would be established. *Id.* ann. 2. arts. 3 & 6, at 1227-1230. DSU rules also stipulate that cases should be resolved within nine months if there is no appeal, or within twelve months of establishing a panel if the case is appealed. *Id.* art. 20, at 1237-1238. One novelty in the DSU is the adoption of arbitration as an alternative method in resolving disputes of issues clearly defined. However, it is unclear in the text how the arbitration will be conducted, under which law or agreement, and whether the members have the freedom to choose their own arbitrators. The fact that any panel decision can be appealed means that the Appellate Body could be flooded with decisions from first-level panel.

[163] *Id.* art. 16.4 & 17.14, at 1235, 1237.

[164] *Id.* art. 21.1, at 1238.

[165] *Id.* art. 22.1, at 1239-1241.

[166] See Eugene Kontorovich, *The Arab League Boycott and WTO Accession: Can Foreign Policy Excuse Discriminatory Sanctions?* 4 Chi. J. Intl. L. 283, 285-286 (2003) (recounting evasiveness of Saudi Arabia in describing the status of the boycott in its accession materials and concluding that allowing nations that enforce a boycott to accede would undermine the WTO's commitment to free trade. The free trade system was designed to promote not just prosperity but peaceful and amicable relations between member states. The Arab League trade boycott on Israel defeats one of the major goals of the WTO. Thus, the U.S. should use its considerable clout in the accession process to require Arab boycotting nations to abandon the secondary and tertiary prongs of the boycott as a condition of membership). As an "informal" condition for joining the WTO, some Arab countries were "expected" not to attend meetings of the Central Boycott Office of the Arab League. Some Arab countries were also "expected" not to invoke article XIII of the WTO Charter which would have allowed an acceding country not to apply its commitments to another WTO member.

dispute settlement case before the WTO. Therefore, discussion of the League of Arab States and its trade boycott of Israel is merited.

The League of Arab States was formed as a part of a United Arabia project. It is a watered-down version of that project. On September 25, 1944, a Preparatory Committee composed of Arab states met in Alexandria to discuss various proposals for the scheme.[167] On October 7, 1944, a protocol was signed by all members of the Preparatory Committee. The protocol provided for the establishment of the League of Arab States for independent Arab countries who desired to join the organization.[168] Based on the Alexandria protocol, a charter was drafted and approved by members of the Preparatory Committee in 1945.[169] Since then, the charter formed the constitution of the Arab League. Currently, the Arab League is made up of 22 countries where it provides a forum to promote economic, political, and cultural cooperation.[170]

The League of Arab States boycott of Israel is based on the League's resolution in 1954.[171] For decades the Arab League has boycotted Israeli goods. No Israeli goods may be imported into the Arab League states and no Israeli firms may do business with firms from Arabic countries. In addition, the Arab League has maintained a secondary boycott against companies from third countries that do business with Israel which contribute significantly to Israel's economic and military development. For example, a member state, or its firms, of the Arab League would not do business with a U.S. company that has a business relationship with Israel. A further prohibition is imposed on dealing with a company that deals with another company which in turn has a relationship with Israel. Foreign companies may be required to provide information about the names and nationalities of the companies' board of directors and officers to determine whether they are Jews or not.[172] One Arab boycott blacklist included 1500 U.S. firms, among them

---

[167] For more on the Arab League see Majid Khadduri, *The Arab League as a Regional Arrangement*, 40 Am. J. Intl. L. 756, 763 (1946) (tracing the history of the Arab League to the pan-Arabism movement that revolted against the Turkish domination. The debate among members of the Preparatory Committee focused on the nature of Arab unity scheme as whether they shall opt for a full union or federal union).

[168] The Arab League would be governed by the Council of the League whose membership is based on sovereign equality of member states with one nation, one vote. The Arab League is also composed of the General Secretariat and various committees to address social and economics concerns. *Id.* 765.

[169] One of the conditions for membership in the League was full independence. Therefore, the original signatories were Egypt, Transjordan, Syria, Lebanon, Iraq, Saudi Arabia, and Yemen. *Id.* 766-768 (discussing the concept of full independence and how it applied to the original members).

[170] The Arab League, headquartered in Cairo, Egypt, comprises: Comoros, Iraq, Lebanon, Saudi Arabia, Syria, Jordan, Yemen, Kuwait, Bahrain, Oman, Qatar, United Arab Emirates, Gaza Strip and West Bank, Egypt, Libya, Sudan, Morocco, Tunisia,, Algeria, Mauritania, Somalia, and Djibouti. In 2003, Syria sponsored Turkey to become an observer at the Arab League.

[171] See Preston L. Greene, Jr., *The Arab Economic Boycott of Israel: The International Law Perspective*, 11 Vand. J. Transnatl. L. 77, 79 (1978) (the resolution is a direct response for what the Arabs perceive as the wrongful expropriation of their land for the creation of the state of Israel. The most potent enforcement tool of the boycott is blacklisting). Before placing a company on the blacklist, the company has to be placed on the watch list. In general, the blacklist is not publicly available.

[172] A blacklist of companies that violated the boycott's guidelines such as failing to comply with certification procedures or to complete a questionnaire is maintained at the boycott office headquarters, a specialized agency for the Arab League. Each Arab Country maintains a national boycott office in certain ministries such as foreign affairs, commerce, or finance ministry. *Id.* 78. Currently, the well-staffed Central

Coca Cola, Ford, and Xerox. There is also an informal boycott on the part of Arab consumers who decide to punish U.S. and Israeli goods regardless of whether a formal boycott is maintained or not.[173]

In response to the Arab boycott of Israel, the U.S. introduced over time several measures designed to undercut it.[174] For example, at first, the U.S. encouraged under the Export Administration Act voluntary reporting by U.S. concerns of demands placed on them to comply with the Arab boycott on Israel.[175] Then, the voluntary reporting turned into mandatory reporting. The Internal Revenue Code provides for reduction in several tax benefits such as foreign tax credit or domestic international sales corporation program for any firm that participates in the Arab boycott.[176] Moreover, the U.S. set up an Office of Antiboycott Compliance in the Commerce Department to follow up and interpret the anti-boycott regulations.[177] Any U.S. concern found in violation of anti-boycott rules could be slapped civil and/or criminal fines.[178] These measures are some of U.S. anti-boycott devices.[179] Usually, the U.S. Department of Treasury issues a quarterly list of

---

Boycott Office of the Arab League, which is headed by a Commissioner General, is located in Syria. The Central Boycott Office meets twice a year to update its blacklist. In recent years, some Arab countries had declined to attend the biannual meeting of the Office.

[173] With regard to consumer perception, some Arab anti-normalization lobbies have for a long period actively discouraged consumers from purchasing Israeli or U.S. products. The anti-American sentiment and media publicity could strain trade and investment between Arab countries and the U.S. with potential backlash affecting the sale of U.S. products in Arab countries. Consumer boycott is not the subject of discussion in this section. The focus is only on formal boycott of Israel.

[174] The Arab League boycott on Israel received prominence especially in the years following the 1973 oil crisis.

[175] See Roy M. Mersky & Michael L. Richmond, *Legal Implications of the Arab Economic Boycott of the State of Israel: A Research Guide*, 71 L. Libr. J. 68 (1978).

[176] *Id.* 69.

[177] The Office of Antiboycott Compliance depends on U.S. companies' self-declaration audits as well as selected auditors that would help it in discovering any violation and fraud.

[178] For example a $5,000 fine was imposed on an attorney, in the course of assisting a client, violated the anti-boycott provisions of the Export Administration Act by completing and submitting a form to Saudi Arabia for trademark registration in which the applicant declared that he had no relations with Israel that would violate the Saudi Arabia boycott. The attorney did not inform the Commerce Department of the boycott declaration which is prohibited under U.S. law. See *U.S v. Meyer*, 864 F.2d 214, 218 (1st Cir. 1988) (although the attorney did not intentionally support the Saudi boycott, his awareness of the applications' boycott declaration supports a finding of violation). Other examples include imposing a $4,500 fine in 1990 on Chrono-Log, an exporter of medical equipment, $6 million in 1993 on Baxter International Inc., a medical supplies firm, $31,200 in 1994 on the Arab Bank Plc, New York branch office, and $6,000 in 2001 on Perry Equipment Corp, a drilling company.

[179] Other anti-boycott compliance measures include warning letters, denial of export privileges, potential extraterritorial application of U.S. antitrust laws such as the Sherman and the Clayton Acts, the Federal Trade Commission regulations for letters of credit of U.S. banks, and disclosure requirements mandated by the Securities and Exchange Commission. Additionally, the Foreign Relations Authorization Act allows the U.S. president to take into account foreign country participation in the Arab boycott in determining whether to sell U.S. military to such a country. See *The Arab Boycott: The Antitrust Challenge of United States v. Bechtel in Light of the Export Administration Amendments of 1977*, 93 Harv. L. Rev. 1440, 1441, 1444 (1979) (American firms which comply with the boycott may violate U.S. antitrust laws. The Department of Justice had taken this position in United States v. Bechtel Corp. in 1979 in which it asserted that compliance by Bechtel, one of the world's largest construction firms, made Bechtel a party to a conspiracy that constituted a "concerted refusal to deal" in violation of section 1 of the Sherman Act. Group boycott and refusal to deal are forms of *per se* illegality under the Sherman Act. The Department of Justice's

Arab countries that may require participation in or cooperation with the boycott on Israel.[180] The U.S. Executive is the only authority to enforce the Export Administration Act. There is no private right of action for damages.[181]

The Arab League formal boycott has changed drastically after the launch of the peace process in the Middle East in the 1990s.[182] The Arab League boycott of Israel may be collapsing on its own weight or relic of the past as more and more Arab countries are ignoring it.[183] For example, the Gulf Cooperation Council announced in 1994 that the secondary and tertiary boycott is no longer a threat for the Council members' interests for all practical reasons. Jordan enacted legislation on August 5, 1995, which repealed Jordan's compliance with the boycott.[184] Despite these trends, complete end of the boycott by all Arab countries has not been officially declared. A state of war in its different manifestations is a fact of life in that region. The Arab League boycott is linked to the political situation in the region. Therefore, any discussion of the Arab league's boycott of Israel has been and is important and not symbolic or historical as some would lead us to believe.[185]

---

enforcement policy toward Arab boycott-related activities is founded under the extraterritorial reach of the Sherman Act. In order for U.S. antitrust law to apply extraterritorially, U.S. courts have required domestic "effects" on American commerce. Domestic effects should be direct, substantial, and reasonably foreseeable). To limit the extraterritorial reach of U.S. antitrust law, American companies may argue on the basis of act of state and sovereign compulsion doctrines.

[180] For example, the list of Arab countries for the fourth quarter in 1994 included: Bahrain, Iraq, Jordan, Kuwait, Lebanon, Libya, Oman, Qatar, Saudi Arabia, Syria, United Arab Emirates, and Republic of Yemen. See *List of Countries Requiring Cooperation with an International Boycott*, 59 Fed. Reg. 65, 572 (Dec. 20, 1994). See also *List of Countries Requiring Cooperation with an International Boycott*, 69 Fed. Reg. 75, 604-01 (Dec. 17, 2004) (the list includes: Bahrain, Kuwait, Lebanon, Libya, Oman, Qatar, Saudi Arabia, Syria, United Arab Emirates, and Republic of Yemen). Some Arab countries are on and off the list several times. For example, Jordan was removed from the list in 1995.

[181] A case involved a joint venture of an Israeli corporation and another company in which it tried to acquire a financially troubled U.S. aircraft company. The principal lender to the aircraft company, which is a subsidiary to a Japanese bank, based on instructions from its parent Japanese bank refused to deal with the Israeli corporation because of the Arab boycott. The U.S. court denied the Israeli corporation's request for relief. See *Israel Aircraft Indus. Ltd., v. Sanwa Bus. Credit Corp.*, 16 F.3d 198, 200 (7th Cir. 1994) (the Export Administration Act did not create a private right of action in favor of victims of foreign boycotts. The Act does not authorize private litigation. It does not mention any particular class of beneficiaries).

[182] See Robert A. Diamond, *U.S. Antiboycott Law and Regulations*, 830 P.L.I./COMM. 721, 730-731 (2001) (the number of boycott requests reported to Office of Antiboycott Compliance by U.S. firms fell during the years 1990 to 1996 from 11,026 in 1990 to 2,493 in 1996. Prohibited requests fell during the same period from 2,812 to 1,025. Total boycott requests from all countries for 1997 and 1998 were 1,666 and 1,780 respectively, with prohibited requests at 532 and 526 for the two years. In 1999, there was a decline in total requests to 1,358 with prohibited requests down to 402. In 2000, there was a further decline to 1,271 total requests and 355 prohibited requests).

[183] Perhaps Syria is the last stronghold of the Arab boycott.

[184] Syria, Lebanon, Bahrain, Oman, United Arab Emirates, Kuwait, Saudi Arabia, Qatar, Yemen, Iraq, and Libya still have Israel boycott laws. Bangladesh, Indonesia, Iran, Malaysia, and Pakistan also have their own boycott laws. *Id.* 730.

[185] It can be argued rightfully that the Arab boycott of Israel is symbolic since there is no much direct trade between Arab countries and Israel. Therefore, the economic impact of the boycott on Israel may be minimal.

It has been the ritual for the USTR to issue a report periodically stating that the Arab boycott to Israel is an impediment to U.S. trade.[186] U.S. firms are being hurt, especially by the secondary and tertiary boycott, since the boycott distorts with whom they trade or source their inputs from. U.S. firms may be at a competitive disadvantage with other Asian or European firms whose countries do not have stringent anti-boycott laws and enforcement. It is the secondary and tertiary Arab boycott that has extra-territorial application because it punishes U.S. companies. The U.S. ought to publish, alongside with its periodic reports, specific figures regarding affected companies and dollar damage that would help readers understand how much trade or potential trade has been lost due to the boycott in order to measure the real impact.[187] Additionally, the report ought to detail the implications of this boycott through country-by-country analysis with their activities.[188]

From a narrow legal viewpoint, the Arab boycott may be illegal. GATT articles I and III, among others, ban discriminatory treatment among like products of WTO members and between imported and domestically produced products. The Arab boycott singles out Israeli products compared with other trading nations. However, one must bear in mind that the purpose of the boycott is not to protect the Arab domestic industry. Rather, it is grounded on foreign policy reasons. Therefore, there might be no violation of WTO non-discriminatory articles.

If one would justify the Arab boycott on the basis of article XXI.c of GATT 1994, it may not pass the exception test. Article XXI.c allows a member to take any "action" in pursuance of its obligations under the U.N charter for the maintenance of peace and security. The U.N did not directly authorize the Arab economic boycott of Israel compared with that imposed on Iraq in the 1990s. However, one can counter-argue that the Arab boycott is legitimate because it can be tacitly based on the U.N Security Council resolutions calling for the withdrawal of Israel from the occupied territories of Arab countries. This sort of argument adopts a tacit approach. The Arab embargo is just taking note of the U.N resolutions.

Moreover, article XXI.b.iii permits a member to take any action which "it" considers necessary for the protection of its essential security interests in time of war or emergency in international relations. The use of the word "it" clearly states that it is for every country to judge on the question of what it is related to with regards to its own essential

---

[186] See USTR, *National Trade Estimate Report on Foreign Trade Barriers 2004*,
http://www.ustr.gov/reports/nte/2004/arableague.pdf (accessed July 15, 2004). The National Trade Estimate Report is mandated by the 1974 Trade Act. Barriers identified in the report are intended to form the basis for trade negotiations and sanctions.

[187] The only time the USTR had quantified lost opportunities and profits arising from the Arab boycott was in 1994. The International Trade Commission study, requested by USTR, showed that U.S. companies lost more than $410 million in potential sales during 1993 as a direct result of the Arab boycott. The cost of U.S. companies for compliance with U.S. antiboycott laws estimated to be an additional $160 million. The effects of the boycott included delays in concluding transactions. See U.S.I.T.C, Effects of the Arab League Boycott of Israel on U.S. Businesses, USITC Inv. No. 332-349 (Nov. 1994).

[188] The section on the Arab boycott of Israel in National Trade Estimate Reports on Foreign Trade Barriers is usually two pages long of a version of the boycott which is copied from a previous year with no new substantive information.

security interests. The second prong of article XXI.b.iii requires that the action is taken in time of war or other emergency in international relations. Although there is no direct war between Israel and some Arab countries, an emergency situation has been the case in that region for quite a time. Thus, under the broader term "other emergency", the Arab boycott may be valid.

The Helms-Burton Act provides also a precedent that would further the argument of the legality of the Arab boycott under the WTO. President Kennedy imposed a trade embargo on Cuba in 1962 under the authority of the Foreign Assistance Act of 1961. The Trading with the Enemy Act reinforced the embargo imposed on Cuba under the authority of the Foreign Assistance Act of 1961. These regulations are still substantially in effect and now codified in the Cuban Liberty and Democratic Solidarity Act of 1996, known as the Helms-Burton Act.[189] Title I of the Helm-Burton Act strengthens the provisions of the prior economic boycott against Cuba.[190] It prohibits the importation of Cuban goods into the U.S., and Titles III and IV of the Act deal with sanctions against persons who use property in Cuba that U.S. nationals assert has been confiscated from them.[191]

Although the EC filed a complaint with the WTO challenging the secondary boycott provisions of Helms-Burton Act, a WTO panel did not have the chance to rule on the boycott. After trade skirmishes between the U.S. and the EC, the matter was settled before the first submissions were due to the WTO dispute settlement panel.

The U.S. economic boycott on Cuba has both similarities and differences with the Arab boycott on Israel. The U.S. boycott to Cuba has been in existence, and strengthened over time, since 1962. It has direct and extraterritorial application. U.S. law prohibits the entry into the U.S., not only of Cuban sugar or rum, but also of goods from other countries which contain Cuban sugar or rum. Thus, U.S. boycott forces foreign countries to change their trade patterns and sources of their production inputs. The intent of the Arab boycott is national security determined collectively by the perceived threat of Israel. In contrast, Cuba "threat" is determined unilaterally by the U.S. Although, the U.S. claims the Cuban boycott is relevant based on national security grounds, the U.S.

---

[189] Shortly before the passage of Helms-Burton Act, named after its sponsors Sen. Jesse A. Helms (R-NC) and Rep. Dan Burton (R-IND), Cuba shot down two American aircraft. See John A. Spanogle, Jr., *Can Helms-Burton be Challenged Under WTO?* 27 Stetson L. Rev. 1313, 1323 (1998). As part of the embargo against the Castro regime, the U.S. Congress enacted a provision that denies protection to trademarks that were seized by the Cuban government after the revolution of 1959, unless the original owner assents. In 2000, Congress passed a legislation intended to facilitate sales of medical and agricultural products to Cuba. The legislation, Trade Sanctions Reform and Export Enhancement Act of 2000, permitted agricultural sales to Cuba through payment of cash in advance but prohibited credit agricultural sales. See *The Trade Sanctions Reform and Export Enhancement Act of 2000*, 22 U.S.C. § 7210 (2000).
[190] See Spanogle, Jr., at 1318.
[191] Section 110.a of Helms-Burton Act prohibits the entry into the U.S., not only of Cuban sugar or rum, but also of goods of other countries which are made in part of Cuban sugar or rum. *Id.* 1320. The Act is enforced through civil damages actions by the owners of the property and by visa restrictions on foreign nationals.

Department of Defense has stated that Cuba is no longer a threat to the U.S. national security defense.[192]

The U.S. claim of passing the Helms-Burton Act of 1996 solely on security grounds solely may be doubtful. An alternative purpose for the boycott was pleasing the U.S. Cuban community in an election year. In addition, the claim of preventing transacting in confiscated property owned by U.S. nationals may be doubtful. Some of those U.S. nationals at time of confiscation were Cubans who only later on obtained their U.S. citizenship.

So where do we depart from here? Since the Arab trade restrictions are just taking note of the U.N Security Council resolutions, it would be more than likely that a WTO panel excuses those restrictions as "action in pursuance of obligations under the United Nations Charter for the maintenance of international peace and security," according to article XXI.c of the GATT. Moreover, Arab trade restrictions are actions taken in time of emergency in international relations. They are considered necessary for the protection of Arab countries and essential to Arab security interests.

The legality of trade sanctions have never been adjudicated under GATT or the WTO. Therefore, it is unlikely for the Arab boycott to come under scrutiny by a WTO panel if the U.S. were to challenge the boycott. It may also be very difficult to bring a case against the Arab boycott drawing on the precedent of the Helms-Burton Act. Even if a case could be brought before a WTO panel, there may be reasons for not doing so. There may be a concern regarding potential future abuses of article XXI national security exceptions. It is also the worrisome having the WTO, a trade institution, addressing a sensitive issue with political ramifications.

It is ironic for the USTR to declare that Arab League's boycott of Israel is restriction on trade, but not the U.S. embargo on Cuba. The U.S., which assumes the leadership mantle for free market, must be aware of that no government has either the power or the right to prevent other independent countries from determining their national security. The U.S. would never permit any other country to interfere with its own national security, so it is bound to respect others in that freedom of national security that she asserts for herself.[193] Arab countries have a sovereign right to impose trade sanctions.

---

[192] *Id.* 1329.

[193] Ileana Ros-Lehtinen, Chair, Subcomm. on International Economic Policy and Trade said, "Therefore, the U.S. Government's right to make decisions about our own foreign policy and our national security is absolute and cannot be abrogated or interfered with by any foreign entity . . . He [EC] who lives in a glass house should not throw stones [at the U.S.]". See H.R. Subcomm. on International Economic Policy and Trade of the Comm. on International Relations, *Hearing on Interfering with U.S. National Security Interests: The World Trade Organization and the European Union Challenge to the Helms-Burton Law*, 105th Cong. 1st Sess. 2-3 (Mar. 19, 1997).

VI. Arab countries Accession to the WTO: Playground of Politics

The absence of some Arab countries, and some Islamic countries for that matter, from participation in the WTO is due to the fact that the U.S. is blocking the establishment of working parties to examine their applications.[194] Since 2000, Jordan and Oman were the last Arab countries to accede to the WTO. Five years have passed so far and no other Arab country has joined the WTO. If the U.S. is sincerely engaged with Arab countries, it should allow them entry into the WTO at accelerated rate.

---

[194] To join the WTO, a working party needs to be established to negotiate terms of accession, and the General Council, which operates by consensus, must agree to form the working party. See Raj Bhala, *Challenges of Poverty and Islam Facing American Trade Law*, 17 St. John's J. Legal Comment. 471, 508 (2003). Islamic countries such as Afghanistan, Iran, and Turkmenistan are not yet members of the WTO. Although Afghanistan did not have an observer seat at the WTO it requested accession to the WTO twice. Afghanistan first requested accession in Apr. 2003, a request which lacked the back up of the Afghani government. In Dec. 2004, Afghanistan also requested accession. On Dec. 13, 2004, WTO members agreed to commence accession negotiations with Afghanistan. Afghanistan, a developing country with few tradable items such as silk, fruits, nuts, spices, tea, and textiles, took several bold steps to promote its integration in the global economy despite a conflict that, among other things, threatened its traditionally strong agriculture sector and its gene- banking system. See Ashraf Ghani, *Afghanistan Craves for Investment*, Wall St. J. A10 (Dec. 1, 2004). See *Special Information Sharing Procedures to Deter Money Laundering and Terrorist Activity*, 67 Fed. Reg. 9889 (Mar. 4, 2002). See *Major Drug Transit or Major Illicit Drug Producing Countries for FY05*, 69 Fed. Reg. 57809 (Sep. 28, 2004). The U.S. adopted several initiatives to boost the Afghani economy by granting Afghanistan normal trade relations status ("NTR") in May 2002. NTR obliges the U.S. to apply tariff rates on Afghani imports at levels equivalent to those enjoyed by other U.S. trading partners. See *Restore Nondiscriminatory Trade Treatment (Normal Trade Relations Treatment) to the Products of Afghanistan*, 67 Fed. Reg. 30535 (May 7, 2002). In 2002, legislation (S.3151) has been introduced in Congress to negotiate FTA with Afghanistan. Additionally, the U.S. in Jan. 2003 provided products made in Afghanistan duty-free access to its market under the GSP scheme. In Sep. 2004, the U.S. and Afghanistan signed a Trade and Investment Framework Agreement. Iran has submitted its application for membership in WTO since Sept. 1996. In May 2001, Iran's request for establishing a working party on accession was for the first time placed on the agenda of the General Council. Earlier, such request had not made it to the General Council agenda. As of 2004, Iran requested accession nineteen times. However, the U.S. still blocks Iran's request on three grounds: Iran supports terrorism, encourages Arab trade embargo on Israel, and develops nuclear weapons. In 2005, however, a WTO working party was established to examine Iran's membership in the trade body. See *WTO Agrees to Begin Accession Talks with Iran, Taps Lamy as Next DG*, Inside U.S. Trade (May 27, 2005) (the U.S. signaled a shift in its position in March, when Secretary of State Condoleezza Rice announced the U.S. would drop its objection to Iran's WTO application in an effort to support EU efforts meant to convince Iran to drop its development of a nuclear weapons program). The U.S. maintains executive orders. Some of these executive orders are extensions of the national emergency with respect to Iran announced in 1979. These executive orders prohibit the importation of goods or services of Iranian origin as part of the International Emergency Economic Power Act of 1988 which gives the U.S. president the authority to regulate or prohibit any foreign exchange transaction. Moreover, the U.S. maintains legislation, the Iran and Libya Sanctions Act (ILSA) of 1996, which imposes penalties on companies, including foreign companies, doing business in the Iran. The ILSA authorizes the U.S. president to impose economic sanctions against foreign companies that invest more than $20 million in Iran to develop its petroleum resources. U.S. companies are barred from doing business in Iran directly, although their foreign subsidiaries can work there. The ILSA is renewed continuously. See *Iran and Libya Sanctions Act of 1996*, 50 U.S.C. § 1701 (2000). See also *Iranian Transactions Regulations*, 31 C.F.R § 560 (1996). Of the fifteen ex-Soviet states, Turkmenistan has had observer status in the GATT/WTO since 1992.

Of the 148 current members of the WTO, there are only eleven Arab countries. Algeria, Comoros, Iraq, Lebanon, Libya, the Palestinian Authority, Saudi Arabia, Somalia, the Sudan, Syria, and Yemen have all lined up for accession to the WTO. However, applications of some of Arab countries for admission to the WTO are "clinically dead".[195] Other Arab countries' applications are at a "standstill".[196] The U.S. supports applications of accession for only handpicked Arab countries that are considered "peaceful", however this term maybe interpreted.[197]

In a leapfrog move, Iraq became an observer at the WTO overnight.[198] It is possible that Iraq will accede to the WTO in a short period of time. Iraq has already adopted several orders that liberalize trade policy.[199] For example, a new foreign investment law

---

[195] See Daniel Pruzin, *U.S. Blocks Iranian WTO Application; Syria Prevented from Placement on Agenda*, 19 Intl. Trade Rep. (BNA) 36 (Jan. 3, 2002) (stating that Syria's request for membership in the WTO was blocked because of Syria's backing for the Arab League trade boycott of Israel).

[196] See Daniel Pruzin, *U.S., EU Push Saudis to Improve Market Access Offers for WTO Entry*, 17 Intl. Trade Rep. (BNA) 1654 (Oct. 26, 2000). See also Daniel Pruzin, *Progress Cited in Saudi Accession But Partners Still Waiting For Details*, 20 Intl. Trade Rep. (BNA) 1324 (July 31, 2003) (Saudi accession has dragged for a decade since 1993. Saudi trading partners are concerned over Saudi legislation that restricts foreign investment in oil exploration, production, insurance, telecommunications, and retail and whole-sale trade. Furthermore, Saudi Arabia maintains import ban on alcohol and pork).

[197] See Grary G. Yerkey, *U.S. and Saudi Arabia Sign Agreement that Could Lead to Free Trade Negotiations*, 20 Intl. Trade Rep. (BNA) 1353 (Aug. 7, 2003) (citing the term "peaceful countries" used by [former] USTR Robert Zoellick).

[198] See *Brussels Resists Demand for Iraq WTO Seat*, Fin. Times 4 (Jan. 26, 2004) (the EC resisted demand by the U.S. and Britain backed by U.S. Vice-President Dick Cheney that Iraq be given WTO seat. The U.S. argues that WTO seat for Iraq would help its reconstruction and adapt to market economy. On the other hand, the EC argues that Iraq does not have a government that has control over its trade policy). Ultimately, however, Iraq was granted, on a silver plate, a seat at the WTO as observer which would allow it to attend WTO meetings but cannot participate in decision-making or table proposals for negotiations. See *Iraq Takes First Step to Join WTO*, Fin. Times 14 (Feb. 12, 2004). Although formally Iraq cannot participate in tabling proposals since it is an observer, it may do so in practicality. For example, China in 1980s was permitted to submit proposals during the Uruguay Round negotiations. Currently, Saudi Arabia is permitted to submit proposals in the Doha Round. Ahmad Al-Mukhtar, director general of foreign economic relations at Iraq's Ministry of Trade declared his country's intention to start accession negotiations as soon as possible. Indeed, in Oct. 2004, Iraq sent a letter to WTO Director General Supachai requesting that its membership request be circulated to WTO members and be placed on the agenda of the General Council in Dec. so as to commence accession negotiations. On Dec. 13, 2004, WTO members agreed on starting accession negotiations with Iraq. Iraq's Trade Minister Mohammed Mustafa Al-Jibouri expressed his government's hope to complete the accession negotiations as soon as possible.

[199] See Judith Richards Hope & Edward N. Griffin, *The New Iraq: Revising Iraq's Commercial Law is a Necessity for Foreign Direct Investment and the Reconstruction of Iraq's Decimated Economy*, 11 Cardozo J. Intl. & Comp. L. 875, 877, 878 (2004) (citing the Coalition Provisional Authority order no. 12 which liberalized trade policy by suspending a number of tariffs and trade restrictions. The Coalition Provisional Authority also issued order no. 39 which instituted far ranging free-market reforms throughout Iraq in every sector, except for natural resources [the government of Iraq still subsidizes gasoline by fixing its price at very low rate], banking and insurance. For banks, after the end of a five-year period, there will be no limitations on the entry of foreign banks). In Oct. 2004, the U.S. Ex-Im bank concluded a framework agreement with Iraq's ministry of finance and Trade Bank of Iraq to finance U.S. exports to Iraq. Discussions are underway for Iraq to enter into aid and economic-reform programs with the IMF and to receive more aid from other countries to smooth Iraq's debt burden. The U.S. also planned for a major write-off of some of Iraqi debt currently totaling about $120 billion. One has to question the imbalance in the form preferential write-off of Iraqi debt over other neighboring countries such as Jordan.

was passed in 2003 permitting 100 percent foreign ownership of firms in all sectors of the economy, apart from oil and other mineral extraction. Iraq has also modernized its existing intellectual property regime, by using the laws of Jordan and United Arab Emirates as examples, to bring it into compliance with international standards. Iraq's overall purpose with these changes is to assist its participation in the WTO.

Opening the fragile Iraqi banking system, where lending to the private sector made up one-half of 1 percent total commercial bank assets lending in 2004, would create a regime more favorable to meg-foreign banks. Iraqi banks may not have enough capitalization to compete with foreign banks. The subsidized agriculture sector is also set for reform.[200] Similarly to example of Iraqi banks, the reform in the Iraqi agricultural sector would benefit the agri-businesses of the U.S. and other major agricultural exporters. Likewise, Iraqi higher education is also slated for market-oriented reform. It is no longer the responsibility of the government to find graduates jobs; graduates would be responsible for their own career searches.

In a country ravaged by war, where only a small percentage of U.S.-appropriated funds have been put into action and prime reconstruction contracts are limited to companies from the U.S. led by Halliburton and Bechtel, Iraq and force-contributing nations such as Australia and Poland has little time for WTO work.[201] Furthermore, with many decades of a paternalistic cradle-to-grave government policy, it is hardly perceivable that such reforms would make life easier for Iraqi citizens. Iraq needs gradual, not an instant trade liberalization, to advance from a closed economy dominated

---

[200] See Ariana Eunjung Cha, *Iraqis Face Tough Transition to Market-based Agriculture*, Wash. Post A10 (Jan. 22, 2004) (Iraq has 5 million agricultural workers mostly family farmers. In old Iraq, the state provided seeds, fertilizers, pesticides, sprinklers, and tractors at low cost. The Coalition Provisional Authority is determined to create a capitalist economy where the state provides little, if any, support. The U.S. and Australia [major agriculture exporters] are taking the lead in rehabilitating the Iraqi agricultural sector. After first purchasing and then destroying Iraqi wheat in 2003 because it was of low quality, the gap in food supply was made up with $190 million worth wheat from Kansas, Oklahoma, and Texas, courtesy of the U.S.).

[201] See *Resolution of Cultural Property Disputes* 23-29 (The International Bureau of the Permanent Court of Arbitration ed., Aspen Publishers 2004) (discussing, in part, the tragic looting of many of Iraq's museums as a recent example of how vulnerable cultural property is to theft, damage, and destruction. As time went by, legal rules have developed for the protection of cultural property during hostilities represented in the 1954 Hague Convention for the Protection of Cultural Property in the Event of Armed Conflict. One of the obligations included in article 5 of the Convention is that occupying forces must as far as possible support the competent national authority of the occupied country to protect cultural property. It is an obligation of stewardship. This did not take place in Iraq. Neither the U.K nor the U.S. is party to the Hague Convention. The experience of UNESCO in many conflict situations shows that only the tiniest fraction of looted materials will be returned). For more on the dispute between the U.S. and EC over procurement bar from bidding on $18.6 billion in reconstruction projects in Iraq see *USTR Argues Iraq Contract Exclusion Fall within WTO Rules*, Inside U.S. Trade (Inside Wash. Publishers) (Dec. 12, 2003) (the U.S. argues that Iraq's Coalition Provisional Authority, along with Defense Department which are responsible for awarding procurement contracts, is not a listed entity covered by the WTO GPA. As such there is no need to invoke [article XXIII of the GPA] "essential security" exception to justify the use of noncompetitive procedures in awarding these contracts. In the alternative, the U.S. can argue that these contracts are foreign aid which is not subject to the U.S. commitments under GPA).

by state-owned monopolies and subsidies toward a competitive and modern economy open to world trade.

Algeria has been seeking WTO membership for seventeen years, beginning in June 1987. Its accession negotiations are moving at snail's pace.[202] A sticking point is dual price energy (gas and electricity), which the U.S. and EC claim provide an indirect subsidy to industrial producers and give them an unfair advantage over foreign competitors. For example, prices of some fertilizers are directly linked to the price of energy. Algeria may want to argue that WTO agreements do not address or prohibit dual price energy policies. If Algeria's argument proves fruitless, it will have to agree to language that requires energy prices to be set according to commercial considerations (production costs and profit), staged increases in gas prices for industrial users, and/or allow exceptions to permit current energy policies for non-industrial users and households, which would be based on social considerations. Another sticking point is the import ban on alcohol.[203] Due to these hurdles, it seems that Algeria might top China in terms of the length of time it has to endure before being able to secure WTO membership.

Lebanon talks are still at early stage. The working party on Lebanon accession met in 2003, for the first time since 1999.[204] If one can draw on the experience of China and Taiwan (or Chinese Taipei as China's delegation to the WTO prefers to the Taiwanese contingent) accession to the WTO, Lebanon may not accede except after Syria's accession to the WTO. Alternatively, Lebanon and Syria may accede to the WTO simultaneously to reduce tensions between the two neighbors. Either way, Lebanon efforts would be handicapped by Syria's own accession.

Libya submitted its accession application in November 2001.[205] Nonetheless, the application was blocked by the U.S. because Libya allegedly supports terrorism. On July 27, 2004, WTO members agreed to set up a working party to examine Libya's accession. However, despite headways in the US-Libyan relationship, Libya still has a long road

---

[202] See Daniel Pruzin, *WTO Members Discuss Accession of Algeria, Lebanon, Iraq Explores Membership Process*, 20 Intl. Trade Rep. (BNA) 2079 (Dec. 18, 2003) (Algeria talks stumbled over its dual price for energy and ban on imports of alcohol. Dual energy policy allows domestic firms to buy gas at lower price than what Algeria charges on the international market. The Algerian parliament introduced a ban, which was proposed by religious factions, on imports of alcohol as part of the budget bill that would expire at the end of 2004). Other stumbling issues in Algeria's accession to the WTO include introducing new agricultural export subsidies, application of tariff-rate quotas, special safeguard on farm imports, and whether WTO agreements would automatically take precedence over any conflicting internal regulation. *Id.*
[203] Other WTO members are likely to argue that the basis of the import ban on Alcohol is not religious but rather to protect the Algerian brewery industry, especially wine.
[204] Lebanon tabled its offer for market access in goods and services. Lebanon would reduce tariffs on agricultural and industrial goods to 12.5 percent. Further, Lebanon promised to liberalize mobile phone services, fixed-line telecommunication, and port services. *Id.*
[205] A ministerial committee has been established to prepare for negotiation with the WTO immediately after Deputy Director-General of the WTO concluded his visit to Tripoli in Oct. 2001.

ahead. The U.S. has adopted a step-by-step approach toward Libyan accession.[206] The U.S. would help Libya modernize its economy and infrastructure, which is largely dependent on gas and oil, and invigorate a working private sector. In this process, Libya would open up oil exploration, privatize roughly 360 states-owned enterprises, and ease price controls. One reason for the U.S. taking these steps is that it wishes to maintain its competitiveness in the Libyan market.

In 2001, the Palestinian Authority sent a twenty-four member delegation for a two-day visit to the WTO to address the issue of its own WTO accession.[207] The Palestinian Authority adopted foreign trade regime similar to that of Israel.[208] However, the U.S. and Israel are still likely to oppose the Palestinian Authority application because of the tension between the Palestinians and Israelis.[209] In 2004, the U.S. downgraded the status of the Palestinian Liberation office in the U.S.[210] Even if tension did not exist between the Palestinians and Israelis, the U.S and Israel may raise a technical point in opposition to Palestinian accession. While under article XXXIII of GATT 1994, a "government" possessing full autonomy in the conduct of its external commercial relations was required for accession, article XII of the WTO Charter allows "state[s]" or "separate customs [territories]" to join its membership ranks. The Palestinian Authority is clearly a government, but whether the Gaza Strip and the West Bank form a state is an open question.[211]

---

[206] The U.S. Liaison Office in Tripoli stated that the pace of travel to Libya is still hampered by visa difficulties. Thus, the U.S. Liaison Office advises those who plan to travel to Libya to apply for visa three to six weeks in advance. See Gray G. Yerkey, *U.S. May Soon Lift Ban on Travel to Libya, Bowing to Pressure from Business, Congress*, 21 Intl. Trade Rep (BNA) 289 (Feb. 12, 2004). In Apr. 2004, the U.S. terminated the application of the ILSA to Libya. In Sept. 2004, the U.S. lifted its eighteen year ban on trade between the two countries, terminating the need for license from the Treasury Department to trade with Libya, allowing direct air service and regular charter flights, and lifting the prohibition against financing through direct loans, credits, and guarantees by the U.S. Ex-Im Bank and other government agencies. In addition, on the same date, the U.S. terminated the national emergency declared in 1986 under the International Emergency Economic Powers Act with respect to Libya and released frozen assets belonging to Libya. New Regulations were issued that would allow U.S. companies to interact with U.S. made products that were illegally exported or re-exported to Libya before the U.S. trade embargo was removed. However, the U.S. still bans programs of the Overseas Private Investment Corporation in Libya. Moreover, the State Department still classifies Libya as state sponsor of terrorism thus prohibiting, with the exception of farm products and medicine, purchasing U.S. military equipments such as radioactive materials and explosives and restricting, through export controls, U.S. high-tech and encrypted exports such as computers and software. In order for Libya to be taken off the list of countries supporting terrorism, there must be efforts by the State Department, notification of Congress, and formal/informal congressional consent.

[207] See Daniel Pruzin, *Palestinian Authority Prepares to Pursue WTO membership; Observer Status First Step*, 18 Intl. Trade Rep. (BNA) 869 (May 31, 2001) (the visit was financed by the U.S. Agency for International Development).

[208] *Id.* As a result of the peace truce, a customs union is formed between Israel, the West Bank, and Gaza Strip.

[209] *Id.* The U.S. and Israeli objections prove that WTO accession is not a rule-based process but rather power-based.

[210] The downgrading was based on the Foreign Relations Authorization Act. See *Foreign Relations Authorization Act of 2002*, Pub. L. No. 107-228, § 604, 116 Stat. 1350, 1395 (2002).

[211] Israel usually refers to Gaza Strip and the West Bank as the Territories or Areas. If the U.S. and Israel raise the technical point, the Palestinian Authority may argue that the U.N gave its predecessor, the Palestinian Liberation Organization (PLO), an observer status, a position that allowed the PLO to participate in its discussions. See Press Release G.A. 9427, U.N. GAOR, 52nd Sess., 89th mtg. (1998).

Saudi Arabia has been an observer since 1986. It formally submitted its admission application in 1993. One would question why the Saudis have extended the period accession to the GATT/WTO despite the fact that they are a prominent player in the World Bank and the IMF, which mandate and advocate liberalization policies.[212] Whether Saudi Arabia's accession to the WTO in 2004 is "imminent reality", the fact remains that one cannot predict when it might happen.[213] Accession could take place as late as 2006 or 2007.

With respect to its WTO application, Saudi Arabia has opened its markets to gas development projects, telegraph and fax services, Vsat and GMPCS services, Internet provision services, and online information and database retrieval services to non-Saudi operators. Saudi Arabia has also passed several trade-related laws, including regulations that liberalize capital markets. However, as a result of the Saudis putting some 100 reservations in market access where liberalization would not apply, negotiations might take a sharp turn.[214] Some of these reservations presented by Saudis can be qualified as measures to preserve Islamic values and traditions. As an example, Saudi Arabia's media interests (audiovisual), which are state-censored for content, are occupied with patriotic programming and are off-limits to non-Saudi interests. Global media interests such as

Moreover, the U.S. extended its GSP scheme to cover Palestinian goods. As such, Palestinian goods would enter the U.S. at preferential rate. Therefore, this implies a statehood status. See *Amendment to the Generalized System of Preferences*, 60 Fed. Reg. 25266 (Mar. 17, 1995). Finally, the Palestinian Authority can counter-argue that WTO agreements are trade agreements and discussions of broader international law issues should be left to other forums.

[212] One can speculate that due to the nature of the Saudi economy and its potential impact on world trade, WTO members are taking tougher stance in its accession to the WTO. See Tomer Broude, Accession to the WTO: Current Issues in the Arab World, 32 J.W.T. 147, 153 (1998) (stating that Saudi economy ranks among the twenty largest economies in the world and among the fifteen largest importers).

[213] The accession negotiations grounded to a halt in early 2001 after Saudi Arabia published a negative list on investment prohibiting access to foreigners in key sectors such as oil exploration. However, Saudi Arabia's accession to the WTO received a new momentum after the departure of Osama Faqih, former Saudi commerce minister who was considered an obstacle for moving the accession talks, and the appointment of Hashim Yamani as the new one. Moreover, the conclusion of some sixteen bilateral deals with trading partners including the one with the EC in Sep. 2003 provided another impetus for negotiations. Some trade diplomats suspect that Saudi Arabia may wrap up negotiations in 2004. See Daniel Pruzin, *In Push to Finalize WTO Accession Deal in 2004, Saudis May Hold Talks Past Dec. 19*, 20 Intl. Trade Rep. (BNA) 2077 (Dec. 18, 2003) (the most contentious negotiations is with the U.S. over market access in financial services and insurance [branching rights for foreign insurers. Generally, branching is preferred over establishing subsidiaries since the latter require more capital and are less efficient]. Feeling sense of urgency the Saudis are ready to travel to capitals to resolve outstanding issues. The Saudis push for accession is due in part to the desire to improve the strained relations with Washington after Sep. 11). An interesting point in Saudi Arabia's accession to the WTO is whether it should be classified as a developing, advanced developing country, or developed country. If it is classified as a developing country, it may qualify for benefits, if any, accruing to developing countries in their accession to the WTO.

[214] See Daniel Pruzin, *Saudi Flexible on Easing Investment Curbs During WTO Accession Talks, Report States*, 21 Intl. Trade Rep. (BNA) 288 (Feb. 12, 2004) (the latest draft report of WTO's working party on accession cites that foreign investment in audiovisual, satellite transmission, land/air transport, real estate are off-limits. The report's annex sets out some seventy-three products that are prohibited from importations. They include alcohol, pork, satellite internet receivers, mobile phones fitted with cameras, video boosters, animal fertilizers, asbestos, used tires, mobile phone chips, prepaid mobile phone cards, and electronic greeting cards).

Viacom will not be allowed to own shares in TV production companies or invest in joint production projects with Saudi media companies. If other WTO members raise objections to these reservations, Saudi can argue that France was permitted a "cultural exemption" clause during the Uruguay Round negotiations. Other Saudi reservations, such as prepaid mobile phone cards, may be more suspicious for justifications as exemptions from trade liberalization on religious grounds.

There are several other concerns with respect to the Saudi application. Dual price for energy and gas is a one issue. The application of customs valuation, import licensing, and precedence of international law over domestic law are also major concerns for trading partners of Saudi Arabia. Other obstacles include the huge subsidies paid to rich farmers for growing wheat in the Saudi desert. In addition, Dominican Republic and Honduras sudden requests for bilateral talks with Saudis mean further delays. Some U.S. congressmen oppose Saudi accession because of its support of Arab trade boycott of Israel, the Saudi human rights record, and fears about terrorism. Finally, the U.S. State Department's designation of Saudi Arabia, under the International Religious Freedom Act of 1998, as a Country of Particular Concern could prove as a sticking point in negotiations.

Regardless of Saudi progress towards trade liberalization, realistically, after accession, Saudi Arabia may need one to two years at minimum to learn the mechanics of the WTO, and develop a large legal staff to assist in pursuing effective membership in the WTO. The latter point seems illusive considering that many Arab countries have small delegations dedicated to the WTO. In addition, Saudi Arabia may need more time to familiarize itself with the thousands pages of WTO trade rules.

The Sudan, usually a forgotten country when speaking about international trade even though it is an important exporter of Arabic gum and the largest country in the African continent, is outside the club.[215] The Sudan has adopted an open-oriented policy that includes trade liberalization.[216] However, the Sudan is unlikely to accede to the WTO anytime soon, especially in light of sanctions imposed on it due to suspicion it supports terrorist organizations. Moreover, proposed legislation (H.R 5414) in the 108th and 109th U.S. Congress could cut off foreign tax credits and tax deferrals to U.S. companics doing business in the Sudan until it ends the genocide in Darfur region. Similarly to Syria, the Sudan is usually considered a pariah state.

Comoros, a small island state, is another forgotten Arab country when speaking about WTO membership. Comoros has been recipient of preferential treatment from developed countries, such as under the Canadian Least Developed Country Tariff treatment and by the U.S. under the GSP program and the African Growth and

---

[215] The WTO had set up a working party on Sudan's accession since 1994.

[216] The policy of Sudan focuses on enhancing the agricultural sector, which employs about 70 percent of the population, attracting foreign investors, including Islamic and Arab funds by reducing taxes and tariffs, reducing the inflation rate from 166 percent to less than 7 percent, and keeping currency prices stable. Nonetheless, over 90 percent of Sudanese people live below the poverty line. See Jim Phipps & Christopher H. Johnson, *Foreign Law in Review: 2001*, 36 Intl. L. 901, 939 (2002).

Opportunity Act.[217] Furthermore, Comoros has taken several steps to reform its trade regime.[218] Since Comoro has a vulnerable economy with weak supply capacity, WTO members must be moderate in their demands with respect to its membership application in the trade body if it requests to join.

Somalia has also been largely overlooked in the context of the WTO. Somalia has undergone market-oriented policies.[219] After years of conflict and chaos, Somalia is experiencing more political stability that would help it revives its shattered economy and rebuilds it manufacturing sector. Since many of its industries would not be competitive internationally, WTO members, when considering Somalia's accession to the global trade body, must also be moderate in their demands for accession.[220]

Syria has taken several steps on the path of economic reform. These include increased imports, such as vehicles, and permitting the private sector to venture into such fields as banking, telecoms, TV production, and higher education. In the context of these reform initiatives, Syria applied for WTO membership in October 2001. However, four years have passed since it submitted its application and its application is at a standstill.[221] Syria is a rogue state, and the U.S. State Department claims that it supports international terrorism and the Arab trade boycott on Israel and harbors elements of the former Iraqi regime.

It is unlikely that Syria's application to the WTO will be welcomed anytime soon, especially after the U.S. Congress passed the Syria Accountability and Lebanese Sovereignty Restoration Act of 2003.[222] The Act orders the U.S. President to impose sanctions against Syria by blocking U.S. exports of any item on the U.S. Munitions List. Moreover, the U.S. President must also choose two or more sanctions from a menu of six options, including: prohibiting all exports of U.S. products to Syria, with the exception of food and medicine; prohibiting U.S. business from operating or investing in Syria; calling for U.S. financial institutions to sever dealings with the Commercial Bank of Syria; freezing assets belonging to certain Syrian individuals and government entities; and

---

[217] See *Trade and Development Act of 2000*, 19 U.S.C. § 3721 (2000). Comoros is dependant on the exports of basic commodities such as spices and official development assistance.

[218] In 1996, Comoros accepted article VIII of the IMF's Articles of Agreement which requires countries to refrain from imposing restrictions on the making of payments and transfers for current international transactions, engaging in discriminatory currency arrangements, or multiple currency practices without the approval of the IMF. Comoros agreed to pursue sound economic policy. Comoros also took trade reforms as part of the IMF-supported programs such as Structural Adjustment Facility. For example, in 1994, Comoros received $1.90 million credit under Structural Adjustment Facility to support its economic reforms. See Robert Sharer et. al., *Trade Liberalization in IMF-Supported Programs* 9, 30 (IMF 1998) (Comoros began Fund-supported programs with relatively restrictive trade regime. However, there was marked reduction in its trade restrictiveness).

[219] See U.S. Dept. Com. *Somalia: A Country Study* (Lib. of Cong. 1993) (stabilization and macroeconomic adjustment programs had been implemented during 1980s under auspices of international credit and aid agencies. There has been a privatization of wholesale trade and financial services).

[220] Crop and livestock production, forestry, and fisheries are Sudan's main items of exports. *Id.*

[221] On Feb. 11, 2004, the day Iraq was granted observership seat at the WTO, Syria circulated a note expressing its interest in joining the organization.

[222] See *Syria Sanctions Bill Passes Senate with Lugar Amendment*, Inside U.S. Trade (Inside Wash. Publishers) 13 (Nov. 14, 2003).

prohibiting aircraft of any air carrier owned or controlled by Syria to take off, land in, or fly over the U.S. The President has the flexibility to waive sanctions if he determines it is in the U.S. national security interest. U.S. trade sanctions on Syria may have little impact on its economy since trade between the two countries amounted to only $472 million in 2003. Additionally, Syria neither does operate flights to the U.S. nor does it receive U.S. aid.

Yemen is another Arab country that is still out in the cold. Modern laws have been enacted that are comparable with those of other Arab countries.[223] Islamic law has been codified in Yemen covering trade, among other areas. Among trade reforms, Yemen removed import restrictions for many products, introduced four-band tariff structure with rates ranging from 5-30 percent, and harmonized excise tax rates. Additionally, Yemen opened its wheat trade and distribution of petroleum products and removed a price-fixing cartel in the trucking sector. Yet, Yemen's accession to the WTO will still face many obstacles.

There have been calls by Arab countries to grant the Arab League as an observer status at the WTO. These calls have so far been received by deaf ears. Admitting the Arab League to the WTO would strengthen the position of Arab countries in the organization. Furthermore, the Vatican has been setting as an observer since 1997 without the intention of applying for membership. It is preposterous to delay granting the Arab League a seat to observe the WTO at work.

As to the boycott on Israel, a precedent exists permitting an Arab country to accede to the GATT while simultaneously maintaining its boycott on Israel. This was the case of the accession of the United Arab Republic, a union between Egypt and Syria, accession to the GATT.[224] Therefore, accession of Arab countries to the WTO should not hinge on dismantling their trade boycott on Israel.

VII. WTO Technical Assistance and Arab Countries

Arab countries, like other developing countries, face a limited capacity to negotiate and implement complex international trade agreements.[225] An indication of this is the dearth of quality research on Arab countries and the WTO. No extensive publications are

---

[223] See Phipps & Johnson, *supra* n. 216, at 953.

[224] The Arab boycott was justified as a reasonable measure considering the state of war between the United Arab Republic and Israel. During the accession negotiations, some contracting parties raised concerns that the United Arabic Republic was participating in the Arab League boycott of Israel. Members of the working party supported the concept that such a boycott did not preclude accession, as long as it was for political purposes and not a disguised trade protection measure. See GATT Analytical Index, *supra* n. 123, at 602-03.

[225] It is no clear than in the Doha Ministerial Declaration which states, "We shall continue to make positive efforts designed to ensure that developing countries, and especially the least-developed among them, secure a share in the growth of world trade commensurate with the need of their economic development. In this context, enhanced market access, balanced rules, and well-targeted, sustainably financed technical assistance and capacity-building programs have important roles to play". See Doha Ministerial Declaration, Nov. 14, 2001, WTO Doc. No. WT/MIN(01)/DEC/1, at para. 2.

available in Arabic. Most publications are based on meetings and conferences. In English, writing articles about Arab countries and international trade in learned journalistic periodicals is a largely new development. Traditionally, articles about Arab countries and international trade in English were limited to a few general and sporadic lines. Today's scene has changed especially, after the September 11th terrorist attacks on the U.S. This proliferation seems to have occurred because of political and commercial reasons. The Arab reader has a quality menu of scholastic articles to choose from.

The WTO uses some of its resources, whether through its regular budget or off-budget, to help developing countries improve their involvement in the WTO work.[226] The broad objectives of technical assistance are to provide general information on the multilateral trading system, improve the country's participation in this system through training on negotiating techniques, use of the Integrated Data Base, and encouraging participation in dispute settlement courses.[227] The further objective is to deepen beneficiary countries' knowledge of the trading system through specialized workshops or seminars. The WTO also organizes a variety of technical assistance activities all over the world. Technical assistance is mainly delivered in the following forms: courses, seminars, workshops and technical missions covering a range of subjects, briefing sessions, Reference Centers, and daily advice to delegations. Examples include Short Trade Policy courses, Dispute Settlement workshops and courses, Trade Negotiation simulations, and establishment of WTO Reference Centers.[228]

Many Arab countries are recipients of the buzzword "capacity building" or technical assistance.[229] One can argue that technical assistance is fairly distributed geographically among Arab countries. The WTO announced cooperation with the Arab Monetary Fund

---

[226] There are four mechanisms employed by the WTO to implement the WTO Agreements: capacity building, monitoring, supervision, and enforcement. The WTO defines the objectives of technical assistance and cooperation as to improve knowledge of multilateral trade rules and WTO working procedures and negotiations and to assist in the implementation of commitments in the multilateral trading system and full use of its provisions, including the effective use of the dispute settlement mechanism. These objectives will be administered by the WTO Secretariat and reviewed by the members. The Committee on Trade and Development approves a three-year plan adjusted on an annual basis, including the budget consideration, and submit the plan to relevant WTO bodies for implementation. See Xin Zhang, *Implementation of the WTO Agreements: Framework and Reform*, 23 Nw. J. Intl. L. & Bus. 383, 387, 395 (2003) (the functions of the WTO will be fundamentally undermined if the majority members cannot implement the WTO Agreements due to lack of capacity). Discussion will be limited to capacity building. Following the Doha Ministerial Declaration's instructions to develop a plan ensuring long-term funding for WTO technical assistance, the General Council adopted on Dec. 20, 2001, a new budget that would increase technical assistance funding by 80 percent and establish a Doha Development Agenda Global Trust Fund with a proposed core budget of CHF15 million.

[227] *Id.*

[228] *Id.*

[229] For example, Algeria, Djibouti, Egypt, Jordan, Kuwait, Mauritania, Morocco, Oman, Qatar, Saudi Arabia, Sudan, Syria, Tunisia, and United Arab Emirates are usual participants in Trade Policy courses and specialized courses. Many Arab countries also have been provided assistance for Trade Reference Centers. For more on the nature of these courses see Committee on Trade and Development, *Technical Assistance and Training Plan 2004*, WT/COMTD/W/119/Rev.3, para.27 (Feb. 18, 2004) (the WTO Secretariat plans to hold regional trade policy courses in regions not yet covered from the year 2005 such as Arab countries).

in 2002.[230] Arab officials are also participants in Doha Development Agenda Short Trade Policy courses, Dispute Settlement courses, Trade Facilitation course, and other regional seminars/workshops.[231]

Even more, in the context of collaboration between Arab countries and the WTO, an important step has been taken to establish an "unofficial" Arabic language website to translate all WTO documents into Arabic.[232] Though it is a welcome gesture, there are two drawbacks for translating these documents into Arabic. First, the information on the website is not updated very frequently.[233] Because it takes a longer period of time to translate documents from English into Arabic. There are certain trade terms and/or phrases for which it might be impossible to translate their intrinsic and subtle nuances into Arabic. As such, the meaning of the whole word or phrase could be lost in the translation. Second, is the reality that reading WTO information available at its Arabic website will not develop comprehensive knowledge or expertise in international trade law. The scarce resources directed toward the WTO Arabic website might be put to better use if they were used for training on international trade, especially considering that English is the language of international trade.

Although WTO technical assistance is appreciated, it is not enough. Generally, the technical assistance is funded by the WTO budget. Contributions to the WTO budget are based on a trade-weighted basis. This means that bigger trading countries, such as the U.S, EC, Canada, and Japan, have a stronger say on the allocation of their contributions. In this way, technical assistance may be limited in scope depending on the availability of funds. In some cases, technical assistance might be affected by the whims in the WTO. For example, the WTO staff initiated a "work to rule" campaign in which they refuse to provide administrative support outside normal hours.[234] Another example is China's blocking of the WTO technical assistance and training plan for 2005 in the Committee on Trade and Development unless provisions are removed allowing the issue of textiles and apparels to be discussed at WTO-financed regional seminars. This is an evidence of the undependable nature of technical assistance delivered by WTO Secretariat.

---

[230] A close cooperation is undertaken with the Arab Monetary Fund (AMF), the Islamic Development Bank (IsDB) and the United Nations Economic and Social Commission for Western Asia (UNESCWA). *Id.* at para. 97.

[231] Seminars/workshops average 19-48 participants and run over 1-5 days. The number of Arab participants for instance increases to 48 in sanitary and phytosanitary course. *Id.* annex. There seems to be more focus and interest in sanitary and phytosanitary course than others. This is logical since many Arab countries face difficulties in implementing the different aspects of the WTO Sanitary and Phytosanitary Agreement which lead to lost export sales. At the Doha Ministerial Conference of 2001, WTO members along with several multilateral organizations including the Food and Agriculture Organization launched a mechanism known as Standards and Trade Development Facility to help countries meet the complexities of food and animal health standards.

[232] The Arab based Talal Abu-Ghazaleh & Co. foundation is administering the website. It can be accessed at < http://www.wtoarab.org/>.

[233] It is unclear how many hits the website receives or how many documents are downloaded from the website. These indicators may measure the popularity of the website.

[234] See Daniel Pruzin, *Staff Action to Push Pay Raise Interrupts Several WTO Meetings*, 19 Intl. Trade Rep. (BNA) 1985 (Nov. 21, 2002) (the U.S. and Germany leading the tough line in keeping WTO budget to a minimum).

Up until now, technical assistance to Arab countries can be summarized in two words: translation and some international trade courses. With respect to translation, WTO members have established an unofficial website in Arabic. However, the WTO is shy of saying that although 280 million people speak Arabic in the Arab countries, Arabic is not a working language along with the other three working languages (English, Spanish, and French) in the trade body. The memorandum of understanding to translate WTO documents into Arabic proves once again the superiority of the WTO, meaning one must receive the blessing of the WTO before translating its documents into another language.[235] In this way, the WTO has resorted to a backdoor policy of pretending to deliver technical assistance to Arab countries but not, in reality, accomplishing very much.

As to WTO trade courses, these are shallow courses. They can be best described as introductory-level undergraduate college courses. Arab participants may not have the chance to delve as deeply as possible into the world of international trade.[236] Furthermore, these courses cover areas that may not be of interest or use for Arab countries. For example, offering an antidumping course to Jordan may not be of help since it uses safeguard measures all the time. In addition, any trade course that is not put to use may be less beneficial because unless Arab countries are involved extensively in international trade on a regular basis, the information may fade away with time. Only the efficient delivery of technical assistance to Arab countries will provide them with the skills needed to successfully negotiate with developed countries.

The WTO is working on a strategy for Arab countries, which is aimed at raising awareness of the WTO in the region and better integrating it into the current multilateral trading system.[237] In other words, the WTO would launch a "public awareness" campaign. Although Arab countries are appreciative for the wishful thinking of the WTO, such a strategy would have to include technical assistance that is frequent, information-rich and deep, and relevant to their trade needs. Moreover, WTO technical assistance must be presented in local languages and spread out throughout each country's region, not strictly concentrated in capitals.

Some WTO technical assistance is confined to a particular event. For example, before WTO Ministerial Conference in Cancun in 2003, there was a local workshop in Jordan covering several WTO Agreements. However, such type of technical assistance

---

[235] Perhaps, the WTO needs to protect its own copyrighted materials from deceptive practices of others who copycat them. The Yes Men, an anti-globalization organization, established a website nearly identical to the WTO website with Andy Bichlbaum acting as the WTO spokesperson who mistakenly on several occasions was invited as speaker in conferences in which he praised slavery and decried Ghandi. Conference organizers thought Andy Bichlbaum was from the WTO Secretariat. In reality, Andy Bichlbaum is an imposter. The web address for the "fake" WTO is available at <www.gatt.org>. See Jerry Useem, *Will the Real WTO Please Stand Up?* 145 Fortune 34 (Jan. 21, 2002).
[236] However, some trade courses that are delivered in Geneva could be beneficial since Arab participants have first hand experience of the WTO.
[237] See Pruzin, *supra* n. 195, at 36 (citing a statement of [then] WTO Director-General Mike Moore).

has its own limitations. If there is a setback at the Ministerial Conference and stalemate, as it happened, any earlier technical assistance directed at that particular event would not be relevant.

Arab countries are offered different sorts of technical assistance from other international institutions and international donors.[238] These institutions and donors include the Beirut-based IMF Technical Assistance Center for the Middle East; UNDP-funded regional projects; ITC matchmaking for business people; UNCTAD programs; USAID technical assistance programs, especially in the area of intellectual property; and non-profit entities such as the International Intellectual Property Institute. The mission statements of all these institutions are directed toward different goals and different methodologies. Each international institution or donor has its own "agenda" that can lead to confusion, redundancy, and lack of uniformity.

An Arab institution, perhaps named the Inter-Arab Academy for International Trade Law, could be created to fill in the gap in the WTO technical assistance programs. The institution will have a budget funded by contributions and donations of Arab countries proportionate to its economic development. The purpose of the Academy would be to send Arab candidates, such as government officials, academia, or representatives from the private sector, from Arab countries, nominated by their countries based on qualifications and not on political affiliation, to be trained in different areas of international trade in different international institutions. Over several years, those Arab candidates will become human capital (knowledge and skill) and would be able to reinforce the ability of Arab countries to defend their interests. These candidates will also be able to transfer their knowledge to others in the Academy, thereby strengthening the ability of Arabs as a group to participate in the international trade regime.

VIII. The Venue of the Fourth WTO Ministerial Conference: Qatar (2001)

The WTO must hold its Ministerial Conference at least once every two years. The General Council of the WTO decides on the date and venue of the Ministerial Conference.[239] The Gulf state of Qatar voluntarily offered to host the WTO Ministerial Conference during the 1999 Seattle Ministerial Conference. The fourth WTO Ministerial Conference held in Doha, Qatar brought the WTO ever closer to Arab countries and was the largest international meeting in the region.[240]

---

[238] See Tamara Cofman Wittes, *The Promise of Arab Liberalism*, Policy Rev. 61, 63, 67 (July 2004) (the Middle East Partnership Initiative launched in 2002 meant to promote, in part, economic reform. Through the initiative the U.S. is supporting WTO membership bids for several Arab countries. Some of the initiative funds, about $1 million, are allocated to translating Algeria's documents submitted to the WTO into English). Once again, the focus of WTO-related technical assistance is on translation.

[239] There are many factors considered in selecting the venue of the WTO Ministerial Conference. Those include the capacity to host the conference, proximity of the conference venue to corporate hotels such as Marriott, Sheraton, and Hyatt and airport(s), transportations, local assistance, and security arrangements. Usually, WTO Secretariat officials visit the prospective city to determine its infrastructure ability to host such a large meeting.

[240] The other WTO Ministerial Conferences were consecutively: Singapore (Dec. 9-13, 1996), Geneva (May 18-20, 1998), Seattle (Nov.-Dec., 30-3, 1999), and Cancun (Sep. 10-14, 2003). The sixth Ministerial Conference will be held in Hong Kong (Dec. 13-18, 2005). The usual date for WTO Ministerial

Qatar is a small country, and it is not an active member of the WTO as other members such as Canada, Chile, Singapore, or South Africa. Despite these limitations, Qatar was found to have the required infrastructure to host the meeting.[241] Since Qatar is not an active member of the WTO, Qatari trade minister, Yousef Hussain Kamal, did not likely have the experience necessary to chair the conference. In practice, the old experienced guards of WTO members would run effectively the procedures of the conference. It is possible that Qatar was chosen for reasons other than its infrastructure and the WTO claim of wanting to integrate Arab countries into the WTO system.

The 1999 Seattle Ministerial Conference was a blow to the efforts of WTO members to launch the "Millennium Round".[242] The WTO could not sustain another failure. As such, Qatar was the proper venue to remove the Seattle stain. In terms of geography, Qatar is a far way from the anti-globalization protestors and anarchists that disrupted the Seattle Conference.[243] Even if protestors decided to travel to Qatar, they were unlikely to flock in large numbers considering travel expenses and other logistical hurdles.[244] Protestors were likely to have a low key profile in Doha. Therefore, to outflank Seattle reoccurrence, Doha was chosen as it is far from demonstrations, riot police, tear gas, and downtown arrests.

Over the course of several WTO Ministerial Conferences, delegations of some Arab countries to the Conferences were small in number. Generally, Arab delegations consisted of a trade minister and with two senior trade officials. This reflects the fact that Arab countries do not have enough financial resources to send full-fledged delegations.[245] The small numbers of Arab delegations could be easily compared with hundreds of trade negotiators representing other countries.[246] Delegations consisting of small numbers put Arab countries at disadvantage, especially when due to an imbalanced calendar, several meetings were held at the same time.

Conferences is the Nov. to Dec. period. During this period in 2001, the Islamic month of Ramadan would come. Being sensitive to Islamic values, it was decided to hold the fourth Ministerial Conference earlier (Nov. 9-13). If WTO members did not decide so, trade negotiators would be hungry. Trade negotiators would not provide the anticipated outcomes.

[241] See Daniel Pruzin, *Chile, Qatar Signal to WTO Interest in Hosting Ministerial Meeting Next Year*, 17 Intl. Trade Rep. (BNA) 1888 (Dec. 14, 2000) (Qatar was prepared to make available 4,440 rooms for attending officials some in terms of luxury villas and cruise ships. The proposed venue was the Sheraton Doha Conference and the International Exhibition Center).

[242] There are many reasons for the failure of the Seattle meeting. At this point, external factors will be counted. Violent protests against the WTO resulted in 600 arrests, $3 million in property damages, and between $12 million and $22 million in lost business for Seattle merchants. *Id*. Protestors delayed and disrupted several Seattle meetings.

[243] The largest jam ever in Qatar in which police interfered was the McDonald-Burger King price war. The two fast-food restaurants engaged in price war after Burger King opened in Qatar.

[244] While if the WTO Ministerial Conference was held in Vancouver, Canada, protestors would have flocked in vans by thousands just across the U.S. borders.

[245] The WTO provides three travel tickets, for more you buy your own ticket. Other international agencies may handle travel expenses such as WIPO or USAID.

[246] For GATT Brussels Ministerial Meeting in 1990, the U.S. sent an army of 600 personnel and Japan 300. Perhaps out of security reasons, U.S. trade delegation to the Doha Ministerial Conference had a low turnout of less than 100.

Non-governmental organizations (NGOs) are permitted to attend WTO Ministerial Conferences.[247] NGOs are subject to accreditation process by specifying how their activities are linked to the work of the WTO and source(s) of finance.[248] However, these requirements are also a potential drawback for NGOs from Arab countries.[249]

Over the course of the five WTO Ministerial Conferences held so far, few Arab business associations and NGOs have participated. Moreover, they are limited in representation to one or two personnel. For example, in the third Ministerial Conference held in Seattle in 1999 among approximately 739 associations and NGOs that took part only three were from Arab countries.[250] The number of Arab associations increased dramatically in the fourth Ministerial Conference held in Doha in 2001.[251] The lack of expansive Arab associations and NGOs participation in WTO Ministerial Conferences can be attributed to lack of interest or understanding of the WTO mechanics or more importantly due to lack of financial resources.

Inter-governmental organizations also participate in WTO Ministerial Conferences. For example, in the Doha Ministerial Conference of 2001, sixty-two inter-governmental organizations were permitted to participate. One noticeable group that was missing from participation in WTO Ministerial Conferences was the League of Arab States, one of the oldest regional organizations of states in the world. Despite various attempts by the League to obtain an observership seat at WTO Ministerial Conferences, as well as

---

[247] NGOs' attendance is limited to plenary sessions but not other meetings.

[248] See Press Release, Non-Governmental Organizations Facilities Provided During the WTO Ministerial Conference in Singapore, PRESS/TF 012 (Aug. 26, 1996). An obvious reason for the accreditation process is to prevent NGOs with "hidden agenda" from participating.
Coincidentally, the title of the document refers to trade and environment. One assumes that some environmental NGOs have hidden agenda.

[249] Perhaps, some Arab NGOs might be interested in the work of the WTO although their activities are not linked to the work of the WTO.

[250] Two were from Egypt (Group of Fifteen-Federation of Chambers of Commerce, Industry and Services and the Central Agricultural Co-op Union) and one from Sudan (Sudanese Business Men and Employers Federation).

[251] Out of approximately 365 associations and NGOs participated in the Conference,12 Arab association participated: six were from Jordan (Arab Knowledge Management Society, Arab Society for Certified Accountants, Arab Society for Intellectual Property, Licensing Executives Society-Arab Countries, National Society for Consumer Protection, PhRMA East/Africa Committee), one from Lebanon (Arab NGO Network for Development), three from Egypt (Centre for Trade Union and Workers Services, Group of Fifteen-Federation of Chambers of Commerce, Industry and Services, National Association for Human Rights and Development), one from Syria (International Confederation of Arab Trade Unions), and one from Saudi Arabia (Women and Children International). The number of Arab associations and NGOs in the fifth Ministerial Conference in Cancun in 2003 dropped back to 8 out of 1002: three from Egypt (Afro-Asian People's Solidarity Organization, Center for Trade Union and Workers Services, Federation of Egyptian Industries), two from Jordan (Arab Knowledge Management Society, Pharmaceutical Research and Manufacturers of America-Jordan), one from Lebanon (Arab NGO Network for Development), one from Iran (Confederation of Iranian Industry), and one from Tunisia (Union Tunisienne de l'Agriculture et de la Pêche).

various meetings, the League's efforts have thus far been fruitless.[252] Several WTO members have objected to such requests on the pretext that the League of Arab States' promotion of boycott of Israel is contrary to WTO rules. Clearly, the objections of these members are politically motivated rather than legally justified. WTO rules provide the means for integrating the functions of international, regional, and country-specific inter-governmental organizations, including the IMF, World Bank, and the OECD (the holy triangle of industrialized countries).[253] In return for blocking the League of Arab States application for observership, Arab countries such as Egypt blocked applications of other inter-governmental organizations.[254] For example, U.N Commissioner for Human Rights was not granted an observer status in the Council for Trade in Services.

At the end of the Ministerial Conference in Qatar, members marked the launch of new round of multilateral trade negotiations. Apart from being considered "developing countries," the question that arises is what had Arab countries achieved during the meeting. One of the immediate benefits, at least from the perspective of Qatar, is that the new round was dubbed "the Doha Development Agenda".[255] Additionally, Qatar boosted its domestic tourism industry, even if such a boost was only temporary.[256] However, there have not been any long-range economic benefits from hosting the Conference. As for other Arab countries, they are now faced with the daunting task of understanding the complex and extensive trade negotiations in which they will participate over the next several years, while still digesting the raw deals of the Uruguay Round.

IX. Trade Patterns of Arab Countries

Despite the fact that Arab countries collectively represent approximately 5 percent of world's population, they are not as integrated in the world economy as other countries. The share of Arab countries in world trade is effectively *de minimis*. It amounted to about 3 percent of export and about 2.4 percent of import in 1999. In total, international trade is about 5.4 percent of all trade in Arab countries. According to *the Economist*, the region's

---

[252] For instance, the League of Arab States was not permitted to participate as an observer in the WTO Ministerial Conference in Cancun in 2003. Hussein Hassouna, Ambassador of the League of Arab States to the U.S., Address, *The League of Arab States and International Law* (Am. U. Sch. L., Apr. 21, 2004) (copy on file with author). On the other hand, Qatar courteously hosted Israel delegation in the Fourth Ministerial Conference in Doha. Usually, the WTO issues invitations to members and other organizations to attend its Ministerial Conferences.

[253] Article V.1 of the WTO Charter states that the General Council shall make "appropriate arrangements" for effective cooperation with other inter-governmental organizations that have responsibilities related to those of the WTO. Thus, members of the WTO recognized, though without any specific reference for any inter-governmental organization, other legal entities as part of the wider economic order.

[254] See Robyn Eckersley, *The Big Chill: The WTO and Multilateral Environmental Agreements*, 4 Global Envtl. Pol. 24 (May 2004) (admission of observers has been dealt with on *ad hoc* basis. The continuing impasse on the observer problem can be resolved only at the General Council level).

[255] The "Doha Development Agenda" will enter the history of trade rounds along with the Tokyo Round and the Uruguay Round. It is of notice that the Doha Ministerial Declaration of 2001 uses the term "work program" instead of the politically sensitive term "trade round". For example, the term "work program" was used seventeen times while round was referred to only one time in the context of the Uruguay Round. See Doha Ministerial Declaration, *supra* n. 225.

[256] Qatar may have built facilities such as rooms that cost million of dollars to be used only for one time.

total GDP is at $531 billion yearly, which less than that of Spain.[257] Despite the fact that Arab countries are geographically giant, they are still economically tiny.

Intra-regional trade, that is, trade among Arab countries, represents just 10 percent of total Arab trade. These figures clearly indicate that external and intra-Arab trade is negligible. There are several explanations for the poor trading performance of Arab countries. One suggestion is that regional conflicts and political tensions, along with large military expenditures, have prevailed over the years.[258] The combination of small markets and high barriers to trade is another factor.[259] Another theory is that Arab countries have not sufficiently diversified their exports, with the exception of oil.[260] Some Arab countries impose cabotage restrictions by limiting the ability of their transportation companies to operate in other countries with full freedom.[261]

Tariff rates in Arab countries are still higher than other regions. For example, the weighted average tariff in Egypt is 28 percent compared with 14 percent in Latin American countries.[262] In Lebanon, tariff accounts for 44 percent of total government revenue, the largest contributor to the budget. Therefore, the revenue impact of trade liberalization differs from country to country, depending on the total tariffs' contribution to the budget. In addition, Arab countries use different forms of para-tariffs that have the equivalent effect of tariffs.[263] Examples of para-tariffs include stamp taxes and consular fees, which increase as the value of imports increases or do not reflect the actual service rendered.[264] Arab countries would have to streamline these para-tariffs, if they have not already done so, in the process of acceding to the WTO.

Internal barriers to intra-Arab trade also leave many economies of scales unexploited. Arab trade usually takes the form of homogenous products (textiles and

---

[257] See *Special Report: Self-doomed to Failure-Arab Development*, Economist 24 (July 6, 2002) (unemployment is about 15 percent of the labor force and growth is stagnant. Arab countries poor performance is not for lack of resources but for shortage of three essentials: freedom, knowledge, and womanpower).
[258] Bernard Hoekman & Patrick Messerlin, *Harnessing Trade for Development and Growth in the Middle East* 7 (Brookings Instn. Press 2002).
[259] *Id.* at 11.
[260] *Id.* at 12.
[261] A survey of companies in Arab countries found that costs of trading in these countries are about 10.6 of value of trade. These costs include slow customs clearance, additional payments to customs officials, and large number of documents and signatures required for processing. *Id.* at 14, 53-56.
[262] See *Trade Policy Developments in the Middle East and North Africa* 118 (Bernard Hoekman & Hanaa Kheir-El-Din eds., World Bank Publications 2000).
[263] *Id.* at 168.
[264] Jordan, for example, imposed fees for customs overtime wage at 0.2 percent of the CIF value of imports or traffic administration fee. Tunisia imposed TD 2 as a computer data word-processing fee on each page of the customs declaration. Egypt imposed statistical tax of 1 percent on all imports. See M. M Kostecki & M. J. Tymowski, *Customs Duties versus other Import Charges in the Developing Countries*, 19 J.W.T. 269-281 (1985) (some Arab countries such as Libya, Algeria, Egypt, and Mauritania impose taxes on foreign trade transactions in the form of compulsory foreign exchange levies and advanced import deposits. Such taxes are not reported in the financial statistics on import taxes).

apparel) competing in the same markets (the U.S. and EC).[265] Finally, one should not ignore developed countries protectionism that contributes to the lack of Arab countries integration in the world market.[266]

The structure of exports and imports of Arab countries clearly indicates that oil products amount to more than half of the total of exports from Arab countries.[267] This is followed by manufactured products, which amount to 15.8 percent. Machinery absorbs the lion share of imports, 34.2 percent, followed by manufactured products, 30.5 percent. In terms of geographical distribution of trade, the EC is the largest Arab trading partner in terms of exports and imports, followed by the U.S. and Japan, which means that there is a trade dependency on the U.S. and EC markets.

The divided circumstances of Arab countries are so varied that generalizations are rendered difficult.[268] However, some trends in export structures are ascertainable. In terms of exports, Arab countries can be divided into two categories.[269] The first category includes countries that depend primarily on oil exports.[270] For example, oil exports amount to 95 percent of Kuwait's total exports and 87 percent of Saudi Arabia's total exports.[271]

The second category includes countries that export foodstuffs, agricultural, and manufactured products.[272] Most manufactured products exported from Arab countries are clothing and textiles. The clothing sector, in pre-Uruguay rounds, was subject to quantitative restrictions imposed by several developed countries.[273] The clothing sector

---

[265] Since the U.S. and EC markets account for much of Arab countries exports, trade policies and practices in these two countries would have a profound impact on Arab countries trade.

[266] If trade in textiles and apparel, agriculture, oil, and movement of people are restricted, one would wonder what Arab countries can trade in.

[267] See Table 2 in appendix 1, page 218.

[268] There is no single formula that would determine how to classify Arab countries. Many Arab countries differ in size, degree of development, trade pattern, and income.

[269] A third group of Arab least-developed countries can be added. It includes Comoros, Djibouti, Mauritania, Somalia, and Sudan. In the WTO there is no specific definition for developed, developing, and least developing countries. Each country may self-select its status, but this does not mean that it would automatically qualify for such status in the WTO bodies. The U.N usually classifies countries as such.

[270] This category includes Algeria, Bahrain, Iraq, Kuwait, Libya, Oman, Qatar, Saudi Arabia, and United Arab Emirates.

[271] See Said El-Naggar, *The Effects of the WTO on Arab Countries*, U.N. Economic and Social Commission for Western Asia, at 2, U.N. Doc. E/ESCWA/CAB/2001/6 (2001) (Arabic Version).

[272] The second category includes Egypt, Jordan, Lebanon, Morocco, Syria, Tunisia, and Yemen. *Id.* 3.

[273] The industries of developed countries were unable to face competition from imports of developing countries. The normal action to protect developed countries' industries, if there was an injury to the domestic industries, was to apply article XIX of GATT 1947. However, according to article MFN treatment, safeguard would have to apply to all countries which in that case would have counteracted by other developed countries. Hence, the Agreement Regarding International Trade in Textiles, known as the Multi-Fiber Agreement, came into existence. It prescribed import quotas for developing countries which signed the agreement.

finally came under the jurisdiction of the WTO.[274] Arab countries are likely to benefit from further liberalization in the clothing sector.[275]

A pattern of countertrade has developed in Arab countries. In 1995, the U.N Security Council, for humanitarian purposes in Iraq, adopted Resolution No. 986, also known as the "Oil for Food Resolution".[276] It provides for the export of specified quantities of Iraqi oil with the proceeds being deposited in an escrow account that may be used for the import of goods, products and technology necessary for Iraq's economic and social development. In other words, it is a trade of a product for another product. This sort of partial barter-trade is beneficial for Arab countries that are under economic embargoes and may not have enough foreign exchange to finance imports.

X. The Impact of the International Trading System on Arab Countries

This section will briefly summarize the implications of WTO on Arab countries in certain sectors.[277] From the outset, it is important to indicate that the multilateral trading system will have profound effects on the Arab countries collectively. For those countries that joined the WTO, this means that they will have to abide by its rules. For those that are outside the WTO, this means that they would have to undertake regulatory reforms. The effects of the WTO on different sectors can be summarized as follows. Benefits are likely to materialize once the Arab countries enact a broad package of laws and regulations. This does not mean that some Arab industries are not likely to be negatively affected. A price must be paid for joining the WTO (no pain, no gain). However, any negative impact on Arab import-competing industries may be compensated by exportable industries. Regardless, one cannot for sure say what the full-portrait of the negative or positive effects will be since these are probabilities.

A. Agriculture

Until the Uruguay Round, agriculture was under softer disciplines. The WTO Agreement on Agriculture contains new regulations in this sector. The WTO Agreement on Agriculture covers market access, export subsidies, and domestic support.[278] The

---

[274] The liberalization of the clothing sector extended over ten years period ending in 2005. The WTO Agreement on Textiles and Clothing contains an annex which has a list of articles that are covered by the liberalization action.

[275] Many developing countries have expressed their dismay as to the pace of the application of the WTO Textiles and Clothing Agreement in its early stage. The phase-out schedule under the Agreement was backloaded so that industrialized countries could maintain nearly half of their quotas until the final implementation period. Therefore, value-added textiles and apparels were not covered until the later stage of liberalization.

[276] See Mark Turner, *Iraq and the U.N.*, Fin. Times 3 (Mar. 26, 2004).

[277] Measuring the impact of WTO accession on Arab countries in different sectors such as services, employment, and telecommunication, just to mention few, requires extensive studies and analysis that are beyond the limits of this section. For some sectoral studies on the WTO and Arab countries see *Opening Doors to the World: A New Trade Agenda for the Middle East* (Raed Safadi ed., Intl. Dev. Research Ctr. 1998).

[278] Without going into the details of the WTO Agreement on Agriculture, restrictions on market access of agriculture were in the form of tariffs and non-tariff barriers. WTO members agreed to tariffy non-tariff

WTO Agreement on Agriculture also establishes a special safeguard mechanism that allows WTO members to impose restrictive measures when facing surging farm imports.

Arab countries' agriculture sectors are in primitive stages. Arab countries are facing an ever increasing challenge to acquire adequate food to feed their populations. Arab countries are experiencing a lack of young farmers. Many farming households derive most of their income from non-agricultural activities. Although some parts of the region have been historically exporters of agricultural products nowadays they are, to large extent, dependent on staple food imports.[279] Many Arab countries post a trade deficit in farm products.

There are many reasons for the decline of agriculture in Arab countries. First, farm policy in Arab countries, which is different from developed countries, plays a role in this state of affairs.[280] Second, Arab agriculture sectors are relatively subsidy-free while developed countries provide massive agricultural subsidies, thus causing lower prices and harming farmers in Arab countries. Moreover, Arab agricultural technology, such as mechanization and large farm operations, is also not at the same level as that of their foreign counterparts, which results in high output costs and low international competitiveness. Additionally, exports of agriculture and fishery products from Arab countries face a myriad of safety and environmental regulations in foreign markets. For

---

barriers in binding recorded schedules with tariffs resulting from this process are to be reduced by average 36 percent in case of developed countries and 24 percent for developing countries, with minimum reductions for each tariff line required. This process is known as the Uruguay Round formula. Regarding export subsidy, developed countries committed to reduction at a level of 36 percent below the 1986-1990 base level and the quantity of subsidized exports by 21 percent over the same period. In case of developing countries the reductions are two-thirds of those of developed countries. The implementation period is six years for developed countries starting Jan.1 1995, and ten years for developing countries regarding direct export subsidy. Some WTO members calculated very high levels of equivalent tariffs in replacement of non-tariff barriers. To alleviate such a problem members provided three approaches: current market access, minimum access quotas where current access is less than 3 percent of domestic consumption, and special treatment for some products such as rice. For more on the WTO Agriculture Agreement see Melaku Geboye Desta, *Food Security and International Trade Law: An Appraisal of the World Trade Organization*, 35 J.W.T. 450-452 (2001).

[279] See Roni N. Halabi, *Stability in the Middle East through Economic Development: An Analysis of the Peace Process, Increased Agricultural Trade, Joint Ventures, and Free Trade Agreements*, 2 Drake J. Agric. L. 275, 284 (1997) (twenty Arab countries purchased $27.3 billion worth of agricultural products in 1993).

[280] For example, Arab countries tax farmers so as urban population would purchase these farm products at lower prices. In order to compensate for taxing farmers, Arab countries subsidize inputs such as irrigation thus providing artificially low-cost water. However, with taking on economic reforms under the aegis of international agencies, subsidizing inputs is no longer a viable approach. Moreover, Arab countries lack foreign exchange to subsidize agriculture. On the other hand, developed countries, such as the EC, tax urban population to insure income support for farmers. Rather subsidizing inputs, developed countries subsidize agriculture output. Therefore, domestic Arab farm products priced higher than imported ones. Of course, developed countries agricultural exporters are more than happy to fill in the gap and "dump" their surplus productions in Arab countries markets. Thus, further eroding what is remaining of the agriculture sector in these Arab countries. Water scarcity in the region is another reason for the decline in agriculture. However, although it is valid, this is not all true. Further reason for insufficient grain harvest could be due to giving more emphasis on value-added crops such as fruits and vegetables. One could argue that this works for Arab countries comparative advantage since they have large pool of labor and little arable land.

example, Oman was allowed to export wild shrimp to the U.S. in 2005, only after the State Department certified that its fishing operations do not threaten endangered sea turtles because Oman harvests shrimp using manual rather than mechanical means to retrieve nets.[281] Other regulatory measures imposed by the U.S. include mandatory country-of-origin labeling for meat and meat products. Safety and environmental regulations make it burdensome for agriculture and fishery products from Arab countries to penetrate foreign markets.

Arab countries, such as Saudi Arabia, have undertaken programs to become self-sufficient in agriculture. To achieve this goal, Arab countries may want to increase farm spending which has little impact on trade and thus does not run afoul of WTO rules. For example, Arab countries could establish support programs that include measures such as income insurance and income safety nets, agricultural research, restructuring aid, disease control, and regional assistance. These support programs could also include certain forms of direct payments to farmers as long as these payments are not linked to the type or amount of crops being grown.

Trade in genetically modified or bioengineered foods involves complex factors. These factors include lack of scientific certainty on the possible impact of agriculture biotechnology on human or animal health and the environment, involvement of huge economic interests in the biotech food trade, and the links that biotech food has to ethical and religious concerns and biodiversity preservation. Arab countries, such as the Sudan, have imposed import bans or tight restrictions on genetically modified organisms (GMOs) products. These Arab countries fear the contamination of local crops by GMO strains that could affect their ability to export agriculture products to the EC, where there are strict controls on bioengineered foods. Arab countries may need to approve biotechnology in order to boost food security. Bioengineered crops provide protection against pests or tolerance to chemicals. For example, in 2004, Algeria and Tunisia experienced a slow-down in economic growth due in part to a locust infestation that curbed agricultural output. Approval of bioengineered crops could be accompanied by adequate labeling laws put in place such as have been put in place in Saudi Arabia. The areas of GMOs crops under cultivation could be separated from other areas of conventional crops. In addition, as a safety measure, GMOs could pass through safety and risk assessments before entering Arab countries.

Accession into the WTO would force the opening up of the domestic agricultural commodity markets. Moreover, as a result of further liberalization in agriculture, it is expected that the price tag of imported food products will increase. Arab net food-

---

[281] Under U.S. law, wild shrimp imports are barred if harvested in ways harmful to endangered sea turtles. However, the import bar is inapplicable if the State Department certifies that the harvesting nation has taken steps to reduce the incidental taking of turtles in shrimp trawl operations such as the use of sea turtle excluder devices or has fishing environment that poses no threat to sea turtles such as fishing in cold water regions not frequented by sea turtles. The shipment of shrimp must be accompanied by the State Department form DS-2031 signed by the exporter, importer, and government official from the harvesting nation. See *Appropriations Act of 1990*, 16 U.S.C. § 1537 (2005).

importing countries would likely to face some difficulties.[282] Therefore, in WTO trade negotiations, one could anticipate that some Arab countries would be in a defensive position or low profile proponents of agricultural trade liberalization. Any reduction in subsidies by developed countries for their agriculture exporters would translate into a higher food import bill for Arab countries.

In WTO trade negotiations, Arab net food-importing countries could be proponents of special and differential treatment in agricultural export credits, offered through export credit agencies of developed countries, by arguing for longer maximum repayment terms, minimum annual repayment of principal and interest, favorable interest rates, and premium terms for food imports. Some Arab countries, such as Jordan and the Sudan, currently are recipients of food aid. As such, these Arab countries could argue for continuing food aid in the form of in-kind donations and cash payments when negotiating new WTO rules regarding the use of food aid. Any agriculture trade reforms should not lead to a reduction in food aid delivered to Arab countries. Arab countries should resist any proposals that would limit food aid given in grants rather than credits and food aid that takes the form of cash donations, rather than in-kind food donations. Cash donation may take a longer time to reach targeted groups as compared with in-kind donations. Moreover, Arab countries could argue that food aid should not be restricted only to defined emergencies and humanitarian crises.

B. State-Owned Enterprises

Arab countries face the dilemma of the public/private sector dichotomy. State-owned enterprises (SOEs) are perceived as a drag on the economy and the budget. Some officials in Arab countries believe in smaller government by reducing the number of civil servants. It is also perceived that Arab countries' economic future depends upon the reform of SOEs. Usually, the public sector opposes trade liberalization and the private sector backs it. When SOEs were set up in 1960s, they were arms of the state, and they generate 40 percent of GDP.[283] These SOEs account for a large share of urban employment.[284]

---

[282] The WTO Agreement on Agriculture recognizes the negative effects of agricultural liberalization. For this reason, WTO members adopted the Ministerial Decision on Measures Concerning the Possible Negative Effects of the Reforming Program on Least-developed and Net Food-Importing Developing Countries. Statistics show that food prices rose sharply after entry into force of the WTO Agreement on Agriculture. Since then prices have been on the decline. For more on discussion the Ministerial Decision and the effects on food security see Desta, *supra* n. 278, at 465-467. The list of net food-importing countries includes Djibouti, Mauritania, Somalia, Sudan, Egypt, Jordan, Morocco, and Tunisia. See Committee on Agriculture, *WTO List of Net Food-Importing Developing Countries*, G/AG/5/Rev.5 (Mar. 26, 2002).

[283] See *Doing Business with Egypt* 11, 17-25 (Marat Terterov ed., Kogan Page 2001).

[284] See Yitzhak Reiter, *The Palestinian-Transjordanian Rift: Economic Might and Political Power in Jordan*, 58 The Middle East J. 72, 77 (2004) (the top 500 private-owned enterprises has JD5,814 million worth of assets with total employment of 44,839). From this article, one can inversely draw the conclusion regarding the large number of employees in public enterprises in Jordan. See also *Doing Business with Saudi Arabia* 5, 21 (Anthony Shoult ed., 2d ed., Kogan Page 2002) (the Saudi economy is currently in a state of transition as a consequence of the need to move from a focus on public to private sector activity.

The arguments then proceed along the following lines: These SOEs suffer from an inability to reduce overmanned offices coupled with bloated payrolls. In these enterprises, political skills are far more important than educational or managerial skills. The dilemma of public/private sector is further complicated if the civil service in Arab countries has ethnic majority, while the private sector has different ethnic structure. SOEs maintain advantages in obtaining government subsidies, land rights, loans from state banks, and legalized monopolies in sectors such as aviation and power. To put it bluntly, the private sector may not enjoy a level playing field.

The balance between the public/private sectors also means that it takes a longer time for reform to maintain the socio-political balance. Taking into account the abilities of the private sector and of all these private/SOEs, the reality is that few may spring out as conglomerates in a nasty international market that recognizes only one thing: being lean and mean. The goal should not be to squeeze one sector over the other. Rather, there must be a potentially a long-term partnership on broad range of activities between private enterprises and SOEs based on communication through workshops, cooperation, shared accountability, and mutual benefit.[285] In other words, a national economy must be a private/public sector-led economy. Moreover, creating a few large SOEs may lead to some Arab multinationals that would be globally competitive and that have reduced their inefficiencies.

The ability of Arab countries to compete in international trade depends on productivity, investment in human and physical capital, and research and development. Several indicators suggest a decline in Arab countries competitiveness. Intra-industry trade between 1985 and 1997 had been relatively slow and show little change when compared with Brazil, Taiwan, and Malaysia.[286] Many firms in Arab countries are dominated by individuals, compete based on price alone, and lack managerial and technological resources. Some domestic industries are mostly composed of family-owned small and medium-sized enterprises.[287] They are concentrated in traditional labor-intensive industries such as textiles and apparel, wood products, and non-metallic mineral products. There are no available data on overall expenditure in research and development or the number of patents awarded in Arab countries.

Arab countries should focus their efforts on developing high-tech industries. Arab countries should also boost their support for research and development and improve their engineering and science education. Competition will lead to increases in efficiency and creativity, which will force domestic industries to adapt with the new climate.[288]

Annual government spending represents one-third of Saudi GDP. For example, in 1994, income payments to public sector employees accounted for around 50 percent of total government spending).

[285] Long-term partnership may include outsourcing of non-essential functions to private sector companies so as to allow SOEs to focus on their essential functions. For example, notary services may be outsourced to private companies.

[286] See *Globalization and Firm Competitivenes in the Middle East and North African Region* 191-195 (Samiha Fawzy ed., The World Bank 2002).

[287] For example, in Jordan 93 percent of establishments are small and medium-sized enterprises. *Id.*

[288] Through mergers companies could be able to compete, invest in their production systems, and strengthen their financial position.

C. International Trade in Oil

Oil is the largest primary commodity traded internationally.[289] Some Arab countries are top suppliers of oil. They have a comparative cost advantage since oil in these countries is cheap to pump. Therefore, oil-Arab producing countries that are not yet members of the WTO such as Algeria, Iraq, Libya, and Saudi Arabia may have concern over subjecting oil to market forces. In acceding to the WTO, these countries may have to bind their tariffs on oil imports, meaning that tariffs cannot increase above certain ceiling. Also, this implies that other oil-importing countries would reduce and bind their tariffs based on reciprocity, thus giving an advantage to oil-Arab exporting countries.[290]

It is a misconception to claim that oil trade, whether crude oil or oil derivatives, is not covered or excluded by the WTO agreements. Over the years, developed and developing countries have increased the number of goods governed by the disciplines of multilateral trading system.[291] As a matter of fact, Kuwait associated itself with a 1987 GATT case that was concerned with oil trade.[292] If oil trade is not governed by GATT, then the GATT panel would not have exercised jurisdiction in the matter. However, that case was limited to the consumer/importer side of the oil trade. There has not yet been a case involving the producer/exporter country side for reasons, such as setting prices or production targets.[293] Additionally, oil trade is subject to domestic trade remedy laws.[294]

---

[289] Fuel exports in 2002 stood at $615 billion accounting for 9.8 percent of world merchandise trade. See WTO Secretariat, *International Trade Statistics for 2003* (2003).

[290] For much of the twentieth century the U.S. maintained a tariff on oil imports to protect its petroleum industry against lower-priced competition from abroad. See Michael A. Toman, *International Oil Security: Problems and Policies*, 20 Brookings Rev. 20, 21 (2002).

[291] In its accession to the WTO in 2001, China committed to allocate tariff-rate quotas for crude oil. China agreed to allow in prescribed amounts of oil at lower tariff levels. Oil imports above the quota levels are subject to higher tariffs.

[292] The Superfund case was brought by EC, Canada, and Mexico. A 1987 GATT panel found that tariffs mandated by the U.S. Comprehensive Environmental Response, Compensation, and Liability Act, known as Superfund legislation, was in violation of article III.2 of GATT (the non-discriminatory article). The U.S. charged imported oil at rate of 11.7 percent per barrel. On the other hand, it charged domestic oil at rate of 8.2 percent. The case is cited briefly in Kwan kiat Sim article. See Sim, *infra* note 1895. The other oil-related case is U.S.-Reformulated Gasoline case of 1996. However, the Reformulated Gasoline case was primarily concerned with an environmental measure. For more on this "environmental" case see *Reconciling Environment and Trade* 163-292 (Edith Brown Weiss & John H. Jackson eds., Transnatl. Publishers 2001).

[293] See Rossella Brevetti, *DeFazio Asks for WTO Case against OPEC Production Cuts*, 21 Intl. Trade Rep. (BNA) 565 (Apr. 1, 2004) (Rep. Peter DeFazio, along with over 30 other House members filed a letter with President Bush asking to launch a WTO case against OPEC. The letter alleges that OPEC supply restrictions are disguised restrictions on international trade violating article XI of GATT 1994. Moreover, the letter states that article XX exception allowing restrictions for the conservation of exhaustible natural resources is inapplicable since OPEC is not restricting oil production due to conservation concerns or to preserve an exhaustible supply). If a WTO case is filed, although it is unlikely for its political and economically-destabilizing ramifications, it would be the first WTO case on the producer/supplier side.

[294] Oil trade includes here crude oil, oil derivatives, and oil country tubular goods that are used in the oil and gas industry such as tubes and drill pipes.

For example, in 1999, a consortium of independent U.S. crude oil producers alleged that companies in Saudi Arabia and Iraq, among other countries, were dumping crude oil that was subsidized by the Saudi and Iraqi governments in the U.S. market.[295]

However, one certainly can claim that oil trade is an "ambivalent" trade.[296] On the one hand, oil trade is supposedly covered by WTO agreements. On the other hand, some oil production is managed by the Organization of Petroleum Exporting Countries (OPEC) through supply control measures such as price targets or production quotas.[297] There are many factors that affect trade in oil.[298] The U.S. and other developed countries should reduce their trade barriers such as high tariffs, discriminatory taxes on fossil fuels, carbon taxes, subsidies for coal, and threats of antidumping orders.[299]

XI. Data on the Application of Arab countries of Selected WTO Provisions

Based on data collected in February 2003, fourteen investigations on the application of safeguard measures have been either self-initiated by the competent authority or initiated upon petition from the domestic industries of Arab countries members of the WTO. Egypt, Jordan, and Morocco are the frequent users of safeguard provisions. Of

---

[295] The U.S. Department of Commerce denied the petition on the ground that there was no sufficient support from the domestic industry to initiate an investigation since opposition from U.S. producers exceeded support. On appeal, the CIT and Court of Appeals for the Federal Circuit affirmed the decision of the Commerce Department. See *Save Dom. Oil, Inc. v. U.S.*, 240 F. Supp. 2d 1342 (Ct. Intl. Trade 2002) (stating that this was the first case the Commerce Department had rejected a petition at the filing petition level). See also *Save Dom. Oil v. U.S.*, 357 F.3d 1278, 1284 (Fed. Cir. 2004) (the Commerce Department does not have a standard practice applicable to all industries of disregarding the opposition of domestic importer-producers with import levels beyond a certain percentage. There is an industry-specific analysis). One may speculate that the Commerce Department rejected the dumping petition because imposing an anti-dumping order would lead to political backlash from oil-producing countries as well as to increase in the price U.S. consumers would pay at the pump.

[296] See Francis N. Botchway, *International Trade Regime and Energy Trade*, 28 Syracuse J. Int'l. L. & Com. 1, 11, 12 (2001) (some of the theoretical reasons for the apparent ambivalent attitude of contemporary international trade regime to energy trade include the definition of energy as good or service which in itself is not without controversy, location of energy at the heart of government economic thinking, and energy as a vital national asset to be left to free international trade trajectories. Movements in international regulation of energy are more likely to come from regional or industry-determined economic blocs. The legal basis for OPEC is article XX(h) of GATT which permits import or export restrictions legislated by commodity agreements. However, OPEC was not submitted for approved of the Contracting Parties as required by article XX(h) of GATT).

[297] See *Oil: A Burning Question*, Economist 71 (Mar. 27, 2004) (citing the OPEC "cartel" and its kingpin Saudi Arabia decision to cut production by 1 million barrel per day). The word "cartel" deserves a pause since developed countries themselves established cartels through the Multi-Fiber Arrangement for textiles with the approval of the GATT itself or through the on-going negotiations of multilateral agreement on steel over-production with the aim of setting production quotas.

[298] For overview of trade in oil see James M. Day, *Petroleum Prices*, 1 Am. U. Bus. L. Br. 52, 53 (2004) (discussing the petroleum industry and factors that affect the industry such as traders, weather reports, expectations of war, OPEC, currency value, taxes, lack of refining capacity, and refiners' profits).

[299] High tariffs are often maintained on processed products to keep value-added production and employment in a certain market, while low tariffs are kept on raw products. This is known as tariff escalation. Some oil-importing countries impose higher tariffs on processed oil in order to keep value-added production and employment in their markets. Exporting raw products may constitute a threat to oil-Arab exporting countries' economic stability because they are natural resources with little value added.

those fourteen petitions, Jordan has investigated nine, Egypt has investigated three, and Morocco has investigated two. Of Jordan's petitions, the competent authority found serious injury in four, terminated four, and there is one outstanding investigation.[300] Of the three petitions of Egypt, the competent authority found merit in all of them.[301] Of the two petitions of Morocco, the competent authority imposed safeguard measures in one and terminated the other without imposing any safeguard measure.[302] Thus, almost 80 percent of the petitions resulted in import restrictions. Other Arab countries members of the WTO have not taken any safeguard action.[303]

Since their accession to the GATT/WTO, many Arab countries still impose safeguard measures as trade remedy measures. There have been no major structural changes in their respective trade remedy policies. If the purpose is to protect Arab countries' industries, then it is more advantageous to use antidumping and countervailing duty laws. For example, if Jordan uses its antidumping law to protect its domestic industry, it can target a particular industry of a country rather than imposing a safeguard measure against all countries as required by article 2.2 of the WTO Agreement on Safeguards. In this way, Jordan will not upset its trade relationship with other countries. Moreover, Jordan does not need to provide compensation to the exporting country(s) in the case of imposing antidumping duty, while under article 8.1 of the WTO Agreement on Safeguard Jordan has to maintain the same level of concession in case it imposes a

---

[300] Jordan found serious injury and applied safeguard measures on imports of biscuits and chocolates, (Aug. 24, 2001, WTO Doc. No.G/SG/N/8/JOR/1, WTO Doc. No. G/SG/N/10/JOR/1), imports of unrecorded media tapes (magnetic tapes) for sound recording or similar recording of other phenomena of a width not exceeding 4 mm, (June 19, 2002, WTO Doc. No. G/SG/N/8/JOR/2/Corr.1, WTO Doc. No. G/SG/N/10/JOR/2/Corr.1), imports of pasta in all its forms, (Jan. 27, 2003, WTO Doc. No. G/SG/N/8/JOR/3, Feb. 24, 2003, WTO Doc. No. G/SG/N/10/JOR/3), imports of sanitary products in all its forms and specifications, (Jan. 31, 2003, WTO Doc. No. G/SG/N/8/JOR/4, Feb. 21, 2003, WTO Doc. No. G/SG/N/10/JOR/4). Jordan terminated safeguard investigation on chocolate containing over 5 percent of coconut butter substitute, (July 3, 2001, WTO Doc. No. G/SG/N/9/JOR/1), imports of cooking appliances and plate-warmers - for gas fuel or for both gas and other fuels, (Oct. 31, 2002, WTO Doc. No. G/SG/N/9/JOR/4, G/SG/N/9/JOR/5), electric accumulators, including separators thereof, whether or not rectangular (including square) lead-acid, of a kind used for starting piston engines, (Oct. 31, 2002, WTO Doc. No. G/SG/N/9/JOR/3), and imports of Unglazed ceramic flags and paving, hearth or wall tiles; unglazed ceramic mosaic cubes and the like, whether or not on a backing and glazed ceramic flags and paving (Oct. 31, 2002, WTO Doc. No. G/SG/N/9/JOR/2). There was an outstanding investigation on imports of aerated waters containing added sugar or other sweeteners or flavors (Sep. 20, 2002, WTO Doc. No. G/SG/N/6/JOR/9).
[301] Egypt found serious injury on imports of matches, (Aug. 11, 1998, WTO Doc. No. G/SG/N/7/EGY/1, Feb. 10, 1999, WTO Docs. No. G/SG/N/8/EGY/1, G/SG/N/10/EGY/1), imports of Common Fluorescent Lamps, (Mar. 1, 2000, WTO Docs. No. G/SG/N/8/EGY/2, G/SG/N/10/EGY/2, Feb. 28, 2001, WTO Docs. No. G/SG/N/8/EGY/3, G/SG/N/10/EGY/3), and imports of Powdered Milk (Sep. 26, 2000, WTO Doc. No. G/SG/N/7/EGY/2, Apr. 3, 2001, WTO Doc. No. G/SG/N/8/EGY/4, G/SG/N/10/EGY/4).
[302] Morocco took safeguard measures on the importation of Bananas (Nov. 1, 2000, WTO Doc. No. G/SG/N/7/MAR/1, May 22, 2001, WTO Doc. No.G/SG/N/8/MAR/1, G/SG/N/10/MAR/1). Morocco terminated the investigation without applying any safeguard measure on rubber plate and sheet products (Jan. 10, 2002, WTO Doc. No. G/SG/N/9/MAR/1).
[303] See for instance UAE (Feb. 3, 1998, WTO Doc. No. G/SG/Q1/ARE/2), Bahrain (Jan. 16, 1998, WTO Doc. No. G/SG/Q1/BHR/2, 13. Oct. 2000, WTO Doc. No. Para. 26. WT/TPR/M/74), Qatar (Jan. 12, 1999 WTO Doc. No. G/SG/Q1/QAT/2), Oman (Apr. 10, 2001 WTO Docs. No. G/ADP/N/1/OMN/1, G/SCM/N/1/OMN/1, G/SG/N/1/OMN/1), and Tunisia (Sep. 11, 2001, WTO Docs. No. G/ADP/Q1/TUN/5, G/SCM/Q1/TUN/5).

safeguard measure. Finally, by imposing an antidumping duty Jordan will tell the world that its industries are just as competitive but because other countries dump in its market, it cannot compete. On the other hand, if Jordan imposes a safeguard measure, that is similar to saying "we confess and declare that our industries are not competitive, so would you please give us more time". Bluntly, safeguard law is a weak defense measure for weak countries.

Based on reports submitted to WTO committees in various periods, no Arab country undertook antidumping duty actions.[304] Egypt is the only Arab country member of the WTO that has taken an antidumping or countervailing duty action.[305] Thus, history shows that Egypt is the only Arab country that has launched and imposed antidumping measures.[306] This is ironic considering that other countries, such as the U.S., imposes antidumping and countervailing duties on exports of Arab countries. For example, the U.S. has imposed countervailing duty on imports of carbon steel wire rods from Saudi Arabia.[307] The EC has also imposed antidumping orders of 40 percent on imports of urea from Libya and Saudi Arabia.[308]

The Gulf countries, in their endeavor to comply with the WTO obligations, are intensifying their efforts, to implement intellectual property protection.[309] For example, although the Kuwaiti Parliament did not make any significant progress from 1995 until 1999, when the parliament was dissolved, the Emir of Kuwait did enact laws regarding foreign investment and copyright protection.[310] The U.S. is concerned about patent

---

[304] See Committee on Subsidies and Countervailing Measures, *Semi-Annual Reports under Article 25.11 of the Agreement*, G/SCM/N/52/Add.1/Rev.5 (Oct. 18, 2002).

[305] For example from the period 1996-2002 the following countries have submitted reports on whether a countervailing duty action has been taken or not: Kuwait, Morocco, Qatar, Tunisia, and United Arab Emirates. No reports have been received from the following Members: Bahrain, Djibouti, and Mauritania. See G/SCM/N/19/Add.1/Rev.10.

[306] See Press Release, WTO Secretariat Reports Significant Decline in Anti-Dumping Investigations, PRESS/374 (Apr. 20, 2004) (the WTO Secretariat stated that in the later part of 2003 115 investigations had been initiated. On the other hand, final antidumping duty orders imposed remained relatively constant. For example, over the same period in 2002 there were 113 final antidumping orders compared with 107 final orders in 2003).

[307] The case involved Saudi Iron and Steel Co. challenging the USITA methodology for determining the amount of Saudi subsidy, loan in that case. See *Georgetown Steel Corp. v. U.S.* 810 F.Supp. 318 (Ct. Intl. Trade 1992).

[308] The European Court of Justice overruled the antidumping order on the basis that the defendants were denied access to information. See Case C-49/88, Al-Jubail Fertilizer Co. & others v. Council, 1991 E.C.R. I-03187 (1991).

[309] For example, the UAE passed a patent law upon compelling from the U.S. There are also extensive efforts to eliminate software piracy and insufficient protection for pharmaceutical products. Bahrain also acceded to the Berne Convention for the Protection of Literary and Artistic Works and Paris Convention for the Protection of Industrial Property. Kuwait informed the WTO that it would enact new laws at short notice. However, no laws were passed. See Meyer Reumann, *The Endeavours of Gulf Countries to Meet WTO Requirements* Vol. 16 A. L Q. 49, 50-52 (2001).

[310] After the old parliament was dissolved, the new parliament rejected both laws on the ground that they were not urgent and under the Kuwaiti Constitution, the Emir may decree laws only in urgent situations. However, the copyright law was then resubmitted to Parliament, with few changes, and passed, but so far, no new foreign investment law has been proposed. See Reema I. Ali & Loubna W. Haddad, *WTO*

protection in Kuwait, especially that part which involves the so-called mailbox procedure and market exclusivity.[311]

The WTO dispute settlement system has been in effect for nearly ten years. Over the span of that period, of total ninety-two WTO members who participated in dispute proceedings, no Arab country has ever initiated a case before a panel as a complainant.[312] Further, through the end of 2004, Egypt has been the only Arab country that had been a respondent in a case.[313] This state of affairs may indicate that Arab countries are not rule breakers. Another interpretation is that Arab countries choose to settle their disputes with other WTO countries through consultations. Reasons for this include high fees charged by international law firms for representation in the litigation or fear of spillover effects on financial aid.

Membership and Compliance in the Middle East countries, Vol. 22 Middle E. Exec. Rep. Newsltr.11 (Sep. 1999).

[311] The mailbox system applies to WTO members that do not make patent protection available for pharmaceutical and agricultural chemical products. Under this procedure, those countries must ensure that an applicant who has filed a patent application under the mailbox procedure has the legal right to claim the benefit of the actual filing date, regardless of when the application is examined. Additionally, Kuwait must extend marketing exclusivity to pharmaceutical and agricultural chemical products that are the subject of an application filed under the mailbox system.

[312] However, four Islamic countries-Indonesia, Malaysia, Pakistan, and Turkey- initiated a dispute in the WTO or were respondents in a dispute. See The International Bureau of the Permanent Court of Arbitration, *supra* n. 133, at 188, 205. See also Dispute Settlement Body, *Overview of State of Play of WTO Disputes*, WT/DSB/W/209/Add.1 (Nov. 18, 2002).

[313] See Panel Report, *Egypt-Definitive Anti-Dumping Measures on Steel Rebar from Turkey*, WT/DS211/R (Aug. 8, 2002). That case involved definitive anti-dumping measures imposed by Egypt on imports of concrete steel reinforcing bar (rebar) from Turkey. Egypt divided foreign exporters for purposes of antidumping investigation into cooperative and non-cooperative companies. The whole case evolved around the relationship between what an investigating authority is obligated by the antidumping agreement to do with regard to procedural issues in an anti-dumping investigation, and what interested parties must themselves contribute in the way of evidence and argument. The panel found Egypt acted consistently with its obligations under the agreement in some parts. However, the panel decided that Egypt acted in violation of the agreement because the investigating authority had "examined" all the relevant economic factors in article 3.4 of the agreement without "evaluation" of these factors. *Id.* para. 7.42-45. The panel also found that in respect of two Turkish companies (Icdas and IDC) out of five companies in the investigation, the Egyptian authority did not provide the two with ample opportunity to defend themselves and inform them that their submissions were being rejected, though they submitted, under article 6.8, all the necessary requested information. *Id.* para. 7.252-266. In that case, in which Egypt presented an excellent argument, its counsel was Van Beal and Bellis of Brussels, Belgium. See The European Commission, *Internet Chat with E.U Commissioner Pascal Lamy and Egyptian Trade Minister Youssef Boutros-Ghali, New WTO Round: Talking Trade-What's Going on?*, http://europa.eu.int/comm/chat/lamy9/index_en.htm (Nov. 21, 2002). The other potential case in which Egypt would have been a respondent was under the Sanitary and Phytosanitary Agreement. See Request for Consultation by Thailand, *Egypt-Import Prohibition on Canned Tuna with Soybean Oil*, WT/DS205/1 (Sept. 20, 2000). Although the WTO document does not elaborate, the case involved a decision by Egypt to prohibit imports of Thai canned tuna with soybean oil because it suspects that the oil is made from genetically modified beans. Thailand is known to be technologically capable of developing genetically modified organisms. Perhaps, Egypt wanted to protect its people, environment, and organic produce. In that case both parties, Egypt and Thailand, started consultations on the matter. However, it is unclear the results of those consultations. Perhaps, the parties did not proceed further in requesting establishment of WTO panel due to the sensitivity of the issue. The case if advanced would have been the first genetically modified organism case to be brought before the WTO.

Lack of participation in WTO dispute settlement proceedings may also be attributed to the minuscule level of the Arab countries' contribution to world trade, contrasted with $1 billion a day of trade between the U.S. and EC.[314] However, this is by no means a completely valid bar to litigation. Argentina, for example, which accounts for only 0.6 percent of world trade, is one of the most challenged nations before the WTO, after the U.S. and the EC. Argentina has also filed 9 complaints in the WTO. Additionally, India is an active participant in the WTO dispute settlement cases despite the fact that its share of world trade is under 0.8 percent.

Another reason that Arab countries are not frequent users of the WTO dispute settlement system is a lack of expertise and knowledge of complicated WTO law with some complaints crossing between several WTO agreements. Bringing a case before a WTO panel is an extensive process that requires preparing commercial data, which in some instances may not be provided by the other party meaning that it must be obtained from other sources, studies, econometric modeling, and substantial documentation. However, with lapse of time and the growing knowledge of the WTO law, one might expect more use of the WTO dispute settlement system. Moreover, litigating a WTO case, which may take years, is very costly. For example, Brazil, in its 2004 case against U.S. upland cotton subsidies, incurred an estimated $2 million in legal fees at the WTO panel level alone.[315] Unless some Arab countries share the legal and financial burdens of proceedings at the WTO it might be very difficult for a single Arab country to initiate a case alone. Therefore, spreading the cost among Arab countries would make the process more affordable for Arab countries to be involved.

In addition, power relations may play role in limiting Arab countries participation in trade disputes. For example, Egypt may have been in a Scylla and Charybdis position when it decided to settle its dispute with the EC out of court.[316] If Egypt supported the U.S. in the sensitive GMO case, it would have upset its relations with the EC. By the same token, if Egypt did not support the U.S., it would have lead to a souring in trade relations between the U.S. and Egypt. Ultimately, Egypt chose to settle the dispute with the EC without litigation. Perhaps, without this pressure, Egypt may have pressed ahead with the dispute against the EC.

---

[314] See Grary G. Yerkey, *U.S. Trade Policy Overlooks Middle East Region, Could Hurt War on Terrorism, PPI Study Says*, 20 Intl. Trade Rep. (BNA) 323 (Feb. 13, 2003) (the Muslim world has experienced a 75% drop in its share of world export since 1980. As of 2001, the entire Muslim world received only $13.6 billion in FDI, barely more than Sweden all by itself).

[315] On appeal, Brazil is likely to incur more costs. For more on the case see WTO Secretariat, *United States - Subsidies on Upland Cotton- Constitution of the Panel Established at the Request of Brazil*, WT/DS267/15 (May 23, 2003).

[316] See Grary G. Yerkey and Christopher S. Rugaber, U.S. and Egypt Beginning to See "Eye-to-Eye" on Need for FTA but No Talks Scheduled Yet, 20 Int'l. Trade Rep. 1145 (July 3, 2003) (quoting Boutros-Gali, Egypt's [former] foreign trade minister, saying that Egypt wants to begin the [US FTA] negotiations "tomorrow". However, the U.S. has been cold toward negotiating FTA with Egypt. Some hint that this so because Egypt withdrew its support of the U.S. in the Genetically Modified Organism case against the EC).

Arab traditions and history may juxtapose all other reasons for the limited participation by Arab countries in WTO dispute settlement cases. International litigation is not a preferred choice for Arab countries. Negotiations and compromises are the traditional path. It is a question of style. One hopes that in the future, the process may become more confrontational so that the Arab countries press their interests in trade disputes. Through litigation Arab countries would send a signal to other WTO members that negotiation is one option for resolving a trade dispute, but it is not the only option. Arab countries should employ litigation and negotiation at the same time because litigation plays an important role in informing negotiations.

As some have alluded, Arab countries can participate in WTO dispute settlement proceedings as a third party, as there is no explicit provision in the DSU requiring a member to have a legal interest to participate.[317] However, usually only countries that have substantial interests at stake participate in these proceedings. Indeed, only Egypt, among all Arab WTO members, has participated as a third party in a WTO case.[318] It remains to be seen how the Appellate Body decision to amend its working procedures regarding the rights of third parties to participate in its proceedings will help Arab countries.[319] Even if some Arab countries can participate as third parties to a dispute, their oral representation would be limited to 3-5 minutes, as that has traditionally been the practice. Also, Arab countries may have the chance to participate through *amicus curiae* briefs.[320] Filing *amicus curiae* briefs does not, however, guarantee that WTO dispute settlement panels will take them into account in deciding cases.

Arab countries can participate in WTO disputes through other venues. Article 17.3 of the DSU requires that the Appellate Body membership be broadly representative of the

---

[317] Peter Van Den Bossche, former counselor to the Appellate Body of the WTO, citing the EC-Bananas III case in which the Appellate Body decided that any member has a broad discretion to bring a case against another member if it considers that this is "fruitful". See The International Bureau of the Permanent Court of Arbitration, *supra* note 133, at 191. However, the Appellate Body qualified its statement by stating that not one or more of the factors would be dispositve in another case.

[318] Egypt participated as a third party in EC-Bed Linen case. See Panel Report, *European Communities-Anti-Dumping Duties on Imports of Cotton-Type Bed Linen from India*, WT/DS141/R (Oct. 30, 2000).

[319] See Appellate Body, *Annual Report for 2003*, WT/AB/1, at 34-37 (May 7, 2004). The new amendments gives a third party an automatic right to appear at the oral hearing even though no written submission has been forwarded if there is a notification to the Body's secretariat compared with the previous practice where a written submission must be filed first before appearing at the hearing. Although the new amendments are a positive step, they did not elaborate or clarify whether WTO members with no substantial interest at stake can participate in the Appellate Body hearing(s). Moreover, the decision to allow a third party to participate in case in which it neither files a written submission nor notifies the secretariat is left to the Appellate Body to decide on a case-by-case basis.

[320] See The International Bureau of the Permanent Court of Arbitration, *supra* n. 133, at 191. One must remember that the WTO is a government contract for governments and governments only. Morocco, as the first Arab country and indeed the first WTO member, submitted *amicus curiae* in the EC-Sardine case with Peru. The Appellate Body in that case allowed Morocco to submit its *amicus curiae* even though it did not participate as a third party at the panel level. See Appellate Body Report, *European Communities-Trade Description of Sardines*, WT/DS231/AB/R, at para. 166-167 (Sep. 26, 2002). It seemed that in the Sardine decision, the Appellate Body added more rights to and obligations on WTO members setting an example for NGOs, academia, industrial associations to file large number of these briefs swaying the attention and limited resources of the Body from resolving the dispute to answering these briefs.

WTO membership. For this reason, two Arab panelists have sat on the bench of the Appellate Body since 1995.[321] In addition, there are nine cases at the panel level for which three Arab panelists were selected.[322] However, Arab panelists are outnumbered

[321] These Arab panelists are: late Said El-Naggar of Egypt (served 1995-2000 in twelve cases: Japan-Taxes on Alcoholic Beverages, Oct. 4, 1996, WTO Doc. No. WT/DS8/AB/R, WT/DS10/AB/R, WT/DS11/AB/R, Appellate Body Report, *Brazil-Measures Affecting Desiccated Coconut*, WT/DS22/AB/R (Feb. 12, 1997), Appellate Body Report, *European Communities-Regime for the Importation, Sale, and Distribution of Banana*, WT/DS27/AB/R (Sep. 9, 1997), Appellate Body Report, *Argentina-Measures Affecting Imports of Footwear, Textiles, Apparel and other Items*, WT/DS56/AB/R (Mar. 27, 1998), Panel Report, *European Communities-Measures Affecting the Importation of Certain Poultry Products*, WT/DS69/R (Mar. 12, 1998), Appellate Body Report, *Australia-Measures Affecting Importation of Salmon*, WT/DS18/AB/R (Oct. 20, 1998), Appellate Body, *Guatemala-Anti-Dumping Investigation Regarding Portland Cement from Mexico*, WT/DS60/AB/R (Nov. 2, 1998), Appellate Body Report, *Brazil-Export Financing Program for Aircraft*, WT/DS46/AB/R (Aug. 2, 1999), Appellate Body Report, *India-Quantitative Restrictions on Imports of Agricultural, Textile and Industrial Products*, WT/DS90/AB/R (Aug. 23, 1999), Appellate Body Report, *Turkey-Restrictions on Imports of Textile and Clothing Products*, WT/DS34/AB/R (Oct. 22, 1999), Appellate Body Report, *Korea-Definitive Safeguard Measure on Imports of Certain Dairy Products*, WT/DS98/AB/R (Dec. 14, 1999), and Appellate Body Report, *United States-Imposition of Countervailing Duties on Certain Hot-Rolled Lead and Bismuth Carbon Steel Products Originating in the United Kingdom*, WT/DS138/AB/R (May 10, 2000)), and George Abi-Saab of Egypt (served 2000-present in fourteen cases: Appellate Body Report, *Korea-Measures Affecting Imports of Fresh, Chilled and Frozen Beef*, WT/DS161/AB/R (Dec. 11, 2000), Appellate Body Report, *United States-Definitive Safeguard Measures on Imports of Wheat Gluten from the European Countries*, WT/DS166/AB/R (Dec. 22, 2000), Panel Report, *European Communities-Anti-Dumping Duties on Imports of Cotton-Type Bed Linen from India*, WT/DS141/R (Oct. 30, 2000), Appellate Body Report, *United States-Transitional Safeguard Measure on Combed Cotton Yard from Pakistan*, WT/DS192/AB/R (Oct. 8, 2001), Appellate Body Report, *Mexico-Anti-Dumping Investigation of High Fructose Corn Syrup (IIFCS) from the United States*, WT/DS132/AB/RW (Oct. 22, 2001), Appellate Body Report, *Canada-Measures Affecting the Importation of Milk and the Exportation of Dairy Products*, WT/DS103/AB/RW (Dec. 3, 2001), WT/DS113/AB/RW, Appellate Body Report, *United States-Definitive Safeguard Measures on Imports of Circular Welded Carbon Quality Line Pipe from Korea*, WT/DS202/AB/R (Feb. 15, 2002), Appellate Body Report, *Chile-Price Band System and Safeguard Measures Relating to Certain Agricultural Products*, WT/DS207/AB/R (Sep. 23, 2002), Appellate Body Report, *European Communities-Trade Description of Sardines*, WT/DS231/AB/R (Sep. 26, 2002), Appellate Body Report, *United States-Safeguard Measures on Imports of Fresh, Chilled or Frozen Lamb Meat from New Zealand and Australia*, WT/DS177/AB/R (May 1, 2001), Appellate Body Report, *European Communities-Anti-Dumping Duties on Imports of Cotton-Type Bed Linen from India*, WT/DS141/AB/R (Mar. 1, 2001), Panel Report, *United States-Definitive Safeguard Measures on Imports of Certain Steel Products*, WT/DS248/R (July 11, 2003), Appellate Body Report, *United States Sunset Review of Anti-Dumping Duties on Corrosion-Resistant Carbon Steel Flat Products from Japan*, WT/DS244/AB/R (Dec.15, 2002), and Appellate Body Report, *European Communities-Conditions for the Granting of Tariffs Preferences to Developing Countries*, WT/DS246/AB/R (Apr. 7, 2004)). For more on biographies of Arab panelists see Press Release, WTO Announces Appointments to Appellate Body, PRESS/32 (Nov. 29, 1995). See also Press Release, WTO Completes Appointment of Appellate Body Members, PRESS/179 (May 22, 2000).
[322] These Arab panelists are: Maamoun Abdel-Fattah of Egypt, Magda Shahin of Egypt, and Nacer Benjelloun-Touimi of Morocco. As of Oct. 2004, Maamoun Abdel-Fattah participated in seven cases (Panel Report, *Brazil-Measures Affecting Desiccated Coconut*, WT/DS22/R (Oct. 17, 1996), Panel Report, *Canada- Measures Affecting the Export of Civilian Aircraft*, WT/DS70/RW (May 9, 2000), Panel Report, *Canada- Measures Affecting the Export of Civilian Aircraft*, WT/DS70/R (Apr. 14, 1999), Panel Report, *United States-Definitive Safeguard Measures on Imports of Wheat Gluten from the European Communities*, WT/DS166/R (July 31, 2000), Panel Report, *United States-Continued Dumping and Subsidy Offset Act of 2000*, WT/DS217/R (Sep. 16, 2002), Panel Report, *European Communities-Anti-Dumping Duties on Malleable Cast Iron Tube or Pipe Fittings from Brazil*, WT/DS219/R (Mar. 7, 2003), and Arbitrator Decision, *United States-Continued Dumping and Subsidy Offset Act of 200-Original Complaint by the*

by panelists from other developed countries such as New Zealand or Switzerland. This indicates a limited pool of Arab expertise.

There are some provisions in the DSU that give special treatment for developing and least-developed countries.[323] An important step has been taken to assist developing countries in WTO dispute settlement through the establishment of the Advisory Center on WTO Law.[324] Four Arab countries are members of the Advisory Center.[325] The Advisory Center resembles a law office that specializes in WTO law. Despite several limitations on the functions of the Advisory Center, Arab countries should consider becoming involved in the Center until they have their own in-house counsels and expertise in international trade law.[326]

XII. Representations in the WTO and Delegations of Arab Countries

Concerning Arab representation in the WTO Secretariat, out of the 550 employees, who are mainly French and Britons, few are from Arab countries. There are three

---

European Communities-Recourse to Arbitration by the United States under Article 22.6 of the DSU, WT/DS217/ARB/EEC (Aug. 31, 2004)) while Magda Shahin participated in one case (Appellate Body Report, *European Communities-Measures Affecting the Importation of Certain Poultry Products*, WT/DS69/AB/R (July 13, 1998)) Nacer Benjelloun-Touimi chairs the panel that will rule on U.S. complaint against EC customs practices (European Communities-Selected Customs Matters, Sept. 27, 2004, WTO Doc. No. WT/DS315/1).

[323] For example, according to article 27.2 of the DSU, the WTO Secretariat provides assistance to developing countries through legal advice of experts in dispute settlement. However, legal assistance of WTO Secretariat is qualified "in a manner ensuring the continued impartiality of the Secretariat". In other words, legal assistance of WTO Secretariat is not full but limited to the extent that the Secretariat's neutrality is not compromised.

[324] The Advisory Center on WTO Law has been established to alleviate article 27.2 of the DSU problem which provides legal advice and assistance through the WTO Secretariat. To fulfill its mandate, the Secretariat dedicated only two legal affairs officers and engaged two consultants who are available one day a week. The Advisory Center is independent from the WTO established as a foundation under Swiss law. The Advisory Center is open to all WTO members, but only developing countries and economies in transition can use its services. The Advisory Center sources of income are: user charges, revenues from an endowment fund, and traditional donor contributions. The Advisory Center organizes seminars on WTO jurisprudence, offers legal advice on WTO law, provides support in WTO proceedings, and permits internships for officials dealing with WTO legal issues. To function, the Advisory Center has an executive director and four experienced professionals who have interest in advancing the interests of developing countries. See Kim Van der Borght, *The Advisory Center on WTO Law: Advancing Fairness and Equality*, 2 J. Intl Econ. L. 723, 724-727 (1999).

[325] Egypt, Tunisia, Jordan, and Oman are members of the Advisory Center. Egypt and Tunisia are original members of the Advisory Center which signed the agreement establishing the Center while Jordan was the first country to accede to the agreement followed by Oman. Late Said El-Naggar of Egypt, former Appellate Body member, held a seat in the management board for two years term starting 2001. See < http://www.acwl.ch/ > (Last visited Mar. 4, 2003).

[326] One of the criticisms directed toward the Advisory Center is that there may be real duplication between its work and the work of the WTO Technical Cooperation Division. Another criticism is the limited number of professionals and estimated hours per case (700 hours for a simple case). Even more, the Advisory Center executive director will have the power to decide whether a case brought to the Center by a developing country has legal merit or not. See Van der Borght, *supra* n. 324, at 728.

Egyptians, one Moroccan, and four Tunisians.[327] However, the lack of representation at the WTO Secretariat should not be apprehended negatively. Even if one appreciates having a large number of Arab representatives at the WTO Secretariat, however one has to take into account the breakdown of posts that Arab employees fill. It may not be necessary to have Arab employees in the trade body if they fill in administrative or secretarial (lower) positions rather than managerial or technical (middle and top) positions.[328] There must be a balance.

Even if an Arab representative(s) is selected to chair a WTO committee, such representation might be just illusory. For example, in the annual rotation of WTO chairs for the year 2004, Naéla Gabr of Egypt, a member of Egypt delegation, was appointed as chair for the WTO Committee on Trade and Environment ("CTE").[329] One should say "wow" too soon. The WTO CTE is to a large extent ineffective because of the political sensitivity and complexity of the matters under its jurisdiction. The WTO CTE is limited in its negotiating mandate and membership, and since its creation in 1994 has not achieved concrete results.[330] So far, the creation of the CTE has resulted in issuing reports.[331] Thus, the CTE is academic in nature. Much more important chairs include the General Council, the negotiating group on agriculture, and the DSB.[332] Finally, albeit that Arab representation in the WTO Secretariat is important, it is of greater importance to have potent and effective Arab delegations who are able to conduct negotiations. The real work is done by the delegations.

A major hindrance facing Arab countries' full participation in the work of the WTO is insufficient human resources dedicated to WTO work. Arab countries representation is limited to a single or a handful of officials. Moreover, delegations of Arab countries in Geneva do not cover the work of the WTO exclusively, but they also participate in other-Geneva based organizations such as U.N and its specialized agencies including UNCTAD, WIPO, ITU, and ISO. Egypt, with its ten professional staff members, has the

---

[327] See Bhala, *supra* n. 194, at 511.
[328] Currently, Abdel-Hamid Mamdouh of Egypt holds a senior position as head of the WTO Secretariat's Service Division. The only other time there was a chance for an Arab candidate to fill in the would-be vacant WTO Director General post was in 1999. Among the candidates that were waiting in the wings to succeed the outgoing Director General of the WTO Renato Ruggiero, a former Italian foreign trade minister, Hassan Abouyoub, former trade and investment minister who led his country's accession to GATT, of Morocco was a candidate. Cutting a long story short, it was decided to end the show by splitting the Director General term into two terms between Mike Moore of New Zealand and then Supachai Panitchpakdi of Thailand.
[329] See Press Release, WTO Chairpersons for 2004, PRESS/371 (Feb. 11, 2004).
[330] The mandate of the CTE covers, among others, facilitating the transfer of environmental technology to developing countries, receiving input from non-governmental environmental organizations, and studying the relationship between environmental policy and the multilateral trading system.
[331] See WTO and UNEP Secretariats, Committee on Trade and Environment-Compliance and Dispute Settlement Provisions in the WTO and in Multilateral Environmental Agreements, WT/CTE/W/191 (June 6, 2001).
[332] The WTO developed a practice in which, during the annual rotation of WTO chairs, the chairman of the DSB heads the General Council in the next rotation. For example, in 2004 Amina Mohamed of Kenya chaired the DSB while Shotaro Oshima of Japan chaired the General Council. In 2005, Amina Mohamed should chair the General Council.

largest delegation among Arab countries.[333] The following list represents the number of professional staff in Geneva-based delegations for other Arab countries: Bahrain- two; Djibouti- one; Jordan- two; Kuwait- two; Morocco- five; Mauritania- four; Oman- two; Qatar- one; United Arab Emirates- two; and Tunisia- three.[334]

Financial resources may constraint the ability of some lower-middle income Arab countries to have full professional staff devoted to the WTO in Geneva, which is one of the world's most expensive cities. What is puzzling, however, is the fact that the United Arab Emirates, a high-income country, has only two professional staff. Mauritania, a low-income country, has four professional staff. This is more than the United Arab Emirates! An issue may arise in the future if poor Arab countries such as the Sudan and Somalia accede to the WTO, they may not have the capabilities to have full-fledged delegations in Geneva. In that scenario, "obligations with representation" would apply.[335]

Being small is only one part of the equation. The other interlinked part is having skilled and versatile delegation. Many of the trade negotiators in Arab delegations are "flying negotiators," attending daily meetings after meetings without the ability to develop, much less maintain mastery knowledge.[336] Arab countries must dedicate even a small portion of their annual budgets, despite their constraints, to train their lawyers if they want to take part in the WTO effectively and avoid being onlookers.

All in all, one can say that Egypt is the only active Arab country active at the WTO. It is a user of trade remedy measures, WTO dispute settlement, and has a large Geneva-based delegation. Egypt also is a member of the G20 countries, which was established to counter US-EC agriculture proposal before the Cancun Ministerial Conference.[337] Even more, Egypt is the only Arab country that is usually invited to WTO mini-ministerial

---

[333] Egypt is one of a handful of developing countries within the WTO that has an ambassador in Geneva appointed by the ministry of foreign affairs and a trade mission, located in different premises in Geneva, whose staff are appointed by the ministry of trade and headed by a minister plenipotentiary. The two ministers and missions have divergent views on trade that lead to internal as well as external conflicts. See Fatoumata Jawara & Aileen Kwa, *Behind the Scenes at the WTO: The Real World of International Trade Negotiations* 21, 171 (Zed Books 2003).

[334] A Geneva-based Arab trade diplomat provided information on Bahrain, Kuwait, Oman, and Djibouti. (Mar. 18, 2004) (on file with author).

[335] To avoid this scenario, Somalia and Sudan could pool their resources with one or several Arab WTO delegations to represent them in certain meetings.

[336] Staffing is very critical because of the need to participate in numerous meetings, often taking place at the same time. The WTO has sixty-seven bodies including thirty-four standing bodies open to all members, twenty-eight accession working parties, and five plurilateral bodies. In 2001, there were nearly 400 formal meetings of WTO bodies, 500 informal meetings (meetings with no records of discussions such as the green room meetings), 90 workshops and seminars sponsored by the WTO. Officials in South Korean delegation complain about the workload of the WTO despite the fact that they have thirty staff. See Jawara & Kwa, *supra* n. 333, at 22. One might add also numerous negotiating groups if WTO members launch a new round of trade negotiations.

[337] Although membership in G20 has been changing, other gang members include: Brazil, China, India, Argentina, Bolivia, Chile, Cuba, Indonesia, Mexico, Nigeria, Pakistan, Paraguay, Philippines, South Africa, Thailand, Uruguay, Venezuela, and Zimbabwe.

meetings.[338] This means that other Arab countries are marginalized. Views of Arab countries may be communicated to Egypt and might find their way to other WTO members at these mini-ministerial meetings. However, one must remember that WTO members are rational. Each country pursues its own interests, and Egypt is no exception.

XIII. Arab Public Opinion and the WTO

Although globalization has no specific definition, the most used meaning is economic globalization. Trends of Arab public opinion regarding globalization, and the WTO specifically are mixed. In public, Arab government officials speak the jargon of economic reform and free trade. In contrast, there are some reported incidents of an Arab anti-globalization movement and its visible presence, the WTO. In 2002, Arab activists from Tunisia, Morocco, Lebanon, and the Palestinian territories met in Beirut and established a permanent Arab network, called the Arab Forum, to resist globalization and implicitly the WTO.[339] The Arab Forum spelled out its objectives: to exchange and coordinate information among the organizations of Arab civil society; to represent a unified Arab position from an unofficial Arab perspective; and to lead protests.

Even though there might not be an effective way to determine the pattern of Arab public opinion regarding globalization and the WTO, there is an evidence leading to the conclusion that anti-WTO/anti-globalization sentiment exists among a large portion of the Arab population. For example, the majority of the population in Jordan has less confidence in globalization than the populations of India, Mali, Argentina, and Bolivia.[340]

Arab activists fight against corporate greed that is destroying jobs and wages. Arab activists consider trade as a threat to jobs. The WTO, as an institution, needs an overhaul to be able to address the interests of Arab countries. Otherwise, the WTO will poison Arab public opinion on globalization and free trade and this is likely to provoke backlash against more open economies.

XIV. Arab Countries Regional Trade Initiatives

Arab countries face the challenge of coordinating among various, often competing, bilateral and regional trade arrangements. These include for example the United States-

---

[338] WTO mini-ministerial meetings are new phenomenon at the WTO, usually held in the run-up to ministerial conferences, in which "key" WTO members are invited to review progress and resolve key issues. It is unclear who organize such meetings whether the WTO or the host country. Other forum with limited membership is the Five Interested Parties in agricultural negotiation that include the U.S., EC, Australia, Brazil, and India.

[339] See Mustafa Abdalla Abulgasem, Presentation, *The Arab-Mediterranean Countries between the Conditions of the Barcelona Process and the WTO: A Comparative Study* (Conference on Arab Countries and the World Trade Organization, Inst. Arab & Islamic Stud., U. Exeter, U.K, Sep. 23, 2002) (copy in file with author).

[340] See Alan M. Field, *Can Trade Bridge the Gap?* J. Com. 18 (July 21, 2003) (a study found that Jordanians ranked last among the forty-four countries surveyed when it came to assessing the effects of globalization on their country. Sixty-four percent of Jordanians said it was bad compared with only twenty-seven percent who said globalization was good).

Jordan Free Trade Agreement, the association agreements with the EC, free trade agreements with the European Free Trade Association (EFTA), and the Arab Free Trade Area.[341] There is "Arab free trade agreements congestion". Of all these competing arrangements, there may not be time to focus on the WTO.

Some of the trade agreements signed by Arab countries are U.S., EC, and EFTA-centric bilateral trade agreements. In other words, these trade agreements are U.S.-plus, EC-plus, and EFTA-plus trade agreements. For example, the U.S. sets certain criteria, standards and linkages to the global war on terror that must be fulfilled to initiate trade talks with Arab countries such as the potential U.S.-Egypt free trade agreement. The EC association agreements include prerequisite provisions concerning the proliferation of weapons of mass destruction. One example of these agreements is the EC-Syria Association Agreement of 2004. Moreover, the EC association agreements adopt selective agricultural import policies by setting limits as to the type and volume of imported farm products into the EC market. EFTA trade agreements, such as the EFTA-Lebanon Free Trade Agreement of 2004, include intellectual property provisions that restrict the rights of poor farmers and limit access to generic medicines. These provisions include patent extensions, 5-10 years of exclusive periods for brand name medicines, patenting biotech inventions that allow for patenting animals and plants, and joining the International Union for the Protection of New Varieties of Plants, which restrict the ability of farmers to trade seeds without permission.

The underlying purpose of bilateral or regional Arab arrangements is to achieve freer trade. However, Arab free trade initiatives can be characterized as "to talk and talk".[342] For example, the Arab Common Market, which supposed to eliminate tariffs, non-tariff barriers, and set a common external tariff regime, did not mature.[343]

The bottom line is that Arab free trade initiatives have imperfections that burden intra-regional trade. These imperfections include a lack of political will, exclusion of certain sectors (farm products) from free trade agreements, weak institutions, absence of serious consequences for violating these agreements, sloppy compliance-monitoring

---

[341] The Arab Free Trade Area of 1998 is the latest attempt among Arab countries for economic integration. The early attempts were the League of Arab States of 1945, Arab Common Market 1964, Trade Facilitation and Development Program 1981, Gulf Cooperation Council 1981, Arab Maghreb Union 1989. The Arab Free Trade Area provides for gradual elimination of internal trade barriers within ten years. For a discussion of Arab economic integration especially the Arab Free Trade Area of 1998 see *Catching up with Competition: Trade Opportunities and Challenges for Arab Countries* 286-288 (Bernard Hoekman & Jamal Zarrouk eds., U. Mich. Press 2000). The Arab Free Trade Area is not amenable to effective follow-up or monitoring and there is lack of information on its practical implementation. It is not even known whether Arab countries have ever made a notification of the agreement to the WTO pursuant to article XXIV.7.a of GATT 1994 or if they obtained a waiver under article XXIV.10 of GATT 1994 since the agreement includes non-WTO members. There is no official journal to follow up and cover the process of integration.

[342] Based on poor record, one is opted not to discuss and analyze extensively pathetic Arab trade agreements that are just inked on paper.

[343] See GATT Working Party Report, Apr. 6, 1966, B.I.S.D. (14th Supp.) at 20 (1966).

schemes, and external forces that do not support such agreements.[344] Earlier attempts at Arab regional integration were largely politically based on the premise of Arab unity.

---

[344] Regarding external forces, one should not forget "divide and rule" tactics and "fight the enemy with the enemy" technique employed by other countries. "Fight the enemy with the enemy" technique applies also in other areas such as the 1980s Iraq-Iran war. The well cited example of successful integrationist policy is the EC. However, one must not forget how the U.S., through billions of dollars in loans and grants, helped that enterprise. The reason for U.S. help was to help the EC contain the spread of communism in Europe. See Mario Esteban Carranza, *South American Free Trade Area or free Trade Area of the Americas? Open Regionalism and the Future of Regional Economic Integration in South America* 15 (Ashgate 2000) (the United States promoted Western European integration as an effective strategy to counter the Soviet threat. The central reality was that West European integration was rooted in a wider security framework). A trade conflict between the two superpowers across the Atlantic, the U.S. and EC, is just an intra-family affair.

Conclusion

The effectiveness of the multilateral trading system may be examined by considering what would have happened in the absence of such a system. Let us assume that the WTO disappears overnight. Arab countries would probably not be better off. The Arabic citizen opinion which criticizes or doubts the WTO, even if he is right to a certain extent, may be able to identify what is wrong. However, that Arabic citizen opinion may be unable to provide a workable alternative. The only other alternative is to perpetuate the mass of hegemony-centered bilateral trade agreements between the U.S. or EC and Arab countries where Arab countries are at disadvantage.

Institutions are never perfect. How the WTO, as an institution, runs its business may not be perfect either. Certainly, the WTO needs a tune-up so as to project a new image towards Arab countries. The WTO should permit accession of Arab countries into the organization at an accelerated rate. In addition, the WTO Secretariat should hire more staff from Arab countries. If the WTO were to hold a future Ministerial Conference in an Arab country, it should do so in a genuine and appropriate manner. To illustrate, the fourth Ministerial Conference was held in Qatar because of fears that anti-globalization protestors would disrupt the proceedings of the Conference, as it happened with the Seattle Ministerial Conference, not because the WTO wanted to integrate Arab countries further into the multilateral trading system, a claim advanced by WTO members. Although for practical reasons the WTO uses "mini-ministerial" meetings, where dozens of members are invited, the WTO should minimize their use, since they exclude Arab countries. The WTO should include Arabic, a language spoken by 280 million people, as a working language along with the other three working languages (English, Spanish, and French) in the trade body.

The path to joining the WTO is a two-way street. Adhering to the rules of the WTO may enhance global confidence in the Arab countries and will likely result in increased flow of investments. Consumers in Arab countries would enjoy access to a wide variety of products that would otherwise be unavailable. Thus, trade can have an overall positive effect. However, the dilemma is how to minimize any losses and capture any benefits that the multilateral trading system has to offer. Economic reform and trade liberalization must also take into account the potential for social upheaval if hundreds of thousands of SOE employees are tossed out of work quickly without adequate guaranteed pensions. There will be losers among Arab import-competing industries, but hopefully winners among exportable industries should compensate for any losses. For example, exportable industries and governments can aid those who could face dislocations because of increased competition by insuring better access to capital. Additionally, government of Arab countries should establish health insurance coverage and training programs to develop the skills of those dislocated.

Legally, all Arab countries should be able to accede to the WTO. According to article XII of the WTO Charter, any state that has full autonomy in the conduct of its external commercial relations may accede to the WTO. This article begins the accession process. However, pragmatically, there are prerequisites for accession, such as protection for human rights, religious freedom, and democracy, and not having any trade boycotts. Since Arab countries have their own cultures and do not share all Western values, they are essentially banned from joining the WTO. It seems that WTO accession is a power-based process, rather than a rule-based process, as some legal scholars and WTO members claim. The U.S. backing-up of Arab countries to accede to the WTO is based on American foreign policy rather than commercial considerations. Syria, for example, is an important trade player in the region but it is still outside the WTO club. Until other Arab countries join the trade body, the universality theme of the WTO is simply a utopian dream.

As Max Weber stated, "Technical knowledge is of extraordinary power." The agreements covered by the WTO and its judicial decisions are voluminous. The results of the Uruguay Round, for example, cover some sixty agreements, which amount to over 30,000 pages. It is understood that every word, sentence, and decision in the context of WTO documents could, by itself, become the subject of an article or a book, without exaggeration. It is important to develop a deep understanding of the WTO texts and their effects on Arab countries and Arab industries to determine what are the benefits and challenges of membership. It is not enough to skim through WTO agreements in two hours in conferences and public seminars. There must be in-depth study and analysis of these over time by Arab experts. Moreover, Arab countries have to balance, as in the case of Egypt, between building their own expertise in WTO law, which is a long-term objective, and their current dependence, for an immediate need, on legal services provided by foreign law firms, which is a more immediate need.

An Arab institution, a kind of Inter-Arab Academy for International Trade Law, may be needed to fill in the gap left by the WTO technical assistance. The Academy would have a budget funded by contributions and donations from Arab countries proportionate to their economies. The purpose of the Academy would be to send Arab candidates to be trained in different areas of international trade and in different international institutions. These candidates could include officials, academia, or representatives from the private sector nominated by their countries based on qualifications not on political affiliations.

An important issue is how to use the WTO rules similarly to other developed countries. That is not to say that Arab countries should adopt protectionist policies. It is rather how to find their way through the current rules of the WTO agreements. Arab countries could use antidumping measures to protect their domestic industries from imports and the WTO dispute settlement mechanism to guard their rights. Arab countries could form a peer group for an extension of special and differential treatment.[345] Arab

---

[345] One may not reasonably understand what is economically common between Jordan, Tunisia and Canada, among other countries, alliance, and Jordan and India alliance in negotiating positions. Canada is a leading country in the Cairns Group which advocates greater agriculture liberalization. On the other hand, Jordan is a net food-importing country, which means that further liberalization in world agriculture will lead to increase in the price of imported food bills. Another alternative interpretation of such an alliance is to achieve a common negotiating position is by logrolling. Perhaps, Jordan and Tunisia agree to support a long list of negotiating objectives, only one or two of which they have an interest in, to get Canada to support their own concerns. However, there seems little incentive to form an Arab alliance. See Christian Bjornskov & Kim Martin Lind, *Where Do Developing Countries Go After Doha? An Analysis of WTO*

countries could use the political mechanisms of the WTO, which include decisions taken by consensus, to block trade matters that may run counter to their development interests of Arab countries.

Arab countries must ensure effective representations in the different meetings of WTO councils and committees. At these meetings, no light decisions would be taken on world trade. How Arab countries would guard their rights would depend on how much their interests are represented at these meetings. Since some Arab countries may not be able to afford the expenses of having "effective" missions in Geneva that are solely dedicated to the work of the WTO, Arab countries should form an Arab alliance so that each Arab country is represented by Arab trade experts. The representation in this alliance shall not be limited to privileged personnel or certain elite individuals. Nothing in the WTO agreements prevents forming an Arab alliance. This alliance should afford the help requested by its constituent members. The presidency of such an alliance would rotate, every year for example, so that each country is responsible to avoid any political sensitivities and to promote the voice of each Arab country. Additionally, Arab trade ministers could become more active early in the process of trade negotiations to provide the necessary feedback and not just leave trade matters solely to Arab trade officials in Geneva.

Intra-trade depends on three factors: economic size (per capita GDP and population), economic distance (transportation costs), and production structure. Arab countries would likely qualify in terms of economic size and economic distance. However, the problem may be in production structure. Restructuring small and medium-sized Arab industries is necessary to increase the competitive conditions of these industries through specialization and division of labor. This could be achieved through consolidation in sectors such as banking and pharmaceutical, automation, downsizing, and the streamlining of production operations. If restructuring small and medium-sized Arab industries does not occur, then bankruptcy looms for inefficient producers.

The unfinished common Arab economic project that began in the 1940s should be revisited seriously, especially in light of the worldwide proliferation of regional trade agreements. The illusive dream of an Arab regional trade agreement has not yet occurred, despite the fact that free trade once profoundly reigned in the region and many Arab countries are bound together by ties of common culture, ethnicity, and language. A critical examination of current bilateral and regional Arab trade agreements must be pursued to identify different possibilities of effective economic integration. Achieving this kind of critical examination of Arab trade agreements leads to a more realistic and practical approach for economic integration and overcoming political barriers to such initiatives.

To improve the competitive position of the region, Arab countries will have to be creative in generating alternative ideas and new solutions. The model of future regional

---

Positions and Potential Alliances, 36 J.W.T. 3, 556 (2002) (many countries in cluster 3, which includes Jordan, do not have official positions on most issues. There was insufficient information on 24 WTO members including Bahrain, Kuwait, Oman, Qatar, and United Arab Emirates.).

Arab free trade agreements must be one that is grounded in economics, not politics. The model should cover agriculture, transportation, financial services, business facilitation, and specific-sector initiatives. The model should move beyond classic tariff reductions to cover unnecessary impediments that currently compromise trade flows between Arab countries. For example, Arab countries must engage in regulatory harmonization for different testing requirements, controls, and inspections. Arab countries should increase labor mobility by lifting visa requirements for certain nationals of these countries. Moreover, Arab countries should enter into mutual recognition pacts where regulatory agencies would agree to accept certification processes carried out in other Arab countries to eliminate the burden of seeking approval in each country.

CHAPTER III

JORDAN BID FOR ACCESSION TO THE WTO

Chapter II argued that the WTO is not a perfect institution. In Arab countries accession to the WTO, politics matters more than trade. To remedy the imperfections, the WTO should involve Arab countries in the work of the organization by accepting membership of Arab countries into the WTO at accelerated rate, hiring more staff from Arab countries at the WTO Secretariat, and using Arabic as a working language along with the other three working languages (English, Spanish, and French) in the trade body.

Chapter III discusses the characteristics of the Jordanian economy and the status of international trade agreements in the legal system of Jordan. In addition, Chapter III analyzes, in detail, the main commitments Jordan undertook in its admission to the WTO. Chapter III contends that the terms and conditions for Jordan's accession were extensive. Jordan enjoyed a special and differential treatment in few areas such as tariff reductions.

I. General Background

The Hashemite Kingdom of Jordan one of the Arab countries sandwiched in a rowdy neighborhood, bordered by Syria on the north, Saudi Arabia on the South, Iraq on the east, and Israel and West Bank on the west. [346] Due to its geographic location as an entrepot between the east and the west, many civilizations, on one time or another resided in Jordan. These civilizations range from the Sumerian, Persian, Nabateans, Greek, to the Roman civilization, just to name a few. [347]

The early inhabitants of Jordan depended on hunting for subsistence. However, with the climatic change and the settlement in communities, the relative peace brought by the Egyptians Pharaohs encouraged international trade, especially with the Mediterranean region. Since the seventh century, Jordan has been ruled by various Arab and Islamic dynasties such as *Umayyad* of Damascus, *Abbasids* of Baghdad, *Fatimids, Ayyubid, Mamluk* of Cairo, the last being the Ottoman Empire (1516-1918). [348] During the rulings of Arab and Islamic dynasties, castles were constructed or rebuilt, and caravan houses were built to host pilgrims and strengthen lines of communication and trade.

Excessive taxation, persecution, and abandoning the pan-Islamic policies by the Ottomans, led to feeling of distrust by the Arabs. During World War I, the Ottoman Empire sided with the Central Powers (Germany, Austria-Hungary, and Bulgaria) against the Allies (Serbia, British Empire, and the U.S.). *Sharif* Hussein Bin Ali, *Emir* of Mecca and King of the Arabs, launched the Great Arab Revolt as he saw it an opportunity to liberate Arab lands from Turkish oppression and trusting the honor of British officials who promised their support for a unified kingdom for the Arab lands. However, the

---

[346] The Hashemite Kingdom of Jordan is the official name of Jordan.
[347] Peter Gubser, Historical Dictionary of the Hashemite Kingdom of Jordan 5-7 (Scarecrow Press 1991).
[348] *Id.*

Allies failed to honor their promise after the victory in World War I. Instead, what was called Trans-Jordan in 1920 was placed under the British mandate by the League of the Nations.[349] The British mandate expired in 1946 through a series of Anglo-Trans-Jordan treaties, and since that time Trans-Jordan, now called the Hashemite Kingdom of Jordan, has been governed as a constitutional monarchy.[350]

According to the 2001 census, Jordan's population is estimated at 5.1 million.[351] The kingdom's area covers about 89.3 thousand sq. km (35 thousand sq. mile). Only 6 percent of Jordan's land is suitable for agricultural use. Jordan is divided into 12 administrative zones.[352] Jordan has, to a variable degree, mineral resources the most common of which are phosphate and potash. The labor force in Jordan amounts to 1.2 million, of which 400 thousand are non-Jordanian workers, where the majority of them are from Egypt. The percentage of illiteracy in Jordan is 10 percent of the population. The contribution of the service sector to the economy amounts to 71.4 percent, followed by manufacturing 21 percent, agriculture 3.8 percent, and mining 2.9 percent.[353] Per capita GDP hovers at US$ 1,703.[354] These figures reflect low level of economic development and dependence on limited number of exports such as phosphate and potash.

II. Characteristics of the Jordanian Economy

Jordan is a small country in terms of geographical area and population.[355] These two factors make Jordanian economy a limited market with limited production capability. Despite these limitations, Jordan has maintained relatively open economy which is greatly affected by external factors such as regional conflicts that are beyond its control. Jordan's economy is characterized by limited resources, reliance on the service sector,

---

[349] Id. 39-40. See *Terms of the British Mandate for Palestine Confirmed by the Council of the League of Nations*, 3 LEAGUE OF NATIONS O.J. 1007, art. 2 (1922). According to the Mandate for Palestine, the British created unilaterally a separate state to the area east of Jordan River as "Trans-Jordan". Trans-Jordan would be administered under the control of *Emir* Abdullah.

[350] See Gubser, *supra* n. 347, at 18.

[351] See Jordan Department of Statistics, *Size of Population*, Jordan in Figures, 1 (No. 4, 2002). Jordan's population tripled over the years, from the addition of almost 800,000 Palestinians in post Arab-Israeli wars (1948 and 1967) to the addition of about 300,000 Palestinians in post Gulf war (1990).

[352] *Id.* 5. These administrative zones are the capital Amman, Zarqa, Balqa, Irbid, Karak, Ma'an, Aqaba, Mafraq, Tafileh, Jerash, Madaba, and Ajloun. Aqaba is Jordan's outlet on the Red Sea. Jordan's climate is characterized by being the climate of the Mediterranean region, warm and dry in the summer, moderate and rainy in the winter.

[353] See Table 4 in appendix 1, page 219.

[354] Per capita income in Jordan is a fraction of the $30,620 per capita GDP of the hydrocarbon-rich Qatar in 2000. For more on the Gulf state of Qatar see *Business in Qatar*, Economist 64, 70 (Mar. 26, 2004). See also *Saudi Arabia on the Dole*, Economist 47 (Apr. 22, 2000) (with growing population, Saudi Arabia's income per person tumbled from $16,650 in dear-oil 1981 to $6,526 in cheap-oil 1998). Jordan per capita GDP is closer to that of many Arab countries. For example, Algeria's per capita GDP was almost $1,600 in 1999 while Egypt's was almost $1,400. Morocco scored last with per capita GDP $1,200 in 1999. See *Morocco: Down in the Dumps*, Economist 48 (Mar. 4, 2000).

[355] However, within Jordan, differentiation exists where some urban regions such as Greater Amman are highly developed, while others are economically less developed. For example, in 1988, a survey of world's expensive cities compiled by Business International Corp., ranked Amman along Geneva, Tehran, and Washington as expensive cities.

continuous budget deficit, dependence on foreign aid, and excessive foreign debt. What follows is a general discussion of these salient features of the economy and development patterns in Jordan starting in 1980s that would help shed the light on the challenges and implications associated with its WTO accession.

With the exception of a number of mineral resources, such as phosphate and potash, the prevalent feature in Jordan is limited resources, if not absolute absence of mineral resources.[356] These ecological factors contribute partly to Jordan's lagging behind other countries in the region. In 1970s and 1980s, Jordan invested heavily in human resources. Remittances from Jordanians expatriates, especially in the Gulf States, have been one of the government's largest sources of foreign exchange.[357] Although Jordan is a major exporter and importer of labor, participation in labor force is limited. Small rigid labor market,[358] high population growth rate,[359] high percentage of youth, growing number of working-age adults entering the labor force at a late stage due to high tendency for higher education,[360] and low percentage of female participation in the labor force, are among the limitations in the Jordanian labor market.[361]

Jordan's economy is a service economy despite growth in the manufacturing sector. For example, the service sector grew at unprecedented rate from 67.5 percent in 1995 to 71.4 percent in 2000.[362] The growth rate of agriculture is in decline while overall modest output is recorded in some industrial sectors such as construction and mining. Unfortunately, rapid expansion in the service sector has not generated adequate employment opportunities to absorb the growing labor force. The civil service continues to play a major role in the economy compared with limited private sector base, although this trend has been changing in recent years. One should not also overlook the

---

[356] Jordan suffers from shortages in water resources whether in terms of annual precipitation fallings or surface water. Jordan is below the Water Stress Level of 500 cubic meters per person per year. See Hillel I. Shuval, *Approaches to Resolving the Water Conflicts between Israel and her Neighbors: A Regional Water-for-Peace Plan*, 17 Water Intl. 133 (1992). One of the points of contention in the peace process between Israel and Jordan was the issue of water. Like many other countries, Jordan depends on ground water.

[357] See United Nations Economic and Social Commission for Western Asia, *infra* note 361, at 55. However, expatriate remittances, among other social illusions, created a social spillover represented in large consumption-based phenomenon (a good recipe for laws and economics of behavior). Logically, if individual's income is $600, he cannot consume $1000 worth of goods or services unless he borrows money or receives grease payments. After all, what an individual consumes is what he produces.

[358] Some of the rigidities of the labor market include fixed wages and full-time positions.

[359] In 1999, population growth rate amounted to 3.9 percent while economic growth rate was 2 percent. Thus, population growth posed challenge in terms of growing pressure on limited resources. During the planning years, Jordan introduced family-planning programs to alleviate soaring population growth.

[360] See Yitzhak Reiter, *Higher Education and Sociopolitical Transformation in Jordan*, 29 British J. Middle East Stud. 137, 141 (2002) (Jordan's higher education system has undergone an enormous expansion. The number of students, some admitted through affirmative action policy, has increased 23 fold in 30 years). It is hardly anymore to see higher education as limitation on the labor market especially in the light of the new economy where knowledge is an asset with higher potential of return. To address unemployment, there must be improvement in education and training. Jordan also must address the rigidities of the labor market.

[361] *The Role of the State in the Globalized Economy, with Egypt and Jordan as Case Studies*, U.N. Economic and Social Commission for Western Asia, at 54, U.N. Doc. E/ESCWA/ED/2000/2/ Add.1 (2000).

[362] See Table 4 in appendix 1, page 219.

contribution to Jordan's GDP of the informal economy, known also as gray economy, parallel economy, underground economy, or shadow economy, such as petty traders, industrialists, self-employed, and street vendors. There are no statistics that capture the contribution of the informal economy to total GDP.

Jordan faces chronic budget deficit. In the fiscal year 2001, for instance, budget deficit reached JD233 million or 6.9 percent of GDP.[363] Jordan also faces trade deficit.[364] In addition, Jordan experiences heavy debt burden. For example, at the end of 2002, foreign debt stood at $8.5 billion compared with $7.1 billion in 1995 with debt-service ratio of 14.4 percent.[365] Jordan receives foreign aid that includes grants, foreign (concessional) aid, and loans.[366] Foreign aid helps reduce budget deficit.

III. Economic Reform

Jordan faced an economic crisis in late 1980s due to reduction in foreign aid, increase in foreign debt, inability to pay debts and debts services, and decline in foreign exchange reserves.[367] In addition, higher population growth coupled with slow economic growth led to decline in standards of living and rise in unemployment.

---

[363] See Table 5 in appendix 1, page 219.

[364] See Table 6 in appendix 1, page 220.

[365] To reduce the problem of foreign debt and avoid default on maturity date, the Jordanian government resorted to several measures such as debt buyback to restructure debts. The reason for repurchasing debts is the fact that by buying the debt at a discount than the original amount of debt, foreign creditors might be able to recover part of their money, otherwise would have not been able due to Jordan's inability to pay the whole outstanding debt. Generally, since the end of the Cold War, there has been decline in foreign aid through loans. The decline in foreign aid is the result of a belief that further new loans would be used to pay old loans and their services. Therefore, new loans will not contribute to the industrialization of a country and is a waste for the lender. For on new strategies of delivering foreign aid see Amy McFarlane, *In the Business of Development: Development Policy in the First Two Years of the Bush Administration*, 21 Berkeley J. Intl. L. 521, 536 (2003) (discussing the U.S. overture on Mar. 14, 2002 for a government-sponsored trust called the Millennium Challenge Account (MCA) that conditions the receipt of foreign aid funds upon the recipient's ability to produce measurable results such as adopting good governance, investing in health care and education, and maintaining free markets. The new strategy is built upon outcomes-based approach which may not necessarily lead to efficient allocation of funds. The MCA proposal affirms the long history of the U.S. avoidance of a multilateral forum regarding foreign aid. USAID changed its philosophy toward free-market approaches to development aid. The agency acts as venture capitalist. Even interestingly, Andrew Natsios, Bush's appointee to head USAID, proposed to drop the term "sustainable development" from the department's official lexicon). In addition, as part of its debt reduction efforts, Jordan resorted to debt forgiveness (write-off), rescheduling debts at concessional interest rates with longer time to pay, or debt-swap agreements. See Debt-Swap Agreement Signed with France, 36 Econ. Rev. of the Arab World 7 (May 2002) (under Jordan's debt-swap agreement with France a portion of Jordan's $64 million total debt was converted into investments). The types of investments that would result from debt-swap conversion depend on the priorities of Jordan and the desire of investors. Debt relief schemes may induce investment thus increase the rate of debt repayment. For the first time in its history, perhaps due to its debt repayment rate among other factors, Jordan in 1990s was given international credit ratings by international rating agencies Moody's and Standards & Poor's assigning Ba3 and B+ respectively. These ratings are indicative of Jordan's trustworthiness in the international market.

[366] See Table 7 in appendix 1, page 220.

[367] The dependence on foreign aid and expatriate remittances during the 1970s and 1980's resulted in a failure to develop productive basis for private industries. In addition, Jordan's trade regime was based on strategy of import substitution or export pessimism which could be characterized by government's reliance

As part of the structural adjustment program, the IMF and World Bank pushed Jordan to reorient its economy with an emphasis on export-led growth and privatization.[368] Due to Jordan's political position during the Gulf crisis in 1990, Jordan's economy was hit with a severe blow. Overnight, exports markets to Iraq and the Gulf states were shut. Moreover, the returning of almost 300.000 workers and their families to Jordan raised unemployment level to 25 percent.[369] Thus, the would-be economic reform program was interrupted. After the early 1990 crisis, Jordan adopted several economic reform programs.[370] As a clear signal to the international economic market of its commitments to outward market policy Jordan decided to accede to the WTO.

---

on tariffs and other import fees for a high percentage of the state's revenue and to protect infant industries. See Timothy J. Piro, *The Political Economy of Market Reform in Jordan* 11, 40, 63 (Rowman & Littlefield Publishers 1998). State planning in Jordan took the form of comprehensive "five-year or three-year plans".
[368] Structural adjustment program involved, *in toto*, slashing subsidies on basic foodstuff and agricultural resources, reducing public investment and expenditure, reducing budgetary allocation for social spending and development, controlling inflation, and freezing public hiring. Additionally, the structural adjustment program involved price rationalization, deregulation, and de-bureaucratization. Structural adjustment programs were financed by loans and donations. For example, the IMF extended $295 million worth of special drawing rights in 1996 under the extended fund facility to support Jordan's economic reform. See *IMF Extends Credits to Jordan*, 13 Intl. Trade Rep. (BNA) 305 (Feb. 21, 1996). International cooperation is needed in the area of structural adjustment due to social, economic, and political implications. Jordan, therefore, cannot afford to pay the price alone. Cutting subsidies, which included increase in prices of certain basic commodities such as bread and launching consumption-based taxes such as sales tax, led to social unrest exemplified in riots in southern Jordan initially started in Ma'an in Apr. 1989. The middle class of Jordan spent, and still spend, a large portion of their income on food. Central to their food consumption was bread. Therefore, the price of bread was key to the cost of living. The introduction of consumption-based taxes such as sales tax would cause higher prices for consumer goods and services since sellers would pass the tax burden to consumers. Rather than military crushing of the social unrest, it had been wisely decided to hold national election for a new parliament in 1989.
[369] United Nations Economic and Social Commission for Western Asia, *supra* n. 361, at 56-58.
[370] For example, the 1992-1998 and 1999-2001 economic reform programs differ from earlier periods of three to five years development plans which were based on government intervention. Generally, the purpose of these economic reform programs is to stabilize the economy from external shocks, broaden the role of private sector, and liberalize trade. Other goals include increasing investment, stabilization of exchange rate, decreasing reliance on external and internal loans, and proceeding with privatization programs. Since 1996, Jordan has been implementing privatization program in order to give the necessary momentum to the private sector. Jordan has completed some 60 privatization transactions netting proceeds of $1,214 million. Some of the sectors that were privatized are: the Jordan Electricity Authority (1996), Amman Water and Wastewater treatment management (1998), Jordan Cement Factories Company (1998), Aqaba Railways Corporation (1999), Jordan Telecommunications Company (1999), Airports Duty-Free Shops Company (2000), Jordan Flight Catering Company (2001), and Jordan Airline Training and Simulation. See The Economist Intelligence Unit, Country Profile: Jordan 23-25 (2002). Additionally, the postal service, Jordan Phosphate Mines Company, Arab Potash Company, and the national carrier (Royal Jordanian) are in the process of being privatized. It is unclear how sectors are selected for privatization purposes. Factors in the selection process may include the size of the enterprise (small, medium, and large), salability, potential market, and profitability. Privatization is one of the few means by which the Jordanian government can generate revenue without incurring more international debt. The government can reallocate the privatization revenue into the state budget to fulfill its needs. Market forces, infrastructure upgrades, and professional management could improve the efficiency of some sectors in Jordan. However, social pressure of civil servants, no clear rule about the responsibilities of private investors to civil servants, long history of subsidized services, and the issue of foreign control may slow the process of privatization. To combat poverty and unemployment, the government may want to create a social protection program to extend help to the poor and the disadvantaged in Jordan through cash fund, institutional infrastructures such as schools and medical centers, and job training. For more on strategies for privatization see Ronald A.

Before discussing Jordan's accession to the WTO, it is worthy to analyze the legal institutions in Jordan and their relevance to international trade. The analysis will be accomplished in comparison with the U.S. legal system.[371] This, it is important, while the main focus of this part is Jordan's accession to the WTO, to explore the legal system of Jordan.

IV. International Trade Regulation in Jordan

Under the Jordanian constitution, the executive power is vested in the king who exercises his authority, as a head of the cabinet and the executive power, through the ministers.[372] Legislative power rests with the king and the National Assembly which consists of the Senate and Chamber of Deputies, Jordan's equivalent of the U.S. House of Representatives.[373] Various committees, with different membership, exist in the National Assembly to examine different issues.[374] The most important committees are the Finance

---

Cass, *The Optimal Pace of Privatization*, 13 B.U. Int'l L. J. 413 (1995) (discussing the concept of privatization in terms of economic efficiency by assessing the benefits as well as the costs that, other things equal, maximize the benefits of privatization at the lowest cost. Privatization is defined differently depending on the country in question. Different strategies for privatization can be employed by selling a state-owned enterprise in its entirety, either by a negotiation with a single buyer or by a public offering of equity shares through an established market for share purchases and sales. Free and discounted stock offerings to employees of companies targeted for privatization, which both reduce resistance to privatization and increase incentives for post-privatization efficiency, have become a common feature of privatization in many countries). Linking privatization with the capital market, where investment funds act as financial intermediaries by offering a state enterprise as shares, would energize the capital market and at the same time create popularism for privatization. Other means of privatization include restructuring state-owned enterprise into joint stock or limited liability companies that remain in the state hands but managed separately from the state budget with the state appointing board of directors who are primary shareholders in the company.

[371] The WTO Appellate Body functions like an American court where U.S. lawyers feel more comfortable and familiar in adjudicating cases. See Raj Bhala, *The Myth about Stare Decisis and International Trade Law*, 14 Am. U. Int'l L. Rev. 845, 848 (1999). The Americanization of the WTO Appellate Body is not limited to *stare decisis*. The Americanization also covers *amicus curiae* and open panel proceedings.

[372] DUSTOUR Al-URDUN [Constitution] art. 26 (Jordan).

[373] *Id.* art. 25. Jordan is divided into a number of constituencies and each constituency is allocated seats specified in a schedule attached to the election law (currently there are 110 deputies). Electoral Districts Regulation No. 42 of 2001, art. 2, al Jaridah al Rasmiyah No. 4498 (Official Gazette) (July 23, 2001). The Senate, whose members are appointed by the king, consists of not more than one-half the number of the Chamber of Deputies members including the speaker of the Senate (55 senators). DUSTOUR Al-URDUN [Constitution] arts. 63 & 67 (Jordan). The U.S. Congress is divided into two houses: the House of Representatives and the Senate. The number of representatives in the House of Representatives varies according to population. Some 435 members of the House stand for election every two years, most of them in individual districts to which states are divided on the basis of population, but for some of them by statewide vote. The Senate consists of 100 Senators on the basis of two senators from each state. U.S. Const. art I, § 2. In addition, 3 delegates represent the District of Columbia in Congress. Thus, bringing the total number of members of Congress to 538.

[374] The Chamber of Deputies has fourteen permanent committees with eleven members in each committee. Among these committees are the legal committee, administrative committee, and international and Arab Affairs committee. Membership in these committees is for two years term. In addition, the National Assembly may prescribe other permanent or temporary committees as it deems necessary. Internal Regulation of the Chamber of Deputies of 1996, art. 35 & 50, al Jaridah al Rasmiyah No. 4106 (Official Gazette) (Mar. 16, 1996).

and Economy Committee in the Senate and the Finance and Economy Committee in the Chamber of Deputies.[375] Their principal role is to deal with the economy with matters such as budget, foreign debt, and fiscal laws. Their jurisdictions also include unemployment, national housing, and social security. It is unclear from the internal regulations of both houses whose committee is responsible for international trade.[376] The Cabinet in Jordan consists of the Council of Ministers headed by the Prime Minister, who must be appointed by the king. Ministers are appointed by the king with the advice of the Prime Minister.[377]

The executive power in Jordan has the right to enter into negotiations of international agreements without the prior approval of the National Assembly.[378] In Jordan, as a unitary country, the sub-divisions authorities in localities such as municipalities are not responsible for matters related to foreign trade such as subsidies, taxation, or other trade measures.[379] Obviously, the reason that sub-divisions authorities in Jordan do not have power in trade relations is to ensure a coherent policy. A country with a federal system of government such as the U.S. faces the dilemma of conciliating states laws and practices with international trade agreements and at the same time preserving states' rights to legislate on local jurisdictions and set public standards.[380]

---

[375] In the House of Representatives, the full Ways and Means committee is the most powerful committee for overseeing trade policy. The Ways and Means committee has several subcommittees such as Trade and Oversight Subcommittees. In the Senate, the Finance committee has similar power with regard to trade policy.

[376] *Id.* art. 37.

[377] DUSTOUR Al-URDUN [Constitution] art. 35 (Jordan).

[378] Under the Commerce Clause of the U.S. Constitution, the Congress has the power to regulate commerce with foreign nations. In addition, Congress has the exclusive power to regulate commerce among the several states and with the Indian Tribes. It also has the authority to "lay and collect Taxes, Duties, Imposts and Excises". See U.S. Const. art. I, § 8, cl. 1. For more on the Commerce Clause see Michael Conant, *The Constitution and the Economy: Objective Theory and Critical Commentary* 11, 87-114 (U. Okla. Press 1991). The U.S. executive must have the authority, delegated by the Congress, in order to negotiate. In United States V. Guy W. Capps, Inc, the court said "We, think, however, that the executive agreement was void because it was not authorized by Congress...The power to regulate foreign commerce is vested in Congress, not in the executive or the courts". See *U.S V. Guy Capps Inc.*, 204 F.2d 655, 658 (4th Cir. 1953).

[379] See Working Party Report, *Report of the Working Party on the Accession of Jordan*, WT/ACC/JOR/33, para. 43 (Dec. 3, 1999).

[380] States have no authority to enter into agreements or compacts with foreign nations without the consent of congress. See U.S. Const. art. I, § 10. However, some U.S. states such as New York or California have economies larger than all but a handful of nations. The WTO agreements cover areas in which U.S. states are actively involved such as services, government procurement, product standards, and subsidies. Therefore, states and local governments may act in international trade arena. See Matthew Schaefer, *Twenty-First Century Trade Negotiations, The US Constitution and the Elimination of US State-Level Protectionism*, 2 J. Intl. Econ. L. 71, 72 (1999). The federal government can preempt state laws. However, U.S. federal officials are reluctant use the constitutional power of the Supremacy Clause in their relations with states because of political considerations. The U.S. federal government prefers to encourage voluntary states' compliance.

The king of Jordan is the one who concludes and ratifies treaties and agreements.[381] Since the WTO accession package and other trade agreements involve financial commitments of the treasury and affect the public or private rights of Jordanians, the National Assembly must subsequently approve such agreements to give them the status of domestic law.[382] Thus, by the language of the Constitution, these kinds of agreements are not executive agreements. Also, one can assume that since these kinds of agreements regulate customs duties, which are taxes, they must be approved by the National Assembly.[383] In order for any international agreement such as WTO agreements to be enforceable the competent authorities must publish the agreement in the Official Gazette so as it is known to the public. Then, and only then, the agreement has the force of law and every local authority, judicial authority, and the individual is obliged to abide by it.[384] The approval requirement by the Jordanian National Assembly for treaties is designed to protect individual rights that treaties might be restricted by granting the Assembly some control over the treaty making power of the executive.

A question arises as to whether every agreement that affects the treasury must be approved by the National Assembly, even if such an agreement is concluded with a

---

[381] The king declares war, concludes peace and ratifies treaties and agreements. Treaties and agreements which involve financial commitments to the Treasury or affect the public or private rights of Jordanians shall not be valid unless approved by the National Assembly. In no circumstances shall any secret terms contained in any treaty or agreement be contrary to their overt terms. DUSTOUR Al-URDUN [Constitution] art. 33 (I), (II) (Jordan). Before modification, article 33 incorporated the right to enter into "trade agreements". One might argue that such agreements, after modification, could fall under the sole jurisdiction of the king without the approval of the National Assembly. However, closer look at the precise language of the current article indicates that the approval of National Assembly is necessary since they affect the treasury. In addition, the practice supports this conclusion. The words "treaties and agreements" in the Jordanian constitution are very broad to include also international trade agreements. There are executive agreements that do not require the approval of the National Assembly. For example, agreements of technical details of diplomacy, agreements detailing the implementation of already approved agreements, or executive agreements that fall within the sole jurisdiction of the executive power. In other words, any agreement that does not affect the treasury is not subject to approval by the National Assembly.
[382] See Id. arts. 33 (II) & 91. The High Court of Justice in Jordan decided that "The king is the one who ratifies treaties provided that the National Assembly approves therein if they would alter the country's lands, or deprive its sovereignty, or involve financial commitments on the treasury…Thus, the agreements concluded between the minister of economy and the U.S. representative to Jordan in 1954 were not operational because they were not approved by the authority prescribed by the constitution". See Decision No. 55/27, Journal of the Jordanian Bar Association p. 622 (No. 11 1955). Also in another decision the High Court of Justice held that the economic and transit cooperation agreement concluded between Jordan and Lebanon was not operative without the National Assembly approval. See Decision No. 57/24, Journal of the Jordanian Bar Association p. 487 (No. 3 1957).
[383] A law must be passed for imposing tax or duty, whether the draft law is self-initiated by the National Assembly or by the Council of Ministers. See Jordan Const art. 111.
[384] See Law Sanctioning Jordan's Accession to the World Trade Organization No. 4 of 2000, al Jaridah al Rasmiyah No. 4415 (Official Gazette) (Feb. 24, 2000). The law sanctioning Jordan's accession to the WTO means that the National Assembly had approved WTO multilateral agreements. Plurilateral WTO agreements were not approved since Jordan is not member to any of them yet. There is no need to approve the "Trade Policy Review Mechanism" of the WTO because it is procedural. In Mexico, the president is authorized to enter into international treaties that are consistent with the constitution, but must be ratified by the Senate to become effective. See Constitucion Politicia de los Estados Unirdos Mexicanos [Mexican Const.] art. 133.

private entity for example an international bank or loan agreement with another country.[385] The Constitution is silent on the question of the number of votes necessary for the approval of international agreements. One can argue that since passing draft laws or resolutions requires a majority of votes of the members present in each the house of Senate and Deputies, then international agreements must be approved by majority of the members present.[386]

Another problem arises when an agreement conflicts with a provision of the Jordanian Constitution. The answer is not clear. There are no cases right on the spot. However, one can maintain that the Constitution supersedes any agreement because if an agreement is given priority over the Constitution, it would mean that the Constitution could be amended by the conclusion of an agreement, which contradicts with the Constitution, without following the prerequisite procedures.[387] This is contrary to the basic doctrine of the sovereignty of people that is regarded as one of the fundamental doctrines in the Constitution.[388] To assume that an agreement prevails over the Constitution would mean that any fundamental right provided in the Constitution could be overlooked if the Council of Ministers enters into an agreement that invalidate such right.

The relationship between national laws and international treaties depend on the constitutional law of each country.[389] There is no specific statement for transformation of

---

[385] The High Tribunal for the Interpretation of the Constitution is a tribunal that consists of the Speaker of the Senate, as President, and eight members, three of them are selected by ballot by the Senate from its members and five members selected from judges of the highest civil court in order of seniority. See DUSTOUR Al-URDUN [Constitution] art. 57 (Jordan). The High Tribunal for the Interpretation of the Constitution faced the question whether the National Assembly approval was necessary for loans. The High Tribunal took a different approach and decided that public loans do not need the approval of the National Assembly. The High Tribunal stated "As to the fact that public interest requires loan agreements be subject to approval of the National Assembly, it requires modification the constitution rather than concluding a decision from the letter of the constitution. It is the task of the High Tribunal to interpret the current provisions of the constitution but not to add new provisions that are within the jurisdiction of the legislator". See Muhammad ʿAbd al-Salʾam & Hanʾi Khayr, *Ahkʾam Al-Dustʾur Wa Al-Swaʾbiq Al-Barlamaʾniah [Rules of the Constitution and Parliamentary Precedents]* 725-726 (1971).

[386] DUSTOUR Al-URDUN [Constitution] art. 84(II) (Jordan). See also Internal Regulation of the Chamber of Deputies of 1996, *supra* n. 374, art. 76.

[387] Any proposed amendment to the Constitution must be passed by a two-thirds majority of the members of each of the Senate and the Chamber of Deputies, or by two-thirds majority of members of both houses if they convene in a joint session. See DUSTOUR Al-URDUN [Constitution] art. 126(I) (Jordan).

[388] The nation is the source of all powers. See DUSTOUR Al-URDUN [Constitution] art. 24(I) (Jordan).

[389] See Paul Reuter, *Operational and Normative Aspects of Treaties*, 20 Is. L. Rev. 123. 129-130 (1985). (There are two systems that demarcate the relationship between international agreements and national law. These are: dualism and monism). In dualism, one imagines international agreements located in somewhere in metaphysical place that need an act of transformation to bring them within the domain of national law. In monism, once an international agreement is concluded it becomes a national law without an act of transformation. In other words, in monism country there is automaticity in the application of an international treaty which becomes directly applicable or self-executive. Additionally, in monism, an international agreement prevails in case of conflict over domestic law and even the constitution.

international treaties into Jordan's legal system.[390] When WTO agreements and domestic laws have conflicting provisions, WTO obligations prevail over domestic laws.[391] This means that international agreements in Jordan have a quasi-constitutional or constitutional status in the sense that every international agreement prevails over domestic law.[392]

Although the triumph of international agreements over domestic law may lead to coherence and effectiveness in international law, the hands of the government of Jordan could be tied especially if the international agreement is concerned with economic activity. If Jordan desires to enact legislation, it must take into account the international agreement in question. For example, if Jordan proposes a legislation that runs afoul of an international agreement, it must refrain from enacting the desired legislation. This will impose rigidity on future government actions. By the same token, some might consider the prevalence of international agreements over national law as an advantage since it would restrain later domestic political attempts to overturn or erode trade liberalization commitments.

A treaty in the US is the supreme law of the land meaning it is on the same footing as the Constitution or a federal statute.[393] The U.S. is a dualist state. In other words, the U.S. Congress must incorporate, implement, or transform them into domestic statutes in order

---

[390] The National Assembly could enact specific legislation to incorporate a treaty or even enact a legislation that is influenced by an international treaty. For example, the National Assembly enacted specific legislation that approved Jordan's accession package to the WTO. See Law Sanctioning Jordan's Accession to the World Trade Organization No. 4 of 2000, *supra* n. 384. An example of a legislation that is influenced by an international treaty is UNCITRAL Model Law on International Commercial Arbitration that was adopted in Jordan by the Arbitration Law No. 31 o 2001. See also *Draft Law on Arbitration of 2001*, Ad-Dustour 5 (June 23, 2001).

[391] Law Sanctioning Jordan's Accession to the World Trade Organization No. 4 of 2000, *supra* note 384, art. 2 (a). When any provision of the WTO found to be not fully applied, the central government will enforce it without requiring the affected parties to bring a case before local courts. See Report of the Working Party on the Accession of Jordan, *supra* n. 379, at para. 43. The High Court of Justice ruled that an international agreement prevails if it conflicts with a provision of domestic law. Even though Jordan is a civil law country, in the case of absence of clear language in the Constitution, the decisions of higher courts serve as guidance. It seems that the amount of confidence that the judiciary and policymakers have in international institutions relative to Jordan's national institutions has important influence on their thinking about these issues. The approval of the National Assembly for international agreements may provide the necessary checks and balances.

[392] The Mexican Supreme Court of Justice held that international treaties are superior to federal law but subordinate to the Constitution. See "Sindicato Nacional de Controladores de de Trafico Aéreo," LXXVII/99 Semanario 46 (9a época 1999).

[393] The U.S. Constitution states: This Constitution, and the Laws of the United States which shall be made in Pursuance thereof; and all Treaties made, or which shall be made, under the Authority of the United States, shall be the supreme Law of the Land; and the Judges in every State shall be bound thereby, any Thing in the Constitution or Laws of any State to the Contrary notwithstanding. See U.S. Const. art. VI, cl. 2.

to have the legal effects of domestic law.[394] This indicates that a free trade agreement by itself is not domestic law.

Jordan does not have a basic trade law. Trade policies are formulated and implemented through specific laws and regulations.[395] The National Assembly must approve all trade legislations, but the executive power holds much of the responsibility for formulating and implementing trade laws.[396] For example, according to the Customs Law, the Council of Ministers decides on matters of tariffs changes upon advice from the Customs Tariff Council. The latter is comprised of Minister of Finance (as chairman), Minister of Industry and Trade, Minister of Supply, and Director General of Customs Department.[397] The Council of Ministers is also empowered to restrict exportation or importation of certain goods, restrict totally or partially the right to import or export goods to certain entities, or exempt goods from import and export licensing requirements upon proposal of the Minister of Industry and Trade.[398]

In the area of foreign or international economic policies, there has been relatively little role played or opposition raised by the two houses of the National Assembly. One reason for this is that these policies are technical and the National Assembly members do not have expertise or interest in the field. In the U.S., the role of the Congress in international trade policy is strengthened by the explicit constitutional grant of power of the Commerce Clause.

The relationship between the executive and the National Assembly in Jordan is based on mutual cooperation and trade policy conflict has rarely emerged.[399] Most of the controversies in the Jordanian National Assembly revolve around political issues such as the October 1994 Peace Treaty between Jordan and Israel and certain social laws such as personal status law.[400] Tensions on trade policy surface among the different ministries and agencies. These tensions are not reported.[401]

---

[394] See North American Free Trade Agreement Implementation Act of 1993, 19 U.S.C. § 3312 (2000). See An Act to Implement the Free Trade Area Agreement between the United States and Israel of 1985, 19 U.S.C. § 2112 n. (2000).

[395] For complete list of the various trade and trade-related laws see http://www.jftp.gov.jo/main.htm (Last Visited December 24, 2002).

[396] However, the National Assembly holds the responsibility of taxes and duties. "No tax or duty may be imposed except by law". See DUSTOUR Al-URDUN [Constitution] art. 111 (Jordan).

[397] Customs Law No. 20 of 1998, art. 13 (b), Official Gazette No. 4305 (Oct. 1, 1998).

[398] Id. art. 15.

[399] In fact, nothing in the Constitution prevents a minister from concurrently holding the office of his ministry and a membership in either house of the National Assembly. See DUSTOUR Al-URDUN [Constitution] art. 52 (Jordan). This could attribute to the rarity of conflict.

[400] See Glenn E. Robinson, *Defensive Democratization in Jordan*, 30 Intl. J. Middle East Stud. 387, 393-396, 405-407 (1998) (the Jordanian-Israeli peace treaty was approved by fifty-five out of eighty in favor and discussing the consequences that emerged in the aftermath of passing that treaty with the widespread popular opposition to Jordan's 1994 peace treaty with Israel).

[401] King Abdullah II, chaired the Economic Consultative Council on December 21, 1999, called on government ministries to avoid "sensitivities" warning that he "will not accept from anyone to place hurdles" on the path of much-needed reforms. Saad G. Hattar, *Economic Council Sets Deadlines for State Institutions to Present Reform Plans*, Jordan Times 1 (Dec. 22, 1999).

Jordan's main agency responsible for regulating international trade is the Ministry of Industry and Trade (MIT). Proposals for national and foreign trade policy usually emanate from the ministry and undergo discussions among relevant ministries before being formulated ultimately by the Council of Ministers.[402] The Foreign Trade Policy Department (FTPD) is the core unit in the ministry to provide assistance for formulating, negotiating, and implementing trade policy.[403] The FTPD consists of seven divisions.[404] Trade in Goods Division, Trade in Services Division, Trade Policy Review Division, and Reference Center (sort of trade library). These divisions cover the multilateral trading system. Additionally, there are the Economic and Trade Relations with Arab Countries Division and Economic and Trade Relations with Foreign Countries Division. These two divisions cover bilateral trade matters. Finally, there is a Legal Affairs Division covering multilateral and bilateral matters.

Although a procedural issue, one of the mismanagement of the Jordanian delegation for the accession to the WTO was selecting private individuals, heads or members of associations as part of the official delegation.[405] The WTO forum is only designed to accommodate governments.[406] The WTO is an inter-governmental organization. Private entities are excluded from the official negotiating process although they can approach in the negotiating process informally. To bring private interests into the negotiations, Jordan can create a trade advisory committee(s).

---

[402] Telephone Interview with Maha Ali, Director of Foreign Trade Policy Department, Ministry of Industry and Trade (May 18, 2004).

[403] The FTPD was established as the WTO Unit in 1998 to coordinate Jordan's accession to the WTO. Then, the FTPD was elevated in 2000 to a status of a department. In the year 2003, the FTPD merged with the Economic Cooperation Department. Now, the FTPD is responsible for bilateral as well as multilateral trade agreements. It is composed of 10 professional and supporting staff (on file with author). With no-brainer, it is the unfortunate reality that the FTPD is undermanned considering the huge mandate it has to cover. At present, economists by profession and some other relevant specialties proportionately play a major part with only one lawyer at FTPD. In the years to come, the FTPD needs more staff, litigators as well as negotiators, to negotiate and enforce trade agreements.

[404] Id.

[405] During WTO accession negotiations, the Jordanian government attempted to obtain the views of the private sector through contact with Jordanian business associations to be in a better negotiating position. Representatives from the chamber of commerce and the chamber of industry were following closely the negotiations. However, on different occasions, private sector representatives attended the formal meetings of accession negotiations as government contractors to provide consultancy for the government, albeit they did not negotiate. Their presence was solely for the purpose of providing negotiators with the position of the private sector. Telephone Interview with Fakhry Hazimeh, Counselor of Economic Affairs, Permanent Mission [now Delegation] of Jordan to the WTO and U.N (July 9, 2004). Although, the WTO Secretariat allowed Jordan to have private sector representatives in the negotiations, the U.S. team objected to and rejected participation of some members of Jordan's delegate because they are not government officials. It is understandable that trade negotiators are economists or lawyers who perhaps never traded in reality. Therefore, private sector representatives provided insights for Jordan's trade negotiators of their needs and options. However, rather than selecting persons with a broad range of views such as consumer groups or unions, or farmers having private representatives from selected associations may indicate less-open trade policy with narrow focus. Moreover, private sectors representative could have been briefed outside the negotiations room. One also wonders if private sector representatives or other interested persons outside the circle of Amman were consulted.

[406] There is neither formal provision in the GATT/WTO that permits representatives of private industries direct participation nor in the practice of any of the multilateral negotiations held within the GATT/WTO.

The Judiciary branch in Jordan is divided into three categories: regular courts, religious courts, and special courts.[407] There is no one special court that hears all WTO related cases in Jordan. However, there are few specialized courts that hear trade cases. For example, administrative decisions related to customs duties and customs-related cases are subject to review before the Customs Court of First Instance.[408]

---

[407] DUSTOUR Al-URDUN [Constitution] art. 99 (Jordan).
[408] See Customs Law No. 20 of 1998, *supra* n. 397, art. 222.

Conclusion

Duality characterizes Jordan's economy. On the one hand, Jordan has a large pool of trained manpower. On the other, Jordan's socioeconomic disparities and the level of poverty have significant implications. Jordan is constrained in its economic development by the small size of the domestic market, small population, and low level of income. The discussion in this section attempted, mainly to tackle the questions of the status of international trade agreements into the domestic law of Jordan. It also attempts to highlight the relationship between the National Assembly, the Executive Power, and the Judiciary in respect of international trade, the bodies in Jordan that have the power to enter into international agreements, the legal effects of an international agreement, and the cases where international agreements prevail over domestic law.

Once the National Assembly approves an agreement it becomes a source of law and even prevails over domestic law. The institutional conflict in Jordan appears in the overlapping jurisdictions of the different executive authorities rather than between the executive and the National Assembly. Fortunately, this turf conflict is somewhat bridged through consultation and reference. This helps the executive power formulate regulations of international trade in Jordan. Additionally, local authorities do not have a role in formulating Jordan's trade policy. Therefore, the executive power is centralized. In contrast, the constitutional and political structure in the U.S. leads to a maze. The U.S. Congress has a greater input into the formulation of U.S. trade policy-making process. The different states in the U.S. have, to some extent, a role in formulating foreign trade policy, especially with regard to evaluating credentials and qualifications for service suppliers. It is fair to say that forming an international trade policy in Jordan is more predictable than that in the U.S.

V. Jordan: The Process of Accession to the WTO

Before the WTO came into existence, a country became a contracting party to the GATT through the article XXXIII full accession procedure and the article XXVI "sponsorship procedure".[409] Article XXXIII provided the general framework for accession to GATT and established the process of accession for countries that are not founding members of GATT. Article XXVI.5 (c) of GATT created a different procedure for accession for customs territories that have full autonomy in the conduct of its external commercial relations.[410] An existing contracting party that is responsible for the customs territory can sponsor it for membership.[411] Most Arab countries acceded to GATT through the sponsorship procedure.[412] For example, if England sponsored Jordan, Jordan would have been a contracting party to GATT. Article XVII of GATT 1994, which refers to state monopolies, also provided the basis for accession of countries with centrally planned economies.[413] Jordan could have also used this provision for its accession given its interventionist trade policy.

Jordan could have acceded to the GATT in 1960's and 1970's and acceded on much easier terms than under the WTO. In those decades, GATT was related mainly to trade in goods. In other words, Jordan would have had to negotiate only on border measures, such as tariffs and quotas. Therefore, there would not have been negotiations on reforming internal regulatory practices in areas such as services, agriculture, and intellectual property.

---

[409] See General Agreement on Tariffs and Trade, *supra* note 105, arts. XXXIII & XXVI.

[410] See Raj Bhala, *Enter the Dragon: An Essay on China's WTO Accession Saga*, 15 Am. U. Int'l L. Rev. 1469, 1476 (2000).

[411] Article XXVI.5 (c) procedure does not require a series of bilateral concession agreements, decision of the Contracting Parties, or protocol of accession. Rather, the customs territory or newly independent country obtains membership on the same terms and conditions as those that had been accepted by its former colonial master on its behalf. Under GATT Article XXVI.5 (c) and procedures adopted during a 1957 GATT meeting, there is a period of *de facto* application of GATT obligations on a reciprocal basis between the contracting parties and the customs territory or newly independent country. During that period, the new country can adjust to the obligations, implement necessary trade policies, and decide whether it desires full GATT membership. An affirmative decision leads to full membership after a prescribed reasonable period. *Id*, at 1477.

[412] For example, Bahrain (1993), Djibouti (1994), Kuwait (1963), Mauritania (1963), Qatar (1994), and United Arab Emirates (1994) entered into the GATT through the sponsorship procedure. On the other hand, Egypt (1970), Morocco (1987), and Tunisia (1990) joined the GATT through the full accession process. Arab countries, like other countries, that were contracting parties in GATT automatically became members of WTO once they ratified the Marrakesh agreement.

[413] Non-market economy is an economy where enterprises make decisions not on the basis of economic factors, but rather on the basis government directives. The purpose of article XVII is to regulate the market behavior of state trading enterprises. However, the drafters of GATT were unsure about their role especially that they emerged from the difficult wartime. Therefore, the drafters maintained flexibility in article XVII so they can apply to state trading countries and not only to state trading enterprises. See Anna Lanoszka, *The World Trade Organization Accession Process, Negotiating Participation in a Globalizing Economy*, 35 J.W.T. 575, 579 (2001).

Article XII of the WTO Charter, which echoes article XXXIII of GATT, governs the WTO accession process.[414] This accession process is based on a case-by-case methodology. The WTO accession process begins with an official notification to the office of WTO Director-General of the intention to join by the country in question.[415] Any application for accession must first be approved informally by the General Council. Thereafter, the General Council formally establishes a working party of countries that are interested in evaluating the application.[416] The working party and the acceding country engage in round(s) of questions and answers in writing before the first meeting of working party. After basic policies have been sorted out with the working party, interested WTO members enter into bilateral negotiations with the applicant over specific commitments that are prerequisites to joining the WTO. Once the bilateral negotiations are finalized, bilateral concession agreements are drafted. The best concessions for market access in goods and services obtained in the bilateral negotiations process extend to all other WTO members.[417]

Jordan wanted to become a WTO member for many reasons. By acceding to the GATT/WTO, Jordan's exports would be subject to lower tariffs and other trade barriers. Consumers would enjoy a wide variety of products.[418] Jordan would be considered on the same footing as any other member of the WTO and would avoid becoming isolated in its relations with other countries, an important consideration in an increasingly interrelated world. It was prestigious for Jordan, as an Arab country, to accede to the WTO,

---

[414] Article XII of the WTO charter provides that any state or customs territory possessing full autonomy in the conduct of its external commercial relations may accede to the WTO on terms to be agreed between it and the WTO.

[415] Usually, a country applies for membership in the WTO after enjoying the status of observer. As an observer, a country can attend WTO meetings and participate in discussion. However, the country may not participate in decision-making process. Some meetings may be confidential and thus an observer may be excluded from such meeting. The observer country must apply for membership within five years of being observer. *Id.*

[416] The applicant submits a trade policy memorandum that describes its foreign trade policies and administrative system that may have bearing on the WTO agreements. It is a fact-finding document that includes relevant statistical data, laws and regulations, the current tariff schedule, domestic support measures and export subsidies in agriculture set in a specific pattern and tabular format, and policies that affect trade in services. This memorandum establishes the basis for negotiations between the applicant and the working party. *Id* at 591-593.

[417] The protocol of accession represents the terms of entry into the WTO.. The protocol outlines the applicant's current trade laws and policies, while noting the differences between that regime and the minimum WTO requirements. It explains how and when the applicant intends to correct these differences. The final package of accession includes the working party report, the protocol of accession, and the annexed schedules of the applicant's commitments. The Ministerial Conference or the General Council, in case the Ministerial Conference is not in session, makes a decision by two-thirds majority on the accession report. If the two-thirds majority favors the accession, the applicant may sign the protocol and join the WTO.

[418] Consumers in Jordan benefit from trade liberalization by purchasing many commodities. Cars are commodities on point. Private car ownership, from affordable compact cars to high-end cars, is ubiquitous. Mobile phones, among several other popular personal electronics, are another hot commodity. Jordan has 24 percent mobile penetration rate. See *Special Report: Telecoms*, 48 Middle East Econ. Dig, 26 (No. 15, Apr. 9, 2004) (citing total number of GSM subscribers as of 2003 as 866,000 gaining 56.50 percent share of total telephone subscribers).

especially in the Arab region where WTO membership or effective participation in the WTO has been the exception rather than the rule.

Jordan started negotiations to join the GATT in January 1994. In 1995, after the WTO was established, Jordan's application was transferred to the WTO working party.[419] At this time, Jordan imposed a self-declared deadline of 1999 for accession. The 1999 deadline was prescribed because 1999 is the year that the WTO would launch the "Millennium Round" at the WTO Seattle Ministerial Conference. Jordan wanted to accede by 1999 because the "Millennium Round" would raise the bar to accede and the terms of entry would become enormous. It was felt that the sooner Jordan acceded to the WTO the earlier it could have a say in future trade rounds.

Many Arab countries, including Egypt, Kuwait, and Morocco, urged other WTO members to accept Jordan at an earlier point in time. Additionally, the U.S. supported Jordan's accession to the WTO. Momentum on Jordan's accession was also provided by the lifting of Jordan from the U.S. watch list of countries that do not adequately protect intellectual property rights.[420] It was anticipated that Jordan's accession package would be ratified during the Seattle Ministerial meeting of the WTO.[421] However, the meeting

---

[419] The working party held five meetings starting Oct. 1996. See Report of the Working Party on the Accession of Jordan, *supra* n. 379, at para. 2. This means that Jordan's delegation had to travel to Geneva five times and incur the costs of traveling and accommodation during its stay there. Originally, the working party consisted of 20 members headed by K. Kesavapany, Singapore's WTO ambassador and former chairman of WTO General Council. As the number can change at any time during negotiations, the working party on Jordan's accession first changed from 20 to 27, and then from 27 to 33. Those 33 members are usually the exporting countries that have interest in the Jordanian market. For example, the working party on Jordan's accession included members as diverse as Argentina, Australia, Morocco, Switzerland, India, the U.S., Canada, and the EC. These countries may not have the same interest as others in Jordan's market. See Working Party on the Accession of Jordan, *Membership and Terms of Reference*, WT/ACC/JOR/5 (Nov. 1, 1996). However, one might say that, pragmatically, the U.S., Canada, and EC geared the working party in which the U.S. and EC, using trade lingo, playing good cop, bad cop in turn. Moreover, since Jordan's accession to the WTO, Jordan has participated as member of a working party only in one case. See Working Party on the Accession of Lithuania, *Membership and Terms of Reference*, WT/ACC/LTU/1/Rev.1 (June 14, 2000). This might be interpreted that Jordan's WTO mission in Geneva is not well-equipped, in terms of finance or human resources, to participate in every acceding country negotiating process, setting aside taking an effective role in the daily hustle and bustle of WTO committees' meetings and negotiations.

[420] *Jordan Cleared to Join WTO: Removed from Watch List* No. 22 Middle E. Exec. Rep. 8 (1999) (page references not avail.). USTR removed Jordan from the watch list (WL) in an out-of cycle review (OCR). Generally, WL is reviewed by the end of March of every year, but provisions allow for OCRs that can take place any time during the year. Although not required by the Omnibus Trade and Competitiveness Act of 1988, USTR publishes lists of countries with various intellectual property concerns: priority foreign country (PFC), priority WL, WL, and under observation. Priority WL country is one notch under PFC which undergoes investigation that could lead to trade sanctions.

[421] The real reasons for the impasse at Seattle meeting was due to multiple factors. Before the Seattle meeting, it took WTO members almost a year to select the new Director General of the WTO agreeing at the end that Mike Moore would assume the post first for three years (non-renewable) followed by Supachai for another three years (non-renewable). Developing countries pleaded for their plight in implementing the results of the Uruguay round, but neither developed countries listened nor the appellate body in its interpretation of special and differential rules for developing countries. They wanted to extend the moratorium on non-violation cases of TRIPS. There was a tension mood even among developed countries themselves exaggerated through the Beef-Hormone case, Banana case, and agriculture. In Seattle meeting,

was interrupted and the approval was delayed. The General Council voted for Jordan's accession package on December 17, 1999. Jordan became a member on April 11, 2000.[422] Thus, Jordan met its self-imposed deadline for accession to the WTO. The following section discusses Jordan's commitments in its accession to the WTO.

VI. Protocol of Accession and WTO Commitments

Jordan agreed on a broad range of obligations in areas such as tariff reductions, services, agriculture, intellectual property rights, and transparency.[423] This section examines some of Jordan's obligations in its accession to the WTO, the extent of Jordan's initial compliance with its WTO obligations, the current status of implementation of these obligations, and the issues of concern that have surfaced in Jordan's WTO membership.

A. Market Access in Goods

1. Tariff Reduction

When a country joins the WTO, it enjoys market access rights, i.e. entry and exit. In return, an acceding country must offer equivalent market access concessions. For purposes of tariff reduction, products and their tariff lines are grouped together into several categories, in what can be seen as a sectoral approach.[424] Jordan made substantial market access commitments as part of its WTO membership negotiations.[425] Jordan has low average tariffs with single or two digit rates, *ad valorem*-only duties with some

---

the USTR adopted the "green room module" by limiting negotiations to some 30 countries while excluding others who felt being marginalized. Then, President Clinton during a late-than-supposed luncheon with representatives of WTO members stated that the U.S. proposes establishing a working party on trade and labor and using trade sanctions to enforce labor rights violations. The failure to launch the Millennium Round was due to internal factors not to the thousands of protestors in the streets. For more see Dilip K. Das, Debacle at Seattle; The Way the Cookie Crumbled, 34 J.W.T. 5, 181-201 (2000).

[422] Jordan ratified the WTO accession package in March 2000. See WTO Director-General, *Protocol of Accession of Jordan: Notification of Acceptance and Entry into Force*, WT/Let/333 (Mar. 14, 2000). Jordan's working party report to the WTO is 114 pages long 8 1/2 x 11-page format (this is compared with the 50 pages of Oman's working party report). It took 35 specific commitments in the working party report covering not only WTO agreements but also pricing rationalization that should reflect cost, privatization programs, and reforming domestic tax system.

[423] Given that some documents on Jordan's accession to the WTO and implementation of its commitments may be restricted to the public, unless one is considered an "insider" whether in the WTO or Jordan's ministries and agencies, most of the materials used are in public. Documents of the WTO working party related to accession are automatically derestricted once the working party report is formally completed.

[424] See WTO, *Goods Schedule of Jordan, Staging Annex*, http://www.wto.org/english/thewto_e/countries_e/jordan_e.htm (Dec. 3, 1999). It is unclear how Jordan made its decision to group products and their tariff lines into categories and/or lower its import tariffs. Perhaps, it fixed reduced import tariffs according to the situation or sensitivity of the domestic industry defined by the level of import penetration, productivity, job losses, and prices.

[425] This is despite Jordan's efforts in convincing WTO members that further tariff cuts would damage its fragile economy in 1998 with mounting trade deficit.

exceptions where specific duties apply, and nearly 100 percent tariff bindings.[426] Jordan may have binding overhangs, which is the difference between bound tariff rates and applied tariff rates, in its tariff schedule.[427] To deal with sensitivities in tariffs reduction, Jordan was granted staging and product exclusion rights.[428] As Jordan has a longer implementation period for tariff reductions, it made some degree of cuts in tariff rates several months after the date of accession, which has the effect of securing for WTO countries some immediate tangible results from the negotiations.

Since, Jordan has acceded to the 1997 WTO's Information Technology Agreement (ITA), it has committed itself to reduce tariffs to zero and bound them at that level on IT products.[429] In other words, computer and computer-related products, including semiconductor chips, are not subject to tariffs. Since Jordan is not a major exporter of ITA products, the ITA provides Jordanians with an access to wide varieties of ITA products at low costs. This should help build up Jordan's IT sector and other IT-related sectors such as telecommunications.

These tariff reductions did not require changes in Jordanian domestic law. The Customs Law of 1998 provides that goods entering Jordan are subject to customs duties as prescribed in the customs law. However, if there is a special provision for a tariff in an international agreement to which Jordan is a party, a tariff shall be imposed in accordance with the provisions of such agreement.[430] Additionally, the Council of Ministers will issue decisions related to tariff changes.[431] Regarding compliance with the WTO's ITA,

---

[426] Jordan agreed to impose zero or very low tariffs on all chemical products perhaps in light of the Chemical Tariff Harmonization Agreement of the Uruguay Round (CTHA). Specific duties, as opposed to *ad valorem* duties, are not transparent and have the effect of increasing trade protectionism.

[427] Bound tariff rates are the maximum tariffs Jordan can apply under its WTO commitments. Applied tariff rates are the actual tariffs in place.

[428] Jordan has a 10-year transition period for implementing reduction commitments. Tobacco and alcohol maintain high tariff peaks. See Daniel Pruzin, *WTO Approves Accession of Jordan to Trade Body*, 17 Intl. Trade Rep. 29 (BNA) (Jan. 6, 2000). See Report of the Working Party on the Accession of Jordan, *supra* note 379, at para. 55. It is noticeable that rather than outright prohibition on imports of tobacco and alcohol, Jordan opted to impose higher prohibitive tariffs between 150 percent and 200 percent.

[429] The ITA provides for the elimination of tariffs on a wide range of some 180 information technology products in five major categories: computers and peripheral devices, semiconductors, printed circuit boards, telecommunications equipment (except satellites), and software. The tariff cuts, which began in July 1997, affect more than 93 percent of world trade in information technology products. Developed countries had until Jan. 1, 2000, to phase out tariffs while developing countries were given extended deadlines to eliminate tariffs on certain products deemed sensitive. The ITA takes account of the rapid pace of development in information technologies by establishing procedures for consultations on, and review of, product coverage, as well as non-tariff measures that might impede market access for information technology products. Under the first ITA review, known as ITA II, U.S. high-technology companies urged the then Clinton Administration to expand the ITA to include hundreds of new products, from photocopying machines, digital cameras, thermistor devices, to multi-chip packages. See Charles Owen Verrill, Jr., Peter S. Jordan, Timothy C. Brightbill, *International Trade*, 32 Intl. L. 319, 323-324 (1998). It is quite obvious that U.S. high-tech companies are major exporters of information technology products. These companies include Cisco Systems Inc., Compac Computer Corp., and Intel Corp., to name few. Therefore, the ITA provides greater market access to Jordan and other countries.

[430] See Customs Law No. 20 of 1998, art. 9, *infra* n. 397.

[431] *Id.* art. 14.

Jordan included its amended tariff schedule in its WTO accession agreements, thus negating the need to make changes in its domestic law and submit separate modification document that indicates its compliance with the ITA.

In total, Jordan made tariff concessions with regard to 2790 tariff lines for industrial products and 462 tariff lines for agricultural products.[432] The imbalance of tariff concessions between industrial and agricultural products is due to Jordan's emphasis on industrial products in international trade rather than on agricultural products.

Jordan can use its tariff rates for several goals. First, Jordan can rely on tariff rates as bargaining leverage in future multilateral trade rounds. Second, Jordan can rely on tariffs as a method by which to protect some domestic industries, raise revenue, and redistribute income. However, there is one potential pitfall for relying on tariffs as bargaining leverage in negotiations. As a result of several trade rounds, a large number of countries might lower their tariffs, thus depriving Jordan of its bargaining power. This is a scenario where the law of diminishing return would apply to Jordan.

In approaching future rounds of trade negotiations, Jordan should argue in favor of a mathematical formula (linear cuts) in which the tariff rate applies across the board with lower tariff cuts per tariff line. The reason for favoring linear cuts is because of the nature of Jordan's current tariff schedule. Close to 2131 tariff lines are above 20 percent tariff rate while about 7110 tariff lines are set below that percentage. Therefore, a harmonization formula, which applies for higher cuts on higher tariffs and lower cuts on lower tariffs, may not be desired. In addition, there is a need to exempt certain imported inputs from tariffs and other domestic taxes. The tariff exemptions would reduce production costs for domestic producers and give them a much needed competitiveness through cost savings.

2. Agriculture

The agriculture sector in Jordan is a recipient of government subsidies.[433] As a result of an economic crisis in the late 1980's, Jordan adopted a structural adjustment program to reform the agriculture sector.[434] In addition, Jordan passed a new law that would abolish the Agricultural Marketing Organization (AMO).[435] This law dismantled the

---

[432] See Jordan Schedule of Market Access on Goods, *supra* n. 424.

[433] In the wheat sector, the government bought wheat production from producers at prices higher than international wheat prices. Jordan also had a history of subsidizing agriculture inputs such as water, electricity, and credit. Farmers could obtain loans either from the Agriculture Credit Cooperation (ACC) or from commercial banks. However, since the ACC provides loans at an interest rate below that of commercial banks, many farmers borrow from the ACC. The average interest rate on loans given by the ACC is below that of commercial banks by 3.5-5.5 percent. See Working Party on the Accession of Jordan, *Introduction to Jordan's Agriculture Sector and Agricultural Policies,* WT/ACC/JOR/14, at 14-17 (July 1, 1998).

[434] In 1996, Jordan adopted the agricultural policy charter. The objective of the charter, among others, is to maximize the role of the private sector in agriculture and limit the government role to the provision of institutional support such as research and infrastructure investments. *Id.* 16.

[435] See Provisional Law on the Cancellation of the Agricultural Marketing Organization No. 22 of 2002 al Jaridah al Rasmiyah (Official Gazette No. not avail.) (May 16, 2002).

AMO authority over import and export sales.[436] Additionally, Jordan abolished the system of fixed prices and allowed the private sector for the first time to import almost any agricultural product.[437]

Partially motivated by WTO accession, Jordan abolished the AMO and the Ministry of Supply. The policies of the AMO and the Ministry of Supply may have violated Article XVII of GATT 1994 or article 4 of the WTO Agreement on Agriculture. However, this does not mean that AMO or the Ministry of Supply themselves are invalid but rather that their respective practices and policies may be invalid. Rather than abolishing these entities, Jordan could have streamlined their operations by resolving internal disputes, removing stalemated bureaucracy and budget constraints, and changing their practices.

In 2002, Jordan introduced a new Law on Agriculture.[438] The new Law on Agriculture defines SPS measures in a manner consistent with the WTO Agreement on the Application of Sanitary and Phytosanitary Measures (SPS Agreement).[439] The Law on Agriculture also authorizes the Ministry of Agriculture to enact SPS measures to the extent necessary for the protection of human, animal, plant life or health, so long as these measures are based on scientific principles.[440] Furthermore, Jordan established an inquiry point or trade desk to provide information on SPS measures.[441] Therefore, it is fair to say that the Law on Agriculture embraces the concepts of the relevant WTO relevant agreements.

Jordan has made several commitments to bring its agricultural practices in line with WTO rules. Jordan has eliminated quotas and other restrictive measures on imports of

---

[436] The AMO set the quantities and types of agricultural products to be imported or exported and the dates of importing or exporting. For example, prior to 1998, it was responsible for determining imports on a monthly and quarterly basis. It also participated in determining the prices of agricultural products. Under market mechanism, prices would be determined by market forces. See Law of the Agricultural Marketing Organization No. 40 of 1988, art. 4(b) & (g) al Jaridah al Rasmiyah (Official Gazette No. not avail.) (1988). See also An Introduction to Jordan's Agriculture Sector and Agricultural Policies, *supra* n. 433, at 21.

[437] Under earlier practice, the Ministry of Supply had exclusive rights in wheat imports and brand distribution of Halibuna, type of dried milk. The Ministry also fixed the prices of essential food such as bread, sugar, and rice.

[438] Provisional Law on Agriculture No. 44 of 2002, al Jaridah al Rasmiyah No. 4558 (Official Gazette) (Aug. 1, 2002).

[439] The Law defines SPS measures as those laws, decrees, regulations, requirements and procedures, which include, *inter alia*, end product criteria, process and production methods, testing, inspection, certification and approval procedures, quarantine treatment including relevant requirements associated with the transport of animals or plants, statistical methods, sampling procedures and methods of risk assessment, and packaging and labeling requirements directly related to food safety. *Id.* art. 2. Thus, article 2 of the Law copies the language of annex A.1 of the SPS Agreement.

[440] *Id.* arts. 6.a & 7. Articles 6.a & 7 of the Law on Agriculture are in compliance with basic rights and obligations under article 2 of the WTO SPS Agreement. *Id.* art. 6.a.

[441] See Notification from Jordan, *Implementations of Transparency Obligations*, G/SPS/27/Rev.7 (Nov. 1, 2000). This is in compliance with annex B of the WTO SPS Agreement which requires members to establish one enquiry point.

agricultural products.[442] In addition, Jordan has committed itself to abolishing double inspection of carcasses.[443] It has also agreed to reduce domestic support for agriculture, which previously amounted to JD1.5 million, to 13.3 percent over seven years period.[444] Jordan does not have a history of export subsidies since it does not have the money to support its domestic agricultural production or agricultural exports as does the U.S. or EC.[445]

The WTO accession has led to the establishment of different bureaucracies in Jordan. Jordan's current food safety and inspection network consists of several government agencies, including the Ministry of Health, Ministry of Agriculture, and Jordan Institute of Standards and Metrology (JISM).[446] The establishment of the Jordan Food and Drug Administration, which is similar to the U.S. Food and Drug Administration, could lead to an overlap in inspection, lack of coordination, and different enforcement tools.[447] It is

---

[442] During 1994-1996, Jordan imposed quotas on imports of olive oil and chicken meat.

[443] It has been the practice in Jordan to inspect imported meat at the border as well as after it cleared the customs. Some WTO members argued that such practice appear to be more trade-restrictive than necessary. The representative of Jordan confirmed that, as from the date of accession, unnecessary inspections of imported meat products would be eliminated and national treatment would be accorded fully to such products. See Report of the Working Party on the Accession of Jordan, *supra* note 379, at 147, 149.

[444] See Report of the Working Party on the Accession of Jordan, *supra* n. 379, at para. 189. See also Notification from Jordan, *Domestic Support of Jordan*, G/AG/N/JOR/1 (Sep. 17, 2002).

[445] The Farm Bill of 2002 sets out U.S. farm spending plans through the 2007 marketing year. It includes export credit guarantees, marketing loan payments, rural development loans for things such as power lines and power plants, countercyclical payments, farm conservation and renewable energy funds, and step 2 programs. It also provides direct payments to producers of nine commodities based on historic acreage and yields. See *Farm Security and Rural Investment Act of 2002*, 7 U.S.C.A. §§ 7901-7918 (West Supp. 2005) See Ann Saccomano, *Free but with a Price*, J. Com. 13, 14 (Dec. 9, 2002) (citing that the new farm bill provides for a subsidy of $180 billion to farmers over the next ten years). For more on the U.S. agricultural policy see J.W. Looney et al., *Agricultural Law: A Lawyer's Guide to Representing Farm Clients* 5-10, 191-205 (ABA 1990) (many of the U.S. support programs date back to the farm financial crises of 1930s and 1980s. Certain reasons may provide as an explanation for the divergent treatment of agriculture in the U.S. First, farming is viewed as a way of life dependant on natural forces which are beyond the farmer's control. Farmers also viewed as stabilizing element in society because of their vital role in food and fiber production. Farmland is a major source of aesthetically and psychologically pleasing open space and locale for many non-farm recreational activities. Farmers are distinct minority in the U.S. They constitute about 2 percent of the total population. Farmers receive specialized legal treatment as an attempt to protect them from the generally urban orientation of law and government. Lastly, their lack of participation beyond the production stage of agriculture is a contributing factor to their inability to attain adequate income).

[446] The new Law on Food Control stipulates that the Ministry of Health is the sole authority responsible for food safety for imported as well as domestically processed products. See Provisional Law on Food Control No. 79 of 2001, art. 3, al Jaridah al Rasmiyah No. 4522 (Official Gazette) (Dec. 13, 2001).

[447] See Michael S. Schumann et al., *Food Safety Law* 2, 8-11 (Van Nostrand Reinhold 1997) (explaining the an ongoing problem involves the division of responsibility between the two primary agencies: the U.S. Department of Agriculture (USDA) which oversees meat and poultry inspection and regulations and the Food and Drug Administration (FDA) which oversees almost all other food products. This arrangement is not quite as simple as it sounds. For example, the two organizations share jurisdiction for egg products. Under the USDA, food products must be pre-approved prior to marketing. Food products under FDA's jurisdiction can be marketed without pre-approval and are subject only to postmarketing surveillance and enforcement. The USDA has the major labeling requirements for food while the FDA's requirements generally refer to artificial flavoring, coloring, and chemical preservatives, as well as saccharin. Regarding

unclear where the line can be drawn between the jurisdictions of these entities. These jurisdictional issues between these entities must be addressed through internal regulations.

Issue that affects trade in food products include shelf-life, i.e. how long a product can stay on the shelf, reclassification (chilled vs. frozen) and other requirements. Usually, U.S. industry cites short shelf-life standards in Jordan and other Arab countries as an important non-tariff barrier to trade in processed fruits and vegetables.[448] Shelf-life requirements in Jordan were considered inconsistent with the WTO agreements.[449] For example, it has been the practice in Jordan that imported foodstuffs must have half the shelf-life at the time of importation.[450] This practice could amount to restrictions on importing fresh food products because of the time required for processing, shipment, and customs clearance, which sometimes lasts several days or weeks. Jordan agreed to phase out the government-mandated shelf life for shelf-stable products.[451] Therefore, Jordan would accept manufacturers who use of their own "sell by" dates or open dating.[452]

Jordan requires that the percentage of imported ewes or yearlings, i.e. female sheep of 1-1.5 year of age, cannot exceed 10 percent of the total number of imported sheep. This age restriction was justified on the ground that imported female sheep of old age are usually more prone to carrying diseases.[453] A WTO member can challenge the age

---

warning labels on food and food products, the FDA has historically mandated relatively few warnings for food products while the USDA has mandated that safe handling instructions appear in labeling).

[448] See U.S. International Trade Commission, Processed Foods and Beverages: A Description of Tariff and Non-Tariff Barriers for Major products and Their Impact on Trade, Inv. No. 332-421, Pub. No. 3455 (Oct. 2001) (In some Middle Eastern countries such as Saudi Arabia, processed fruit and vegetable products are given a shelf-life of 12 months, without regard to the packaging technology used, and must have 50 percent of their shelf-life remaining upon entry into the country. However, many of these products are produced once a year from fresh products harvested in season and distributed from inventory. Shelf-life restrictions prevent the year-round distribution of these products. Moreover, these standards are in place regardless of the packaging technology employed that may give a product a longer shelf-life than those listed in the shelf-life standards of these countries).

[449] Shelf-life requirements were based on Jordan Standard 288/1994 for foodstuff and Jordan Standard 401/1997 for infant and children's foodstuff specifically. The working party on Jordan's accession stated that such requirements do not have a sound scientific justification. See Report of the Working Party on the Accession of Jordan, supra n. 379, at 144. Jordan can impose restrictions on imports of food for safety reasons but not for quality concerns. Generally, shelf-life standards function as quality indications.

[450] Id.

[451] Shelf stable means that the product's life is too short, i.e. must be consumed within 5 days. Jordan confirmed in its accession that it would eliminate shelf-stable products from the coverage of these standards by June 30, 2000. See id. at 145. Jordan's move to processors' dates from the government-mandated shelf life standards would be accomplished without an interim period over a short period of time ending in 2000.

[452] In the U.S., product dating is not required by the federal government except for poultry, infant formula, and baby food. However, there are some 20 states that mandate dating for some food. Dates are applied by either the manufacturer or the store. The terms used for dating are flexible since there are no standards. For example, "best by" is a quality and flavor assurance date. It does not mean that the food is unsafe after that date. This kind of date is often placed on cereals. The term "sell by" is indication for the retailer to pull off the product on the shelf by the last date. The term "packaged date" is the date for food such as meat in which it was packaged or processed. It is not indication of safety. Expiration date refers to the date on which food must be used or eaten. "Born on" refers to the freshest beer and "coded" date refers to letters or numbers that allow the manufacturer to track food. See The Dating Game, Consumer Rep. 9 (Mar. 2004).

[453] See Report of the Working Party on the Accession of Jordan, supra n. 379, at 176.

restriction unless it is scientifically proven that there is a basis to distinguish between female sheep imported at the age of 1-1.5 years and older female sheep. In other words, Jordan's age restrictions claim must be scientifically supportable. Otherwise, the distinction could be considered arbitrary.

In its accession negotiations, Jordan attempted to apply for certain agricultural products such as olive oil, sheep, and poultry meat as special safeguard goods (SSG).[454] If Jordan were able to designate those agricultural products as SSG, the WTO Agreement on Agriculture would have applied to them.[455] However, Jordan was not able to designate olive oil, sheep, and poultry as SSG. Instead, WTO working party members determined whether a product of an acceding country such as Jordan merited designation as SSG or not but not for Jordan itself. Other WTO members were concerned that if Jordan was able to designate certain agricultural products as SSG, it would set a precedent for future acceding countries who would request designating their own agricultural products as SSG. This would have created a situation that seemed to be unacceptable for members of the working party on Jordan's accession to the WTO.

---

[454] Even after Jordan acceded to the WTO, Jordan argues for SSG designation for olive oil, sheep, and poultry meat. See Proposal by Jordan, *WTO Negotiations on Agriculture*, G/AG/NG/W/140 (Mar. 22, 2001) (page references are not avail.).

[455] Article 5 of the WTO Agreement on Agriculture is a special safeguard article for agricultural products. However, in order to apply this special safeguard provision, any non-tariff measure imposed on the imported agriculture product in question would have to be converted into tariff. Additionally, the agricultural product must be designated as SSG. Moreover, there are two conditions the presence of either one of them is sufficient to trigger the special safeguard. First, the volume of imported agricultural product will have to exceed a trigger level. Second, the price of imported agricultural product must fall below the trigger price in the base period (1986-1990). If the first condition is satisfied, then an additional duty will be applied for the rest of the year in question (the additional duty may not exceed 33.3% of the ordinary tariff in effect the year the action was taken). If the second criterion is met, then additional duty will be imposed on a shipment-by-shipment basis. Article 5 of the WTO Agreement on Agriculture is a special provision since it does not require a serious injury test, the safeguard measure will in the form of additional duty only, and no retaliation is allowed. This is contrary to the WTO Safeguards Agreement which requires an injury test, a safeguard measure could be in the form of tariff or quota, and there could be counter-retaliation. In order to obtain SSG status, an acceding country has to convert non-tariff trade measures into tariffs. Jordan did not convert non-tariff trade measures into tariffs as required under article 4 of the WTO Agreement on Agriculture, a condition that is vital for applying SSG measure. Rather, Jordan set tariffs on agricultural imports at lower levels and bound them.

3. Trade Remedy Laws[456]

The WTO Agreement on Safeguards prescribes that each member to adopt appropriate domestic legislation before it imposes safeguard measures.[457] On the eve of its accession to the WTO, Jordan enacted the first WTO-compatible safeguard law, known as the National Production Protection Law No.4 of 1998 (NPP Law) and Regulation on Safeguard of National Production.[458] In 2002, Jordan enacted the NPP Law No. 50 of 2002.[459] The NPP Law of 2002 is a framework law that does not cover, as its name might suggest, all trade remedy legislations, including antidumping and countervailing duties.[460]

The organization in charge of the NPP Law is the Directorate of National Production Protection.[461] In particular, the Safeguards Department, a non-independent organ under the umbrella of the MIT, is in charge of administering safeguard cases.[462] The Safeguards

---

[456] Discussion in this section will be limited to fair trade laws and regulations since Jordan invokes safeguard measures frequently and it has never applied an antidumping or countervailing duty order. Therefore, this section does not deal with antidumping, subsidies and countervailing regulations. Moreover, considerations of time and space do not permit for treating antidumping and countervailing laws and regulations. For more on unfair trade regulations see Provisional Anti-Dumping and Subsidies Regulation No. 26 of 2003, al Jaridah al Rasmiyah No. 4587 Official Gazette (Mar. 2, 2003). There could be a number of reasons for the passive use of antidumping or countervailing measures. First, the Jordanian market, until recently, was protected from foreign imports through high tariffs and other non-tariff trade barrier. Second, by the time of trade liberalization, some Jordanian industries may be adjusting to open market. Third, there could be lack of experience (legal, accounting, and human resources) in administering a complex anti-dumping or countervailing investigation and/or enforcing antidumping or countervailing duty orders. However, as more sectors in Jordan are opened to foreign competition, it becomes likely that some industries may petition the government to initiate antidumping or countervailing proceedings.

[457] Jordan committed in its accession to the WTO that it would not apply an anti-dumping, countervailing, or safeguard measure to imports from WTO members until it had notified and implemented appropriate laws in conformity with the provisions of the WTO agreements on safeguards, subsidies and countervailing measures, and antidumping. See Report of the Working Party on the Accession of Jordan, *supra* n. 379, at 107.

[458] See Regulation on Safeguard of National Production No. 55 of 2000, al Jaridah al Rasmiyah No. 4465 Official Gazette (Nov. 16, 2000). The Regulation on Safeguard of 2000 has a total of thirty-nine articles. In these articles, the Regulation sets forth basic principles and concepts. It stipulates the conditions, investigation, forms, time limits, and review of safeguard measures.

[459] See Provisional Law on National Production Protection No. 50 of 2002, al Jaridah al Rasmiyah No. 4560 (Official Gazette) (Aug. 15, 2002). The new NPP Law is essentially modeled on the old NPP Law of 1998. However, the new NPP Law has been elaborated upon in terms of adding new articles such as article 3 which states explicitly that NPP Law of 2002 applies to agricultural as well as industrial products or new definitions such as that of like products and serious injury.

[460] Jordan had to follow up the adoption of the NPP Law with implementing regulations. It seems that Jordan was not able to counter-argue that no implementing regulations were needed given that the NPP Law contained description of investigation concepts such as injurious practices, increase imports, and serious and material injury.

[461] The National Production Protection Directorate, which was set up in 2001, is divided into two departments: the Safeguards Department and the Anti-dumping Department (on file with author). There is also the Council on Tariff which is entrusted in recommending the application of safeguard measures to the Council of Ministers.

Department conducts safeguard investigations with regard to serious injuries caused by increases imports, recommends initiation of investigations, and suggests relief measures.[463]

The NPP Law of 2002 and the Regulation on Safeguard reflect, to a large extent, the WTO Safeguards Agreement. However, there are certain shortcomings regarding Jordan's safeguard law and practice. For example, the NPP Law defines domestic industry for the purposes of a safeguard investigation. However, the NPP Law does not address the case when a domestic producer imports one product and produces a different kinds of products including the one subject to a safeguard investigation. Additionally, an issue is whether or not domestic industry should be interpreted to include producers who have special arrangement, through joint ventures for example, with importers or exporters and there is a coincidence of economic interests between them. Since Jordan is a small country, the case of a regionally dispersed industry in a safeguard invesitgation, as supposed to national market, would not raise a controversy.[464] Therefore, Jordan would not have a regional industry.

In principle, safeguard measures cannot be targeted at imports from a particular country and safeguard investigations should not be country specific. In other words, safeguard measures should be applied to an imported product irrespective of its source.[465] However, in the case of China, a safeguard measure could be country/product-specific.[466] Therefore, Jordan may want to implement paragraph 16 of China's Protocol of Accession to the WTO into domestic law.

---

[462] As of 2004, the Safeguards Department comprises seven permanent staff who presumably is appointed by the minister of industry and trade. It includes persons experienced in cost accounting and economics (on file with author).

[463] See Regulation on Safeguard of National Production No. 55 of 2000, *supra* n. 458, arts. 6, 11 & 23.

[464] In the U.S., in some instances the ITC may conduct a regional market analysis in dumping or countervailing duty investigations. See *Venez. Cement v. U.S.*, 372 F.3d 1284, 1287-1288, 1290 (11th Cir. 2004) (in performing a regional market analysis, the ITC must find on a case-by-case basis a concentration of dumped imports into the regional market. In this context, the ITC must decide whether the ratio of subject imports to consumption is clearly higher in the regional market such as in Florida region than the rest of the U.S. market. Additionally, the ITC must find that imports in the region in question must account for a substantial portion of total subject imports entering the U.S.).

[465] See Provisional Law on National Production Protection No. 50 of 2002, *supra* note 459, art. 19.

[466] Paragraph 16 of China's Protocol of Accession provides that where products of Chinese origin are being imported into the territory of any WTO Member in such increased quantities or under such conditions as to cause or threaten to cause "market disruption" to the domestic producers of like or directly competitive products, the WTO Member so affected may request consultations with China with a view to seeking a mutually satisfactory solution, including whether the affected WTO Member should pursue application of a measure under the Agreement on Safeguards. If consultations do not lead to an agreement between China and the WTO Member concerned within 60 days of the receipt of a request for consultations, the WTO Member affected "shall be free", in respect of such products, to withdraw concessions or otherwise to limit imports only to the extent necessary to prevent or remedy such market disruption. The application of China's safeguard provision shall be terminated 12 years after the date of accession. See Decision on China's Accession, *Accession of the People's Republic of China*, WT/L/432, para. 16 (Nov. 23, 2001). Rather than adopting a "market disruption" standard, the WTO Agreement on Safeguards in article 2.1 requires that a product is being imported under such conditions as to cause or threaten to cause "serious injury" to the domestic industry.

The Regulation on Safeguard of 2000 does not refer to article XIX of GATT 1994.[467] There is no reference in the Regulation of the circumstance of "unforeseen developments," as stipulated by article XIX.1(a) of GATT 1994, which is a prerequisite for imposing other safeguard conditions.[468] As it stands, the Safeguards Department is not obligated by the NPP Law of 2002 or the Regulation to examine the existence of "unforeseen developments" in its investigations.[469] Requiring a WTO member to define establish import surges as "unforeseen developments" as a condition for its application of safeguards could make it difficult for a member to utilize safeguard measures because such import surges may not easily be said to be unforeseen.

Proper and accurate translation seems to be an issue with respect to NPP Law and Regulation on Safeguard in Jordan.[470] Mistranslation could affect the application of the NPP Law. For example, precision in translating one of the most important terms in the safeguard provisions, serious injury, could pose a problem. Mistranslation of certain terms should not be regarded as inconsequential. Inaccurate or deliberately misleading translations of WTO safeguard provisions may make the translated law or regulation subject to criticism by other trading partners. Therefore, Jordan would have to update its vocabularies to reflect the WTO Safeguards Agreement or utilize equivalent terminology to be found in the WTO Safeguards Agreement.

In effect, Jordan adopted a unified system in its safeguard law. In other words, one organ, the Safeguards Department, investigates increases in imports and serious injuries to the domestic industry.[471] This unified system is reasonable because the Safeguards

---

[467] The WTO Agreement on Safeguards and article XIX of GATT 1994 must be read cumulatively. This is supported by article 1 of the WTO Agreement on Safeguards which states that the Agreement establishes rules for the application of safeguard measures which shall be understood to mean those provided for in article XIX of GATT 1994.

[468] According to some commentators, earlier in the history of article XIX of GATT, the requirement of "unforeseen development" was not required. See Ezra Ginzburg, *An Analysis of Article XIX: The Safeguard Problem after the Uruguay Round*, 17 Neb. L. Rev. 566, 568 (1992) (the unforeseen development requirement has little meaning. It has been read out of existence under the GATT). However, recent WTO Appellate Body decisions have restored the requirement of "unforeseen developments" in applying safeguard measures. See Appellate Body Report, *United States-Safeguard Measures on Imports of Fresh, Chilled or Frozen Lamb Meat from New Zealand and Australia*, WT/DS177/AB/R, at para. 69 (May 1, 2001).

[469] In actuality, the Department had factored "unforeseen developments" requirement in all safeguard cases it examined. However, this practice may not be satisfactory until the Regulation is amended to explicitly make reference to "unforeseen developments" requirement. The WTO Appellate Body in the Lamb case rejected the U.S. argument that the "unforeseen developments" needed to justify a safeguard measure could be inferred from the factual record of the investigating authority and demonstrated during WTO dispute settlement proceedings. See United States-Safeguard Measures on Imports of Fresh, Chilled or Frozen Lamb Meat, *supra* n. 468, at paras. 67 & 74. Sources in the Safeguards Department indicated that it currently prepares a daft regulation implementing the requirement of "unforeseen developments".

[470] See Notification from Jordan, *Committee on Anti-Dumping Practices-Committee on Subsidies and Countervailing Measures-Notification of Laws and Regulations under Articles 18.5 and 32.6 of the Agreements*, G/ADP/N/1/JOR/2/Corr.1 (June 8, 2004) (stating that a material error affected the translation of article 11(a) (2) [in the NPP Law of 2002] as the word "public" was replaced by "personal"). Certain linguistic characteristics such as the use of passive voice sentences and different tenses could contribute to further problems in translation.

Department can perform its function quickly and efficiently. In contrast, this could be disadvantageous because by centralizing the authority into the same Department, the investigation of increased imports and judgment regarding injuries may lack objectivity.

Jordan, in its attempt to improve its regime of safeguard measures, must take note that the WTO Agreement on Safeguards is a procedural agreement establishing certain minimal procedural requirements.[472] Jordan does not have to adhere to the exact words of the provisions of the Safeguards Agreement. In other words, Jordan could modify its law in a way that is different from the Agreement. For example, athough the WTO Agreement on Safeguards allows the use of safeguards for up to eight to ten year, Jordan could apply safeguards measures for only three years. Moreover, Jordan must take into account the WTO panel decisions. For example, recent WTO panel decisions have brought to life both the requirement of "unforeseen developments" as well as the requirement that competent authority must provide "explicit" findings that are "clear and unambiguous" and "do not merely imply or suggest an explanation".[473]

To meet the future demand of relief measures, Jordan must put in place a plan to help small and medium-sized firms access the safeguard system. The current system may pose problems for these companies with respect to the costs of complying with the NPP Law of 2002 or Regulation on Safeguard requirements, which include paper burdens, the formality, complexity, duration of the process, lack of knowledge and expertise about the safeguard law and its procedures, the need to work with other small producers or producer associations, and the cost of hiring external counsel.

In certain instances, the Safeguards Department should self-initiate safeguard investigations rather than wait for the domestic industry itself to petition for an investigation. Self-initiation of a safeguard investigation may enable the Safeguards Department to limit imports more quickly. If the domestic industry petitions for safeguard measures, it would take a longer period of time to impose restrictions on imports because the safeguard investigation would require a longer process. Therefore, self-initiation of safeguard investigation could produce faster results by cutting the time needed to conduct an investigation. Courts in Jordan have not yet developed an extensive jurisprudence in the area of trade remedy laws. This state of affairs reveals the inexperience of Jordanian courts in reviewing remedy law cases. This also indicates that the trade remedy system is relatively young; it was not until 2000 that Jordan introduced trade remedy laws and regulations.

---

[471] This is compared with the dual system in which two organs, whether independents or not, conduct the investigation of increase imports and the judgment of an injury.

[472] The WTO Agreement on Safeguards does not impose a simple arithmetic standard for determining increased imports or requires a certain pattern of imports.

[473] None of these terms appears in article 3.1 of the WTO Agreement on Safeguards which requires only publication of the findings and reasoned conclusions reached on all pertinent issues of fact and law. The ordinary meaning of these terms does not establish any level of clarity for the competent authority or require that it states its findings with a particular explicitness.

4. Customs Law

Customs laws and procedures are considered an important part of the trade system in Jordan. These laws and procedures regulate the flow of goods across the borders. One of the main functions of the Customs Department is the clearance of goods. Importers seeking to introduce goods into Jordan must file the appropriate documents and follow certain procedures and entry techniques. In some instances, traders could face opaque customs procedures that re associated with customs transactions.[474] For example, Jordan requires consularization or legalization of commercial bills by Jordanian consulates and chambers of commerce in the country of exportation for goods intended for export to Jordan.[475] Consularization or legalization of commercial bills may not be warranted because it adds to the costs of traders and could be considered, in effect, a non-tariff trade barrier.

Goods may enter Jordan for consumption, transit, warehousing, temporary importation, inward processing, or entry into a foreign trade zone.[476] These different forms of entry could be designed to serve the different interests of importers. Warehousing, entry into a foreign trade zone, and inward processing share one common feature- the deferral of customs duties.[477] Deferral of customs duties may help the financial situation of importers.

The owner of imported articles or the owner's designated customs broker must file a customs declaration at the port of entry.[478] The customs declaration could be accompanied by certificate of origin, bill of lading, or air waybill. Imported articles cannot be withdrawn unless customs procedures are completed and duties are paid.[479] However, the Customs Law of 1998 has provisions for releasing imported articles before final payment of tariffs or settling other customs issues, so long as the payment of tariffs can be insured through cash, bonds or other financial guarantees.[480] A system of posting financial guarantees separates between clearance of goods and customs matters such as tariffs. Depositing financial guarantees protects the government by securing tariffs owed

---

[474] See Pete W. Moore, *Doing Business in the Middle East: Politics and Economic Crisis in Jordan and Kuwait* 162, 166 (Cambridge U. Press 2004) (stating that some traders are concerned about the increase in the size and power of the Customs Department. They claim that bureaucratic problems with the Department are legion. Sometimes, completing a customs importation document requires 17 signatures).

[475] Jordan committed to phase out consularization of commercial bills by Dec. 31, 2002. See Report of the Working Party on the Accession of Jordan, *supra* note 379, at 72. Jordan has yet to rectify the practice of consularization as it committed itself. For example, as of 2005, the Embassy of Jordan in Washington, D.C requires legalization of commercial bills and charges $84 per document as a legalization fee. Commercial bills must also be legalized by the National U.S.-Arab Chamber of Commerce.

[476] Customs Law No. 20 of 1998, art. 65, al Jaridah al Rasmiyah No. 4305 (Official Gazette) (Oct. 1, 1998) as amended by Law No. 27 of 2000, al Jaridah al Rasmiyah No. 4443 (Official Gazette) (July 2, 2000).

[477] *Id.* arts. 88, 104, 122 & 133.

[478] *Id.* art. 61.

[479] Customs procedures include inspection and laboratory testing and analysis. *Id.* arts. 69, 73 & 82. Inspection and testing of imported articles suggest delays depending on the number of samples.

[480] *Id.* arts. 75, 82, 83, 85 & 87.

whereas at the same time expedites the clearance of goods for importers. However, small importers may find it difficult to deposit financial guarantees.

The Customs Law of 1998 provides the right of appeal against Customs rulings initially lies within the Customs Department.[481] Additionally, decisions of the Customs Department may be contested before the Customs Court.[482] The emphasis should be placed on administrative appeal, rather than on judicial appeal, as administrative procedures could resolve any customs-related dispute more quickely with lower costs for importers.

Because of the WTO, the Customs Department of Jordan has been aggressively overhauling its customs procedures by moving to upgrade its customs facilities and automate some aspects of the paper-based customs system. Moreover, the Customs Department has adopted many concepts and practices of trade facilitation. For example, the Customs Department provides green lane treatment to companies through expedited shipments free of or with *de minimis* inspections upon arrival at ports of entry.[483] Movement and clearance of imported articles would be based on a risk-management technique, which is essentially a methodical process for identifying high-risk shipments.[484] The risk-management system allows for the speedy clearance of low value or low volume imports. The risk-management system also allows for the speedy clearance for articles imported by a reliable company that has a long history of compliance with Customs Department rules.

Although the adoption of risk-management techniques is a step in the right direction, it will take time and resources to truly activate these techniques. Additionally, since Jordan depends to a certain degree on tariffs, the role of the Customs Department would be devoted largely to collecting revenue for the Treasury. Customs officials may delay imported articles for hours or days while waiting verification as to classification and valuation.[485]

The Customs Department makes available customs related laws, regulations, administrative rules, information on customs process, conditions for importation, charges applicable to Customs Law, tariff rates, tariff classification opinions, and bilateral and

---

[481] A committee of three senior officials within the Customs Department would examine disputes concerning value, origin, characteristics or tariff classification of imported articles. *Id.* art. 80.a.

[482] Customs Law of 1998 establishes Customs Court of First Instance and Customs Court of Appeal. In certain circumstances, decisions of the Customs Court of Appeal could be appealed before Court of Cassation. *Id.* arts. 80.d, 222.a, 224.a & 225.

[483] See Jordan Customs Department, *Selectivity in the ASYCUDA System*, http://www.customs.gov.jo/ publication.asp (accessed Mar. 4, 2005).

[484] See Customs Law No. 20 of 1998, *supra* note 476, art. 84. The idea of inspecting all imported articles is impractical and a poor use of limited resources. The risk-management technique limits the physical inspection of imported articles. It includes random sampling at different rates. The technique starts with the Customs Department when goods are imported and continues through inspection. All information related to goods will enter into a computerized system that would enable inspectors for later retrieval.

[485] Until there is further lowering of tariffs, there could be mistrust between customs officials and importers regarding smuggling and under-valuation for purpose of evading payment of tariffs.

regional trade agreements.[486] The Customs Department provides advanced rulings based on requests from traders who seek clarification on specific matters, such as classification and applicable tariff rates. Advance rulings prior to importation provide certainty and reduce delays. Advance rulings may also help small and medium-sized companies ascertain their respective risks before they enter into commercial transactions.

4.1 Tariff Classification and Valuation

Customs standards in Jordan have been streamlined in accordance with WTO rules. Among the most important changes was the development of a standardized method for imposing duties. While in the past questionable methodologies were used in customs valuation, now customs duties have become more predictable and are based on the WTO Customs Valuation Agreement.[487] Every imported product that enters into Jordan must be classified and valued. Selecting the appropriate tariff classification is significant for an importer because the classification determines which tariff rate will be imposed. Usually, an importer categorizes an imported article in such a way that provides the lowest tariff rate.

There are several methods to classify imported products. These methods include the description, physical characteristics, and usage. The issue of tariff classification may lead to divergent administrative and judicial interpretations. Courts in Jordan render their decisions based upon the proper classification of imported products using one or more of the above listed methods. For example, the question presented in one case related to the appropriate classification of imported tractors for semi-trailers.[488] The Customs Department divided the imported tractors for semi-trailers into tractors classified under item 87/4 of the tariff schedule subject to 400 fils per kilo weight and semi-trailers classified under item 87/14 subject to 40% *ad valorem* duty rate. The plaintiff contested the classification given and claimed that imported tractors for semi-trailers should be properly classified under item 87/1/b and be duty-free.[489] The Court of Cassation concluded that imported tractors for semi-trailers fell under item 87/1/b based upon the name, description, and the specific use of tractors for hauling semi-trailers, noting that a coupling device, located behind the chassis, is used to hold semi-trailers.[490] The Court of Cassation seemed to consider tractors for semi-trailers in their entirety rather than divided into parts because each part could not be used independently.

In essence, customs classification of imported products is usually about choosing between two or more competing tariff lines. The Court of Cassation may consult with

---

[486] The information is available at the Customs Department website with translation in English. See <http://www.customs.gov.jo>.
[487] Jordan confirmed that it would fully implement the WTO Customs Valuation Agreement from date of accession without recourse to any transitional period. Report of the Working Party on the Accession of Jordan, *supra* note 379, at 94. According to article 20.1 of the WTO Customs Valuation Agreement, developing countries were given until Jan. 1, 2000 to implement its provisions. However, the Customs Valuation Agreement contains provisions for extending the deadlines.
[488] See Decision No. 95/1554, Journal of the Jordanian Bar Association p. 1368 (No. 6 1996).
[489] *Id.* 1369.
[490] *Id.* 1370.

rules of interpretation of the integrated tariff schedule of the Arab League, opinions of the Customs Cooperation Council, scientific authorities, testimony of witnesses, and other information to determine the meaning of a specific tariff provision.[491] The Court of Cassation's reasoning in classification cases deserves some discussion. The Court of Cassation has, in some cases, agreed with the lower court decisions, while in other cases it has overruled their decisions. In a different set of cases, the Court of Cassation upheld and respected the decisions of the Customs Department. In customs classification cases, the plaintiff has the burden of proving that Customs Department's classification is not correct and that its claimed classification is valid. The Court of Cassation has used, on a case-by-case basis, different means to classify imports due the wide variety of products.

Once an imported product is properly classified, its customs value must be determined for the purpose of assessing the appropriate tariff. To comply with WTO rules, Jordan has shifted from a normal value scheme and database pricing to compute tariffs to transaction value methodology.[492] The normal value scheme calculates tariffs based on the price that goods would theoretically fetch in an open market between a buyer and a seller independent of each other. In database pricing, customs officials used prices stored and collected in databases to determine tariffs for imported products. Under the new customs valuation system, transaction value means that tariffs levied on imports are based on the invoice price of the item, as agreed upon by the importer and exporter.[493]

Customs valuation rules in Jordan mirror the language set out in the WTO Customs Valuation Agreement. The new Jordanian valuation system has the advantage of stability and consistency in evaluating the value of imported products and will hopefully encourage trade. The new Jordanian valuation system could also help speed the movement of goods as it requires the Customs Department to release imported goods immediately. Under the old valuation system, customs officials could have more discretion. Normal value and databases pricing could be fixed at levels higher than the actual price of imported products, which resulted in higher tariffs. The new valuation system would leave little room for the discretion of customs officials. Additionally, the new valuation system will likely contribute towards greater transparency in the Jordanian customs valuation system.

Since Jordan did not have the advantage of additional time to set up the necessary infrastructure to ensure compliance with WTO rules, it could face technical,

---

[491] See Decision No. 89/669, Journal of the Jordanian Bar Association p. 1193 (No. 6, 7 & 8 1991). Decision No. 95/1067, Journal of the Jordanian Bar Association p. 1620164 (No. 1, 2 & 3 1996). See also Decision No. 90/1104, Journal of the Jordanian Bar Association p. 2332 (No. 12 1991).

[492] In mid-1996, a reference price database for valuation of products had been initiated, but this database no longer existed. See Report of the Working Party on the Accession of Jordan, *supra* n. 379, at 90.

[493] Customs value could include the cost of loading, transport, and insurance as long as this is made on the basis of objective and quantifiable data. Transaction value is the primary basis for determining customs value. However, Customs Law of 1998 lays down rules and guidelines on how to determine customs value whenever customs officials have reasonable ground to doubt the authenticity of the declared import value. Customs officials could use the price of product when sold domestically in cases where transaction value cannot be determined or the computed value of the product. See Customs Law No. 20 of 1998, *supra* n. 397, arts. 28 & 29.

administrative, and financial problems in implementing and complying with the complicated WTO Agreement on Customs Valuation.[494] The implementation of the WTO Customs Valuation Agreement could stretch the capabilities of the already understaffed Customs Department. The Customs Department has to retrain its personnel for the new valuation system. To meet concerns regarding fraud and undervaluation, Jordan could introduce post-entry audits that would give customs officials authority to audit accounts and commercial documents to help verify the accuracy of customs declarations. Moreover, Jordan could also exchange information with the exporting country regarding the value of export products to ensure accuracy and reduce fraud.

4.2 The Harmonized Tariff Schedule of Jordan

Jordan uses the Convention on the Harmonized Commodity Description and Coding System as a basis for its national customs tariffs.[495] The Harmonized System is an international six-digit commodity classification developed under the auspices of the Customs Cooperation Council.[496] Individual countries can extend the classification to 8 digits for export purposes and to ten digits for customs purposes.[497]

The Harmonized Tariff Schedule of Jordan (JHTS) is updated regularly and extends to over 9241 tariff lines.[498] JHTS is represented in a tabular format incorporating 4 columns, each with specific information.[499] The first column is the H.S Code, which has 4 and/or 6 digits. In other words, this column is the Heading/Subheading column. As part of its HS system, Jordan has, in some cases, replaced the fifth and/or the sixth digit with

---

[494] See Lael Brainard, *Ready for Launch? The Prospects for Global Trade Negotiations*, 19 Brookings Rev. 14, 16 (2001) (implementing trade agreements can be extremely costly for developing countries. Some estimate that a typical developing country must spend $150 million to implement just three of the WTO's many agreements on intellectual property, customs valuation, and technical standards).

[495] The Convention entered into force on January 1, 1988 with 36 contracting parties, including Jordan, ratified it. See Hironori Asakura, *The Harmonized System and Rules of Origin*, 27 J.W T 5, 8 (1993).

[496] The Harmonized System is divided into 21 sections. Each of these sections groups together goods produced in the same sector of the economy. Each section comprises one or more chapters, with the entire nomenclature being composed of 97 chapters. Some chapters are reserved for future use. For example, section one (Chapters 1-5) covers live animals and products thereof, section two (Chapters 6-14) covers vegetable products, and section three (Chapter 15) covers animal and vegetable fats and oils. In the Harmonized System goods are classified by what they are. The Harmonized System nomenclature is logically structured by economic activity or component material. For example, animals and animal products are found in one section and machinery and mechanical appliances, which are grouped by function, are found in another. Chapters of sections I to XV are grouped by biological structure or by the component material from which articles are made. For those chapters in which goods are grouped by raw material, a vertical structure is used in which articles are often classified according to their degree of processing: raw materials, semi-manufactured, and manufactured products. For example, Chapter 44 contains items such as rough wood, wood roughly squared and some wooden finished products such as wooden tableware. Articles may also be classified according to the use or function. The classification by function mainly occurs in section XII and sections XVI-XXI. For example, section XVII contains chapters 88 (aircraft) and 89 (ships). See *International Convention on the Harmonized Commodity Description and Coding System* (June 14, 1983), 1035 U.N.T.S. 3.

[497] *Id.* art. 3.3.

[498] The tariff schedule is accessible at the Customs Department website. See <http://www.customs.gov.jo/downloads.asp> (last visited Mar. 31, 2004).

[499] See Table 8 in appendix 1, page 221.

"0" or "00" in accordance with article 4.3 of the Harmonized System Convention. The second column is the "article description" column and contains a description of the product. The third column is the "Collection Unit," which determines the appropriate unit of measure. The entire collection unit column in JHTS is based upon the value of the item. The fourth column appears under the heading "Duty Rate" and contains the different tariff rates that apply to the product in question.[500] JHTS does not contain a column marked "stat. Suffix" for the collection of trade data.

Approximately 98 percent of JHTS is based on *ad valorem* tariff set as a percentage of the value of the imported product.[501] The JHTS does not contain quotas, that is to that Jordan has abolished quantitative import restrictions. The JHTS is a rationalized tariff schedule, but not a complex one.[502] Tariffs rates are in the following six bands: zero, 5, 10,15, 20,and 30 percent, with the exception of tobacco, manufactured tobacco substitutes and alcoholic beverages that are subject to prohibitive rates in the range of 50 percent to 180 percent, and unwrought gold which is subject to a 0.5 percent tariff. One should immediately notice that Jordan's tariffs are concentrated on few levels and are not on a wide range. There is no multiplicity of tariff rates that would involve many different types and levels of tariffs. Thus, the JHTS structure renders greater tariff uniformity.

In addition, products imported into Jordan are subject to general sales tax (GST). Because of the national treatment principle, the same GST must also be imposed on domestic products. However, if there is no local production of the imported product, then the general sales tax on imported products will be a tariff-equivalent rate. A special sales tax is imposed on certain imported products such as vehicles in addition to GST.

The only complex aspect of Jordan's tariff system relates to imported vehicles. Currently, imported automobiles are taxed, excluding general and/or special sales taxes,

---

[500] The U.S. bases its rates of duty into three different tariff levels for all importable goods based on classifications of countries. Column 1 tariffs apply on the basis of MFN to all countries. Column 1 tariffs have been lowered over time through the GATT/WTO rounds of negotiations. Within column 1 there is a special rate of duty for imports from countries that the U.S. has a free trade agreement with such as Israel, Mexico, Canada, and Jordan or recipients of the Generalized System of Preferences, the Caribbean Basin Initiative, and the Andean Initiative. Column 2 tariffs, the highest level of tariffs, apply to countries denied MFN status such as non-market economies. Column 2 tariffs were enacted at the peak of the U.S. trade protectionist era in 1930s. They have not been lowered since their implementation. See *Tariff Act of 1930*, 19 U.S.C. § 1202 (2000). The U.S. harmonized tariff schedule is prepared for publication by the Office of Tariff Affairs and Trade Agreements and published by the Office of Statistics of the ITC.

[501] *Ad valorem* tariff rate is assessed on the basis of CIF which includes the costs of imported products in the country of origin at the time of clearance plus any other costs incidental to delivery at the port of entry in Jordan such as insurance and freight. For example, if imported pocket-size radio cassette-players, tariff line 852712000, valued JD100 were subject to 30 percent *ad valorem* tariff, then JD30 must be paid upon importation. In few cases, Jordan's HS has mixed or compound tariff that consists of *ad valorem* tariff and specific tariff, the latter being flat rate set per quantity or unit. For example, tariff line 010410000 of imported sheep is subject to 5 percent *ad valorem* tariff and JD2 per head. Therefore, one could say that *ad valorem* tariffs cover most tariff lines in Jordan.

[502] For example, Jordan's tariff schedule does not have complex tariffs that would assess a tariff rate on the basis of a maximum or minimum rate or on the basis of a product's attributes.

at a 10 percent to 30 percent duty rate depending on vehicle age or weight.[503] For example, passenger cars that are less than five years old are subject to a 25 percent tariff rate. Trailers may be subject to a 10 percent tariff rate. Buses and cars for the transporting of ten people or more and that have diesel engine would be subject to a 15 percent tariff rate. This vehicle tariff system does not use a flat rate of, for example, 10 percent on all vehicles. Moreover, the vehicle tariff system does not allow for a special tariff section for fuel economy or hybrid vehicles.[504] Customs personnel would compute the value of imported vehicles as a function of basic characteristics of the vehicle.[505]

Jordan's vehicle tariff system raises two interesting points. First, the vehicle tariff system presumes that the declared value of a car is dubious. The vehicle tariff system presumes that the importer is guilty of fraud. Second, the vehicle tariff system indicates that the Customs Department uses price catalogues to determine the customs valuation of imported vehicles. The use of price catalogues may result in arbitrary customs values. Moreover, the use of reference prices in catalogues is contrary to the WTO Customs Valuation Agreement, which requires the use of the actual transaction value of imported products, unless Jordan has asked for WTO permission to continue applying reference price on imported vehicles. Jordan uses price catalogues for imported vehicles because of consistent undervaluation by importers.

5. Pre-shipment Inspection

Jordan, in its protocol of accession to the WTO indicated that it i non-user of WTO Pre-shipment Inspection (PSI).[506] However, Jordan agreed that if in the future it uses PSI services, it will comply with the PSI.[507] This would involve hiring PSI companies to carry out their activities in a non-discriminatory manner and ensuring that such inspections do not result in less favorable treatment to the inspected goods as compared to like domestic products.[508] Furthermore, PSI services should take place in the exporting country or, if that is not possible, in the country where the goods are manufactured.[509] Moreover, Jordanian hired PSI companies would have to apply pre-shipment inspection services in a transparent manner.[510]

---

[503] See Jordan Customs Department, *How can you make a Self-Assessment of Duties and taxes Payable on your car*, http://www.customs.gov.jo/viewins.asp?id=222&title=Instructions (last updated Jan. 26, 2005).

[504] However, a note attached to the calculation method states that standard safety and environment equipments value is exempted from tariffs and general sales tax, provided it does not exceed 15 percent of the car value. *Id.*

[505] For 2004 models, price lists represented by car agents in Jordan would be used. To calculate duties/taxes payable on a car, the customs department states "you should know the value of your car, which may not necessarily be the value you declared or the car purchase price. It is in fact the price lists presented by car agents in Jordan for the brand new (2005) models". *Id.* Prior to 2004 models pricing must cover depreciation of equipment using a depreciation schedule. For example, while for 2005 models there is no depreciation, for 2004 models an 85 percent depreciation rate applies.

[506] See Report of the Working Party on the Accession of Jordan, *supra* n. 379, at 102.

[507] *Id.* 103.

[508] See WTO Agreement on Pre-shipment Inspection, art. 2.1 & 2.

[509] *Id.* 2.3.

[510] *Id.* 2.5. The WTO established a London-based entity to deal with disputes arising from pre-shipment inspections.

No obvious reason exists to explain why Jordan is not a user of the PSI procedure. Pre-shipment inspection involves an inspection by a private firm in the country of export before exportation to Jordan.[511] The inspection will help alleviate some of the bottlenecks in customs procedures. It is possible that Jordan felt that its Customs Department and other government agencies have the administrative institutional capacity to undertake the same functions that PSI companies would do and there have been few cases of corruption of customs officials or custom duty fraud.

In 2003, Jordan contracted with Bureau Veritas/BIVAC International to conduct pre-shipment inspection and issue certificates of conformity for products that meet the required standards.[512] Products subject to mandatory pre-shipment inspection include vehicles, electrical and electronic products, toys, and personal safety devices.[513] Food products are subject to voluntary pre-shipment inspection. Pre-shipment inspection of these products had lead to shipping delays.[514]

B. Market Access in Services

Jordan has agreed to extensive liberalization undertakings under the General Agreement on Trade in Services (GATS), which would open some sectors which were previously closed or restricted to foreign investment and participation.[515] Jordan has undertaken horizontal commitments in the cross-border movement of individuals and commercial presence covering all types of services. For example, in cross-border movement of individuals, Jordan attached requirements related to duration of stay, pre-employment conditions, recognition of professional qualifications, economic and labor market needs tests, and work permits.[516]

Jordan has made specific commitments in eleven major service sectors and 128 sub-sectors and activities. For example, in the business sector, Jordan has agreed to eliminate restrictions on market access and national treatment in legal services in the four modes of

---

[511] PSI companies check the shipment details of goods purchased abroad such as price, quantity, and quality in order to ensure that tariffs are fully paid on the goods.

[512] Jordan pre-shipment inspection system is similar to that of Saudi Arabia which was established in 1996, named International Conformity Certification Program. Saudi Arabia contracted with Inchicape Testing Services of Britain. The certification fee was set at 0.4 per $10,000 or above and 0.5 percent for less than $ 10,000 f.ob. The Saudi system is designed to insure product quality and safety. The Saudi system requires inspection and certification of seventy-six kinds of imports such as food, electric goods, and vehicles. See See Ex. Ref. Man. (BNA) 95:33 (Jan. 22, 2004).

[513] Id.

[514] On several occasions, Jordanian companies claim that Bureau Veritas has not been adhering to standard requirements and its activities have become obstacles to international trade. Jordanian companies have voiced specific complaints about what they see as unwarranted demands and unnecessary delays in clearing shipments.

[515] In addition to GATS, WTO members negotiated sectoral agreements such as the Agreement on Basic Telecommunication Services of 1997 and the WTO Financial Services Agreement of 1997. The detailed undertakings of Jordan for trade in services are included in a 39-page report. See Working Party on the Accession of Jordan, *Report of the Working Party on the Accession of Jordan*, WT/ACC/JOR/33 (Dec. 3, 1999).

[516] Id. 3-6 (paragraph references not avail.).

supply.[517] Thus, Jordan eliminated its rules, if any, that could restrict the rights of Jordanian and foreign lawyers to enter into partnerships or that could impose restrictions on the nationality of a foreign law firm. However, legal services of foreign law firms are limited to "advice" on "foreign law" only.[518] As a result, a U.S. law firm can advise or consult on international or U.S. law but it cannot advise clients on Jordanian domestic law.[519] Other fields of legal services, such as domestic litigation are not open to foreign lawyers.[520] Only Jordanian lawyers are allowed to litigate or plead before Jordanian courts. Although at first glance, it may seem that Jordan has opened its legal service sector to foreign lawyers, but, upon closer scrutiny, most legal activities remain off limits to foreign law firms.[521]

Jordan has granted limited market access to foreign auditing firms.[522] Auditing of financial records or verification reports of domestic companies by foreign auditors are restricted. Auditing must be performed by resident Jordanian auditors who pass qualification tests. However, foreign accounting firms can give opinions on company results, open representative offices in Jordan, or invest in joint ventures. These activities should help enhance transparency and improve accountancy standards.

In addition, Jordan has made concessions in architectural, engineering, urban planning, and landscape architectural services by allowing up to a 50 percent ceiling on foreign shareholding.[523] Foreign firms, however, are required to train and upgrade the technical and management skills of local employees. This seems to be an offset requirement for undertaking commitments in these service areas. In the field of medical services and health care, Jordan has removed all foreign equity restrictions, which means that foreign-owned medical services can offer medical services without these restrictions.[524] As a result, Jordan has two-tier health care system: the state-run medical system provided through state-owned enterprises or directly from the state and the private sector, which specializes for rich clients and high-end services.

Jordan has provided market-opening commitments in telecommunication services by opening its government-controlled telecommunications system to unfettered competition and foreign telecommunications companies.[525] In the audio-visual and related delivery

---

[517] *Id.* 5. The four modes of supply are: cross-border supply, consumption abroad, commercial presence, and presence of natural persons.

[518] *Id.* 6.

[519] A foreign law firm can advise or represent Jordan in its accession to the WTO since its international law but cannot do the same regarding domestic family law in Jordan.

[520] *Id.*

[521] Jordan permitted foreign law firms to advise on foreign law only in order to preserve the integrity of the legal profession in Jordan by prohibiting the entry of unqualified foreign lawyers or protect the domestic legal bar against global law firms. See *International Trade in the 21st Century* 227-228 (Khosrow Fatemi ed., Elsevier Sci. 1997) (the United States leads the world by a wide margin on the total number of lawyers and lawyers per million. It is also very interesting, or perhaps frightening, to further note that 35 percent of the lawyers in the world in 1992 lived, and presumably practiced law, in the United States).

[522] *Id.* 6.

[523] *Id.* 7.

[524] *Id.* 8, 25.

services, Jordan has made commitments, regarding market access and national treatment, in motion picture and videotape productions services, motion picture projection services, and sound recordings.[526] Jordan has, however, imposed foreign ownership restrictions and a nationality requirement for distribution services in this sector.[527] It is unclear whether the commitments scheduled by Jordan in this sector cover radio and television services or note.

Jordan has imposed several restrictions on distribution services, defined as commercial agency, wholesaling, retailing, and franchising services. Some of the restrictions include commercial presence requirements for cross-border trade, restrictions on the type of corporate entities that may be established, and foreign ownership restrictions.[528] Despite these restrictions, foreign wholesalers and retailers, through joint ventures, may be able to establish outlets, chain stores, and wholesale operations in Jordan in which they may sell their goods.

Jordan has removed and reduced obstacles of the transmission of educational services across its borders or the establishment of educational facilities including schools and offices.[529] Thus, Jordan has created favorable conditions for suppliers of higher education and adult education services. Additionally, education consumers can purchase their education abroad. Jordan has hoped that education liberalization may help lure foreign universities into establishing branches in Jordan.[530] It is my belief, however, that education in Jordan is and must be a government function. Liberalization of educational services should not erode the government ability to regulate education. Private education services ought to supplement and not displace public education. For example, private education could offer services that are not currently offered by government schools. Permitting private and public education to coexist in Jordan may help inject competition in the education system; but universities should not act more like commercial firms rather than academic institutions.

Jordan has also scheduled several commitments that cover areas such as life and non-life insurance services (e.g. transport, aviation, and accident insurance) and banking and other financial services (e.g. derivative trading and the provision and transfer of financial information).[531] There are no limitations on the number of service suppliers in the form of

---

[525] All restrictions on market access would be phased out by the end of 2004. Jordan commitments cover basic services which include mobile and wireline voice and data services, local and long distance domestic telephony, mobile radio (cellular, paging and personal communications services), international telecommunications, satellite services, private leasing services, network carrier and network access business and value-added services defined as email, voice mail, online information database storage and retrieval, online data processing, internet access service, internet content service, and videoconferencing services. *Id.* 13-16.

[526] *Id.* 16.

[527] *Id.*

[528] *Id.* 18.

[529] *Id.* 18-19.

[530] In 2005, the Chicago-based DePaul University opened a branch in Jordan offering programs in information privacy and secrecy, software engineering, knowledge management, and information system management (on file with author).

[531] *Id.* 20-25.

quotas, exclusive providers, or economic needs tests, local currency lending restrictions, restrictions on geographical expansion, and capital requirements. Jordan has, however, imposed several restrictions such as the type of establishment allowed.[532] Therefore, suppliers do not have the freedom to choose a preferred form of commercial presence whether a branch, subsidiary, or joint venture. Other restrictions include the level of equity participation and permitted business lines.[533] Liberalization of financial services may allow suppliers to supply certain financial services on a cross-border basis in reinsurance and retrocession services, insurance intermediation services, and services auxiliary to the provision of insurance.

Under article II of GATS, MFN treatment means that measures should be applied to all service transactions without discrimination among countries. However, members are permitted to list MFN exemptions in the service sector. Jordan listed 12 MFN exemptions.[534] Four exemptions are cross-sectoral exemptions related to movement of natural persons such as work permit fees or investment such as preferential measures and purchase of land. Eight of the exemptions are sector-specific exemptions. These sector-specific exemptions are related to professional services, audiovisual services, travel-related services, press services, and land-based transport services.

Jordan made market-opening commitments across a whole range of services ranging from business and telecommunications to education and transportation. The coverage of the service sector is relatively complete. However, there are differences in terms of broad liberalization and full bindings in different service sectors. For example, Jordan liberalized its education, telecommunications, and recreational services while imposed limits on financial services, auditing services, and architectural and engineering services. Many of Jordan's limitations on market access are in the form of residency limits, form of legal entity, foreign equity, and nationality.

GATS provided some flexibility to Jordan in scheduling its commitments to liberalize trade in services. However, this flexibility can be challenged by recent WTO dispute settlement cases such as Mexico's telecom case and the U.S. gambling case.[535] Therefore, Jordan must take care in scheduling future commitments. Alternatively, Jordan can liberalize its service sectors without being written in its schedule of specific commitments. Moreover, Jordan can modify or withdraw some of its commitments under GATS, but other countries would seek compensatory trade concessions. Jordan is building a new economy based on knowledge-based industries. Trade in services may offer Jordanian service providers, small and medium-sized businesses, great potential for opportunities. At the same time, liberalization of the service sector in Jordan could harm service firms, since they have weaknesses in resources, management, and know-how.

---

[532] Id. 20.

[533] Id. 22.

[534] Id. 36-39. The twelve MFN exemptions apply indefinitely. Therefore, Jordan may not need to phase out these exemptions. However, in future trade negotiation rounds, Jordan could eliminate MFN exemptions. It is unclear to what extent some of these exemptions are applied in reality or have substantial significance.

[535] See Panel Report, *Mexico-Measures Affecting Telecommunications Services*, WT/DS204/R (Apr. 2, 2004). See also Panel Report, *United States-Measures Affecting the Cross-border Supply of Gambling and Betting Services*, WT/DS285/R (Nov. 10, 2004).

C. Protection of Intellectual Property in Jordan

The intellectual property regime in Jordan proved to be a stumbling block for Jordan's accession to the WTO. Jordan committed in its accession to the WTO to comply fully with the WTO Agreement on Trade-Related Aspects of Intellectual Property Rights (TRIPs), from the date of accession, without recourse to any transitional period.[536] The question of Jordan's compliance has gained importance, especially given the decision by the USTR to unlist Jordan from the watch list of Special 301 in 1999.[537] Compliance with TRIPS and the un-listing from the U.S. watch list of Special 301 helped Jordan accede to the WTO.

It is beyond the scope of this section to give a very comprehensive analysis of the history and various forms of intellectual property rights. Therefore, it suffices to highlight the main areas where changes in Jordan's intellectual property regime were driven by TRIPs. This section seeks to compare Jordan's current intellectual property laws with its obligations under the TRIPs Agreement. The main intellectual property rights are set out below.

1. Copyright Law

The international conventions that protect copyright works are the Berne Convention and the TRIPs Agreement. Countries acceding to the WTO must comply with the TRIPs Agreement as well as the Berne Convention.[538] However, the TRIPs Agreement does not recognize moral rights of copyrighted works.[539] Moreover, the TRIPs Agreement addresses aspects of copyright related to new technologies, such as computer programs.

Jordan's copyright law can be primarily found in the Copyright Law of 2001. Under the Copyright Law, the subject matter of copyright protection is literary, scientific, and artistic works.[540] These conventional works include written materials, music, works of fine arts, such as paintings and photography, and technology-based works such as

---

[536] See Report of the Working Party on the Accession of Jordan, *supra* n. 379, at 230. Despite several attempts by Jordanian officials and negotiators, Jordan was not given a transition period to comply with its TRIPs obligations. The U.S. and EC firmly held their no-transition position by arguing that every acceding country must comply with TRIPs immediately upon accession.

[537] Jordan had been on the U.S. watch list for quite sometime, where the U.S. has closely watched Jordan's intellectual property regime. The situation worsened when there was discussion in 1998 on whether Jordan would be targeted with trade sanctions under Special 301 of the 1988 Omnibus Trade and Competitiveness Act for failing to adequately protect U.S. copyrights, patents, and trademarks. However, one could say that imposing sanctions against Jordan under Special 301 would have been counterproductive because that would interfere with other U.S. foreign policy priorities.

[538] Article 9.1 of TRIPs requires members to comply with articles 1 through 21, with the exception of article 6bis, of the 1971 Paris Act of the Berne Convention and the Appendix thereto (that is, the substantive provisions of that Convention). Jordan joined the Berne Convention in 1999.

[539] In fact, the TRIPS Agreement explicitly excludes article *6bis* of the Berne Convention on moral rights from its application. See TRIPS, art. 9.1.

[540] See Provisional Copyright Law No. 52 of 2001, art. 3.a, al Jaridah al Rasmiyah No. 4508 (Official Gazette) (Oct. 1, 2001). This is in compliance with article 2 of the Berne Convention.

computer programs.[541] In addition, Jordan's Copyright Law of 2001 includes software within the ambit of copyright protection. Foreign software developers would rely on explicit provisions for protection before licensing their best technologies. Article 3.d of the Copyright Law also mandates protection for encyclopedias, an area not previously covered, which by reason of selection or arrangement of contents constitute intellectual creations as such. The list in the Copyright Law is not at all inclusive, but illustrative.[542]

Copyright protects the expression of thoughts but not the ideas itself.[543] For example, if somebody writes a book about Jordan's accession to the WTO, his/her expressions are protected, but not the idea or the topic of Jordan's accession to the WTO, since anybody could write about Jordan's accession to the WTO.[544] Under Jordan's Copyright Law, innovative expressions are protected.[545] The inquiry that must be pursued by courts and commentators in Jordan is whether the Copyright Law should protect a work as a whole (for example a statistical form), including original expressions, non-original expressions, and facts, or if it should protect the original expressive elements of a work so as to identify them with as much certainty as possible. In other words, the question is whether to adopt the "work as a whole" approach or the "element by element" approach.

The Copyright Law applies to published or unpublished works of Jordanians and foreigners.[546] The Copyright Law requires Jordan to extend its copyright law protection to nationals of other countries in a non-discriminatory manner.[547] Thus, the Copyright Law recognizes the personal status of the author as a Jordanian citizen or national (including resident) of another country as a connecting factor to secure copyright protection in Jordan.

There are certain works that are excluded from protection under the Copyright Law. For example, legislations, regulations, judicial decisions, and other official texts of a

---

[541] *Id.* art. 3.b.

[542] This is supported by the use of the word "in particular". *Id.*

[543] See TRIPS, art. 9.2.

[544] A Copyright does not preclude others from independently creating similar expressions.

[545] Copyright Law of 2001 provides that a work is made when it is reduced to writing or other material form. There are no other formalities for copyright to be acquired or as pre-condition of filing a lawsuit. For example, there are no requirements for registration of the work, recordation, or copyright notice. See Provisional Copyright Law No. 52 of 2001, *supra* note 540, art. 3.a &b. Article 38 of the Copyright Law addresses filing of best edition of a published work with the Filing Center in the National Library Department. However, it seems that the Law established a policy of flexibility by stating in article 45 that non-filing cannot be considered a violation of the Law. As such, filing is considered a procedural step and not condition to secure copyright protection. Depositing a published work in the Filing Center would help the flow of materials to the Department, evidentiary use in the judicial system, and serve the public interest in an open and comprehensive registry.

[546] *Id.* art. 53.a.

[547] However, under article 53.b of the Copyright Law of 2001, copyright protection would apply based on reciprocity, not national treatment, for non-members of an international copyright agreement (the Berne Convention). In any case, Jordan will have to apply its copyright law to works of all TRIPs members even if they are not parties to the Berne Convention by virtue of the principles of national treatment and MFN incorporated in the TRIPs. On this basis, one can argue that Jordan is obliged to protect works of TRIPs parties who may or may not be parties to the Bern Convention.

legislative, administrative or legal nature are not protected.[548] However, these official texts are protected to the extent that they involve innovation in their arrangement. For example, if a person compiles Jordan's trade laws, bilateral trade agreements, and WTO Agreements in a supplementary book by providing indices, certain selections for publication, or brief commentaries at the end of each article, then the compilation could be copyrighted. There is no copyright in news information *per se*. Political or legal speeches are copyrightable if they are literary works reduced to writing or other material form.

Folklore communicated to the public by performers are protected under the Copyright Law.[549] The Minister of Culture will exercise his/her authority as the owner of folklore by providing protection against distortion or misrepresentation.[550] In other words, the Minister of Culture will exercise his authority over these works as "moral rights". Thus, protection of the vast, ancient and invaluable cultural expression is afforded, when there is distortion or misrepresentation, by all means without limitation in time. The provisions the Copyright Law, however, do not speak of the Minister of Culture exercising economic rights over these works, although he could.

1.1 Exclusive Rights

There are two types of rights under the Copyright Law. These are economic rights, which allow the author of a work to derive financial reward (through licensing) from the use of his/her work by others, and the other is moral rights, which allow the author to take certain actions to preserve the personal linkage between him and the work.[551] The Copyright Law sets out a number of exclusive rights which are to be granted to an author. The right of the author of a copyrighted work to exclude others from making copies of his/her work is the basic right under copyright law. Economic rights involve commercial exploitation of protected works including the right of publishing.[552] Other economic rights include the right of broadcasting, the right to authorize distribution, the right of reproduction, the right of commercial rental, and the right of public recitation.[553]

The Copyright Law protects acts of translation and adaptation.[554] Since translation and adaptation are works protected by the Copyright Law, an authorization must be

---

[548] *Id.* art. 7.a.

[549] Examples of folklore include such artistic expressions as a tribal dance, folklore pillow covers, and folklore wall hangings.

[550] Because works of folklore do not have a single identifiable author capable of exploiting these works, the Copyright Law gives ownership of such works to the Minister of Culture.

[551] *Id.* arts. 8 & 9.

[552] *Id.* art. 9.a, b.

[553] The right of rental is not available under the Berne Convention. However, it is made available under article 11 of TRIPs. The right of rental is important because technological advances such as digital audio tape made it very easy to copy computer-based programs, films, or sound recordings by customers of rental stores. Therefore, the right to control commercial rental practices is necessary in order to safeguard the copyright owner's sales market and royalties.

[554] *Id.* arts. 9.c & 5.a. Translation means the expression of a work in a language other than that of the original version. Adaptation means the modification or conversion of a work to create another work such as converting a novel into a motion picture.

obtained for any reproduction or publication of translated or adapted copy from both the owner of the copyright of the original pre-existing work as well as the adaptator or translator. Furthermore, article 23 of the Copyright Law covers neighboring or related rights.[555] The Copyright Law confers rights on performers, broadcasting organizations, and producers of phonograms.[556] In principle, the rights of holders of these related rights are similar to the rights of holders of other copyrighted works.

1.2 Moral Rights

Moral rights of authorship and integrity are distinct from the bundle of economic or exploitation rights that are usually associated with copyright. Economic rights of the type mentioned earlier can be transferred or assigned to others in return for royalties. However, the second type of rights, moral rights, cannot be transferred. Moral rights are inalienable and perpetual. Moral rights always remain with the original author of the copyrighted work.

Article 8 of the Copyright Law recognizes moral rights.[557] The basis for these rights is the personal linkage between the work and its author. The author has the right to claim/disclaim a work as his own (authorship or paternity) and to safeguard the work from distortion, mutilation, and other amendments which would be prejudicial to his reputation or honor (integrity). Based on moral rights, an author in Jordan can prevent others from passing off his work as theirs or he can block usage of a work, such as in parody, which he feels will prejudice his honor.

1.3 Exceptions

There are certain exceptions or limitations to the general rule of prior authorization from the owner of a work. Some of these exceptions fall under a three-step test of article 13 of the TRIPs Agreement. Other limitations fall under article 9.1 of the TRIPs Agreement that include the appendix of the Berne Convention of 1971. The former limitations could be labeled as "fair uses", and the latter as "non-voluntary licenses". Both of these exceptions are covered under the Copyright Law.[558] The difference between the fair use and non-voluntary license is that under free use exploitation of a copyrighted work is carried out without any authorization or an undertaking to remunerate the owner of copyrighted work for the use. On other hand, exploitation under

---

[555] Neighboring rights is named as such because they build upon and relate to already protected copyrighted works. For example, a singer that performs a composer's work to the public is considered a holder of a neighboring right.

[556] The right of performers is recognized because their creativity gives spirit to the body of poems for example. The same recognition also applies to broadcasting organizations because of their contribution of making works available to the public. Additionally, producers of sound recordings are recognized because their creativity in contributing to the work.

[557] The often-used translation in Arabic (in Jordan) for the word "copyright" is the author's right. The use of the term "author's right" places more emphasis on moral rights (with a personality link), as opposed to only economic rights of the author, such as reproduction, of the author. Article 6bis of Berne Convention requires members to recognize the author's moral right of integrity and the right to claim authorship.

[558] Article 11 of the Copyright Law governs non-voluntary licensing and article 17 governs fair use.

the non-voluntary license is carried out without any authorization, but with the obligation to compensate the owner of rights.[559]

For example, under the fair dealing defense of the Copyright Law, individuals are allowed to make a single copy of the work for private personal purposes, provided that such reproduction does not conflict with a normal exploitation of the work and does not unreasonably prejudice the legitimate interests of the author.[560] Other examples supporting the fair dealing defenses include reproduction of articles published in newspapers or periodicals on current economic, political or religious topics, reproduction for research, illustration for teaching purposes, library use, short extracts for criticism, or review within the limits justified and with proper citation.[561] There are certain factors that courts in Jordan take into account when judging whether the case in question involves a fair use defense. These factors could include the purpose of the use, nature of the work used, amount of quotation or use of the copyrighted work, and amount of financial gain, if any.

The other limitation on the exclusive rights of the owner of a copyrighted work is the non-voluntary license, which allows for the use of works under certain circumstances and conditions without the authorization of the owner.[562] Article 11 of the Copyright Law sets out a scheme whereby citizens of Jordan can apply under certain conditions to the Minister of Culture or his assignee for permission to translate foreign works for the purposes of teaching, scholarship and research.[563] However, for any work translated or reproduced via a non-voluntary license, by virtue of the Copyright Law, fair compensation must be paid in respect of the use.[564] The purpose of non-voluntary licensing in the Copyright Law is the dissemination of copyrighted works to the public where the national legislature fears that the non-availability of these works could hinder the dissemination and development of knowledge.

---

[559] *Id.* art. 11.d.

[560] *Id.* art. 17.b. This is in compliance with article 13 of the TRIPs Agreement. In Jordan, fair use defenses are limited to "published" works. It seems that there is a distinction between published and unpublished works for fair use purposes. As such, a biographer or historian may not cite excerpts from an unpublished biography.

[561] *Id.* arts. 17.d, 18 & 20.

[562] The Copyright Law in article 11 authorizes non-voluntary licenses. Therefore, non-voluntary licenses are determined specifically in the law and do not result from the discretion of any person including the copyright owner. Article 11 is in line with the Appendix of the Berne Convention of 1971 that allows these exceptions for developing countries. Article I of the Appendix limits the application of the Appendix to countries which are regarded as developing in conformity with the established practice of the General Assembly of the U.N. Any developing country member of the Berne Convention which wishes to introduce the special compulsory licenses is required to deposit a declaration notification with the Director General of WIPO.

[563] *Id.* art. 11.a &c.

[564] *Id.* art. 11.d.

1.4 Copyright Term

The copyright period required by the Copyright Law is the life of the author and 50 years after his death. [565] The term of protection for cinematographic and television works, any work whose author or right holder is a legal entity, any work published for the first time after the death of its author, and anonymous and pseudonymous works is 50 years from the date of publication.[566] However, photographic and applied art works are protected for 25 years.[567] This is because the Copyright Law does not assimilate applied art and photographic works, for example to other literary works, but rather provides them with protection for shorter periods.

The period of protection for performers and producers of phonograms is until the end of 50 years from the end of the year in which the fixation was made or the performance took place.[568] The term of protection for broadcasting organizations is 20 years from the end of the year in which the broadcasting took place.[569] As stipulated under the TRIPs Agreement, the Copyright Law granted the minimum period of protection.

1.5 Remedies

The Copyright Law expressly deals with the question of available remedies for a copyright infringement.[570] Enforcement provisions are to be found in articles 46-52 of the law. These measures could be divided into provisional measures, civil remedies, criminal penalties, and measures taken at the border. Provisional measures include search and seizure of infringing copies, and evidence of infringement on a protective basis in an interlocutory proceeding. These measures have the purpose of preventing infringements from occurring and preserving relevant evidence.[571] Civil remedies compensate the owner of rights for economic injury suffered because of infringement.[572] Criminal sanctions are intended to punish those who commit acts of infringement, theft, or piracy of copyright and related rights and, as in the case of civil remedies, to deter further infringement.[573] The final category of remedies is measures to be taken at the borders.[574]

---

[565] *Id.* art. 30. Term of protection under Jordan's Copyright Law is in line with article 7.1 of the Berne Convention which provides protection for lifetime plus 50 years after death. It is also in compliance with article 12 of the TRIPs Agreement.

[566] *Id.* art. 31.

[567] *Id.* art. 32.

[568] *Id.* art. 23.d. The TRIPs standard is higher since the period of protection under the Rome Convention for the Protection of Performers, Producers of Phonograms and Broadcasting Organizations is only 20 years.

[569] *Id.* art. 23.e.

[570] The Copyright Law grants the staff of the Copyright Protection Office within the National Library Department the status of judicial police. The staff of the Copyright Protection Office, which is limited in number and finance, can search premises without the need for a warranty or being accompanied by police officers, or stop and board a vehicle suspected of having in its possession goods which violate intellectual property rights. *Id.* art. 36.

[571] *Id.* arts. 46.c & d.

[572] *Id.* art. 49.

[573] The Copyright Law requires an intention, for purposes of imposing criminal penalties. *Id.* art. 51.a. The purpose of punishment is served by imposing a substantial fine or sentencing that corresponds to the seriousness of the crime particularly in cases of repeat offenses. Under the Copyright Law, criminal

The Copyright Law does not cover border measures, but rather such measures are covered under the Customs Law.[575]

2. Trademarks

Jordan passed the Trademarks Law of 1999 to comply with the TRIPs Agreement and its obligation to comply with the Paris Convention for the Protection of Industrial Property (1967). The Trademarks Law describes a trademark in the broadest sense as any visually perceptible sign, such as a word, logo, number, letter, slogan, or color.[576] The Trademarks Law does not apply to nontraditional trademarks such as sound or smell.[577] The Trademarks Law recognizes service marks, which is an area that was previously not recognized.[578] Given the fact that almost 70 percent of Jordan's GDP comes from services, protection of service marks is essential in the services industry.

The Trademarks Law determines the conditions and procedures for the filing and registration of trademarks. Under the Law, a trademark has to meet the requirement of being distinctive.[579] For example, the word "vegetable" cannot be registered as a trademark for carrots, since it is a generic term for carrots. However, factual distinctiveness, as supposed to inherent distinctiveness, could be acquired through use.[580] In other words, these marks could be protected if they acquire secondary meaning.

The Trademarks Law addresses the intent-to-use system, and does not require actual use of a trademark as a condition for filing a registration.[581] An intention to use the

penalties are imprisonment for a period between 3 months to 3 years and a fine of JD1000-3000, or one of these two sentences. In cases of repetition, penalties would be applied to the maximum.

[574] Border measures are different from other enforcement measures in that they involve actions by customs authorities at the borders, rather than by the judicial authorities.

[575] The rights holder may petition the court, after depositing a cash or bank guarantee and submitting sufficient evidence, to suspend the release of suspected infringing products. In case of suspected infringement of intellectual property rights related to copyright and trademark, the clearance of imported goods can be suspended if there is a *prima facie* case of infringement. See Customs Law No. 20 of 1998, *supra* n. 397, art. 13.

[576] The Trademarks Law defines a trademark as any visually perceptible mark used or shall be used by any person to distinguish his goods or services from the goods or services of others. See Trademarks Law No. 34 of 1999, arts. 7, 7.1, 4 & 12 al Jaridah al Rasmiyah No. 4389 Official Gazette (Nov. 1, 1999). This is in compliance with article 15 of the TRIPs Agreement which states that a member "may" require, as a condition of registration, that a sign be visually perceptible. In respect to colors, the limitation of a trademark to a color(s) may be a basis for the establishment of distinctiveness. Colors themselves such as the color orange could be treated as trademarks.

[577] For example, a fragrance trademark can never be registered. The registration of fragrances or sounds would present complex challenges for trademark examiners in MIT in Jordan. It is unclear how fragrances or sounds would be categorized, catalogued, preserved during the registration period, or searched and tested for confusing similarity.

[578] When a mark is used in connection with services, it is sometimes referred to as a service mark. See *Trademark Law Amendment Enacted, Published*, 14.3 World Intell. Prop. Rep. (BNA) (Mar. 15, 2000) (prior to the amendment of Jordan's Trademarks Law, applicants could only protect service marks under class 16 for publication and printed material).

[579] See Trademarks Law No. 34 of 1999, *supra* n. 576, art. 7.1.

[580] *Id.* arts. 7.3 & 8.7.

[581] *Id.* art. 11.1.

trademark for the goods, with respect to which the trademark is to be registered is sufficient. The intent-to-use requirement may lead to an increase in the number of trademark applications. Evidence of intent-to-use could be demonstrated through an on-going business.

The Trademarks Law allows opposition during the prosecution of a trademark application.[582] In such cases, a petitioner must show a valid ground as to why the applicant is not entitled to register his trademark.[583] The Trademarks Law does not specify statutory grounds which would negate the entitlement to the registration, such as the requirement that the opposer proves fraudulent information or economic damage.

Concurrent use of a trademark on identical or similar goods does not prevent registration.[584] However, a concurrent use registration may be granted upon the discretion of the Registrar. Moreover, the Registrar determines the circumstances and conditions for such registration.[585]

Under the principle of territoriality, a trademark has to be registered in Jordan before being protected.[586] The Trademarks Law grants protection in 10-year renewable terms.[587] The owner of a registered trademark has the exclusive right to prevent third party not having obtained his/her consent from usage in the course of trade, identical or similar signs for goods or services which are identical or similar to those registered trademarks where such use would result in a likelihood of confusion.[588] This means that the burden of proving consent of the proprietor would fall on the defendant.

The Trademarks Law provides penalties against offenders who misrepresent goods or use counterfeit trademarks.[589] The Trademarks Law provides for a cease and desist order.[590] The Trademarks Law also provides for an interlocutory seizure of goods, which would take place at the request of the owner of a trademark. Moreover, the Trademarks Law specifically provides for destruction or disposal of materials or tools used in the infringement of trademarks.[591]

2.1 Well Known Marks

---

[582] *Id.* art. 14.
[583] *Id.* art. 14.2.
[584] *Id.* art. 18.
[585] For example, a registration could be granted if the use does not result in misleading the public and is not contrary to the public interest.
[586] *Id.* art. 34.1.
[587] *Id.* art. 20. The pre-1999 Trademarks Law set the initial term of registration and subsequent renewal terms at seven and fourteen years respectively.
[588] *Id.* art. 26. 1. Where an identical sign is used for identical goods or services, a likelihood of confusion is to be presumed. This is in compliance with article 16 of TRIPs.
[589] The Trademarks Law provides penalties that include JD100-3000 fine, 3 months-1 year imprisonment, or both.
[590] *Id.* art. 39.
[591] *Id.* art. 39.4.

Protection of well known marks in Jordan an area where some reform was needed to ensure compliance with the Paris Convention and the TRIPs obligation to protect well known marks. Due to the lack of explicit provisions preventing the registration of well known marks, many local Jordanian companies filed applications to register well known marks under their own names.[592] The simplistic approach to register trademarks in Jordan contributed to the registration of well known marks.[593] Trademark rights were granted to the first persons or entities to register in Jordan regardless to prior use in Jordan or elsewhere.[594] This approach allowed a third party to acquire rights to internationally famous marks by registering them in Jordan as their own.

Many foreign owners of well known trademarks had to litigate in Jordan because of the trademark registrations by Jordanian persons. For example, Shaheen International Corporation Co. filed an application to register the mark PILLSBURY in its name in Jordan.[595] In another example, Hani Al-Qudsi & Partners, a Jordanian Company, filed a trademark application to register the mark "7ELEVEN" in class 16.[596] Farid Khalaf Company, a Jordanian company, filed to register the mark "MILLER" in Jordan in class 32 for beers.[597] In other cases, foreign owners of well known marks were unable to prevent registration of similar marks by Jordanian persons. For example, a Jordanian company, Jordanian Trico & Yarn Factory Co., filed a trademark application for "AL

---

[592] See Amir H. Khoury, *The development of Modern Trademark Legislation and Protection in Arab Countries of the Middle East*, 16 Transnat'l Law. 249, 269, 321 (2003) (this is not to say that well-known marks were without protection. In fact, two practical defenses against unauthorized use of well-known marks were employed. First, an examiner that identifies a certain mark as being owned by a third party may, based on his own personal knowledge, refuse to register the mark in the name of the applicant. Second, any party who claimed right to a well-known registered mark was entitled to institute opposition proceedings against its registration).

[593] The Jordanian law is rather lax regarding documentation that is required when applying for a trademark. All that is required is a general or specific power of attorney. *Id.* 271.

[594] *Id.* 309.

[595] However, the Pillsbury Company filed an opposition contesting such registration and contending that its PILLSBURY mark is a well known mark used to market its ready-made dough and bakery products worldwide including in Jordan. As a result, a settlement was reached whereby Shaheen agreed to assign the trademark registration over to the Pillsbury Company in return for the latter's agreement not to initiate legal action for damages or compensation. *Id.* 321.

[596] The Southland Corporation, a U.S. corporation, filed an opposition claiming that the Jordanian applicant was not entitled to such registration since it uses and owns registrations of the mark "7ELEVEN" in various countries worldwide. The Southland Corporation prevailed in its opposition not so much on the merits but rather on points of procedure. The Jordanian Company did not submit its response to the opposition on time. *Id.*

[597] Miller Brewing Company, owner of the famous mark MILLER, filed an opposition and contended that it was the owner of the famous MILLER trademark that is registered and used in several countries worldwide. It further contended that the fact that its MILLER mark was not registered in Jordan should not adversely affect the opposition. The Jordanian trademark registrar ruled in favor of Miller Brewing Company and rejected Khalaf's application. The registrar reasoned that Khalaf's registration would cause consumer deception and constitute unfair competition and false indication of origin of the goods bearing the mark. The Jordanian High Court of Justice affirmed the registrar's decision. *Id.* 322. In another example, Al-Nasser & Mosely Company, a Jordanian company, filed a trademark registration in "SUBWAY" trademark in class 30. The Registrar also cancelled the registration of ten other trademarks, which included the characters of WINNIE THE POOH, DUMBO, ALADDIN, and LION KING, registered in the name of the Jordanian Halawani Industrial Company for potato chips because they were well known marks owned, registered, and used worldwide by the Walt Disney Company.

TIMSAH" mark, in class 32, which means a crocodile in Arabic, similar to that filed by La Chemise Lacoste, a French company.[598]

Since 1999, well known marks are expressly protected. The Trademarks Law sets out special provisions to protect well known marks. The Law defines well known trademarks as marks that are widely known to the relevant public in Jordan and that enjoy a high international reputation.[599] Therefore, in judging whether a mark is a well known or not, one determine whether the mark has surpassed the borders of its country of origin and that the mark is well known to the relevant consumer segment in Jordan.

The Trademarks Law prohibits the registration of a trademark which constitutes a reproduction or translation, liable to create confusion, of a well known mark on identical or similar goods.[600] Moreover, the Trademarks Law prohibits the use of a well known but unregistered trademark on dissimilar goods and services, provided that the use of that trademark in relation to those goods or services would indicate a connection between those goods or services and the owner of the trademark, and provided that the interests of the owner of the trademark are likely to be damaged by such use.[601] Thus, a well known mark may be defended even if it is not registered or the owner does not carry on a business in Jordan.[602]

2.2 Parallel Importation

The Trademarks Law does not clearly address whether parallel imports infringe trademark rights. The Trademarks Law provides the trademark owner, who registered his/her mark in Jordan, the exclusive right to "use" that trademark.[603] However, there is no clear definition of the word "use" *per se* in the Law. Courts in Jordan have yet to interpret the term to determine its scope.

A commercial agent is an importer, distributor, and trader and a foreign supplier is an exporter.[604] Therefore, a corollary dimension arises in relation to the application of the

---

[598] The Registrar rejected Lacoste's opposition for the registration of "AL TIMSAH" mark on the basis that the two marks, AL TIMSAH and LACOSTE, were in different classes and there was no likelihood of confusion. *Id.* 324. In another case, Time Warner Entertainment Company filed an opposition against the registration of the trademark TOTO, a depiction of the famous cartoon character Tweety, in Jordan. The Jordanian application was filed by Sobhi Jabri & Sons Co and was intended to cover goods in class 30 (food). In its opposition, Time Warner contended that it owned the rights over its famous "Tweety" character and its opposition should be accepted. However, the Registrar rejected the opposition ruling because no convincing evidence was submitted to prove that Time Warner was using the "Tweety" character with respect to goods in class 30. In addition, the Registrar reasoned that this cartoon character is only protected by copyright law and not trademark law.

[599] See Trademarks Law No. 34 of 1999, *supra* n. 576, art. 2.

[600] *Id.* art. 8.12.

[601] *Id.* art. 26.1.

[602] It could be better to register well marks to avoid any dispute.

[603] See Trademarks Law No. 34 of 1999, *supra* n. 576, art. 26.1.

[604] Commercial Agency Law No. 28 of 2001, art. 2, al Jaridah al Rasmiyah No. 4496 (Official Gazette) (July 16, 2001).

laws on agency, which is the controversial subject of parallel importation.[605] Customs officials in Jordan do not bloc parallel imports. There is no blanket policy of blocking such parallel imports officially, though they may be blocked privately by agreement between the supplier and the distributor. If there is a violation of the terms of a commercial agency/exclusive license agreement, the agent/distributor could enforce his rights in courts but not through Customs.[606]

Many parallel import cases in Jordan involve trademarks and commercial agency laws.[607] The Commercial Agency Law deals with exclusive agency contracts, distribution of goods, distribution channels, and territorial limits. In one case, Jordan Mechanical Engineering Company, a Jordanian company, acted as an agent and distributor of "Maggi" chicken stock cubes, which is a product of Nestle, a Swiss company.[608] It came to the knowledge of Jordan Mechanical that some Jordanian traders, such as Abdul-Fattah Qinno, imported about 1000 boxes of Maggi cubes (a product of Egypt), which did not conform to the required specifications. The Court of Cassation found that Jordan Mechanical was entitled to preserve its rights as the authorized agent of the manufacturing company for marketing certain goods. In addition, the Court found that Jordan Mechanical company was entitled to protect its rights in the trademark that was registered for Maggi cubes.

As the facts of the Maggi case illustrate some parallel importers such as Abdul-Fattah Qinno imported genuine goods that are subject to an agency agreement probably with the purpose of circumventing the agent. The effect of the Court of Cassation decision is that as the Swiss company could not enjoin sales of gray market goods in Jordan, its agent and distributor succeeded in obtaining remedies by having the goods of the parallel importers impounded, destroyed, exported, or requested compensation. Apparently, the quality of Maggi differs from Maggi cubes specifically designed for the Jordanian market. Maggi of Egypt was not designed to comply with consumer specifications in Jordan. By bringing the Maggi case, the agent sought to protect regular trade channels. In this context, the agent raised violations of trademarks and agency laws.

Another lesson learned from the Maggi case is that Customs may not seize gray market goods at the borders. This means that an authorized agent or distributor has to bring a private action against the importer of gray market goods, a task that could prove

---

[605] Parallel imports or gray market goods are genuine goods and not counterfeits, whereby a trademark is misappropriated. Parallel imports involve the importation of genuine goods outside the authorized distribution channels. In other words, a parallel import is the importation of these goods from a foreign source by bypassing the authorized local distributor and trademark licensee therefore allowing the sale of goods directly to retailers or consumers. See Keith E. Maskus, *Parallel Import*, 23 World Econ. 1269 (2000).

[606] The Commercial Agency Law vests in courts the jurisdiction over any dispute involving agency agreement. See Commercial Agency Law No. 28 of 2001, *supra* n. 604, art. 16.1.

[607] Copyright law does not mention the right to import, although the right to distribute may include importation rights. Moreover, there is no mention for parallel importation among exceptions from copyright protection. See Provisional Copyright Law No. 52 of 2001, *supra* note 540, arts. 9, 11 & 17. There have been no cases addressing parallel imports in copyright law. Courts in Jordan can protect the copyright owner in regards to parallel importation. based on court decisions in trademark cases.

[608] See Decision No. 95/1418, Journal of the Jordanian Bar Association p. 957 (No. 6 1996).

difficult for several reasons. First, the distributor has to identify the identities of parallel importers.[609] Secondly, bringing a private action is time consuming. Second, a Jordanian authorized distributor can bring a lawsuit based on an array of theories which embraces trademark, unfair competition, consumer concerns, and agency law.

Neither the Trademarks Law nor Customs Law does address clearly parallel importation. In reality, foreign manufacturers appoint as their agent/distributor a Jordanian firm which is the exclusive importer and distributor of their goods. Therefore, parallel importation could be practically blocked. The matter of parallel importation can be addressed through case law. Since the current intellectual property regime in Jordan is new, it remains to be seen how court decisions will interplay with many treaties signed by Jordan, parallel imports, trademarks law, commercial agency law, public interest, and free trade.

Some merchants in Jordan argue that exclusive agents or distributors abuse the domestic market. Parallel imports would not be sold in competition with goods subject to an exclusive agency agreement. Prohibiting parallel imports in connection with goods subject to exclusive agency agreement can only benefit powerful merchants and local elites. As a result, small merchants are not able to benefit from price differences in different markets. Closed distribution channels impede free trade, competition, and consumer choice in terms of product and price.

The opposing view to parallel imports counter-argues that local agents or distributors have built the goodwill of imported products by offering marketing plans, promotional efforts, and product warranty through after-sale servicing. The purpose of all these plans and efforts is to maintain clients and increase the sale of goods. Agents provide services and incur costs that parallel importers may not provide or incur.[610] Therefore, parallel importers get a free ride at the expense of authorized distributors. In addition, parallel importers could damage product quality control, which causes consumer confusion and can diminish the reputations of the manufacturers and agents.

3. Patents

In 1999, Jordan introduced its patent legislation, Patents Law of 1999, replacing the Patents and Designs Law which had been in effect since 1953. The 1999 Patents Law was further amended in 2001.[611] The Patents Law sets out the definition for a patentable invention. All inventions, whether products or processes, in all fields are covered.[612] The

---

[609] For example, in the Maggi case it seems that in some way it came to the knowledge of Jordan Mechanical that some traders imported Maggi cubes.

[610] The agent or distributor is required to provide spare parts and other items which are necessary and sufficient for maintenance of the imported goods. See Commercial Agency Law No. 28 of 2001, *supra* n. 604, art. 11.

[611] As was typical of former colonies and protectorates of the United Kingdom, Jordan followed the laws of England in many areas, including patent law. See Provisional Patents Law No. 71 of 2001, al Jaridah al Rasmiyah No. 4520 (Official Gazette) (Dec. 2, 2001).

[612] *Id.* art. 2.

Patents Law requires inventions to be new, inventive, and capable of industrial application.[613] Novelty is assessed on a worldwide basis, as supposed to an assessment on what has been disclosed in Jordan, as was the case under the old Patent Law.[614]

The Patents Law requires applicants to disclose the invention in their application in a manner sufficiently clear and complete, so that for the invention can be carried out by a person skilled in the art.[615] Additionally, the Patents Law requires applicants to disclose the best method of making the invention work, and any existing foreign applications and grants.[616] The Patents Law requires one invention per application.[617]

The Patents Law set outs the search and examination procedures.[618] In practice, patent examiners in Jordan rely on the substantive search and examination results of a corresponding application of a foreign patent office, such as the U.S. Patent and Trademark Office (USPTO) or the European Patent Office that may have granted the corresponding patent. The reasons for such practice could be to expedite the process and facilitate the task of examiners in Jordan who would only examine the application with respect to formal requirements. However, it is preferable if such a practice is codified so as to set forth the procedures under which patent examiners in Jordan may accept the examination carried out by other foreign offices. Moreover, it remains to be seen how a court would rule on a patent granted in Jordan based on this practice.

The Registrar can deny patentability for an invention on the grounds of public policy, public order or morality.[619] For example, the Registrar can disallow patents on inventions involving gambling devices or products used to perpetrate fraud, because they would not be socially acceptable. Other non-patentable inventions include discoveries, diagnostic, therapeutic and surgical methods necessary for the treatment of humans or animals, and living matters such as plants and animals other than microorganisms.

A patentable invention grants its inventor or owner certain rights. In the case of product patents, these rights include preventing non-authorized making, using, offering for sale, or importing for these purposes, the product in question.[620] In the case of process patents, these rights include preventing non-consensual use of the process, use, offer for

---

[613] *Id.* art. 3. These requirements meet those stated in article 27.1 of the TRIPs Agreement.

[614] Patents Law of 2001 grants a one year grace period to file a patent application for an invention that has been disclosed. It provides cases of how the disclosure happened such as actions taken by the applicant or abuse by third parties. *Id.*

[615] Insufficiency of specifications is a ground for revocation *Id.* art. 8.a & c.

[616] *Id.* art. 8.a. Article 29 of TRIPs permits members to require applicants to indicate the best mode of carrying out the invention. Thus, this is an optional matter but Jordan does require it to be disclosed.

[617] If there are related inventions, then documents must show a unity of invention. This would allow claims to different inventions that fall under the same inventive concept. All the claims in the application must be clear. *Id.* arts. 8.a & 9.a.

[618] *Id.* art. 8. In addition, articles 18-24 of the Patents Regulation of 2001 addresses examination procedures.

[619] The Patents Law further clarifies that invention shall not be so regarded only because it is prohibited by any law in force in Jordan. *Id.* art. 4. This is in compliance with article 27.2 of TRIPs.

[620] *Id.* art. 21.a.

sale, sale, and importation for these purposes, products obtained directly by the process.[621] Patent protection lasts twenty years from date of filing.[622] In patent infringement proceedings, the court may impose jail terms, monetary fines, or award damages.[623] The Patents Law sets out special provisions regarding the burden of proof in civil proceedings in infringement of process patents.[624]

3.1 Compulsory Licensing

The Patents Law governs granting compulsory licensing without the permission of the patent holder to prevent an abuse of patent rights.[625] Jordan does not have broad or general compulsory licensing provisions because the Patents Law sets out specific cases where the granting of a non-voluntary license is allowed. The Patents Law authorizes granting a compulsory license for the services of the government for national defense, emergency, or for public noncommercial use purposes.[626] However, to date, there has never been a single national defense case that would justify a compulsory license. The Patents Law stipulates another case for granting a compulsory license whereby the patentee abuses his rights by preventing others from competing fairly.[627] Finally, the Patents Law grants compulsory licenses in cases of a failure to work the patent or insufficient working.[628]

The Patents Law requires certain conditions for granting a compulsory license.[629] First, these conditions include the attempt to seek a voluntary license from the patent holder and then offering adequate remuneration to the patent holder. In addition, the Patents Law requires the license to be non-exclusive and non-transferable, and that the use of the license meets the demands of the local market only. The compulsory license would be terminated if the circumstances that led to it ceased to exist.[630] The High Court of Justice will review decisions relating to compulsory licensing.[631] The Patents Law does not specify which products can be covered by a compulsory license. For example, a

---

[621] *Id.*

[622] *Id.* art. 17. Previously, patents were protected for a period of sixteen years. Thus, the Patents Law of 2001 extended the term to twenty years. This is in compliance with article 33 of TRIPs.

[623] *Id.* art. 32.

[624] Where a process patent is allegedly have been infringed through the use of a product made directly by that process, it can be very hard for the patentee to prove that the defendant's product, though identical, was made through the use of the patented process. Accordingly, the Patents Law provides that any identical product when produced without the consent of the patent owner shall be deemed to have been obtained by the patented process if there is a likelihood that the identical product was made by the process and the owner of the patent has been unable through reasonable efforts to determine the process actually used. *Id.* art. 34. This is in compliance with article 34 of TRIPs.

[625] *Id.* arts. 22-26.

[626] *Id.* art. 22.a.

[627] *Id.* art. 22.c.

[628] However, no compulsory license may be granted on this ground before expiration of a period of four years from date of filing or three years from date of grant whichever is later. *Id.* art. 22.b (1).

[629] *Id.* art. 23. The conditions for granting a compulsory license under the Patents Law must meet the requirements of article 31 of the TRIPs Agreement.

[630] *Id.* art. 24.

[631] *Id.* 26.

compulsory license could be issued for pharmaceuticals, medical technologies, or other products and services.

3.2 The Jordanian Pharmaceutical Industry and the TRIPs Agreement

Pharmaceutical industry in Jordan is several decades old, where the first domestic maker started business in the early 1960s.[632] Today, the pharmaceutical industry consists of seventeen small to medium-sized private firms employing approximately 8,000 people.[633] Domestic drug makers export about 60 percent of their production while the rest is destined for local consumption.[634] Hence, the pharmaceutical industry is an important source of foreign exchange. However, the industry's export intensity makes it risky if foreign markets are closed or restricted.

The pharmaceutical sector has been highly fragmented and its profits squeezed by competition. Some companies witnessed their operating income drop. Thus, the pharmaceutical industry was poised for a change. In recent years, there has been a consolidation spree among pharmaceutical firms motivated by cost-cutting savings and market expansion.[635] One could anticipate that industry consolidation would continue as the enhanced financial strength of the largest producers provides the means to actively explore potential takeover targets. Mergers and acquisitions could be an important step to weather competition and expand the market. Small producers, competitive as they may be, might not be able to remain as stand-alone operations. Jordanian firms could explore partnerships with foreign firms as strong patents offered by Jordan ought to make vigorous partnerships that would speed the advance of technology.

Pharmaceutical manufacturers in Jordan face several obstacles in accessing neighboring countries' markets such as Saudi Arabia and Egypt, as these countries create home-grown pharmaceutical industries. These obstacles include registration procedures, market authorization, and procedural barriers. One way to help manufacturers is for Jordan to engage in bilateral negotiations that could eventually lead to a reciprocal market access agreement that would standardize rules and procedures. The agreement could be open to other incomers into the region.

The regulatory drug pricing system in Jordan relies on some forms of price controls. One form of price controls is the use of reference pricing, involves establishing a price based on a basket of prices in other countries. Other direct methods used involve setting the sale price and barring sales at a price higher than those in other countries. Although

---

[632] See *Implications of WTO TRIPS for Technology Transfer in the Pharmaceutical Industry*, U.N. Economic and Social Commission for Western Asia, at 31, U.N Doc. E/ESCWA/TECH/1997/7 (1997).
[633] *Id.*
[634] Production is confined to generics, packaging of imported formulations, and production of formulations based on imported active ingredients. Most raw materials, packaging equipment, and other auxiliary materials are imported. Some drug formulation and packaging activities are conducted under licensing agreements with multinational corporations. *Id.* 32-33, 35.
[635] See *JMP and Al Razi Mark Jordan's First Merger in the Pharmaceutical Sector*, Jordan Times 11 (Nov. 27, 2002). See *Down the Aisle Again*, Jordan Times 11 (Jan. 12, 2003). See also *Merger Announcement Applauded by Bankers but Urge Incentives*, Jordan Times 11 (Feb. 24, 2003).

these price controls yield lower revenue for drug firms by preventing them from charging market-based prices, they address wider health policy considerations such as access and affordability. Price controls are used to maintain and ensure drug prices are in check. If prices increase drug consumption could decrease. These price controls could also be used to manage spending on pharmaceuticals in government health budget.

The problem of the intellectual property regime in Jordan was acute in the pharmaceutical sector, where patented drugs were manufactured without licenses. The Patents and Designs Law of 1953 was deemed as an inadequate.[636] This state of affairs led to patent infringements of pharmaceuticals.[637]

After modifications, the Patents Law permits the granting of patents for foodstuffs and pharmaceuticals.[638] However, these modifications will only come into effect three years after Jordan becomes a WTO member.[639] In the meantime, a provision was made for securing a filing date for applications for pharmaceuticals.[640] Additionally, a provision was made for obtaining exclusive marketing rights during this period.[641] Therefore, pharmaceuticals, drugs, and agriculture chemicals, previously not patentable, are now patentable under the Patents Law.

The Patents Law will bar domestic firms from copying patented drugs. Jordanian drug firms will no longer be able to reproduce patented medicines simply by using a different process. It is early to predict the impact of Jordan's Patent Law on its pharmaceuticals industry. The shift to product patent system could make prices of medicines increase.

4. Enforcement of Intellectual Property Rights

Having laws that comply with the TRIPs Agreement is half the story of compliance with WTO rules. The second half is the enforcement of these laws. The point often argued is that intellectual property rights are included in the WTO for the benefit of the "big three" in the developed countries, namely pharmaceuticals, recorded entertainment, and software.[642] This is supported by the fact that the U.S. has been the most persistent in

---

[636] See 1997 Special 301 Report, *available at* http:// www.ustr.gov/pdf/special.pdf (Apr. 30, 1997) (citing the shortcomings of the patents law regarding pharmaceuticals).

[637] See 1998 Special 301 Report, *available at* http:// www.ustr.gov/pdf/special.pdf (May 1, 1998). See also 1999 Special 301 Report, *available at* http:// www.ustr.gov/pdf/special.pdf (Apr. 30, 1999).

[638] See Provisional Patents Law No. 71 of 2001, *supra* n. 611, art. 36.a. Even though the TRIPs Agreement does not directly extend patent protection to pharmaceuticals, they are however afforded patent protection by virtue of article 27.2 & 3 which specify what products are non-patentable. In that list pharmaceuticals are not included.

[639] *Id.* art. 36.e.

[640] *Id.* art. 36.b.

[641] *Id.* art. 36.d.

[642] Many observers argue that the main effects of TRIPS are to redistribute economic rents from the poor countries to the rich. See Keith E. Maskus, *Regulatory Standards in the WTO: Comparing Intellectual Rights with Competition Policy, Environmental Protection, and Core Labor Standards*, 1 World Trade Rev. 135, 137-138 (2002). In return for agreeing to include intellectual property rights within the WTO, the developing countries were able to secure other trade advantages from the developed countries in terms of

promoting the adoption and enforcement of intellectual property regimes. However, it is argued that adhering to a stronger policy of protecting intellectual property rights is a key for the dissemination of technology by developed countries. For example, intellectual property protection increased production and employment in Jordan ever since it adopted or reformed IP laws to meet international standards.[643]

Although intellectual property laws in Jordan are in conformity with the TRIPs, they are considered to be relaxed and not enforced. Enforcement of intellectual property rights in Jordan is an area where many factors inform policy enforcement which reflects the current status of enforcement of intellectual property rights. Enforcement of intellectual property rights is not cheap.[644] Enforcement of intellectual property rights requires appropriation of millions of dollars that would capture a good portion of the annual budget of Jordan. Therefore, any action plan such as raids, seizures, arrests, or education campaigns, to reduce intellectual property infringement is constrained by limited financial resources.

Jordan also experiences lack of sufficient human resources. For example, the Industrial Property Protection Directorate at MIT has thirty-five professional, trademark and patent examiners, and support staff equipped with computers.[645] Until recently, examiners were not required to be lawyers with intellectual property knowledge and expertise, having background in science and technology, or taking patent bar-like exam. Moreover, an effective intellectual property regime requires an effective well-trained customs service.[646] In Jordan, there is no special court for intellectual property.[647]

Other factors that are attributed to the plight of enforcement of intellectual property rights in Jordan include the sentiment that a religiously-based law is necessary barrack against Westernization and the domination of Western culture.[648] Therefore, violating

---

increase market access in textiles and apparel, and liberalization in agriculture. See also May L. Harris, *TRIPS: Historical Overview and Basic Principles*, 12 J. Contemp. Legal Issues 454, 457 (2001).

[643] After the 1990's reform, the total sale of software IT-related services were $22.3 million. In 2001, IT companies in Jordan generated $130 million in total revenue, over half generated through software, employing about 5,000 IT workers. Moreover, Jordan attracted $60 million in FDI. See Eric Garduno & frank J. Pietrucha, *Intellectual Property Rights in the Arab World*, 4.1 Geo. J. Intl. Aff. 60-62 (2003).

[644] See *Patents and the Poor*, Economist 22 (June 23, 2001) (the cost for a poor country to build just a bare-bones infrastructure to implement TRIPS is roughly $1.5-2 million. WIPO gives technical assistance to countries trying to draft intellectual property legislation or set up their patent offices).

[645] See Report on Industrial Property Protection Directorate of Ministry of Industry and Trade 3 (on file with the author). This number constitutes a fraction of the some 7000 employee at the USPTO. However, this is understandable since the U.S. patent system has been in existence since 1790.

[646] Among the new tasks for modern customs service, there is a focusing on smuggling, accurate goods classification and tariff collection, compliance with security measures, and enforcement of intellectual property. For example, while caring about the rights of intellectual property right holders may be important, it is also of equivalent importance not to restrict trade. The customs service in Jordan may adopt a "selective" system as in the health and food safety rules whereby certain selected imports maybe examined to detect intellectual property violations.

[647] Article 41.5 of TRIPs does not require members to establish a special judicial system for intellectual property rights.

intellectual property rights are a means of revenge for the West's colonization. Moreover, relationships in Jordan are based on mutual cooperation and sharing in common. There are different segments of the Jordanian society which would be affected by the high cost of acquiring intellectual property product because intellectual property is based on individual rights and paid access for those who can afford it.[649]

In Jordan, effective enforcement of intellectual property rights has increased by establishing educational programs.[650] Moreover, in the past it has never published that law enforcement was officially rading pirates' places to clamp down on intellectual property violations.[651] Moreover, there are news accounts of dispatching teams of inspectors nationwide. [652] In the period of 2000-2004, the National Library prosecuted 985 copyright-related cases, with an estimated of 75 percent of these cases ending in individual convictions.

Despite the *de jure* protection of intellectual property rights in Jordan, a *de facto* system operates. Some local software houses only sell originals of local software as a gesture of support to the local software industry.[653] This could be a form of local protectionism.

Taking into account the different approaches adopted by Jordan, enforcement of intellectual property should be a success. However, hardcore, street-level, and result-oriented enforcement activities will hardly change the mentality or belief of Jordanians that intellectual property rights are not imposed by developed countries. These developed countries did not protect intellectual property while they were in the stage of developing their economies.[654] Developed countries took decades to improve their norms, standards, and enforcement while Jordan changed its norms and standards in only a few years. The acceptability of intellectual property is critical for Jordan because the enforcement will depend upon the legitimacy of intellectual property.

---

[648] See John Carroll, *Intellectual Property Rights in the Middle East: A Cultural Perspective*, 11 Fordham Intell. Prop. Media & Ent L.J 555, 574 (2001)..

[649] See Suha Ma'ayeh, *Improved IPR Enforcement Gets Mixed Reviews*, Jordan Times 10 (May 10, 2001) (Without pirated software, my son could not have excelled in an Auto Cad program which I purchased for JD3, said one Jordanian citizen, adding that the price of the original software is way beyond his reach).

[650] In addition to the statutory changes [in Jordan's intellectual property laws to comply with TRIPs] national intellectual property associations and intellectual property courses have proliferated in collaboration with WIPO.

[651] See *Jordan Police Intensify Action Against Piracy*, Jordan Times 18 (May 15, 2001). One solution to the problem of paid access would be to engage into agreements with foreign software developers to sell their software at discounted prices. This solution would be reasonable especially if the software would be used for educational purposes. This solution would encourage Jordanian individuals to buy legal software at a reasonable price without having to pay a large sum.

[652] See *Copyright Infringements Referred to Courts*, Jordan Times 5 (Nov. 14, 2003) (the National Library has referred 729 cases to prosecution since 2000. Infringed items include tapes, pirated books, software, and satellite smart cards).

[653] See Carroll, *supra* n. 648, at 592.

[654] See Marco C.E.J. Bronckers, *The Impact of TRIPS: Intellectual Property Protection in Developing Countries*, 31 CM. L. Rev. 1245, 1247 (1994) (when developed countries, like the Netherlands, were industrializing in the nineteenth century, they chose not to protect intellectual property. For example, from 1869 to 1910 the Netherlands abolished patent law).

D. Commitments of Jordan in Relation to Transparency

The concept of transparency is a core component of the WTO. Generally, every WTO agreement contains a provision related to transparency.[655] Article X of GATT 1994, which is based to a large extent on the U.S. Administrative Procedures Act, forms the basis for commitments on publication of laws, regulations, judicial decisions, administrative rulings, and trade agreements. Moreover, article X of GATT 1994 requires the administration of laws, regulations, and administrative and judicial decisions that affect international trade in a uniform, impartial, and reasonable manner.

The purpose of article X of GATT 1994 is to ensure predictability in an open multilateral trading system, as it embraces the rule of law. The rule of law, *siyadat al-qanun* in Arabic, means authority would be exercised in a fixed and predictable way, rather than one based on unlimited personal discretion. In other words, rule of law means that the government would act according to a set of rules promulgated in advance. Rule of law is a necessary foundation for free trade and economic development. Rule of law undercuts corruption and cronyism. Absence of rule of law discourages investment and commerce. Therefore, free trade and rule of law are not only linked but they also ought to be used interchangeably.

Jordan has committed in its accession to the WTO to publish all laws, regulations, and judicial decisions and administrative rulings of general application as they pertain to international trade.[656] Currently, there are three journals that publish laws, regulation and judicial and administrative decisions.[657] In some instances, laws, regulations, and judicial and administrative decisions could be published in daily newspapers.[658]

---

[655] Article 7 of the SPS Agreement, article 6 of the TRIMS Agreement, and article 63 of TRIPS address transparency.

[656] See Report of the Working Party on the Accession of Jordan, *supra* n. 379, at 239.

[657] These are the Official Gazette, Journal of Jordanian Bar Association, and the Judicial Journal. The Department of Official Gazette in the Prime Ministry publishes the Official Gazette. The Ministry of Finance distributes the Official Gazette. The Jordanian Bar Association issues the Journal of Jordanian Bar Association covering final judicial decisions of the Court of Cassation and the High Court of Justice, news of the Bar Association, and selected research. The Judicial Institute of Jordan publishes the Judicial Journal which covers decisions of the Court of Cassation and High Court of Justice. A published judicial decision, identified by number, covers names of judges who issued the decision, parties, brief time line for the case until appeal, reasons for appeal, summary of the decision, and dissenting opinion, if any. Journal of Jordanian Bar Association and Judicial Journal do not detail the entire decision. These journals publish a summary of the arguments and the decision. Decisions of inferior courts and courts of appeals are usually not reported or published. Decisions of inferior courts and courts of appeals are filed with the clerk of the court and available for inspection by interested persons. Published judicial decisions in Jordan are not a replica of published judicial decisions in the U.S. According to the U.S. style of publishing judicial decisions, defined by names, of state courts of appeals are published in consecutively numbered volumes called "reports". West Publishing Company publishes states reports in regional reporters such as Atlantic (A. or A.2d). Federal district courts decisions are published in the Federal Supplement (F.Supp.). Decisions of the U.S. Courts of Appeals are found in the Federal Reporter (Fed. , F.2d). Decisions of the U.S. Supreme Court are published in the United States Supreme Court Reports (U.S.), Supreme Court Reporter (S.Ct.), and Lawyers Edition (L. Ed). The difference between the U.S. style of publishing judicial decisions

The administration of laws, regulations, and administrative decisions affecting international trade in a uniform, impartial, and reasonable manner could prove difficult in Jordan. Discrepancies in the interpretation and application of laws and regulations involve several factors. Jurisdiction lines among agencies and ministries may overlap. Moreover, some laws or regulation are drafted in a way so as to leave some terms ambiguous. Authorities could exploit ambiguity to implement laws and regulation as they see fit.

The circumstances and the level of development of the legal system in Jordan affects the rule of law. The constitution may not be considered a living legal document.[659] Usually, laws emanate from the executive authority which has extensive control over drafting laws.[660] Judge-made law does not exist in Jordan. Therefore, judges do not make public policy statements. Additionally, Jordan needs to revise and improve the legal profession which includes more than 8,000 lawyers, some of whom are poorly trained and underpaid.

Publication of laws and regulations, though important, are not enough. Consistent and fair application of existing laws and regulations are of utmost importance. Transparency and rule of law commitments will improve the trading system in Jordan. Moreover, transparency and rule of law are effective modes to limit government abuse that would disrupt trade.

---

and Jordan's style could be attributed to the fact that the U.S. legal system is a case law based system. On the other hand, Jordan is a civil law country where case law is of secondary value.

[658] See for example, *Draft Law implementing the Free Trade Agreement between Jordan and the U.S.*, Al-Rai, 27 (Feb. 28, 2001). See also *Draft Law on Arbitration of 2001*, Ad-Dustour, 5 (June 23, 2001).

[659] Constitutions in Arab monarchies as well as republics, are symbols of independence. They were enacted on the eve of independence or the prospect of independence. Constitutions serve the purpose of organizing state authority especially in succession. The Arab constitutional experience and practice allow freedoms to be defined by laws rather than constitutions. Arab constitutions do not go beyond mere description of the political society. See Nathan J. Brown, *Constitutions in a Nonconstitutional World* 35, 49, 61-63 (St. U. N. Y. Press 2002).

[660] See Nathan J. Brown, *The Rule of Law in the Arab World: Courts In Egypt and the Gulf* 57 (Cambridge U. Press 1997) (some Arab governments use certain techniques to contain the legislative authority. For example, the parliament consists of two branches; deputies and senate. People would select deputies while the head of state would select the senate. The senate would act as a counterbalance against some un-welcomed proposals from deputies. Members of the legislative branch are given shorter periods of time to speak in parliament. If they exceed their time, the speaker will exercise his privileges to quiet members. Deputies may not have knowledge or experience in all the matters set before them. Many proposals, including draft laws, emanate from ministries and the deputies can agree to them. Some deputies may also be ministers. Thus, it would be hard to counter-argue the government where these deputies hold seats in it. If parliament exceeds its authority, it is dissolved). The fact that members of parliaments in Arab countries may not have knowledge or experience in all the matters set before them such as international trade is not limited to Arab countries. In the U.S., some congressmen may not have the knowledge or experience in a subject matter. However, each U.S. congressman has a staff that would advise and assist him. There no equivalent staff readily available for members of parliaments in Arab countries is available because of limited financial resources.

E. Other Selected Commitments

Jordan's WTO working party accession report covers fiscal and monetary policy, foreign exchange and payments, privatization, and price policies.[661] Price rationalization or privatization policies are not explicitly covered in the WTO agreements. Moreover, Jordan undertook commitments in trading and distribution rights.[662] Trading and distribution rights allow private Jordanian and foreign companies to import, export, set up after-sale networks, and sell their goods throughout Jordan.[663] These trading rights will enable U.S. companies to import and export goods without using Jordanian trading companies. Distribution services will allow U.S. companies to sell their goods without establishing joint ventures with Jordanian companies.

Jordan committed itself to observe the requirements of article XVII of GATT 1994 which govern state trading enterprises.[664] Currently, there are five state trading enterprises that have the exclusive right to import or export.[665] These state trading enterprises must observe the conditions stipulated in article XVII of GATT 1994 in their purchase or sale. For example, purchases of state trading enterprises must be conducted in a non-discriminatory treatment, based on commercial considerations, and afford enterprises of other countries the opportunity to compete in such purchases or sales based on customary business practice.

Jordan agreed in its accession protocol to the WTO that it would request an observer status under the WTO Government Procurement Agreement (GPA).[666] Moreover, Jordan confirmed that, upon accession to the WTO, it would initiate negotiations for membership in the GPA.[667] It also confirmed that, if the results of the negotiations were

---

[661] Report of the Working Party on the Accession of Jordan, *supra* n. 379, at 9-32. A price control system is designed to ensure the poor can afford basic commodities and prevent price skyrocketing. In the past, the government of Jordan determined a fair price for dozens of essential goods and services in intricate detail. The list of goods included meat and flour. However, price-setting system could be inefficient and prone to corruption. Moreover, the government cannot effectively monitor price compliance. A price control system is for countries that are not yet ready for a completely free market just yet. It is a system used in central planning.

[662] *Id.* at 50.

[663] Under Jordan's trading rights regime, foreign equity in Jordanian trading companies is limited to 50 percent. Jordan committed to permit foreign companies exercising trading rights without limitation on foreign equity or capital. *Id.* at 45.

[664] *Id.* para. 161.

[665] These state trading enterprises are: Jordan Tanning Company, Jordan Petroleum Refinery Company, Jordan Cement Factories Company, Jordan Phosphate Mining Company, and Vegetable Oil Industries.

[666] *Id.* 169. The GPA, signed by some two dozen countries, applies only to those countries which are members of the Agreement. The GPA applies to contracts for purchasing goods and services worth more than $175,000 for central government procurement tenders and about $270,000 for contracts with provincial and state authorities. The GPA contains substantial and procedural obligations. In terms of the substantial obligations, members of the GPA are required to extend the MFN and national treatment rules to goods and services of other members. The procedural obligations included in the GPA are related to transparency through the publication of notices inviting tenders, post-award notices, and establishing an independent review body to consider complaints by domestic or foreign suppliers related to any violation of the Agreement.

[667] *Id.* 170. Currently, Jordan is in the process of accession to the GPA. See Application from Jordan, *Application for Accession to the Agreement on Government Procurement*, GPA/38 (July 19, 2000).

satisfactory to the interests of Jordan and the other members of the agreement, it would complete negotiations for membership within a year of accession. However, Jordan is not a member yet, and it has to offer a detailed plan or timetable.

In its accession to the GPA, Jordan will weigh the possible benefits to its budgetary efficiency and industries, as a result of opening its government procurement sector to foreign competition. First, the share of Jordan's industries in the government procurement market of other countries is negligible. Moreover, Jordan's industries lack experience in competing in contract tendering. Therefore, the benefits from joining the GPA are marginal. U.S. companies are not interested in the small Jordanian government procurement market. Rather, U.S. companies are interested in major projects that are worth billions of dollars, such as the Kansai airport of Japan or valuable procurement markets such as that of Hong Kong. In addition, in acceding to the GPA, Jordan must modify its current practices which give preference to domestic suppliers of goods and services.[668] Jordan acceded to the WTO multilateral agreements which are considered the most important step and thus there is little interest in joining the GPA.

Finally, Jordan is committed in its accession to the WTO to observe the provisions of article XXIV of the GATT 1994 in its trade agreements.[669] The purpose of free trade areas and customs unions is the liberalization of international trade. Jordan is a member to a myriad of international and regional trade agreements. For example, Jordan signed a free trade agreement with Egypt and a member of the Arab Common Market Agreement.[670] In addition, Jordan signed other trade agreements such as the U.S.-Jordan Free Trade Agreement.

---

[668] These practices are tied to industrial, political, and social policies that are difficult to modify.
[669] See Report of the Working Party on the Accession of Jordan, *supra* n. 379, at 247.
[670] *Id.* at 243

Conclusion

Jordan's accession to the WTO was a lengthy and costly process. Jordan did not accede to the trade body until other WTO members were satisfied that Jordan made sufficient concessions. The terms and conditions for accession were easier prior to the creation of the WTO.[671] Jordan agreed to reduce tariffs, open its service market, reform its intellectual property regime, and accede to the ITA. Jordan enjoyed special and differential treatment in few areas. For example, Jordan was granted an adjustment period to cope with the implementation of tariffs reduction, but was not granted transitional periods for the implementation of the TRIPs and customs valuation. Moreover, Jordan was not able to designate olive oil as a special safeguard good. Other WTO members did not grant Jordan special and differential treatment so as not to set a "bad" precedent for other acceding countries and to maintain the "integrity" of the WTO system by not creating a two-tier system for developed and developing countries. In its accession to the WTO, Jordan turned from an applicant to a supplicant.

The degree of open market commitments Jordan undertook in its accession to the WTO was the culmination of several factors, which included domestic policy-making debates, interest groups, and pressure from foreign governments such as the U.S., EC, Australia, and Switzerland. Generally, countries acceding to the WTO are required to make changes to their laws and regulations prior to joining the trade body. Jordan met some of its commitments at the time it joined the WTO. In addition, Jordan committed to meet other requirements after its accession. Therefore, Jordan should meet many of its commitments in the post-accession period.

The WTO agreements required fundamental changes in the domestic laws and regulations of Jordan. For example, nearly 100 laws were new or fundamentally changed.[672] Many of the laws promulgated were provisional and adopted in haste in prior to the 1999 self-imposed deadline for accession to the WTO. In the months ahead, the National Assembly must approve the laws and regulations in order to honor Jordan's commitments. However, the National Assembly, for the sake of proving that it is not a rubber-stamp Assembly and to ensure good legislative practices, may strike down or modify these laws and regulations in a degree less consistent with Jordan's obligations under the WTO. In Jordan, there are many layers of ministries and administrative agencies entrusted with implementing these laws and regulations, and the enforcement of these laws and regulations largely depends upon the discretion of these ministries and agencies access to their decrees.

Counsels must research several bulletins and sources to access laws and regulations. Unfortunately, even the most exhaustive investigation can miss important points because

---

[671] See Doha Ministerial Conference, Doha Ministerial Declaration, WT/MIN(01)/DEC/1, para. 9 (Nov. 14, 2001) (We [WTO members] also welcome the accession as new members, since our last session, of Albania, Croatia, Georgia, Jordan, Lithuania, Moldova and Oman, and note the "extensive" market-access commitments already made by these countries on accession).

[672] See *Nail-Biting: Jordan's Fairly Fair Election*, Economist 38 (June 21, 2003) (some 160 laws have been promulgated, which some say they are good for promoting a program of economic liberalization in the absence of the parliament).

there is no central location where all the necessary information is available. Therefore, a functional website should be established, so that all the laws and regulations of Jordan can be accessed to the public, both in Arabic and English.

In Jordan, many areas of implementation of the WTO agreements require heavy administrative and financial investment. For example, the implementation of the TRIPs required the introduction of new laws, the creation of administrative bodies, the training staff, and the establishment of buildings and equipments, which all costs millions of dollars. However, financial aid from international donors and technical assistance from the WTO can alleviate the difficulty of implementing Jordan's commitments.

The government of Jordan must introduce policies aimed at cushioning the most vulnerable groups from the effects of trade liberalization. These policies include re-employment projects, diversified education, and funds to offset the extreme adverse effects of trade liberalization. Alternative sources of revenue must be developed that include decreasing military expenditures and establishing an effective system of value-added and sales taxes.

Jordan will undertake Trade Policy Review in 2006 which will provide Jordan and its trading partners the chance to examine its trade policies and practices.[673] The Trade Policy Review will present a challenge considering the volume of documentation and information needed to draft a national report. Jordan, however, can draw on the experience of Morocco, one of the first countries that underwent Trade Policy Review in the 1989 cycle.

Jordan will compete in the international market on the basis of the rule of comparative advantage. Many products that Jordan cannot produce it can purchase from other countries, and vice versa. The process of trade liberalization could inject new dynamism into the stagnant industry sector. Moreover, the process of trade liberalization will create winners and losers. Jordan's membership in the WTO is only five years old and is still in the pipeline of liberalization. Since this researcher is not a futurologist, the coming years will show whether the optimists' or pessimists' position on Jordan's accession to the WTO have credence.

---

[673] In the Trade Policy Review, Trading partners of Jordan and the WTO Secretariat would praise Jordan's progress on trade liberalization, and take notice of matters, and air concerns over certain issues

CHAPTER IV

THE U.S.-JORDAN FREE TRADE AGREEMENT

Chapter IV gives a step-by-step account of the legislative history and text of the U.S.-Jordan Free Trade Agreement (US-JO FTA). In addition, Chapter IV includes a comparison between the US-JO FTA, the U.S.-Israel Free Trade Agreement (US-Israel FTA), and North American Free Trade Agreement (NAFTA).[674] Chapter IV also provides an analysis of the elements of the US-JO FTA, including rules of origin, trade in services, and trade remedy laws. Finally, chapter IV examines the extent to which the US-JO FTA achieves its stated objectives and provides a viable model for the proposed US-Middle East Free Trade Agreement (US-Middle East FTA).[675]

Since the US-JO FTA is a treaty, the starting point for the analysis is to consult the relevant rules of the Vienna Convention on the Law of Treaties.[676] This approach is similar to that followed by the WTO panels and Appellate Body.[677] The terms of the US-JO FTA are interpreted in good faith and in accordance with the ordinary meaning given to such terms in light of their context, object, and purpose.[678] An interpreter of the US-JO

---

[674] These FTAs were chosen for the purposes of analysis because only the US-Israel FTA and NAFTA had preceded the US-JO FTA. In addition, Israel is a next-door neighbor.

[675] President Bush announced the U.S. intent to launch a 10-year effort to form a US-Middle East free trade area. See Mike Allen & Karen DeYoung, *Bush Calls Trade Key To Mideast; President launches Plan For U.S. Pact in Region*, Wash. Post A01 (May 10, 2003). See also Grary G. Yerkey, *President Bush Lays Out Broad Plan for Regional FTA with Middle East by 2013*, 20 Intl. Trade Rep. (BNA) 856 (May 15, 2003) (stating that the U.S. will employ a "building-block" approach. This approach requires, as a first step, a Middle East country to accede to the WTO or concluding Trade and Investment Framework Agreement(s) (TIFA). Afterward, the U.S. will negotiate FTA with individual countries. Finally, preferably before 2013, a critical mass of bilateral FTAs would come together to form the broader US-Middle East FTA). It is unfortunate that the U.S. adopted such approach by concluding bilateral free trade agreements rather than a joint free trade agreement at the outset (bundling approach). The U.S. approach will place these Arab countries in weak position on the bargaining table. In FTA negotiations using the bundling approach, Middle East countries would be represented by a panel of representatives from each Middle Eastern country. Moreover, one has to question the utility of negotiating FTAs with small Middle East countries such as Bahrain rather than with the Middle East as a whole. In addition, it seems that the U.S. follows the EC footsteps by adopting hub and spoke system in which the U.S. would conclude a series of bilateral agreements with relatively small countries. In such a system, trade between each spoke and the hub will be more than trade among the spokes themselves. Since achieving U.S. goal of U.S.-Middle East FTA takes time, some members of Congress proposed enacting the Middle East Trade and Engagement Act of 2003 (H. 1121, S. 1121), a trade preference program, that provide immediate improved access to the U.S. market for qualifying Middle Eastern countries.

[676] The terms "agreement" and "treaty" are used here in the manner defined and described in article 2 of the Vienna Convention on the Law of Treaties. See *Vienna Convention on the Law of Treaties* (May 23, 1969), 1155 U.N.T.S. 331.

[677] The Appellate Body in the United States-Reformulated Gasoline case stated regarding article 3.2 of the DSU that "that direction reflects a measure of recognition that the General Agreement is not to be read in "clinical isolation" from public international law". (Emphasis added). See United States-Standards for Reformulated and Conventional Gasoline, Apr. 29, 1996, WTO Doc. No. WT/DS2/AB/R, at 17.

[678] The context for the purpose of the interpretation of a treaty shall comprise, in addition to the text, including its preamble and annexes:
(a) any agreement relating to the treaty which was made between all the parties in connexion with the conclusion of the treaty;

FTA should analyze the text in honesty, fairness and reasonableness, adopting a literal or textual interpretation of the FTA's words, and in light of the intentions of the FTA's drafters.[679]

I. The US-JO FTA: Introduction

The US-JO FTA was the "first" FTA in two respects. First, it was the first FTA to be concluded with an Arab country. Second, it was also the first FTA to include labor and environment within the text of the FTA itself, compared with the side agreements on environment and labor in NAFTA. The FTA was the "second" FTA between the U.S. and a low middle-income country, after the U.S. and Canada expanded their FTA to include Mexico.

There are several reasons that led the U.S. to negotiate a free trade agreement with Jordan. The failed WTO Ministerial Conference in 1999 lead U.S. trade officials to analyze the possibilities for a free trade agreement that would include certain provisions that are resisted at the multilateral trading level.[680] Moreover, the U.S. and Jordan had

---

(b) any instrument which was made by one or more parties in connexion with the conclusion of the treaty and accepted by the other parties as an instrument related to the treaty.
3. There shall be taken into account, together with the context:
(a) any subsequent agreement between the parties regarding the interpretation of the treaty or the application of its provisions;
(b) any subsequent practice in the application of the treaty which establishes the agreement of the parties regarding its interpretation;
(c) any relevant rules of international law applicable in the relations between the parties.
4. A special meaning shall be given to a term if it is established that the parties so intended. Moreover, article 32 is related to the supplementary means of interpretation. It states that recourse may be had to supplementary means of interpretation, including the preparatory work of the treaty and the circumstances of its conclusion, in order to confirm the meaning resulting from the application of article 31, or to determine the meaning when the interpretation according to article 31:
(a) leaves the meaning ambiguous or obscure; or
(b) leads to a result which is manifestly absurd or unreasonable.
See Vienna Convention on the Law of Treaties, *supra* n. 676, art. 31.
[679] Moreover, an interpreter is not free to adopt a reading that would result in reducing whole clauses or paragraphs of a treaty to redundancy or inutility. See Appellate Body, *Japan-Taxes on Alcoholic Beverages*, WT/DS8/AB/R, at 12 (Oct. 4, 1996). Thus, the interpretation of the US-JO FTA is based solely on the Vienna approach, including the use of judicial economy, excluding consideration for making interpretation that satisfy both parties or responding to political signals (whispers) that he has gone far than supposed to. In other words, the principle of effective interpretation will be followed, *effet utile*, by giving the terms their full meanings. Additionally, little attention will be paid to preparatory work or negotiating history of the FTA because of lack of records and the possibility of conflicting negotiating statements by both parties. Moreover, where necessary, reference will be made to decisions of the WTO panels and Appellate Body especially that some articles of the US-JO FTA refers directly to WTO agreements or indirectly to WTO panel and Appellate Body decisions. Finally, the U.S. and Jordan are assumed to share a relatively common legal understanding of precedents.
[680] In the wake of protests by environmentalists and human rights activists at the WTO summit in Seattle in late 1999, then president Clinton promised to link future trade accords to labor, environmental, and human rights issues. See Eric M. Uslaner, *The Democratic Party and Free Trade: An Old Romance Restored*, 6 NAFTA: L & Bus. Rev. Am. 347, 359 (2000).

signed a trade and investment framework in 1999, which is usually a precursor for a FTA.[681]

Jordan was also the right candidate for a FTA in terms of economicas and politics. Economically, U.S. exports to Jordan would increase as a result of the FTA while Jordanian imports to the U.S. would not threaten U.S. industries.[682] The FTA could also spur Jordan's economic growth, allowing for the possibility that it would become less dependant on foreign aid. Moreover, the U.S. needed to negotiate a FTA because it was losing ground to the EC which, which had concluded association agreements with several Mediterranean countries.[683] By signing the FTA, the U.S. could catch up to the EC with respect to economic dominance in Arab countries.

---

[681] See Grary G. Yerkey, *U.S., Jordan Sign Framework For Trade and Investment Pact*, 16 Intl. Trade Rep. (BNA) 468 (Mar. 17, 1999) (then USTR Charlene Barshefsky stated that the agreement would put in place institutional foundation for trade relationship. The agreement opened dialogue on issues such as agriculture, intellectual property, services, investment, and trade-related aspects of labor and environmental policy).
[682] A study conducted by the Office of Economics and the Office of Industries of the USITC, found that "Jordan's exports to the U.S. would not have a measurable impact on U.S. industries, U.S. employment, and production. Based on 1999 trade figures, U.S. imports from Jordan totaled $31 million as compared to total US imports of $1 trillion. See U.S. International Trade Commission, Economic Impact on the United States of a U.S.-Jordan Free Trade Agreement, 5-1 Pub. No. 3340 (Sep. 2000) (an FTA with Jordan is not expected to have a measurable impact on U.S. imports from Jordan for the 15 sectors reviewed. For one sector, textiles and apparels, a likely rise in U.S. imports of apparel is expected to have a negligible effect on total U.S. imports).
[683] The official movement towards a closer relationship between the EC and its Mediterranean neighbors was launched at a meeting of the European Council in Lisbon in 1992. It takes place between the EC and 12 countries to the east and south of the Mediterranean. The major premise of the partnership is to create an enormous zone of free trade between Europe and several countries of the Middle East by the year 2010. The Euro-Mediterranean Partnership was created in 1995 in Barcelona with the signing of the Barcelona Declaration by the EC and 12 Mediterranean Countries. The 12 Mediterranean countries are as follows: Morocco, Algeria, Tunisia, Egypt, Jordan, Israel, The Palestinian Authority, Lebanon, Syria, Cyprus, Malta, and Turkey. This partnership will lead to a series of Euro-Mediterranean association agreements. The purposes of this partnership is EC's recognition that peace and security in the Middle East is of great interest and concern to the EC (EC efforts to create policy in the Middle East could create considerable tension in Washington, DC, where the administration believes it has a strong role to play in the development of peace in the Middle East), creation of the world's largest free trade zone-comprising more than 800 million people-by the year 2010 to rival NAFTA, and providing Middle Easterners with greater opportunities within their own countries, thus they will be less likely to want or need to immigrate to the EC for employment reasons. Euro-Med trade zone provides free trade in industrial goods and services. However, certain sectors where some countries have a comparative advantage are excluded. For example, agriculture is excluded and would be subject to quotas (Tunisia for example has been granted tariff concessions of 46,000 ton per marketing year for olive oil. The EC made concessions for Israel on cut flowers and citrus). Moreover, Euro-Med trade zone has restrictive rules of origin. In order for a product to access the EC market duty free, the majority of it must be produced in the country of export. The EC intends to permit "diagonal cummulation" among the Mediterranean countries. This will allow inputs originate in one country to be incorporated in the final product of the other party to have free access to EC markets, provided that both countries belong to the free trade area. The EC pursues selective cooperation with Middle Eastern countries, which could eventually lead to increasing tensions. Already, Arab countries have argued forcibly that Libya, the Arab country with the longest Mediterranean coastline, should be included. These efforts have been rejected by the EC. See Jacqueline Klosek, *The Euro-Mediterranean Partnership*, 8 Intl. Leg. Persp. 173 (1996). It seems that the EC and the U.S. view Middle East countries as markets not as trading partners since there is rivalry between the U.S. and the EC.

Politically, the FTA reflects the U.S.'s appreciation for Jordan's role in the Middle East peace process and cooperation with international counter-terrorism activities. In addition, the FTA signals to other Arab countries the benefits to maintain peace. Economic growth will also enhance political stability and encourage peace in the Middle East. For its part, the U.S. would be able to market Jordan's economic growth as a product of Jordan's peaceful relationship with its neighbors, especially Israel. In other words, a wealthy Jordan is good for Israel.[684] So long as Jordan remains poor its citizens, who are mostly Palestinians, will continue to blame their poverty on Israel. Therefore, the FTA would also help alleviate the pressure on Israel and reduce its security risk.

On June 6, 2000, King Abdullah II and then President Clinton declared that the U.S. and Jordan would launch negotiations for a free trade agreement.[685] The US-JO FTA was signed in a record time on October 24, 2000.[686] It was the first FTA to be concluded in the absence of fast track authority, which had lapsed since 1994.[687] Without fast track authority, congressional approval for the FTA would be subject to regular procedures. Congress could have made amendments to the FTA, voted it down, delayed its passage, added amendment(s) and filibustered (unlimited debate) it.[688] The FTA negotiators took a

---

[684] Of particular importance are the opportunities the agreement potentially provides Palestinians living in Jordan and operating in QIZs. For these individuals, nearly all of whom at present live in poverty and have little chance to improve their lives, FTA changes the equation and offers real hope. Significantly, it offers a tangible alternative to violence. President Kennedy who said "trade, not aid". See Sen. Comm. on Finance, *Hearing on Jordan Free Trade Agreement*, 107th Cong. 1st Sess. (Mar. 20, 2001) (statement of Sen. Bingaman). That view is held by Israeli Prime Minister Sharon, who, on his first visit to Washington as prime minister, urged Congress to pass this historic trade agreement. See statement of Sen. Daschle. *Id.* at 9693.

[685] See Gary G. Yerkey, *U.S., Jordan Make "Substantial" Progress in Talks on Free Trade Agreement, USTR Says*, 17 Intl. Trade Rep. (BNA) 1224 (Aug. 3, 2000) (stating agreement to initiate negotiations was announced by U.S. officials following a meeting between President Clinton and King Abdullah on June 6 in Washington, D.C.).

[686] This record time of approximately four months can be compared with the 15 months of intensive debate between the U.S. and Israel which resulted in the conclusion of the US-Israel FTA. See Andrew James Samet & Moshe Goldberg, *The U.S.-Israel Free Trade Area Agreement* 1.02 (Bus. L. 1989). NAFTA parties completed negotiations in 1992 after 14 months of negotiations. Along the lines of the US-JO FTA, the US-Bahrain FTA of 2004 was concluded within four months starting January 2004 and ending in May of the same year. Early conclusion of the US-JO FTA negotiations could be attributed to the fact that probably there were not matters that would hold up the negotiations. The ground for the FTA had been laid down in Jordan's economic reforms, its accession to the WTO, and in talks with the U.S. under the existing Trade and Investment Framework Agreement.

[687] The fast track authority is a procedure, delegated by the U.S. Congress, gives the U.S. executive the authority to enter into trade negotiations under certain procedural requirements. It was used to conclude the Tokyo Round of 1979, the US-Israel FTA of 1985 whereby a specific section (section 401) of the U.S. Trade and Tariff Act of 1984 was designed as "trade with Israel", the US-Canada FTA of 1988, NAFTA of 1993, and the Uruguay Multilateral Trade Round of 1994. Since then, the fast track authority was not revived, despite various attempts, until the year 2002. For more on fast track authority see I.M DESTLER, *Renewing Fast-Track Legislation* 8 (Inst. Intl. Econ. 1997). Section 401 of the Tariff and Trade Act of 1984 required the FTA negotiated with Israel to be submitted to Congress under fast track authority. For negotiating with other countries, the country in question must first request to negotiate an FTA with the U.S. and that the House Way and Means Committee and Senate Finance Committee approve such negotiations.

gamble when they concluded the FTA without clear indications that it would be accepted by the U.S. Congress.[689] However, these fears were unfounded as the FTA moved through Congress largely as negotiated. This is an indication that the absence of a fast track authority may not prevent the conclusion of an FTA, although this may also depend on the country with whom the FTA has been concluded.[690]

The National Assembly of Jordan ratified the US-JO FTA by acclamation in May 2001.[691] The U.S. House of Representative approved the US-JO FTA Implementing legislation in July 2001.[692] The U.S. Senate approved FTA Implementing legislation in September 2001.[693] President Bush signed the FTA into a law on September 28, 2001.[694]

---

[688] The following represent the chronicle and timeline for the passage of the US-JO FTA implementing legislation: 1/6/2001 then-president Clinton submitted the FTA along with implementing legislation to Congress (despite that the U.S. President had no time limit for submitting implementing legislation to Congress after concluding negotiations, then-president Clinton could not submit the FTA implementing legislation earlier than 1/6/2001 since it would had taken time to customize the FTA, the Congress was in winter recess which would make it difficult to pass it in a lame duck session, there might be no enough time to finalize the implementing legislation, and U.S. elections. The Clinton administration could not submit the implementing legislation of the FTA until 2 months after the FTA was signed), 7/24/2001 the bill (H.R. 2603) was referred to the House Committee on Ways and Means, and in addition to the Committee on the Judiciary, 7/26/2001 Committee consideration and Markup Session Held (mark-up session is where the bill is formally introduced as it is or a new version, amended if any, considered line by line, section by section, and page by page, and voted on by members of the committee. Non-mark up session focuses mainly on draft legislation), 7/27/2001 Referred to the Subcommittee on Immigration and Claims, 7/31/2001 House Committee on Judiciary Granted an extension for further consideration ending not later than July 31, 2001, 7/31/2001 Mr. Thomas, chairman of the House Ways and Means Committee, moved to suspend the rules and pass the bill (when the House moves to suspend the rules, floor amendments are not permitted. A move to suspend the rules indicates that the bill is not controversial), 7/31/2001 Received in the Senate and Read twice and referred to the Committee on Finance, 9/24/2001 Senate Committee on Finance discharged by unanimous Consent (unanimous consent means that senators all agree to follow certain procedures and ignore standing rules. It also indicates that the bill is uncontroversial. Thus, there is no need to file for cloture on the legislation. Cloture requires 60 votes and if approved the holds on a legislation are overcome the legislation can be considered on the floor), 9/24/2001 Passed Senate without amendment by Voice Vote (Voice vote, as the name indicates, means the implementing legislation of the FTA was approved through a public decision in which congressmen approved the legislation by voicing their votes loudly, not by a show of hands. It is the fastest voting method), 9/24/2001 Message on Senate action sent to the House, 9/24/2001 Cleared for the White House, 9/25/2001 Jeff Trandahl, clerk of the House, presented the bill to the President, 9/28/2001 Signed by President, and 9/28/2001 Became Public Law. During consideration of the US-Jordan FTA implementing legislation, hours of debate were reduced to 2 hours in the Senate. For more on U.S. Congressional terms see Charles Tiefer, *Congressional Practice: A Reference, Research, and Legislative Guide* 167-186, 349-351 (Greenwood Press 1989).
[689] The Clinton Administration, during former USTR Mickey Kantor office, considered negotiating an FTA with Jordan in 1994, but later it decided not to do so because it was too ambitious and the administration lacked fast track authority.
[690] Interview with Edmund R. Saums II, Director for Middle East Affairs, Office of the United States Trade Representative, in Washington, D.C (Oct. 27, 2004).
[691] The US-JO FTA was approved during the extraordinary session of the National Assembly starting April, 22, 2001. See Royal Decree, Official Gazette No. 4486, page 1664 (Apr. 1, 2001).
[692] A bill (H.R. 1484) cosponsored by 30 Democrats and 0 Republicans to implement the US-JO FTA was presented on April 4, 2001 to the House. The House bill, nevertheless, died.
[693] See *The United States-Jordan Free Trade Agreement Free Trade Area Implementation Act*, Sen. 2603, 107th Cong. (2001) (enacted).

II. The Terms of the US-JO FTA

The US-JO FTA is comprised of a preamble, nineteen articles, three annexes, joint statements, memorandums of understanding, and side letters. The preamble of the US-JO FTA lists the aims of the agreement. For example, the FTA partners desire to further the historic bonds of friendship between them.[695]

A. Trade in Goods

The US-JO FTA is designed to "eliminate" substantially all tariffs between the two parties by 2010.[696] This means that products eligible for tariff elimination will enter the customs territory of the other party duty free. For the purpose of tariff reductions, the parties adopted a tariff cut formula that divides their tariff schedules into four baskets. Each basket of products has its own implementation schedule. To facilitate a smooth transition toward freer trade and minimize the economic and social costs associated with such movement, the elimination of tariffs will be fully implemented in four separate stages over a period of ten years.[697]

Tariff concessions of the FTA parties are balanced in baskets A and B. For example, Jordan has more items in basket D (approximately 2384 tariff items) and basket B (approximately 1016 tariff items), while the U.S. put more items in basket A (approximately 2920 tariff items) and basket B (approximately 1765 tariff items).[698] Although the FTA parties divided their tariff schedules into baskets, which have their own tariff implementation schedule, under the general mandate the FTA, the parties can agree to accelerate the removal of tariffs on any range of products.[699]

---

[694] See *United States-Jordan Free Trade Agreement Implementation Act of 2001*, 19 U.S.C. § 2112 n. (2000).

[695] See United States (U.S.)-Jordan: Agreement Between The United States of America and the Hashemite Kingdom of Jordan on The Establishment of a Free Trade Area, Oct. 24, 2000, 41 I. L. M. 63 (entered into force Dec. 17, 2001), preamble.

[696] *Id.* art. 2.1.

[697] The US-Israel FTA provides for the elimination of tariffs on non-agricultural products as of 1995. NAFTA provides for the elimination of all tariffs and other trade barriers within 15 years. See NAFTA, annex 302.2, 32 I.L.M 289, 299 (1993). Additionally, article 308 of NAFTA provides for harmonization of MFN rates among NAFTA parties for certain automatic data-processing goods and their parties. Perhaps, it was thought that it would contribute to deeper integration.

[698] With this in mind, one must notice that tariff lines of the U.S. and Jordan may vary from 6 to 10 digits due to disaggregation. As such, the U.S. tariff schedule has two or three as many tariff lines as Jordan with different item definition.

[699] The FTA allows the Joint Committee "to review the results of the agreement in light of the experience". See United States (U.S.)-Jordan: Agreement Between The United States of America and the Hashemite Kingdom of Jordan on The Establishment of a Free Trade Area, *supra* n. 695, art. 15.2. If Jordan desires to accelerate tariff commitments under the FTA, it ought first to identify its priority products and secondly secure acceptance of the U.S.

The U.S. has adopted a "pay-as-you-go" budget rule to fund the US-JO FTA.[700] The U.S. Congressional Budget Office (CBO) has estamited that the probable loss of revenue resulting from the FTA would be about $15 million over a five fiscal year window. Considering the minimal loss of revenue as a result of the FTA, the U.S. Office of Management and Budget will not likely consider imposing fees or taxes on U.S. citizens to pay for the FTA during the five fiscal years. Jordan, in contrast, could offset loss of revenue resulting from lower import tariffs through economic growth that would be generated by the FTA. For Jordan, the FTA may be a tax cut, but it is not tax expenditure as it will make goods and services less expensive.

B. Trade in Services

The multilateral trading system of the WTO not only covers trade in goods but it also covers trade in services. The US-JO FTA also includes a provision regarding trade in services.[701] As the two parties expect the FTA to expand trade, it was important to insure that trade in services also flows freely between the two countries.

The purpose of the service provision in the US-JO FTA is to prevent discriminatory treatment between foreign and domestic suppliers of services.[702] Moreover, the FTA ensures that there is a minimum threshold of treatment below which one party cannot treat a service provider of the other party. For example, a U.S. firm operating in Jordan will market its services under the same conditions as a Jordanian firm marketing like services.

In the US-JO FTA, Jordan agreed to more liberalization commitments for trade in services more than it had made in its accession to the WTO. Jordan gave U.S. suppliers of services preferential treatment in many sectors. For example, Jordan made new

---

[700] The "pay-as-you-go" rule of the Balanced Budget and Emergency Deficit Control Act of 1985 requires the government to offset any loss of revenue from reduced import tariffs through the FTA by raising taxes, cutting on tax subsidies, or by reducing mandatory/discretionary spending. See *Balanced Budget and Emergency Deficit Control Act of 1985*, 2 U.S.C. § 904 (2000).

[701] See United States (U.S.)-Jordan: Agreement Between The United States of America and the Hashemite Kingdom of Jordan on The Establishment of a Free Trade Area, *supra* n. 695, art. 3. The US-Israel FTA covers trade in services. However, The US-Israel FTA provides a general rule, rather than a detailed provision. For example, the US-Israel FTA states that the parties recognize the importance of trade in services and the need to maintain an open system of services exports which would minimize restrictions on the flow of services between the two nations. To this end, the parties agree to develop means for cooperation on trade in services pursuant to the provisions of a [Declaration] to be made by the parties. See US-Israel FTA, 24 I.L.M. 657,664 (1985). NAFTA has multiple chapters that are related to the service sector. NAFTA liberalizes trade-related services, in chapter 12, by applying the basic principles of national treatment and MFN treatment to the service sector. Chapter 12 of NAFTA does not address telecommunication and financial services since chapter 13 and 14 of NAFTA respectively cover these two sectors. Moreover, chapter 12 of NAFTA does not apply to energy and petrochemical service sector since chapter 6 governs energy. For more see Harry G. Broadman, *International Trade and Investment in Services: A Comparative Analysis of NAFTA*, 27 Int'l Law. 623, 624 (1993).

[702] See United States (U.S.)-Jordan: Agreement Between The United States of America and the Hashemite Kingdom of Jordan on The Establishment of a Free Trade Area, *supra* n. 695, art. 3.2.b.

commitments in veterinary services.[703] In addition, Jordan liberalized the research and development subsector.[704] Jordan also made commitments in leasing and rental services, advertising, public opinion polling services, services incidental to agriculture, manufacturing, services incidental to fishing, services incidental to energy distribution, convention services, audiovisual sector, environmental services, and maritime services.[705]

The movement of natural persons (Mode 4) was of particular importance to Jordan. However, temporary entry into the U.S. is limited to executives, managers, or specialists of a Jordanian company that has a physical presence in the U.S. in the form of branch, subsidiary, or affiliate.[706] Such entry is limited to three years with a one-time two years extension. The U.S. commitment, while covering the intra-corporate movement of senior personnel, does not extend to other categories of workers. Moreover, a corporate employee cannot move to the U.S. his company already maintains a commercial presence in the U.S. The commercial presence requirement makes it difficult for Jordanian workers to enter the U.S. service market.

The US-JO FTA permits trade in a wide range of services offered by U.S. institutions. While Jordan made new commitments that covered veterinary, audiovisual, health and education, and maritime transportation services, the U.S. did not make any new commitments. Rather, the U.S. incorporated its GATS service schedule in the FTA without modifications.[707] In contrast, in the FTA, Jordan made further commitments that went beyond those it made under GATS. Therefore, Jordan's service commitments in the US-JO FTA may be considered "GATS-Plus".

Trade in services is a major trade issue for the U.S. The U.S. is a major service exporter in areas such as motion pictures, banking, and franchising. Indeed, the U.S. was among the leaders to recognize the importance of trade in services and to push for its inclusion in the Uruguay Round. It may be impossible to analyze precisely what effects the FTA commitments will have on Jordan's marketplace and infant service sector.

C. TRIPs-Plus Commitments in the US-JO FTA

One of the objectives of the US-JO FTA is to emphasize the relationship between trade and intellectual property.[708] The TRIPs agreement of the WTO sets minimum standards for the protection of intellectual property rights. The US-JO FTA builds on the

---

[703] See US-JO FTA, Jordan Schedule of Specific Commitments, annex 3.1, page 7, at <http://www.ustr.gov/regions/eu-med/middleeast/ann31Jor.pdf >.

[704] *Id.* at 9.

[705] *Id.* at. 11-28.

[706] See U.S. Service Schedule, 4, at <http://www.ustr.gov/regions/eu-med/middleeast/ann31US.pdf>.

[707] Indeed, the U.S. services schedule of the US-JO FTA makes reference to liberalization dates for certain sectors such as road transport as of 1997 knowing that the US-JO FTA was concluded in 2000. *Id.* at. 90. For comparison see U.S. Schedule of Specific Commitments, Apr. 15, 1994, WTO Doc. No. GATS/SC/90.

[708] The preamble of the US-JO FTA emphasizes the desire of both parties to foster creativity and innovation and promote trade in goods and services that are subject of intellectual property right. See United States (U.S.)-Jordan: Agreement Between The United States of America and the Hashemite Kingdom of Jordan on The Establishment of a Free Trade Area, *supra* n. 695, preamble.

commitments Jordan made in acceding to the WTO. Article 4, which is TRIPs-Plus, of the US-JO FTA occupies five pages out of twenty pages of the FTA and is the longest article in the whole text of the FTA.[709]

The US-JO FTA defines the nature and the scope of intellectual property rights.[710] The US-JO FTA protects copyrights, trademarks, and patents and encourages each party to make "its best effort" in ratifying or acceding to the Patent Cooperation Treaty of 1984 and the 1989 Madrid agreement concerning the international registration of marks.[711] The FTA provides the possibility of protecting geographical indications through trademarks. The US-JO FTA requires each party to provide to the nationals of the other party treatment no less favorable than it gives to its own nationals with respect to the protection

---

[709] The US-Israel FTA which has only one general paragraph addressing intellectual property. See US-Israel FTA, *supra* note 704, art. 14. NAFTA chapter 17 (Intellectual Property) has twenty-one article. Chapter 17 covers copyright, sound recordings, encrypted program-carrying satellite signals, trademarks, patents, layout designs for semiconductor integrated circuits, trade secrets, geographical indications, and industrial designs. See Kent S. Foster & Dean C. Alexander, *Opportunities for Mexico, Canada, and the United States: A summary of Intellectual Property Rights under the North American Free Trade Agreement*, 20 Rutgers Computer & Tech. L.J. 67 (1994). See also David Price, *The U.S.-Bahrain Free Trade Agreement and Intellectual Property Protection*, 7 J.W. Intell. Prop. 829, 830 (No. 6, 2004) (the FTA between the U.S. and Bahrain derives its detail from the US-Jordan free trade agreement. Many of the required changes go far beyond the TRIPs).

[710] Each party to the FTA will have to give effect, at minimum, to the provisions of article 4. See United States (U.S.)-Jordan: Agreement Between The United States of America and the Hashemite Kingdom of Jordan on The Establishment of a Free Trade Area, *supra* n. 695, art. 4.1.

[711] As of 2004, Jordan is not a party to the PCT and the Madrid protocol while the U.S. is party to both of them. *Id.* art. 4.2. Since all intellectual property rights are territorial, an inventor for example has to file a patent application in every country that he/she wishes to protect its invention within. To ease this burdensome process, WIPO administer the patent cooperation treaty, better know as PCT, for the filing, searching, publication and examination of international applications. The PCT makes it easier to obtain patents in other countries by providing for the filing of one international application, which may be subsequently prosecuted in the different designated national or regional offices of countries party to the PCT. However, the ultimate decision to grant a patent is left to those designated offices. Thus, the purpose of the PCT is to facilitate the filing of patent application. See Daniel Pruzin, *WIPO Members Agree to New Filing Fees Under Treaty, Reduced Electronic Filer Fees*, 20 Intl. Trade Rep. (BNA) 1649 (Oct. 9, 2003). By the same token, WIPO administers an international registration of trademarks through what is known as the Madrid system. It is composed of two treaties that complement each other. These two treaties are the Madrid agreement of 1891 and the Madrid protocol of 1989. The Madrid system works in the same manner as the PCT by filing an international application for the registration of a trademark, but the ultimate decision is left to the designated countries whether to afford protection to a trademark or not. To apply for international registration under the protocol, an applicant must be a national, or domiciled, or have an effective and real business or commercial establishment in one of the countries that are members of the protocol. The registration of a trademark in one of the members serves as the basis of an international application (known as the basic application). The international application must be submitted through the trademark office of the basic application. Then, after verification, the international application is submitted to the International Bureau of WIPO. The International Bureau then examines the international application to determine whether the filing requirements and fees have been met. If the application is regular then the International Bureau registers the mark and publishes it in the WIPO Gazette of International Marks. Every designated country in the international application will examine the application under its own laws. See *PTO Issues Rules, Amendments To Implement Madrid Protocol Act*, 20 Intl. Trade Rep. (BNA) 1647 (Oct. 9, 2003).

and enjoyment of all intellectual property rights.[712] The US-JO FTA requires Jordan to undertake commitments and regulatory changes that go beyond what Jordan agreed to in its accession to the WTO. For instance, the FTA protects through patents business methods. The FTA does not address folklore protection and technology transfer.

1. Trademarks and Geographical Indications

The FTA specifically addresses trademarks and geographical indications (GIs). Trademarks include service marks, and collective marks and certification marks.[713] According to the FTA, trademarks may include GIs.[714] Thus, the FTA merges GIs and trademarks, meaning that a GI could be trademarked.[715] The U.S. exported its complex intellectual property statutes and judicial decisions into the language of the US-JO FTA. U.S. courts have developed goods/place association test to distinguish between primarily geographical descriptive marks and primarily geographical deceptive misdescriptive marks.[716] The language in the FTA affirms the U.S. opposition for the protection of GIs. The U.S. does not have a geographical indication law, but rather it protects geographical indication through trademark law.[717]

The FTA obligates each party to afford owners of registered trademarks the exclusive right to prevent any party from using an "identical or similar" mark for a

---

[712] See United States (U.S.)-Jordan: Agreement Between The United States of America and the Hashemite Kingdom of Jordan on The Establishment of a Free Trade Area, *supra* n. 695, art. 4.3.

[713] *Id.* art. 4.6. The FTA parties are not obliged to treat certification marks as a separate category in their national laws, as long as such marks are protected.

[714] A GI will be considered a trademark if it "consists" of any sign, or any combination of signs, capable of identifying a good or service as originating in the territory of a party, or a region or locality in that territory, where given quality, reputation or other characteristic of the good or service is essentially attributable to its geographical origin. *Id.*

[715] Under TRIPS, the distinction between the two concepts is that trademarks indicate a single source of goods while geographical indications can indicate multiple sources of goods, as long as they come from the same geographical origin. See John R. Renaud, *Can't Get There from Here: How NAFTA and GATT Have Reduced Protection for Geographical Trademarks*, 26 Brook. J. Intl. L. 1097, 1115 (2001).

[716] In re Nantucket, Inc. case, the U.S. Court of Customs and Patent Appeals decided that in determining whether the mark is geographically deceptive misdescriptive it adopted goods/place association test. In other words, if the goods do not come from a geographical area and consumers do not associate the goods from that place, then consumers will not be deceived and the mark is not deceptively misdescriptive. Moreover, it must be proved that the alleged misrepresentation would be a material factor in the decision of consumers to purchase the product. See *In re Nantucket, Inc.*, 677 F.2d 95 (C.C.P.A.1982). The current U.S. statute reads that primarily geographical descriptive mark can be registered as a trademark if it obtains a secondary meaning. On the other hand, geographically deceptively misdescriptive mark can never be registered. See Robert P. Merges et al., *Intellectual Property In the New Technology Age* 559 (3rd ed., Aspen Publishers 2003).

[717] The U.S. did not historically placed cultural or economic importance for geographical indications, many geographical indications developed as generic terms when early European immigrants came to the U.S. and brought with vine to plant in the U.S. The U.S. is hostile to geographical indications because they provide protection indefinitely, and it believes that no one can obtain an exclusive right to use geographic name to preclude others from using the geographical term. See Stacy D. Goldberg, *Who Will Raise the White Flag? The Battle between the United States and the European Union over the Protection of Geographical Indications*, 22 U. Pa. J. Intl. Econ. L. 107, 136 (2001). Examples of GIs in the U.S. protected by trademark law include Chablis, Darjeeling tea, Florida citrus, Vidalia onions, Maine lobsters, and Budweiser beer.

"related" good or service for which the trademark is used.[718] The US-JO FTA also protects against the use of a well known marks.[719] The protection of well known marks is an area of concern in Jordan.

The FTA addresses the non-recordal of a trademark license.[720] The FTA stipulates that the non-recordal of a license does not affect the validity of the registration of a trademark or protection of rights for that trademark.[721] If a trademark holder licenses the use of his mark to a licensee, any use by the licensee may constitute a use by the holder and any subsequent rights would accrue to the holder.

2. Copyright and Related Rights

The US-JO FTA addresses copyright and related rights. The FTA also addresses how these rights function in cyberspace.[722] The US-JO FTA covers the right of reproduction, exclusive importation, and broadcasting. There is also a provision relating to the communication of works of producers of phonograms and performances.[723]

---

[718] See United States (U.S.)-Jordan: Agreement Between The United States of America and the Hashemite Kingdom of Jordan on The Establishment of a Free Trade Area, *supra* n. 695, art. 4.7.

[719] *Id.* 4.8.

[720] Non-recordal is a problem area in the ongoing negotiations of amending Trademark Law Treaty of 1994 by WIPO membership.

[721] *Id*, art. 4.9.

[722] The US-JO FTA incorporates article 1(4) of the WCT and articles 7 and 11 of WPPT. Both treaties, WCT and WPPT of 1996, have no parallel in TRIPs. It should come at no surprise that these two treaties are absent from TRIPs since they were concluded in 1996, two years after TRIPs came into existence. *Id.* art. 4.10. WIPO's Diplomatic Conference on Certain Copyright and Neighboring Rights Questions convened in 1996. In the end, the participants reached a consensus on treaties dealing with copyright and performances and phonograms. The treaties were created in response to the arrival of the digital age and known as the "Internet treaties". See Susan A. Mort, *The WTO, WIPO & the Internet: Confounding the Borders of Copyright and Neighboring Rights*, 8 Fordham Intell. Prop. Media & Ent. L.J. 173, 176, 195 (1997). See also See Julie S. Sheinblatt, *The WIPO Copyright Treaty*, 13 Berkeley Tech. L.J. 535 (1998).

[723] See United States (U.S.)-Jordan: Agreement Between The United States of America and the Hashemite Kingdom of Jordan on The Establishment of a Free Trade Area, *supra* n. 695, arts. 4.10-12. The WCT and WPPT do not incorporate the exclusive right of importation. The right of importation, which would have given copyright holders the exclusive right to authorize importation of their works, fell during the negotiations of the WCT and WPPT. The U.S. supported the proposal to include the right of importation during the negotiations of the WCT and WPPT. See Basic Proposal on the Substantive Provisions of the Treaty on Certain Questions Concerning the Protection of Literary and Artistic Works to be Considered by the Diplomatic Conference, Aug. 30, 1996, WIPO Doc. CRNR/DC/4, at 8.10-12. Additionally, the TRIPs Agreement does not mention importation rights for copyright or trademark owners. The exclusive right of importation under article 4.11 of the US-JO FTA is very broad. It gives the copyright holder the exclusive right to authorize or prohibit the importation of copies even if they were made with the authorization of the copyright holder. The FTA provides performers and producers of phonograms the "exclusive right" to authorize or prohibit the whether delivered through a cable, a satellite dish, a terrestrial broadcast, or streamed via the Internet. The language would allow performers and producers of phonograms to control and/or to be compensated for the various ways in which their creations are used and enjoyed by others. In order to achieve a balance of interests, article 4.12 makes it clear that parties have the flexibility in establishing exceptions to the exclusive right of performers and producers of phonograms. For example, a party may provide exceptions for analog transmissions and non-subscription over-the-air programming. As such, free broadcast signals are not compensable. Moreover, a party may provide, through legislation, licenses for non-interactive services that do not conflict with the normal exploitation of phonograms or

The US-JO FTA covers anti-circumvention measures by prohibiting the circumvention of effective technological measures that protect copyright.[724] For example, under the FTA it is illegal to disable a technology that is designed to prevent burning of the content of a CD. The source of the FTA language is the U.S. Digital Millennium Copyright Act of 1998, which protects intellectual property in the digital environment.[725] The FTA requires each party to prohibit both civilly and criminally the manufacture, importation, or circulation of any technology, device, or service that is designed, produced, performed or marketed for engaging in such prohibited conduct or has only limited commercially significant purposes or uses other than enabling or facilitating such conduct.[726] As a result of the FTA anti-circumvention provisions, manufacturer may face uncertainty as to whether a device is "used" for commercial purposes or to circumvent technological measures.

The FTA allows copyright owners to assign economic rights by any means that are considered appropriate without limitations and restrictions.[727] The FTA requires that the U.S. and Jordan enact appropriate laws, regulations, or other measures that provide all government agencies use "only" computer software authorized for a legitimate use.[728] The purpose of requiring government agencies to use legitimate computer software is to set an example for private parties, which is a step towards combating copyright piracy. The use of legitimate software by government agencies means that American software companies, such as Microsoft Corp., will provide products and services to the small Jordanian government software procurement market.

---

performances. A key element in granting statutory license is the requirement that the service must be non-interactive. Unless a service meets this criterion, it is ineligible for the statutory license. In that case, it must negotiate a voluntary agreement with performers and producers of phonograms. An example of non-interactive service could be the traditional practices of FM radio broadcast stations through which individuals can request the station to play a sound recording as part of its general programming available to members of the public at large. The determination as to whether a service is interactive or not requires a case-by-case analysis.

[724] See United States (U.S.)-Jordan: Agreement Between The United States of America and the Hashemite Kingdom of Jordan on The Establishment of a Free Trade Area, *supra* n. 695, art. 4.13.

[725] See *U.S. Digital Millennium Copyright Act of 1998*, 17 U.S.C. §§ 512, 1201 (2000). The DMCA makes exceptions from the anticircumvention measures language for nonprofit libraries, reverse engineering to make software interoperable, encryption research, protecting personal information, security testing, and preventing minor access to inappropriate materials. These exceptions are not included in the FTA. The FTA incorporates article 11 of the WCT and article 18 of the WPPT by reference. However, the WCT and WPPT provide general obligation to adequately protect against circumvention of technological measures.

[726] Article 4.13 of the US-JO FTA prohibits "manufacture" of a device that is designed to circumvent technological measure. This language could be called "anti-production" provision. Moreover, article 4.13 of the FTA prohibits "importation" or "circulation" of such a device. This is could be called "anti-commercial activity" provision. Moreover, article 4.13 of FTA distinguishes between two cases. The first case is the prohibition against a device that is "designed", "produced", "performed", or "marketed" for engaging in such prohibited activity. In other words, the primary purpose of the device is to circumvent technological measure. The second case is where the device has "only" limited commercial significance purpose or use other than enabling or facilitating the prohibited conduct. The second case requires weighing whether the device has significant commercial purpose, other than to circumvent technological measures.

[727] See United States (U.S.)-Jordan: Agreement Between The United States of America and the Hashemite Kingdom of Jordan on The Establishment of a Free Trade Area, *supra* n. 695, art. 4.14.

[728] *Id.* art. 4.15.

The FTA provides an exception to the exclusive rights of copyright holders. Any exception, however, must be confined to certain cases that do not conflict with the normal exploitation of the work and do not unreasonably prejudice the legitimate interests of the right holder.[729] An example of an exception to the exclusive rights of copyright holders is the creation of back-up copies of a computer program. Few cases have been decided by WTO panels regarding the interpretation of these exceptions.[730] Thus, WTO panel decisions may provide guidance as to how a U.S. or Jordanian citizen can act within the exception of the FTA.

3. Patents

The US-JO FTA also covers patents and determines the conditions for patentability. Any invention in any field of technology if it is new, involves an inventive step, and be capable of industrial application is patentable.[731] In addition, the inventor must disclose the information pertinent to the creation of his invention so that others skilled in the art to may be able to carry out the invention.[732] The FTA excludes from patentability any invention the exclusion of which is necessary to protect *ordre public*, morality, human, animal or plant life or health, or to avoid serious prejudice to the environment.[733] In addition, the FTA excludes from patentability diagnostic, therapeutic and surgical methods for the treatment of humans or animals.[734] However, the FTA does not exclude

---

[729] *Id.* art. 4.16. The FTA language is identical to article 10 of the WCT, article 16 of WPP1, and article 13 of TRIPS.

[730] The WTO panel in the US-Section 110(5) of the Copyright Act case defined article 13 of the TRIPS agreement as exception that articulates the scope of the so-called "minor exceptions" doctrine. The panel further delineated that limitations or exceptions to exclusive rights can only be made if three conditions are met: (1) the limitations or exceptions are confined to certain special cases; (2) they do not conflict with a normal exploitation of the work; and (3) they do not unreasonably prejudice the legitimate interests of the right holder. See United States-Section 110(5) of the US Copyright Act, June 15, 2000, WTO Doc. No. WT/DS160/R, para. 6.58.

[731] See United States (U.S.)-Jordan: Agreement Between The United States of America and the Hashemite Kingdom of Jordan on The Establishment of a Free Trade Area, *supra* n. 695, art. 4.17.

[732] *Id.* 4.21. The US-JO FTA stipulates that if it is not possible to provide "sufficient written description" of the invention to enable other skilled in the art to carry out the invention, the U.S. or Jordan shall require a deposit with an international depository authority as defined in the Budapest Treaty on the International Recognition of the Deposit of Microorganism for the Purposes of Patent Procedure of 1980. The Budapest Treaty is primarily concerned with procedural matters associated with microorganism-related inventions and leaves substantive rules to national laws. The Treaty provides for the establishment of International Depository Authorities (IDAs) to collect cultures. Under the regulations of the Budapest Treaty, samples of biological materials deposited with an IDA may be furnished to interested industrial property offices, the depositor or those authorized by the depositor and parties which are legally entitled to obtain a sample. A single deposit with an IDA satisfies the deposit requirement in all countries that are members of the Budapest Treaty. In addition, the application must prove that the sample and any information accompanying or resulting from it will be used only for the purposes of said patent procedure. See Richard I. Gordon, *Facilitating the Exchange of Scientific Information: Institut Pasteur v. United States*, 6 B.U. Intl. L.J. 179, 207, 212 (1988).

[733] See United States (U.S.)-Jordan: Agreement Between The United States of America and the Hashemite Kingdom of Jordan on The Establishment of a Free Trade Area, *supra* n. 695, art. 4.18.a.

[734] *Id.* art. 4.18.b.

from patentability life forms, which is an issue of tremendous importance for U.S. biotechnology companies.[735]

The Memorandum of Understanding of the FTA expands the patentability provisions to include business methods and computer-related inventions.[736] The issue of patenting business methods is derived from U.S. laws and practices. In 1998, the U.S. introduced the concept of patenting business methods.[737] Moreover, U.S. courts granted patents for methods of doing business.[738] Under the FTA, anything under the sun made by man is

---

[735] The TRIPS agreement in article 27.3.b excludes from patentability plants and animals, and biological processes for the production of plants or animals. The U.S. proposed, in a document submitted to the WTO in preparation for the Seattle Ministerial Conference of 1999, that the TRIPS Council should initiate a work to see whether it is desirable to modify the TRIPS agreement to eliminate the exclusion from patentability of plants and animals. See Communication from the United States, *Preparation for the 1999 Ministerial Conference*, WT/GC/W/115 (Nov. 19, 1999). In 1988, the U.S. Patent and Trademark Office issued a patent covering an animal, known as Transgenic Mouse. Thousands of gene-related patent applications have been filed with the U.S. Patent and Trademark Office. Although products of nature are not patentable, various courts in the U.S. have upheld patents on isolated and purified natural substances. For example, the 1912 case of Parke- Davis & Co. v. H.K. Mulford & Co. upheld a patent on adrenaline, a natural hormone that was found in animal glands. The patent applicant identified, isolated, and purified the active ingredient, adrenaline. This discovery created a product that did not exist in nature in that precise form and that could be used for medical treatment. On the other hand, the EC's Biotechnology Directive considers certain subject matter to be per se unpatentable including processes for modifying the genetic identity of animals which are likely to cause them suffering without any substantial medical benefit to man or animal, and also animals resulting from such processes. See Lori B. Andrews, *The Gene Patent Dilemma: Balancing Commercial Incentives with health Needs*, 2 Hous. J. Health L. & Policy 65 (2002) (publication page references not avail.). The divergent views of the U.S. and EC are due to different legal standards of patentability. Generally, the U.S. law entertains broad subject matter patentability, while the EC is more circumspect in the subject matter of patentability. See Barbara Looney, *Should Gene be patented? The Gene Patenting Controversy: Legal, Ethical, and Policy Foundations of an International Agreement*, 26 Law & Policy Intl. Bus. 231, 234 (1994).
[736] Paragraph 5 of the Memorandum reads "Jordan shall take all steps necessary to clarify that the exclusion from patent protection of "mathematical methods" in article 4 (B) of Jordan's Patent Law does not include such "methods" as business methods or computer-related inventions". See Memorandum of Understanding on Issues Related to the Protection of Intellectual Property Rights, http://www.ustr.gov/regions/eu-med/middleeast/memopro.pdf (Mar. 15, 2003). To meet this requirement, Jordan could modify its patent law to state clearly that business methods or computer-related inventions are patentable, it can adopt a regulations that clearly state the same, or adopt any other measure that would meet its requirements under the Memorandum.
[737] A business method can be defined as a method of administering, managing, or otherwise operating an enterprise or organization. The term "business method" means:
(1) a method of -
(A) administering, managing, or otherwise operating an enterprise or organization, including a technique used in doing or conducting business; or
(B) processing financial data;
(2) any technique used in athletics, instruction, or personal skills;
(3) any computer-assisted implementation of a method described in paragraph (1) or a technique described in paragraph (2). See the Business Method Patent Improvement bill of 2000, 2000 H.R. 5364, 106th Cong., 2d Sess. (2000).
[738] In a case involved a method for processing financial data in hub and spoke system for mutual funds accounting and administration, the Court of Appeals for the Federal Circuit held that such method is not excluded from patentability. See *St. St. Bank v. Signature Fin. Group, Inc.*, 149 F.3d 1368 (Fed. Cir. 1998). In another case, Amazon.com and other inventors filed with the U.S. Patent and Trademark Office a patent application for a method and system for placing an order to purchase an item via the Internet, known as the

patentable.[739] The provisions relating to the patentability of business methods were drafted to meet the interests of the U.S.

The US-JO FTA permits the use of a subsisting patent by a third party to support his application for the marketing approval of a product.[740] A subsisting patent should be used for the purpose of obtaining marketing approval only and not for sale. The US-JO FTA also addresses compulsory licensing.[741] It allows the issuance compulsory licensing in only three cases: to remedy a practice determined to be anti-competitive; for public non-commercial use or national emergency or other circumstances of extreme emergency; and if there is a failure to meet working requirements.[742] In contrast, the TRIPs Agreement left open the grounds for issuing compulsory licensing.[743] The compulsory licensing language of the US-JO FTA reflects U.S. policy. The U.S. treats compulsory licensing as an exceptional policy tool to be used only in limited cases rather than a standard part of the intellectual property regime.

4. Data Exclusivity and Pharmaceuticals

The FTA requires that the U.S. and Jordan protect confidential clinical test data in marketing approval applications from misappropriation.[744] The FTA does not limit the protection foreign companies receive for their clinical test data of pharmaceuticals. Data exclusivity, however, can delay the introduction of generic competition for life saving

---

"1-click" method. In 1999, Amazon.com filed suit against Barnesandnoble.com, claiming that Barnesandnoble.com's "Express Lane" ordering feature infringed Amazon.com's patent. Amazon.com obtained a preliminary injunction against the use of its business method by barnesandnoble.com. In 2001, however, the Court of Appeals for the Federal Circuit vacated the preliminary injunction and remanded the case, ruling that all the necessary prerequisites for granting a preliminary injunction were presently lacking. The Court of Appeals decided that the District Court erred by not recognizing prior art reference. For example, CompuServe's Trend Service, which allowed CompuServe's subscribers to purchase stock charts, appeared to use a single-action ordering technology. Another prior art reference, a book, copyrighted in 1996 and entitled Creating the Virtual Store addressed the single-action method. See Sue Ann Mota, *Internet Business Method Patents-The Federal Circuit Vacates the Preliminary Injunction in Amazon.com v. Barnesandnoble.com*, 19 John Marshall J. Computer & Info. L., 523, 528 (2001). In 2002, Amazon and Barns and Noble eventually reached a confidential settlement. See Robert C. Scheinfeld & Jeffrey D. Sullivan, *Internet-Related Patents: Are they Paying Off?* N.Y L.J. 5 (Dec. 10, 2002).

[739] See *Diamond v. Chakrabarty*, 447 U.S. 303, 309 (1980) (the case held that an engineered oil-eating bacteria is patentable).

[740] See United States (U.S.)-Jordan: Agreement Between The United States of America and the Hashemite Kingdom of Jordan on The Establishment of a Free Trade Area, *supra* n. 695, art. 4.19.

[741] *Id*. art. 4.20.

[742] *Id*. The FTA does not define national emergency for purpose of invoking compulsory licensing. The FTA considers importation of the patented product as working. See Paul Champ & Amir Attaran, *Patent Rights and Local Working under the WTO TRIPS Agreement: An Analysis of the U.S.-Brazil Patent Dispute*, 27 Yale J. Intl 'l. 365, 366, 369 (2002) (the U.S. sought in TRIPS negotiations to bar any possible obligation or remedy there might be for a patentee's failure to work locally. It also sought to restrict compulsory licensing to national emergencies and anti-competitive abuses).

[743] Article 31 of the TRIPS agreement sets specific conditions for grant compulsory licensing but does not list or define the cases where a license may be granted. Daniel Geravis, *The TRIPS Agreement: Drafting History and Analysis* 250 (2d ed., Sweet & Maxwell 2003).

[744] See United States (U.S.)-Jordan: Agreement Between The United States of America and the Hashemite Kingdom of Jordan on The Establishment of a Free Trade Area, *supra* n. 695, art. 4.22.

drugs for example. Under the FTA, drug regulatory authorities will not allow a drug originator's registration files to be used to register a therapeutically equivalent generic variation of a medicine for a fixed period of time. The FTA effectively extends monopolies by drug originators and affects access to medicines. Generics will effectively be barred from entering the market, even if patent terms have expired and even if a country has issued a compulsory license for a product that is on patent, until the monopolies on the use of the data expire.

The US-JO FTA extends the patent term for pharmaceutical products.[745] Extending the patent term vindicates the expectations of inventors who did not receive a twenty-year term at the time the patent was first filed. Extending the patent term especially applies in the case of pharmaceutical products that undergo human and animal tests to ensure their safety for use before being granted marketing approval. The use of patent extension depends on the existence of an efficient drug approval system in Jordan.

The FTA mandates that the U.S. and Jordan "make available" an extension of the patent term, which indicates that patent term extensions were not intended to be mandatory. The U.S. and Jordan are obliged to provide access to an extension by giving the inventor the chance to file an application for an extension. The FTA does not determine the period of extension of a patent term. However, textually, the use of the term an "extension" in a singular form may be textually interpreted to mean that an extension of the patent term is allowed only once.

5. Enforcement of Intellectual Property Rights

The US-JO FTA includes provisions governing private enforcement of intellectual property rights, including the availability of injunctions, damages, and other remedial measures.[746] In cases of a knowing infringement of trademark, copyright and related rights, judicial authorities can order the infringer to pay the right holder "adequate damages".[747] The FTA makes use of a mathematical formula to compute how much injury the right holder sustained in order to calculate the amount of damages. An injury determination is based on the value of the infringed-upon item according to the suggested retail price of the legitimate product (SRP) or other equivalent measures established by the right holder for valuing authorized goods.[748] Using the SRP will increase the value of the product and thus increase the amount of damages awarded beyond what could have been awarded if actual retail price have been used.

The FTA imposes statutory fines on infringers. It requires the U.S. and Jordan to increase their statutory-based fines sufficiently to deter future acts of infringement

---

[745] *Id.* art. 4.23.a.
[746] *Id.* arts. 4.24-28.
[747] The right holder must prove that the infringer has engaged in the infringing activity "knowingly". In other words, the infringer must posses the intention to engage in the infringing activity.
[748] *Id.* art. 4.24.

169

through the removal of the monetary incentive of the infringer.[749] Furthermore, the FTA requires authorities to seize all suspected pirated copyright and counterfeit goods, related implements that are used predominantly to commit the offense, and documentary evidence of infringement.[750] With respect to criminal actions and border measures, the FTA requires national authorities to act *ex officio*, i.e. upon their own initiative, without the need for a private party or right holder to lodge a formal complaint. This allows rights holder to protect their rights while avoiding time-consuming legal proceedings. The FTA also establishes a rebuttable presumption that the author, producer, performer, or publisher of a work whose name appears on the work is the person entitled to bring a civil infringement case to protect his copyright.[751]

The FTA changes the conventional definition of piracy. It defines willful copyright piracy on a commercial scale as involving significant willful infringement that has no direct or indirect motivation of financial gain.[752] Piracy is a term that has no uniform definition. While it is most often used to refer to an egregious infringement of copyright, it is also used to refer to the intentional and systematic infringement with the purpose of profit-maximization.[753] According to the FTA, an infringer with no direct or indirect financial motive is liable for copyright piracy, similar to a willful infringer motivated by financial gain.

The US-JO FTA sets a timetable for the parties to comply with their intellectual property obligations. Each party is required to comply with article 4.1.c (WCT), 4.1.d (WPPT), and articles 4.10-16 (copyright and related rights) within two years from the date the FTA enters into force.[754] Each party should also comply with article 4.1.b (UPOV) within six months from the effective date of the FTA. The FTA further mandates that each party shall promptly protect undisclosed data or tests for purposes of marketing approval of pharmaceutical or agricultural chemical products. Finally, each party is required to protect new chemical entities within three years form the date the FTA enters into force.

The transitional period given to Jordan to implement its intellectual property obligations is a form of special and differential treatment. However, the TRIPs Agreement allows developing countries special treatment with respect to fulfilling their obligations; thus similar provisions in the FTA are not unique. Moreover, the FTA does not define how Jordan should implement its obligations. For example, to comply with the FTA, Jordan can redraft its domestic laws or simply make additions or clarifications to those laws. There is a vacuum, however, because it does not determine a transitional period for compliance with the Memorandum of Understanding on Issues Related to the

---

[749] *Id.* art. 4.25.

[750] The use of the term "predominant use" is unclear. For example, it is unclear if 60 percent use of the tool is for committing piracy suffices the FTA requirement.

[751] *Id.* art. 4.27.

[752] *Id.* art. 4.28.

[753] J. Thomas McCarthy, *McCarthy's Desk Encyclopedia of Intellectual Property* 325 (2d ed., Bureau Natl. Affairs 1995).

[754] See United States (U.S.)-Jordan: Agreement Between The United States of America and the Hashemite Kingdom of Jordan on The Establishment of a Free Trade Area, *supra* n. 695, art. 4.29

Protection of Intellectual Property Rights, which include provisions relating to the patentability of business methods.

6. General observations

There are certain points worth mentioning about the FTA intellectual property provisions. Some of the intellectual property provisions are very general. For example, the FTA does not specify in which cases an invention may be excluded from patentability. Furthermore, under the FTA, there are only three cases in which a compulsory license may be issued. In contrast, subsequent to the TRIPs Agreement, WTO members adopted a Declaration on the TRIPs Agreement and Public Health, which grants countries the right to issue compulsory licenses and the freedom to determine the grounds upon which such licenses are issued.[755] As party to the US-JO FTA., Jordan cannot benefit from the Declaration because it locked in the cases in which a compulsory license may be granted. Moreover, there are many exceptions to the intellectual property rights codified in the TRIPs Agreement. In contrast, the FTA includes only few exceptions.

The intellectual property provisions of the FTA are one-sided. They were drafted to protect U.S. intellectual property rights. The FTA does not address communal rights, such as traditional knowledge and folklore expressions. As party to the FTA, Jordan adopted a U.S.-style intellectual property regime. For example, the FTA affords patent protections to business methods. The FTA represents a homogenization of intellectual property laws between the U.S. and Jordan. This harmonization of standards may not be a desirable objective. It is preferable to have separate policy instruments for each party rather than one single policy instrument covering both parties.

The US-JO FTA does not contain provisions relating to the transfer and dissemination of technology. The preamble of the FTA focuses only on "creativity and innovation" but does not refer to the transfer and dissemination of technology or the interest of the public. The FTA should have linked the enforcement of intellectual property rights with the transfer of technology and investment.

D. Balance of Payments

In order to prevent either party of the US-JO FTA from circumventing its obligations under the FTA, a provision was needed to discipline trade restrictions imposed to improve a country's balance of payment.[756] For this end, the US-JO FTA requires that

---

[755] See Doha Ministerial Conference, Declaration on the TRIPS Agreement and Public Health, WT/MIN(01)/DEC/2, para. 5(b) (Nov. 14, 2001).

[756] The term "balance-of-payments" refers to a "statement showing all of a nation's transactions with the rest of the world for a given period. It is divided into current and capital accounts. While current account flows consist primarily of goods and services, capital account flows are flows in the ownership of foreign and domestic assets. In other words, current account is concerned with trade and capital account is concerned with portfolio foreign direct investment. A balance-of-payments problem occurs when a drop in demand for a country's currency, as result of reduction in export earning and/or investment, is so steep that it creates downward pressure on its currency value. This problem renders citizens unable to purchase

any measure imposed for balance of payment purposes has to be in compliance with the WTO.[757] In fact, the US-JO FTA balance of payments provision utilizes the language of the similar WTO provision and does not add further restrictions.

E. The US-JO FTA and Electronic Commerce

The US-JO FTA is the first FTA to include a provision concerning electronic commerce (e-commerce).[758] The US-Israel FTA and NAFTA do not contain parallel provision regarding e-commerce.[759] This is understandable as the US-Israel FTA and NAFTA are fifteen and six years older, respectively, than the US-JO FTA. In the time since since the drafting of the US-Israel FTA and NAFTA, e-commerce has become more developed with the advent of the internet.[760]

The e-commerce provision of the US-JO FTA applies to goods and services traded over the medium of the Internet. The FTA covers e-commerce but does not define the term.[761] The FTA also uses the term "digitized products" without providing a definition. The FTA could have listed illustrative examples of digitized products, such as

---

everyday necessities, known as "consumption crisis". To prevent balance of payment crisis, a government can use monetary policy to increase demand and reduce supply of domestic currency by exchanging foreign currency for domestic currency. A government can fund these exchanges with its foreign reserves, or with borrowed money. Another possible solution is the use of trade policy to counterbalance the increased demand for imports by imposing import restrictions to force a reduction in the trade deficit. For more on the dynamics of balance of payment see Chantal Thomas, *Balance-of-Payment Crises in the Developing World: Balancing Trade, Finance and Development in the New Economic Order*, 15 Am. U. Intl. L. Rev. 1249, 1251-1254 (2000).

[757] See United States (U.S.)-Jordan: Agreement Between The United States of America and the Hashemite Kingdom of Jordan on The Establishment of a Free Trade Area, *supra* n. 695, art. 11. Two principal articles of the WTO relate to balance of payments (article XII and XVIII. section b GATT 1994) Article XII can be invoked by all WTO members, developed and developing countries. However, article XVIII.1 can be imposed by the developing countries only.

[758] Thomas Cottier, *The Impact of New Technologies on Multilateral Trade Regulation and Governance*, 72 Chi.-Kent L. Rev. 415, 426, 435 (1996) (concluding that the new technologies are the most important driving force in the process of globalization of the economy).

[759] However, article 1302 of NAFTA's chapter 13, Telecommunications, could be considered an article related to e-commerce. It contemplates in its subparagraphs access to and use of public telecommunication networks for information services, privacy, security, and confidentiality.

[760] The Internet has changed the way international trade is conducted. National boundaries become secondary to network borders. For example, a simple transaction may involve data captured in one country, a transaction authorization system at a remote computer site located in a second country, and settlement of the transaction in a third country on another computer system. See Joel R. Reidenberg, *Electronic Communications and Legal Challenge: Rules of the Road for Global Electronic Highways: Merging the Trade and Technical Paradigms*, 6 Harv. J.L. & Tech. 287, 304 (1993).

[761] There is no universally agreed definition of e-commerce. However, in the WTO Work Program on Electronic Commerce, e-commerce is understood to mean the production, distribution, marketing, sale or delivery of goods and services by electronic means. A commercial transaction can be divided into three main stages: the advertising and searching stage, the ordering and payment stage, and the delivery stage. Any or all of these stages may be carried out electronically and may therefore be covered by the concept of e-commerce. In other words, a buyer may purchase a book via the Internet and be delivered physically later on or he can purchase and download the book via the Internet. In either case, the purchase of the book could be said that it is conducted through e-commerce means. See WTO Secretariat, *Development Implications of Electronic Commerce*, WT/COMTD/w/51 (Nov. 23, 1998).

electronically traded software, books, and music. The FTA requires that the parties do not deviate from their "existing practice" of not imposing tariffs on electronic transmissions.[762] This language is based on the U.S. Internet Tax Freedom Act of 1998.[763] The FTA also requires that the parties do not establish "unnecessary" barriers on electronic transmissions, which include digitized products. The FTA requires the U.S. and Jordan to make publicly available all laws, regulations, and requirements affecting e-commerce.

The e-commerce provision of the US-JO FTA does not extent to all e-commerce matters, such as domain name, Internet security, and intellectual property.[764] The FTA covers border trade measures only such as, tariffs, unnecessary trade barriers, and services that facilitate e-commerce. The FTA does not determine if digital products should be treated as goods or as services.[765] Determining whether an e-product is a good or service is a crucial assessment. If an e-product is a good, then it will be subject to the

---

[762] See United States (U.S.)-Jordan: Agreement Between The United States of America and the Hashemite Kingdom of Jordan on The Establishment of a Free Trade Area, *supra* n. 695, art. 7.1.a.

[763] The act, which has the purpose of promoting universal access and less burdensome Internet tax policy, imposes a moratorium on all taxation of Internet access and on "multiple" or "discriminatory" taxes on e-commerce. The act also includes a declaration that the Internet should be free of tariffs, trade barriers, and other restrictions. Moreover, the act asks the U.S. President to pursue "international agreements" to ban such tariffs and other trade barriers. See *Internet Tax Freedom Act of 1998*, 47 U.S.C. §151 (2000). The moratorium begins on Oct. 1, 1998 and ends on Nov. 1, 2003. On Nov. 19, 2004, the Congress passed legislation S.150 that reinstated a four year moratorium on Internet access taxes and multiple and discriminatory taxes on e-commerce. The new legislation applies retroactively to Nov. 2003. Thus, the new legislation will expire in 2007.

[764] Legal questions brought about by e-commerce but not discussed here include, but are not limited to, domain names in cyberspace and trade marks. See Suzanna Sherry, *Haste Makes Waste: Congress and the Common Law in Cyberspace*, 55 Vand. L. Rev. 309 (2002). See also Serge G. Avakian, *Global Unfair Competition in the Online Commerce Era*, 46 UCLA L. Rev. 905 (1999). For the effects of new methods, such as price comparison, cookies, exclusive provision by Internet Service Provider (ISP), and business alliances, used by e-retailers to sell their products online that may raise issues of anticompetitive practices see Alan E. Wiseman, *The Internet Economy: Access, Taxes, and Market Structure*, chapter four (Brookings Instn. Press 2000). For discussion of privacy issues such as cookies on user's personal computers and unsolicited commercial communications without the consent of the addressee (opt-in system) in the age of e-commerce and the U.S. reliance on market oriented industry self-regulation approach of handling personal data see Joel R. Reidenberg, *Restoring Americans' Privacy in Electronic Commerce*, 14 Berkeley Tech. L.J. 771 (1999) For discussion on consumers concern regarding identity, privacy, data collectors, and security of financial information see Nicole Ladouceur, *Calibrating the Electronic Scale: Tipping the Balance in Favor of Vigorous and Competitive Electronic Market for Consumers*, 25 Can.-U.S. L. Rev. 295 (1999). For discussion of cyber-security issues and how not only legal but architectural responses are needed see Neal Kumar Katyal, *Digital Architecture as Crime Control*, 112 Yale L.J. 2261 (2003).

[765] There is disagreement among WTO members on this point. In other words, it is unclear whether digital products delivered over the Internet should be classified as goods or as services for the purpose of WTO regimes and rules. E-products include books, music, videos, software, and other newly emerging media, which in a rapidly growing digital market may arguably be developed in strictly computerized forms simply to avoid tariffs and strict international legal standards on physical goods and services. See Kristi L. Bergemann, *A Digital Free Trade Zone and Necessarily-Regulated Self-Governance For Electronic Commerce: The World Trade Organization, International Law, and Classical Liberalism in Cyberspace*, 20 J. Marshall J. Computer & Info. L. 595, 600-601(2002) (discussing the option for self-governance of the Internet based on existing quasi-legal norms within the cyber-community, rather than regulatory framework within national governments or supranational organization).

national treatment rules of the FTA. In conrast, if an e-product is a service, then each party may impose restrictions on market access and national treatment.[766]

The vagueness of the e-commerce provision of the US-JO FTA suggests that negotiators faced a dilemma while drafting it. On the one hand, the FTA parties had to recognize the importance of e-commerce to world trade. On the other, there is no universal regulatory system for e-commerce within the WTO that would have guided the FTA negotiators.[767] The U.S. and Jordan adopted an approach whereby the current rules of trade that apply in the physical world would also apply in the virtual world. For example, the e-commerce provision of the US-JO FTA holds to the existing rules regarding market access, services, and transparency. Thus, the drafters of the US-JO FTA did not create entirely new rules for the new virtual environment.

The next question that must be addressed is how to identify the party benefits from the e-commerce provision of the US-JO FTA. The U.S., as of 2004, has the largest number of internet users, estimated at 200 million, and about 70 percent of all Internet websites are based in the U.S.[768] Even more, 85 percent of the world's internet revenue in 1996-97 was generated in the U.S.[769] In 2003, online retail sales in the U.S. were $55 billion.[770] In contrast, in Arab countries, including Jordan, online commerce is negligible.[771] In 2001, Jordan had only 120,000 internet users.[772] Most commercial websites in Jordan are aimed at cataloging and advertising products rather than selling online. Online commerce requires use of modern financial and credit transactions and payments via consumer credit cards. One of the obstacles for the development of e-

---

[766] The U.S. has been the primary advocate of the position that digitized products should be classified as goods. See Stewart A. Baker et al., *E-Products and the WTO*, 35 Int'l. Law 5,7 (2001).

[767] The first time the WTO addressed Internet trade, although under GATS, was its ruling on U.S. restrictions on cross-border Internet gambling services. The ruling found that online gambling restrictions imposed by the U.S. at the federal and state levels violated its market access commitments under sub-sector 10.D (other recreational services) of its GATS schedule which corresponds to CPC heading 96492. The restrictions denied Antiguan-based gaming operators access to the U.S. market. See Report of the Panel on United States-Measures Affecting the Cross-border Supply of Gambling and Betting Services, Nov. 10, 2004, WTO Doc. No. WT/DS285/R.

[768] See *E-Commerce Takes Off*, Economist 3, 20 (May 15, 2004) (In the U.S., women outnumber men online).

[769] See WTO Secretariat, *supra* note 870, at para.21. See also Catherine L. Mann et al., *Global Electronic Commerce: A Policy Primer*, 16 (Inst. Intl. Econ. 2000).

[770] See The Economist, *supra* n. 768, at 3 (the figure, according the U.S. Department of commerce, excludes online travel services. For example, the owner of Seattle-based expedia.com and hotels.com sold $10 billion worth of travel in 2003 (some 20 percent of travel in the U.S. is bought online). It also excludes pornography which made $ 2 billion in the U.S. in 2003. The figure excludes also sales of financial services, ticket-sales agencies, online dating, tracing ancestors, and gambling. The gambling business is worth $ 6 billion. About $ 24 billion worth of trade was done in 2003 on the California-based ebay, the biggest online auctioneer. Used-car sales are now one the biggest online growth areas). See also Barrett J. Willingham, *Electronic Commerce and the Free Trade of the Americas*, 6 NAFTA: L. & Bus. Rev. Am. 483, 491 (2000) (by 2003, business-to-business trade within the U.S. would soar to $1.3 trillion, an amount that would represent more than nine percent of total U.S. business).

[771] See *Trade Facilitation and E-commerce in the ESCWA Region*, U.N. Economic and Social Commission for Western Asia, at 5, U.N Doc. E/ESCWA/ED/2001/2 (2001).

[772] *Id.* at 36.

commerce in Jordan is the fact that the number of credit card holders is small.[773] One can describe Jordan as a cash-transaction society.[774] In contrast, the U.S. is cashless society. The differences between the U.S. and Jordan with respect to internet accessibility, efficient telecommunication infrastructure, and volume of e-commerce should have been an indication for the FTA negotiators that a more balanced provision would be needed to accommodate the e-commerce environments in each country. The FTA lacks legal obligations or recommendations that the two parties share information and experience regarding policies intended to encourage the development of e-commerce.

F. Visa Obligations in the US-JO FTA

The US-JO FTA addresses entry of nationals of one party into the territory of the other.[775] The FTA allows nationals of one party to enter into the territory of the other party solely to engage in "substantial trade," including trade in services and technology. The FTA does not define "substantial trade". The U.S. Department of State regulations define "substantial trade" as the quantum of trade "sufficient" to ensure a "continuous flow" of trade items between the U.S. and the treaty country.[776]

The FTA also allows nationals of one party to enter into the territory of the other to establish, develop, administer, or advise on the operation of an "investment".[777] The FTA qualifies investment by requiring that a national or the companies that employ that national to "have committed" or be "in the process of committing" a "substantial amount of capital or other resources to that investment. Thus, the FTA requires a significant amount of up front investment, which may take the form of transferring money before the national of Jordan can obtain a visa. The purpose of such language is to prevent fraud. The FTA does not define "investment" or "substantial amount of capital". However, the U.S. Department of State regulations define investment to mean that an investor places of capital, including funds and other assets, "at risk" in a commercial sense with the objective of generating a profit.[778] An investor under the FTA must play a key role in the

---

[773] Id.

[774] Buying through using credit card is not the norm. Cash is the norm. Generally, credit cards are accepted at major hotels, restaurants, and other establishments. There might be a lack of system of credit history check.

[775] See United States (U.S.)-Jordan: Agreement Between The United States of America and the Hashemite Kingdom of Jordan on The Establishment of a Free Trade Area, *supra* n. 695, art. 8.

[776] See *Treaty Trader, Treaty Investor, or Treaty Alien in a Specialty Occupation*, 22 C.F.R. § 41.51 (j) (2005).

[777] See United States (U.S.)-Jordan: Agreement Between The United States of America and the Hashemite Kingdom of Jordan on The Establishment of a Free Trade Area, *supra* n. 695, art. 8.2.

[778] The U.S. regulations require treaty investors to be "in possession" of and "have control" over the capital invested or being invested. Additionally, the U.S. regulations condition that capital in the process of being invested or that has been invested must be "irrevocably" committed to the enterprise. Moreover, the investment must not be passive or virtual but rather a "real" and "active" commercial or entrepreneurial undertaking, producing some service or commodity for profit and must meet applicable legal requirements for doing business in the particular jurisdiction in the U.S. Finally, the Department of State regulations require that the projected future capacity of the enterprise should generally be realizable within five years from the date the alien commences normal business activity of the enterprise.

investment whether through its establishment, development, administration, or advice in order to be eligible for a E-2 visa. The purpose of this language is to prevent visa fraud.

For the first two years of the operation of the FTA, there have been no E-visas issued to Jordanian nationals under the visa provisions of the FTA.[779] This could be interpreted as to lack of interest in or understanding of these visa provisions by Jordanian nationals. Traders in Jordan may also face obstacles in meeting the threshold requirements of "substantial trade" or "substantial amount of capital" for investment.

Chapter 16 of NAFTA is dedicated to temporary entry for business persons.[780] It created four categories of business persons who may be granted temporary entry. These four basic categories are: business visitors; traders and investors' intra-company transferees; and professionals. Business visitors who are engaged in international business activities may enter a NAFTA member country for the purposes of conducting research and design, and participating in growth, manufacture and production.[781] NAFTA also provides E-1 and E-2 visas for traders and investors. The third category of NAFTA visas is a L-1 visa for a business person employed by an enterprise that seeks to render services for that enterprise or a subsidiary or affiliate thereof, in a capacity that is managerial, executive or involves specialized knowledge.[782] The last category of visas under NAFTA is professional visa (TN category), which is a unique kind of visa for NAFTA nationals and is not available for nationals of other countries.[783] One year after NAFTA came into force, 220 accountants from the U.S. entered Canada independently, and 62 U.S. accountants entered as intra-company employees. In addition, 965 engineers from the U.S. and 7 from Mexico, and 224 American intra-company engineers and 3 Mexicans were issued entry documents. There were 34 lawyers independently and 9 as

---

[779] Ltr. from Cher Young, Consular Assoc., U.S. Embassy in Amman, Jordan, to Bashar H. Malkawi, Student, Am. L. Sch., *Number of Visas Issued under the U.S.-Jordan Free Trade Agreement* (Aug. 5, 2003) (on file with author).

[780] See NAFTA, *supra* note 697, art. 1601. Chapter 16 of NAFTA consists of eight Articles and supplemented by annexes. Chapter 16 of NAFTA was modeled on chapter 15 of the US-Canada FTA of 1989 titled "Temporary Entry for Business Persons". However, with the implementation of NAFTA, chapter 15 of the US-Canada FTA was suspended. See Kenneth A. Schultz, *The North American Free Trade Agreement: The Provisions for the Temporary Entry of Canadian and Mexican Business Persons into the United States*, 15 SPG Intl. L. Practicum 50 (2002).

[781] For a description of the four categories of temporary entry of business persons see William J. Benos, *The Movement of Professionals, Technicians, and other Workers across NAFTA Borders*, 8 US-Mex. L. J 25, 26 (2000).

[782] See NAFTA, *supra* n. 697, appendix 1603.C.1.

[783] See Benos, *supra* n. 781, at 27. H-1B status, which also provides for the entry of professionals, should not be confused with TN category under NAFTA. The preamble to the INS interim rule specifically stated that admission pursuant to NAFTA to engage in professional level activities does not imply qualification as a "professional" under the Immigrant and Nationality Act. The H-1B category is for "specialty occupations", namely, those in occupations for which an entry level requirement is customarily a university degree at the American baccalaureate level. On the other hand, NAFTA seeks to simplify the admission process for a select and "precisely" defined group of Canadian and Mexican professionals. See Schultz, *supra* n. 780, at 52. Under NAFTA, certain categories of professionals who meet minimum educational requirements, or posses designated credentials or licenses and experience, and who seek to engage in professional occupations in a NAFTA member country, may be admitted for example into the U.S. for up to one year.

intra-company employees came from the U.S.; no Mexican lawyers moved to work in Canada.[784]

The U.S. could have incorporated provisions in the US-JO FTA similar to the TN category of NAFTA. This would have given Jordanian professionals an opportunity to acquire contacts and experience, which could translate into an increase of trade between the U.S. and Jordan. However, it seems that immigration issues and problems with the recognition of credentials prevented the incorporation of such a provision. The U.S. was concerned that Jordan may dump its citizens in the U.S., although placing a cap on the number of TN visas issued annually would have mitigated this concern. U.S. trade negotiators feared a potential backlash from Congress if a provision relating to professional visas was incorporated in the FTA, as this could have been seen as setting a precedent for future FTAs especially in light of the fact that the US-JO FTA is an agreement with a low-income country.[785] The U.S. could have permitted entry of Jordan's traders or investors as long as they submitted a declaration containing a good business plan. A similar declaration could be submitted to extend the length of business visas. Jordanians are human beings and have a baccalaureate degree. They are part of free trade.[786] As the language of the US-JO FTA currently stands and practice so far proves, the US-JO FTA is a trade agreement concerned with the movement of goods and services, but not the movement of persons.

G. Government Procurement

The US-JO FTA addresses government procurement by requiring the parties to enter into negotiations with regard to Jordan's accession to the WTO GPA.[787] As of this date, Jordan has not acceded to the GPA.[788] Until Jordan accedes to the WTO GPA and its firms are able to compete in bidding, Jordanian firms will face discrimination in supplying goods and services to U.S. governmental agencies.[789] However, Jordan may be

---

[784] *Id.*

[785] The power over immigration rests in Congress. Congress has the power to establish a uniform rule of naturalization. See U.S. Const. art. I, δ 8, cl. 4. See also *Lung v. Freeman*, 92 U.S. 275, 280 (1875) (The passage of laws which concern the admission of citizens and subjects of foreign nations to our shores belongs to Congress. It has the power to regulate commerce with foreign nations).

[786] Mr. Mazzoli, then chairman of the House of Representatives Subcommittee on International Law, Immigration and Refugees, during a heated debate over NAFTA chapter 16 and the differential treatment for Mexicans under that chapter said, "what is the difference? They are human beings, and they have a baccalaureate degree. They are part of the free trade operation". See H.R. Subcomm. on International Law, Immigration, and Refugees of the House Judiciary Comm., *Hearing on Immigration-Related Issues in the North American Free Trade Agreement*, 103d Cong. 1st Sess. 134 (Nov. 3, 1993).

[787] See United States (U.S.)-Jordan: Agreement Between The United States of America and the Hashemite Kingdom of Jordan on The Establishment of a Free Trade Area, *supra* n. 695, art. 9.

[788] Earlier section discussed, among others, Jordan's accession to the WTO Agreement on Government Procurement and some thoughts on its hesitance to accede. Hence, the current section will discuss the U.S. law on government procurement.

[789] The U.S. law overtly "bans any country" that is not member of the WTO Agreement on Government Procurement from participating in bidding to supply goods and services to U.S. governmental agencies. See *Trade Agreements Act of 1979*, 19 U.S.C. § 2513 (2000).

able to gain access to the U.S. government procurement market if the U.S. president designates Jordan as a beneficiary country.[790]

H. Trade Remedy Measures of the US-JO FTA

According to the US-JO FTA, parties can apply safeguard measures based on bilateral or global basis.[791] Either party can take safeguard measures against originating goods of the other party in situations in which such goods may cause or threaten to cause serious injury. The imposition of a safeguard measure under the FTA is tied to obligations. There must be a link between increased imports and the FTA's tariff concessions.[792] However, such a link is subject to a proviso that "only" the reduction or elimination of a duty is a "significant cause" that leads to an increase in imports, but need not be equal to or greater than any other cause.[793] The requirement that tariff concession be a "significant cause" of increased imports is extracted from U.S. law.[794] To imose a safeguard measure, Jordan will have to meet what could be christened as "double test". First, Jordan must prove that tariff concession is a "significant cause" of increased imports.[795] If successful, then Jordan will have to prove that increased imports are "substantial cause" of serious injury. There is a presumption that increased imports are not the result of tariff concessions, unless proven otherwise.

To impose safeguard measures under the FTA there must be an importation of goods in increased quantities, in either absolute or relative terms.[796] Moreover, imports of goods must constitute a "substantial cause" of serious injury, or threat thereof to a domestic industry that produce like or directly competitive product. The term "substantial cause" is defined as a cause that is "important" and "not less than any other cause," a definition derived directly from U.S. trade remedy law.[797] According to this definition of substantial

---

[790] Id. at § 2511.

[791] The terms safeguard measures, escape clause, and emergency actions are interchangeable. Chapter eight of NAFTA is titled "emergency action". See NAFTA, *supra* note 697, at 383. They carry the meaning that a country can escape its obligations of a free trade agreement under certain conditions. NAFTA also establishes two safeguard actions. Safeguard actions can be imposed on "originating goods" from NAFTA region that are imported in such quantities that cause or threaten to cause serious injury. Additionally, NAFTA party can impose safeguard measures on imported goods from "all countries", including NAFTA region. Id. arts. 801& 802.

[792] See United States (U.S.)-Jordan: Agreement Between The United States of America and the Hashemite Kingdom of Jordan on The Establishment of a Free Trade Area, *supra* n. 695, art.10.1.

[793] Id.

[794] See *Trade Act of 1974*, 19 U.S.C. § 2436 (2000). Section 406 of the Trade Act permits safeguard measures to counter market disruption from communist countries where rapid imports is "significant cause", but need not be equal to or greater than any other cause, of material injury.

[795] Absence the test for the link between tariff concession and increase imports, the safeguard provision of the US-JO FTA would be a mere measure for determining what is an unacceptable level of imports without the need to meet such a difficult test. Moreover, "significant cause" is not defined in the FTA. Is it the same as "substantial cause", less, or more? Does significant cause require cut-off such as 50 percent or 60 percent threshold among other causes? Significant cause requires analysis on a case-by-case basis.

[796] Under NAFTA, a party may impose a safeguard measure if there is increase in import in absolute quantities only. See NAFTA, *supra* n. 697, art. 801. 1.

cause, two prongs must be met. First, imports must be an "important" cause of serious injury. Second, imports must be "not less than any other cause". This "substantial cause" test has so difficult to overcome that section 201 of the the U.S. Trade Act has fallen largely into disuse. Aggrieved industries now rely upon the less stringent burdens of the countervailing and antidumping provisions of U.S. trade law to address injuries and threats from imports.[798]

Under the FTA, a safeguard measure may be imposed for a period of time no more than four years.[799] After the expiration of the transition period for imposing a safeguard measure, neither party can impose such a measure unless the other party consents. One can reason that this discrepancy in the ability to apply a safeguard measure without consent during the transition period and the requirement of obtaining consent after the transition period is based on the thought that the free trade area formed by the US-JO FTA would make a safeguard measure less necessary. It is also thought that local industries will have adjusted to trade competition by the time that the transition period ends.

Article 10 of the US-JO FTA establishes procedural obligations for conducting a safeguard investigation and providing notification and consultation with respect to that investigation.[800] The US-JO FTA stipulates that an investigation must be conducted by a competent authority.[801] For purposes of conducting an investigation, the US-JO FTA also incorporates some provisions of the WTO Agreement on Safeguard. For example, while conducting an investigation, either party to the FTA must provide reasonable public notice, a public hearing, and publish a report that sets forth the "findings" and "reasoned conclusions" reached on all pertinent issues of facts and laws. Moreover, either party to the FTA must evaluate all relevant factors of an "objective and quantifiable" nature that have a bearing on the situation of the industry seeking protection.

---

[797] Section 201 of the U.S. trade act of 1974 permits imports to be restricted, for a limited time, and on a non-discriminatory basis, if they are substantial cause of serious injury to U.S. firms or workers. Under the U.S. Trade Expansion Act of 1962, imports must have been "the major factor" causing injury. The Tariff Commission, now called the ITC, has interpreted this to mean that the increased imports were a more important cause of injury than all other causes combined. It is obvious that this interpretation was too restrictive. See Peter Bernardi, *The Great Escape*, 7 D.C.L. J. Intl. L. & Prac. 69, 80 (1998). By adopting, the substantial causation test, the U.S. Congress intended to provide a lower burden of proof than that contained in the 1962 Trade Expansion Act. Moreover, article 2 of the WTO Agreement on Safeguards allows a member to apply a safeguard measure to a product only if that member has determined that such product is being imported into its territory in such increased quantities as to "cause" or threaten to cause serious injury to domestic industry. It is noticeable the absence of "substantial cause" from the language of the WTO Agreement on Safeguards.

[798] The only success story recalled for section 201 petitions is Harley-Davidson case of 1983 of imposing tariffs on inventories of motorcycles from Japan of 700cc models. See Annual Report of the United States International Trade Commission 1-2 (1983) (tariffs increased on completed heavyweight motorcycles by 45 percent *ad valorem*, declining to 35, 20, 15, and 10 in subsequent years). In 1987, before the end of the safeguard protection period, Harley-Davidson requested the termination of the safeguard since the company has adjusted to competition from Japan.

[799] United States (U.S.)-Jordan: Agreement Between The United States of America and the Hashemite Kingdom of Jordan on The Establishment of a Free Trade Area, *supra* n. 695, art. 10.2.d.ii.

[800] *Id.* art.10.2.c.

[801] *Id.* 10.2.

The US-JO FTA covers "global action" safeguards.[802] Any safeguard measure imposed according to the "global action" provision must comply with the requirements of article XIX of GATT 1994 and the WTO Agreement on Safeguard. Any safeguard measure must be applied on a MFN basis.[803] The "global action" provision allows a party to impose a safeguard against the other as part of a multilateral safeguard action taken under article XIX of the GATT and WTO safeguard agreement. However, imports of one party to the FTA may be excluded from an MFN safeguard measure if such imports are not a substantial cause of serious injury or threat thereof. The FTA is silent as to whether imports from a party alone constitute substantial cause of serious injury to the domestic industry, what should the form of the safeguard measure be, or the type of compensation to be provided.[804] The FTA parties could have agreed that imports less than 10 percent of total imports would not be considered substantial.

The US-JO FTA has an industrial policy language aimed at protecting some industries that initially cannot offer competitive prices and quality as competing imports but nonetheless by giving them breathing room can develop over time into competitive price and quality industries.[805] An infant industry is defined, in the US-JO FTA, as an industry that has recently begun to produce like or directly competitive product. It is not clear whether the infant industry provision applies to infant industries that existed prior to the conclusion of the FTA or is limited only to infant industries established after the FTA came into existence. Based on the FTA language, an infant industry is a new industry. This definition does not include an already established industry that produces a new line of product or an expansion of an already existing industry supplying small proportion of the domestic market, or an industry that had previously been destroyed as a result of hostilities or natural disasters. The definition of an infant industry has a narrow scope.[806]

The FTA infant industry provision suggests that Jordan can shield its domestic industries by keeping out U.S. competitors. Depending on how a panel may interpret the infant industry provision, the provision may be found to have little value. First, even assuming that the FTA gives preferential consideration for Jordan's infant industry

---

[802] "Each Party retains its rights and obligations under Article XIX of GATT 1994 and the WTO Agreement on Safeguards". *Id.* art.10.8.

[803] "Safeguard measures shall be applied to a product being imported irrespective of its source". See WTO Agreement on Safeguard, art. 2.1.

[804] Under NAFTA for example, in order to determine in global action whether imports from NAFTA party are substantially cause serious injury to the domestic industry, imports from that NAFTA party must be among the top five suppliers of the good. See NAFTA, *supra* n. 697, art. 802. 2.a.

[805] The FTA states that the Parties recognize that, because it has recently begun to produce a like or directly competitive product described in paragraph 1 [originating good of the other party], an infant industry may face challenges that more mature industries do not encounter. As such, each Party shall ensure that the procedures described in paragraph 2 [the procedures for safeguard investigation] do not create obstacles to infant industries that seek the imposition of such measures". See United States (U.S.)-Jordan: Agreement Between The United States of America and the Hashemite Kingdom of Jordan on The Establishment of a Free Trade Area, *supra* n. 695, art.10.5.

[806] The definition of an infant industry in article XVIII.2 of GATT 1994 is broader. It includes new industry, a new branch of production in an existing industry, substantial transformation of an existing industry, expansion of an existing industry supplying a relatively small proportion of domestic demand, and an industry destroyed or substantially damaged as a result of hostilities or natural disasters.

preferential treatment is limited to procedures used in conducting a safeguard investigation. In other words, the investigation authority in Jordan may give an infant industry more time to respond for a request for a public hearing, present its evidence, or provide a counter-argument against an exporter or importer. The preferential treatment does not mean that an infant industry will be guaranteed a positive determination by imposing a safeguard measure. Second, the ultimate purpose of the US-JO FTA is to liberalize trade; the industrial policy article is at odds with this objective. While article XVIII of GATT 1994 allows additional facilities for infant industry such as tariff protection, government assistance through non-tariff measures, and subsidies, the FTA 's infant industry provision restricts in scope and time Jordan's ability to provide protection for its infant industries.[807]

The only import relief mechanisms available under the US-JO FTA are safeguard measures. The FTA does not have a provision on antidumping or countervailing duties. The inclusion of a safeguard measures under the US-JO FTA reflects the U.S. requirement that all trade agreements must have, at minimum, a provision for safeguard measures.[808] Thus, the US-JO FTA leaves domestic antidumping and countervailing duty laws untouched.

I. Rules of Origin in the US-JO FTA

The FTA contains provisions relating to preferential rules of origin. These rules are designed to guarantee that tariff concessions are enjoyed only by products of the countries that are parties to the FTA.[809] The FTA contains two types of rules of origin: a general rule that applies to all exported industrial and agricultural products, and a specific rule for textiles and apparel that are considered import-sensitive.

Under the FTA general rule of origin, in order for products to qualify for preferential treatment, the product must be "wholly" the growth, production or manufacture of Jordan.[810] The concept of "wholly growth" is interpreted narrowly since all the inputs

---

[807] The discussion has focused so far on the assumption that the FTA article applies only to infant industry of Jordan. The question that arises is whether the FTA infant industry language applies also to the U.S. which is often acknowledged as having no industrial policy. See *Fair Trade and Harmonization: Prerequisites for Free Trade* 306-309 (Jagdish Bhagwati & Robert E. Hudec eds., MIT Press 1996) (the United States has not had an avowed industrial policy. However, some critics have contended that the U.S. does in fact have an industrial policy in the broad sense. The U.S. has an implicit and decentralized industrial policy. The U.S. government and laws do advantage some industries over others).

[808] Following World War II, the U.S. president continued this policy by issuing an executive order requiring the presence of an escape clause in all future trade agreements. See Paul C. Rosenthal & Robin H. Gilbert, *The 1988 Amendments to Section 201: It is not Just for Import Relief Anymore*, 20 Law & Policy Intl. Bus. 403, 406 (1989).

[809] Paragraph 1 of article 14 of the US-JO FTA states "The parties recognize that the rules regarding eligibility for the preferential tariff treatment... are crucial to the functioning of this Agreement...shall strive to administer such rules effectively, uniformly, and consistently with the object and purpose of this Agreement and the WTO Agreement". See United States (U.S.)-Jordan: Agreement Between The United States of America and the Hashemite Kingdom of Jordan on The Establishment of a Free Trade Area, *supra* n. 695, art.14.1.

must be produced in the exporting country to qualify for preferential treatment; third party inputs are not allowed. Moreover, constituents of a product must not have undergone processing in any other country at any stage of production. The "wholly growth" rule of origin applies to agricultural products, primary products, and processed or manufactured products using raw materials solely from Jordan.[811]

If a product is "not wholly the growth, product, or manufacture of the party", then it must be "substantially transformed" into a "new and different article of commerce", having a new name, character, or use distinct from the article or material from which it was transformed.[812] The disjunctive "or" means that one of three parts of substantial transformation test (change in name, use, or characteristic) must occur.[813] The "substantial transformation" test is subjective as it leaves to the custom authorities of the importing country the discretion to determine whether a certain product has undergone substantial transformation. Because of this subjectivity, it is unclear at what time and to what extent a product has to undergo a substantial transformation.[814]

---

[810] *Id.* annex 2.2, art. 1.a. Wholly growth, product, or a manufacture of a party means a product that has been "entirely" grown, produced, or manufactured in a party and to all materials that are incorporated in the product, that have been entirely, grown, produced, or manufactured in the party's territory.

[811] A list of primary products for example would include mineral products, vegetable plants, and sea fishing products such as fish or shellfish.

[812] The language of the US-JO FTA regarding rules of origin is based on U.S. law. Country of origin means country of manufacture, production or growth of article of foreign origin and that further work or material added to article in another country must effect a substantial transformation in order to render such other country the "country of origin". Substantial transformation means fundamental change in form, appearance, nature or character of article which adds to value of article an amount or percentage which is significant in comparison with value which article had when exported from country in which it was first manufactured, produced or grown. See *Tariff Act of 1930*, 19 U.S.C.A. § 1304 (West 1930). Moreover, the U.S. Supreme Court defined substantial transformation further in Anheuser-Busch Brewing Association case. See *Anheuser-Busch Brewing Assn. v. U.S.*, 207 U.S. 556, 561 (1908) (the case involved corks imported from Spain to be incorporated in bottles for re-export. The court decided that manufacture implies a change, but every change is not manufacture, and yet every change in an article is the result of treatment, labor, and manipulation. There must be transformation: a new and different article must emerge, having a distinctive name, character, or use. Therefore, the careful selection and thorough treatment of corks would render corks a new article of commerce). The phrase "substantial transformation" is composed of two words. First, "transformation", whether modified by an adjective or not, means a fundamental change, not a mere alteration, in the form, appearance, nature, or character of an article. Second, "substantial" means more than "fundamental" because if that were its only meaning it would be redundant because transformation also means fundamental change. Therefore, "substantial" means a very great change in the article's "real worth value".

[813] Change in name only could not be in and of itself the determinative factor to meet the "substantial transformation" test. The CIT decided that the name factor in meeting the "substantial transformation" test is the weakest evidence of meeting the test. See *Juice Prod. Assn. V. U.S.*, 628 F. Supp. 978, 989 (Ct. Intl. Trade 1986). Change from producer's product to end-use product may not be of significance in determining that an imported product has undergone substantial transformation. See *U.S. V. Murray*, 621 F.2d 1163, 1170 (1st Cir. 1980) (Although Chinese glue was blended with other glues in Holland that changed from processor's good to consumer's good, it did not increase in value).

[814] For example, suppose that Jordan imports orange from Syria. Then, it manufactures or transforms the orange into orange juice in a factory in Jordan. In this case, it is clear that the orange juice is of Jordanian origin, with different name, use, or characteristics, which makes it eligible for preferential tariff treatment by the U.S. However, suppose that Jordan imports frozen concentrated orange juice from Syria. Then, it processes the frozen concentrated orange juice into liquid orange juice. In the latter case, it is not that obvious whether the liquid orange juice has undergone substantial transformation in Jordan.

Since the substantial transformation test may not suffice by itself to confer origin, the FTA also contains a mathematical requirement, known as the value-added rule or percentage rule.[815] The value-added rule requires, in conjunction with the substantial transformation rule, that the sum of 1) the cost or value of materials produced in Jordan plus 2) the direct cost of processing operations performed in Jordan must not be less than 35 percent of the appraised value of the product at the time it enters into the U.S.[816] The value-added test is designed to ensure that the process of transformation has resulted in the inclusion of a significant degree of Jordanian content. The value-added test may be internally discriminatory when evaluated in light of Jordan's cheap labor. For example, if a U.S. worker applies eight hours labor to an imported input, the valued-added test could be met easily because of high productivity. A Jordanian worker, on the other hand, may fail to raise the value of the product when employing the same amount of hours because of low level of productivity.

The FTA requires that an exported product must be shipped directly from Jordan to the U.S.[817] Technically, this requirement does not mean that the product cannot pass other countries on its way from Jordan to the U.S. As long as the product does not enter into the channels of commerce in other countries, the product will likely be deemed to be a product imported directly from Jordan.[818] This requirement that products be transported directly from Jordan to the U.S. also means that Jordan is forced to transport its products through other countries, which will likely be members of the EC. The "direct import" rule may discriminate against Jordan, which is landlocked and distant from the U.S. In rules of origin, physical proximity matters, and transportation costs may have effects similar to those of tariffs. Moreover, Jordan may lack adequate transportation infrastructure, which may add to transaction costs.

One may argue that the cumulation rule in the FTA, which states that the costs or values of materials produced or originated in the U.S. may add up to 15 percent of the 35 percent, may lessen the impact of 35 percent value added test. There are several points that illustrate the abortive nature of the cumulation rule. First, firm costs and structures in the U.S. are different from those of Jordan. In other words, the industrial structure in the U.S. is different from Jordan. As such, it is unlikely that U.S. inputs would end up as inputs final products of Jordan. Second, U.S. inputs may be priced at a high level that would make it difficult for Jordanian manufactures to produce final products at a reasonable profit margin. Finally, U.S. inputs may not be suitable quality and price for

---

[815] In some instances substantial transformation may confer origin by itself, but with low value such as 10 percent.

[816] See United States (U.S.)-Jordan: Agreement Between The United States of America and the Hashemite Kingdom of Jordan on The Establishment of a Free Trade Area, *supra* n. 695, 1.c.

[817] *Id.* 1.b. Imported directly means that the shipment passed from Jordan to the U.S. without passing through an intermediate country.

[818] If the bills of lading do not indicate that the U.S. is the final destination, then there are three tests that must be met. First, the shipment must remain under the control of the customs authority of the intermediate country. Second, the shipment does not enter into the commerce of the intermediate country except for sale other than at retail and imported as a result of an original commercial transaction between the importer and the producer or his agent. Third, the shipment did not go through any activity other than loading and unloading.

Jordanian manufactured products. Inputs from other perhaps more efficient non-FTA sources will be excluded because only U.S. inputs may be incorporated in the final products destined for the U.S.

While the US-JO FTA applies the "substantial transformation" test if a product is not wholly the growth, product, or manufacture of one party, NAFTA adopts the "tariff shift" rule, i.e. non-originating materials must shift from one tariff heading/subheading into another as a result of production that occurs in a NAFTA party.[819] Moreover, under the US-JO FTA the value added content is at lower threshold than under NAFTA. For example, the RVC is 62.5 percent for certain vehicles based on net cost method of the product. The high threshold for rules of origin under NAFTA may be explained by a long expressed concern that Asian companies were using Mexico as an "export platform," from which Asian parts and components would undergo "final assembly" and then be exported to the U.S. duty-free.[820] Additionally, the US-JO FTA does not incorporate a *de*

---

[819] For the first time in the U.S., the concept of change in tariff heading was used first in the US-Canada FTA and then NAFTA. Chapter Four (rules of origin) in NAFTA has a general rule that applies to all products exported from one party to the other. The general rule determines that a good is considered to originate in North America if 1) the good is wholly obtained or produced entirely in the territory of one or more of the parties to NAFTA 2) the non-originating materials used in the production of the good undergoes an applicable "change in tariff classification" as a result of production occurring entirely in the territory of one or more of the parties to NAFTA 3) the good is produced entirely in the territory of one or more of the parties exclusively from originating materials in NAFTA region 4) the good is produced entirely in the territory of one or more of the parties to NAFTA but one or more of the non-originating materials provided for "as parts" of the good does not undergo a change in tariff classification because the good 1) was imported into the territory of a party in an unassembled or a disassembled form but was classified as an assembled good or 2) the heading for the good describes both the good itself and its parts and is not further subdivided into subheadings, or the subheading for the good describes both the good itself and its parts provided that the regional value content (RVC) is not less than 60 percent under transaction value method or 50 percent under net cost method. Under the transaction value method, RVC = TV - VNM / TV X 100. RVC is the regional value content, expressed as a percentage, TV is the transaction value of the good adjusted to a F.O.B. basis, and VNM is the value of non-originating materials used by the producer in the production of the good. Under the net cost method, RVC = NC - VNM / NC X 100. NC is the net cost of the good and VNM is the value of non-originating materials used by the producer in the production of the good. NAFTA defines the net cost as the total cost less the following specific costs: sales promotion, marketing and after-sales service costs, royalties, shipping and packing costs, and non-allowable interest costs that are included in the total cost. In calculating the net cost, the producer may use several allocation methods. The difference between the two RVC methods in NAFTA is that the transaction-value method includes some costs that are excluded in the net cost method. NAFTA bases the transaction-value method on the price actually paid or payable for a good or material, and may thus include all costs plus profits. To compensate for this difference, the transaction value method requires a higher percentage of RVC. NAFTA rules provide for calculations based on the total price or the total cost, with deductions for certain cost items and/or the value of non-originating materials. See Marie Kately St. Fort, *A Comparison of the Rules of Origin in the United States under The U.S.-Canada Free Trade Agreement (CFTA), and Under the North American Free Trade Agreement (NAFTA)*, 13 Wis. Intl. L.J. 183 (1994).

[820] See Gantz, *supra* n. 817 (NAFTA is best understood if it is recognized as a "preferential" trade agreement rather than a free trade agreement. Mexico desired to make certain that NAFTA will serve as a tool for medium- and long-term economic development and industrialization). Final assembly operations by Asian companies in Mexico are described as "screwdriver" facilities. See David A. Gantz, *Implementing the NAFTA Rules of Origin: Are the Parties Helping or Hurting Free Trade?* 12 Ariz. J. Intl. & Comp. L. 367, 376 (1995).

minimis rule as in NAFTA whereby the tariff shift rule does not apply to non-originating materials if they account for no more than 7 percent of the transaction value of the goods.

The second set of rules of origin in the US-JO FTA is specific to for textile and apparel products. These specific rules of origin for textile are protectionist and were enacted to mitigate the likely effects of textiles and apparels trading on the U.S. clothing industry.[821] These rules were taken verbatim from U.S. regulations on rules of origin for textile products.

The old U.S. rules of origin for textiles and apparel products are found in subparagraph 9.b.iv of annex 2.2 of the US-JO FTA.[822] The old U.S. rules of origin for textiles and apparels are known as the "four operations" rule.[823] Under the "four operations"rule, a textile product will be considered a product of Jordan if the fabric is dyed *and* printed in Jordan and the dyeing *and* printing is accompanied by two or more of the following operations: bleaching, shrinking, fulling, napping, decating, permanent stiffening, weighting, permanent embossing or moireing. Under the "four operations" rule, it does not matter if the fabric is actually woven in Jordan. For example, the fabric could be woven in Syria, but the dyeing, printing, bleaching, and shrinking can occur in Jordan.

Under the FTA, the application of the "four operations" rule is limited to silk, cotton, man-made fiber, or vegetable fiber. Wool is excluded from the "four operations" rule, but subject to the Breaux-Cardin rule.[824] Under the Breaux-Cardin rule, it may not enough for

---

[821] The reasons for protectionist policies in the textile sector are to be found in the importance of the textile sector for employment policy in developed countries. Textile is a labor-intensive industry which requires low skilled workers who if laid off could encounter hard time to find a new job. See Franklin Dehousse et al., *The EU-USA Dispute Concerning the New American Rules of Origin for Textile Products*, 36 J.W.T. 1, 69 (2002).

[822] See *Textiles and Textile Products*, 19 C.F.R. § 12.130.(e) (i) (2005).

[823] See Dehousse, *supra* n. 821, at 71. In a case of first impression, first before the U.S. CIT and then the United States Court of Appeals for the Federal Circuit in 1987 elaborated more on the U.S. textiles country of origin rules. The Court decided that "marginal operations" performed on the cotton fabric in Hong Kong did not substantially transform the fabric originated in China allowing it to enter to the U.S. duty-free. An article "usually" will not be considered to be a product of a particular country by virtue of merely having undergone dyeing and/or printing of fabrics or yarns. The court decided that there must substantial transformation: dyeing of fabric and printing when accompanied by two or more of the following finishing operations: bleaching, shrinking, fulling, napping, decating, permanent stiffening, weighting, permanent embossing, or moireing. See *Mast Indus., Inc. v. U.S.*, 882 F. 2d. 1069 (Fed. Cir.1987) (the case involved cotton fabric in greige form [fabric before it is bleached, dyed, or processed] from China processed in Hong Kong. The court noticed that the textile regulation was adopted in a regulatory vacuum where *ad hoc* determinations had been the rule of the day, resulting in inconsistent import treatment).

[824] In order to offset the liberalization the U.S. took by agreeing to the WTO Agreement of Textiles and Clothing, it hardened the rules of origin for textile. The new U.S. rules of origin for textile products, the same as in annex 2.2 of the US-JO FTA subparagraph (a)(i), (a)(ii), or (a)(iii), under title "general rule", states that a product is considered to originate in Jordan for example if the product is 1) "wholly obtained" or "produced" in Jordan 2) the product is a yarn, thread, twine, cordage, rope or braiding, and the "constituent staple" fibers are "spun" in Jordan or the continuous filament is extruded in Jordan 3) the product is a fabric and the "constituent fibers", filaments or warns are woven, knitted, needled, tufted, felted, entangled or transformed by another fabric-making process in Jordan "or" 4) the product is any other textile or apparel product that is "wholly assembled" in Jordan from its component pieces.

the fabric to be dyed and printed in Jordan in some cases the constituent fibers actually must be woven in Jordan.

The restrictive rules of origin for textiles and apparels in the US-JO FTA are not an exceptional. NAFTA has even more restrictive rules of origin for textiles. Under NAFTA, textiles and apparels must be produced from yarn or fiber produced in the NAFTA region, which is known as the "yarn or fiber forward" rule.[825] This means that everything from the yarn forward up the production chain of an article must be of U.S., Mexican, or Canadian origin.The "yarn forward" rule restricts the ability of a manufacturer to source its inputs.[826] The "yarn or fiber forward" rule may also cause tariff escalation since the cost of using foreign yarn from a non-NAFTA party results in a higher tariff for the entire product. The US-JO FTA adopts the "fabric forward" rule, allowing the use of unlimited third-country yarn, fiber, or fabric components in the making of apparels that may be eligible for preferential treatment.

Rules of origin in the US-JO FTA are difficult to use and protectionist in nature.[827] The most challenging aspect of these rules is the "substantial transformation" test, which is based on U.S. common law.[828] The FTA rules of origin leave importers and exporters with uncertainty. Minimum differences in manufacturing processes or techniques may affect the treatment of products exported from Jordan. Theoretically, the "tariff shift" rule adopted in NAFTA is easier to administer than the "substantial transformation" test in the US-JO FTA. In the "tariff shift" rule, the customs authorities of the importing country can look at the tariff schedule to see if non-originating materials shifted from one heading to another as a result of the manufacturing process.[829] The FTA rules of origin for textiles

---

[825] See Renee T. Legierski, Out in the Cold: The Combined Effects of NAFTA and the MFA on the Caribbean Basin Textile Industry, 2 Minn. J. Global Trade 305, 314 (1993). See David. A. Gantz, A Post-Uruguay Round Introduction to International Trade Law in the United States, 12 Ariz J. Intl. & Comp. L. 7, 141 (1995). NAFTA establishes a Subcommittee on Labeling of Textile and Apparel products for purposes of harmonization of textile and apparel labeling among NAFTA parties. See Joshua A. Escoto, *Technical Barriers to Trade under NAFTA: Harmonizing Textile Labeling*, 7 Ann. Surv. Intl. & Comp. L. 63, 82 (2001) (for example, the U.S. in 1998 as part of the harmonization process, the FTC amended the U.S. Textile, Wool, and Fur Regulations to harmonize and eliminate the disclosure "Fiber Content on Reverse Side".) NAFTA contains an exception, known as tariff preference level three (TPL 3), that allows up to 25 million square meter equivalents of apparel made from yarn originating outside NAFTA region to be imported into the U.S. duty-free as long as the fabric is first cut in the U.S. and then sent to Mexico for assembly before shipped again to the U.S. TPL 3 for NAFTA is scheduled to expire on Jan. 1, 2005.

[826] However, the yarn forward rule may allow for third party inputs such as thread, trim, or elastic other than major components of an article to benefit from preferential treatment.

[827] The US-JO FTA has 12 different rules and sub-rules of origin.

[828] See John Simpson, *Reforming Rules of Origin*, J. Com. 12A (Oct. 4, 1988) (the rule of substantial transformation is too imprecise, too subjective requiring further interpretation. It is based on a case-by-case basis. The law of origin in the U.S. is highly confused). See also Paul Demaret et al., *Regionalism and Multilateralism after the Uruguay Round: Convergence, Divergence and Interaction* 349 (European Interu. Press 1997) (the substantial transformation rule is familiar to common-law legal system by building upon precedent, reasoning by analogy, and taking one step at a time. The rule will work in a court charged with deciding appealed cases that will create case law upon which the rule will depend. Consequently, substantial transformation is likely to be unworkable as a rule of origin for a free trade area). Thus, the substantial transformation rule works well in the U.S. but may not work that well in the Jordanian legal system.

and apparels are restrictive rules designed to protect the U.S. textiles industry.[830] For certain groups of textiles and apparel products, separate rules of origin may apply for each individual product, which makes production and exports way too complicated. These complex rules of origin offset the benefits of tariff reduction. The US-JO FTA does not include a *de minimis* rule that allows a percentage of non-originating inputs to be incorporated in the final product without undergoing substantial manufacturing process to confer origin. Additionally, the FTA does not provide an advance ruling for origin purposes, which may allow exporters or importers to know the origin of their products before trading.[831] The *de minimis* rule and advance origin ruling could provide more certainty for exporters and importers.

The U.S. could have adopted a more enlightened, transparent, and fairer approach tailored to Jordan's specific circumstances. The U.S. not only adopted the "four operations" and Breaux-Cardin rules for most textiles and apparel products, but also the U.S. designated that textiles and apparels are subject to longer tariff phase-outs. Rules of origin under the US-JO FTA seem to be contrary to their proclaimed purposes of ensuring affectiveness, uniformity, consistency, and administrability.[832] Fortunately, article 14.2 of the US-JO FTA requires consultation, when appropriate, to comply with the FTA's rules of origin.

One method to reduce the complexity and costs of rules of origin is to liberalize these rules for certain products that are subject to very low or zero MFN tariff rates. Whether these products are exported from Jordan or a non-FTA party is irrelevant because these products will enter the U.S. at a low tariff rate. Alternatively, the U.S. or Jordan may conduct a study of different industries and use the results as a basis to potentially allow deviations from rules of origin of the FTA. These alternatives seem workable when compared with other suggestions, such as lowering value-added content, creating a government-sponsored trade manuals published via the internet, or establishing FTA education and outreach activities to educate small and medium size Jordanian firms about the FTA. This is because exporters still have to meet the other rules of origin requirements.[833]

---

[829] As a matter of fact, the advantage of the harmonized tariff schedule is its classification of goods into heading and subheading of four digits that would make it easier to certify shifting among headings as a result of manufacturing processes.

[830] One may add that changes made to U.S. rules of origin for textile and apparel products were made to meet EC exporters' interests especially Italian designers and producers.

[831] An advance ruling could start by a letter from the importer/exporter to district director of customs in certain state inquiring on the origin of certain products. The letter would contain brief or detailed description of the product and the manufacturing process that would be conducted on the product. It may provide also cost information, if necessary.

[832] See United States (U.S.)-Jordan: Agreement Between The United States of America and the Hashemite Kingdom of Jordan on The Establishment of a Free Trade Area, *supra* n. 695, art. 14.1.

[833] For example, the U.S. embassy in Jordan maintains a manual on the FTA rules of origin. See Embassy of the United States in Jordan, *Rules of Origin Manual*, http://www.usembassy amman.org.jo/FTA/Rulso.pdf (Aug. 2001).

J. Consultations and Dispute Settlement Mechanism

Articles 15, 16, and 17 of the US-JO FTA are related to the dispute settlement mechanism.[834] Theses articles provide an umbrella under which any dispute may be resolved. The provisions apply to all legal disputes arising from the FTA, with the exception of matters involving services, which is found in article 3, and intellectual property rights, which is found in article 4.[835]

1. The Joint Committee of the FTA

Articles 15 and 16 of the US-JO FTA emphasize the settlement of disputes through consultations. The US-JO FTA establishes a permanent body, called the Joint Committee, to review the implementation of the FTA.[836] The Joint Committee plays a conciliatory role in the dispute settlement process, and any consultation to resolve a dispute that arises under the FTA must pass through this committee.[837] According to the FTA, any dispute that is not resolved through a bilateral consultation may be referred to the Joint Committee.[838]

2. Consultations

The FTA parties are required to exert every effort to settle any contentious matter through cooperative consultations, which are intended to be cooperative and negotiated in

---

[834] Articles 17 (Joint Committee), 18 (Notice and Consultation), and 19 (Dispute Settlements) of the US-Israel FTA are related to the dispute settlement mechanism. See US-Israel FTA, *supra* n. 701. Chapter 20 of NAFTA (Institutional Arrangements and Dispute Settlement Procedures) covers disputes settlement under the agreement.

[835] Subparagraph 17.4.a of the FTA provides "A Party may invoke a panel under paragraph 1.c of this Article for claims arising under Article 3 [services] only to the extent that a claim arises with regard to a commitment that is inscribed in the Party's Services Schedule to Annex 3.1 to this Agreement, but is not inscribed in the Party's Schedule of specific commitments annexed to GATS. Such commitment may include a market access or national treatment commitment in a sector, a horizontal commitment applicable to a sector, or additional commitment". Additionally, subparagraph 17.4.b provides "Except as otherwise agreed by the Parties, a Party may invoke a panel under paragraph 1.c of this Article for claims arising under Article 4 [intellectual property] only to the extent that the same claim would not be subject to resolution through the WTO Understanding on Rules and Procedures Governing the Settlement of Disputes".

[836] The Joint Committee has a vast authority to review all issues pertinent to the FTA. The Joint Committee reviews the general functioning of the agreement and the results of the agreement from experience gained during its functioning, considers and adopts any amendment or modification to the agreement subject to the domestic legal requirements of each party, and develops guidelines, explanatory materials, rules on the proper implementation of the agreement, and discusses the review performed by each part as to the environmental effects of the FTA. In summary, the Joint Committee conducts a stock-taking exercise. The Joint Committee is composed of representatives of the parties headed by the USTR on behalf of the U.S. and Jordan's minister that is primarily responsible for international trade, or their designees. See United States (U.S.)-Jordan: Agreement Between The United States of America and the Hashemite Kingdom of Jordan on The Establishment of a Free Trade Area, *supra* n. 695, art. 15.2.

[837] *Id.* art. 15.2.c.

[838] *Id.* 17.1.b.

nature, rather than adversarial and litigious.[839] Any party can request these consultations.[840] However, any party may also recourse directly to the dispute settlement mechanism under the FTA without first undertaking bilateral consultations.

3. Standard of Review

Article 17 of the FTA provides for a formal dispute settlement mechanism if other methods fail to resolve the matter at issue. The FTA provides the basis of the dispute settlement mechanism and a standard of review.[841] It provides for the comprehensive coverage of matters that could fall under the dispute settlement mechanism. The determination of whether a party has failed to carry out its obligations under the FTA depends on the judgment of the other party bringing the claim.[842]

The FTA covers violation and non-violation cases. A party can bring a case where the other party takes an action that severely distorts the balance of trade benefits or undermine the fundamental objectives of the FTA.[843] Even if the one party to the FTA takes an action that is consistent with the letter of the FTA, the other party may still claim

---

[839] "The parties shall at all times endeavor to agree on the interpretation and application of this Agreement, and shall make every attempt to arrive at mutually satisfactory resolution of any matter that affects the operation of the agreement". *Id.* art. 16.1.

[840] The FTA requires that each party affords the other party adequate opportunity for consultations, prompt reply to the request for consultations, and good faith in negotiating. These technical requirements are mandated to ensure that each party has the chance to present its views and accommodate a solution within reasonable period of time. *Id.* art. 16.2.

[841] The basis of a dispute under the US-JO FTA is related to the interpretation of the agreement, if either party has failed to carry out its obligations under the agreement, or any party considers measures taken by the other party as severely distorts the balance of trade benefits or substantially undermine fundamental objectives of the agreement. *Id.* art. 17.1.a.

[842] This is supported by the use of the sentence that a party "considers" that the other party failed to carry out its obligation. *Id.* art. 17.1.a.ii.

[843] *Id.* art. 17.1.a.iii. The language of this article is borrowed from article XXIII.b of GATT 1994. However, article XXIII.b of GATT uses "nullification and impairment" language. Thus, it seems that the GATT language imposes a lower bar since a measure can nullify or impair a benefit though not severely distort the balance of trade benefits. In considering the application of the non-violation provision, it is important to note that it must be interpreted narrowly as set under GATT practice. In order to make a successful claim under the non-violation provision, a FTA party must demonstrate the following elements: (1) taking of a measure by another party, (2) a benefit accruing under the FTA, and (3) sever distortion of the benefit or substantial undermining of the fundamental objectives of the FTA resulting from taking of the measure. The GATT panel in the oilseed case recognized that article XXIII:1(b) serves mainly to protect the balance of tariff concessions. Furthermore, it confirmed that the non-violation nullification or impairment remedy should be approached with caution and treated as an exceptional concept. The panel justified its reasoning on the ground that the idea underlying article XXIII is that the improved competitive opportunities that can legitimately be expected from a tariff concession can be frustrated not only by measures prohibited by the GATT but also by measures consistent with GATT. See GATT Panel Report, *European Economic Community-Payments and Subsidies Paid to Processors and Producers of Oilseeds and Related Animal-Feed Proteins*, Jan. 25, 1990, GATT B.I.S.D. (37th Supp.) at 86 (1991). Non-violation cases not only covers tariff concessions but also other cases. See GATT Panel Report, *United States- Restrictions on the Importation of Sugar and Sugar- Containing Products Applied Under the 1955 Waiver and Under the Headnote to the Schedule of Tariff Concessions*, Nov. 7, 1990, GATT B.I.S.D. (37th Supp.) at 228, para. 5.21 (1990).

that that action is inconsistent with the spirit of the agreement and thus severely distort the balance of trade benefits.

4. Establishment of a Panel and its Procedures

If the FTA Joint Committee does not resolve the dispute within 90 days, either party may refer the matter to an *ad hoc* dispute settlement panel.[844] The FTA does not require notice to establish such a panel. The panel consists of three members.[845] The FTA does not prescribe a time limit within which the panel should be called or what happens in the case when the parties do not agree on the panel's membership. However, according to the FTA, within 180 days of the entry into force of the FTA the parties should develop rules for the selection and conduct of the members of the panel and model rules of procedure for such panels.[846] By creating these rules, the FTA parties can determine the qualifications, expertise, nationality, and remuneration for panelists serving on a panel. Model rules of procedures may include policies, practices, and procedures for receiving initial and rebuttal written submissions, and how oral hearings will be conducted before a panel.

The FTA dispute settlement panel issues only one non-binding final report.[847] The panel's report includes "findings of facts" and a determination as to whether either party has failed to carry out its obligations under the FTA or that a measure taken by either party severely distorts the balance of trade benefits or substantially undermines the fundamental objectives of the FTA.[848] If the panel finds that either party has failed to honor its obligation, it may provide recommendations as to how to resolve the dispute. However, such recommendations depend on the request of both parties. The panel has only the authority to make a finding of whether a party has failed to carry out its obligation, but it does not have the authority to determine how either party would bring its laws or regulations into compliance with the FTA

The FTA requires the Joint Committee resolve disputes taken into account the panel report when appropriate.[849] In most cases, the panel report will be taken into consideration because it represents an objective and articulate decision that may help to

---

[844] See United States (U.S.)-Jordan: Agreement Between The United States of America and the Hashemite Kingdom of Jordan on The Establishment of a Free Trade Area, *supra* n. 695, art. 17.1.c.

[845] Each party appoints one member and the two panelists will appoint the third one who will serve as a chairman of the panel. *Id.* art. 17.1.c.

[846] See United States (U.S.)-Jordan: Agreement Between The United States of America and the Hashemite Kingdom of Jordan on The Establishment of a Free Trade Area, *supra* n. 695, art. 17.3. In the FTA text, the article number is "17.2", which is followed immediately by 17.4, instead of "17.3". This discrepancy might be response to a typographical error.

[847] It is unfortunate setback that the FTA does not require an interim report issued by the panel and submitted to the parties for comments before it issues a final report. It is important to issue an interim report because the panel would estoppel the parties from coming backing and accuse the panel of misstating their arguments, ignoring their point of view, or denying them the right to present their argument. Therefore, the panel by issuing an interim report would give the parties once and for all the last chance to present their comments.

[848] *Id.* art. 17.1.d.

[849] *Id.* art. 17.2.a.

resolve the dispute. Further, due to the publicity surrounding the panel decision, the Joint Committee may face pressure to comply with it or, at minimum, take the report under review.

If the Joint Committee does not resolve the dispute within 30 days from the date the panel presented its report, the affected party is entitled to take any "appropriate" and "commensurate" measures.[850] The FTA establishes the right to take countermeasures unilaterally and without authorization of the Joint Committee. However, the right to take countermeasures is contingent upon the exhaustion of alternative methods, including consultations, panel procedures, and joint committee deliberations.

To ensure transparency, a Memorandum of Understanding between the U.S. and Jordan requires the publication of parties' submission to the panel, publicity of oral hearings before the panel, the acceptance and consideration of *amicus curia* briefs, and releasing the panel's report to the public at the earliest possible time.[851] In theory, the dispute settlement process takes approximately nine months to reach a conclusion.[852] The table below illustrates the timeline of the dispute settlement process under the US-JO FTA.

60 days	Bilateral Consultations
90 days shorten this period)	Joint Committee Consultations (It can agree to extend or
90 days	Panel Report
30 days	Joint Committee Endeavor after Panel Report

It is difficult to evaluate the effectiveness of the dispute settlement mechanism under the FTA because there is no enough data that shows how many disputes are settled

---

[850] The use of the term "commensurate" after "appropriate" is to emphasize that the measure taken must be in proportion to the violation. The term "commensurate", which is a quantitative term, is hard to quantify practically. *Id.* art. 17.2.b.

[851] The US-JO FTA adopted the Appellate Body approach of the WTO by ruling that WTO dispute resolution panels may accept *amicus* briefs from well-monied, western-type of non-governmental organizations. See Report of the Appellate Body on United States-Import Prohibition of Shrimp and Certain Shrimp Products, *supra* note 138, at 82, 100 (The Appellate Body decided in that case that a panel has the "discretionary" authority either to accept and consider or to reject information and advice submitted to it, whether requested by a panel or not). Under the FTA, a panel is "obliged" to accept and consider *amicus curia* of whatever type filed by individuals, legal persons, and non-governmental organizations. See USTR, *Memorandum of Understanding on Transparency in Dispute Settlement Under the Agreement Between the United States and Jordan on the Establishment of a Free Trade Area*, para. 2.c, http://www.ustr.gov/regions/eu-med/middleeast/memodis.pdf (accessed Apr. 29, 2003). For more on amicus curiae see Padideh Ala'i, *Judicial Lobbying At the WTO: The Debate over the Use of Amicus Curiae Briefs and the U.S. Experience*, 24 Fordham Int'l L.J. 62, 67, 84, 86 (2000).

[852] It is not unusual for specified dispute settlement process deadlines to be disregarded in certain cases for many factors such as the significance of the case, political ramification, and lack of resources to draft panel reports on time.

through consultations, brought before panels, or withdrawn. The absence of such data indicates that the dispute settlement system of the FTA is under-utilized. One reason for this may be that Jordan cannot retaliate against the U.S in the case of a violation. However, one could argue that Jordan could retaliate against the U.S. by disregarding the protection of intellectual property rights in the FTA because the FTA is silent on the sectors in which either party may retaliate.

K. General and Security Exceptions under the US-JO FTA

The FTA includes exceptions that are the same as those found in the WTO. The FTA negotiators, especially the U.S. negotiators, did not consider it necessary to modify the existing WTO exception rules. The FTA parties did depart from the WTO language by specifically referencing to "living and non-living" exhaustible natural resources.[853] However, by inserting the language of the WTO into the FTA, the U.S. adopted new developments in international trade, which is articulated by the WTO panel and Appellate Body decisions.[854]

The FTA allows the U.S. or Jordan to adopt or enforce measures necessary to protect public morals or human, animal, or plant life or health.[855] The FTA, also, allows a member to adopt a measure that "relates" to the conservation of exhaustible natural resources if this measure is made effective in conjunction with restrictions on domestic production or consumption. The US-JO FTA states that article XX (g) of GATT 1994 applies to "living and non-living" exhaustible natural resources.[856] The U.S. in the FTA effectively adopted the "not static but evolutionary" test, which was developed by the Appellate Body decision in the United States-Shrimp case.[857]

---

[853] *Id.*

[854] See GATT Panel Report, *Thailand-Restrictions on Importation of and Internal Taxes on Cigarettes*, Nov. 7, 1990, GATT B.I.S.D (37th Supp.) at 200 (1990), GATT Panel Report, *United States- Restriction on Imports on Tuna*, Sep. 3, 1991, GATT B.I.S.D. (39th Supp.) 155 (1991), Appellate Body Report, *United States-Standards for Reformulated and Conventional Gasoline*, WT/DS2/AB/R (Apr. 29, 1996), Report of the Appellate Body on United States-Import Prohibition of Certain Shrimp and Shrimp Products, Oct. 12, 1998, WTO Doc. No. WT/DS58/AB/R, Report of the Appellate Body on European Communities-Measures Affecting Asbestos and Asbestos-Containing Products, March. 21, 2001, WTO Doc. No. WT/DS135/AB/R. These cases involve article XX exceptions of the GATT 1994. The decisions of these cases erupted a volcanic controversy toward the WTO. For discussion of these cases, except the Asbestos case, see Padideh Ala'i, *Free Trade or Sustainable Development? An Analysis of the WTO Appellate Body's Shift to a More Balanced Approach to Trade Liberalization*, 14 Am. U. Int'l L. Rev. 1129, 1171 (1999) (arguing that the Appellate Body proposed a balancing test to be applied on a case-by-case basis between article XX exceptions and the WTO goals of market access and trade liberalization…even though supporters of article XX interests may have lost the case, the prospects look good for winning the war).

[855] Other exceptions include measures relate to the importation or exportation of gold, the products of prison labor, the protection of national treasures of artistic, historic or archeological value. See United States (U.S.)-Jordan: Agreement Between The United States of America and the Hashemite Kingdom of Jordan on The Establishment of a Free Trade Area, *supra* n. 695, art. 17.1.c.

[856] *Id.* art. 12.1. By comparison, article XX (g) of the GATT 1994 does not define whether a measure applies to "living and non-living" exhaustible natural resources.

[857] In the United States-Shrimp case, the appellee, India, Pakistan, and Thailand, argued that the term "exhaustible" refers to finite resources such as minerals rather than biological or renewable resources. However, the Appellate Body was not convinced by the appellee argument. It stated that exhaustible natural resources are not limited to mineral or non-living natural resources. Living resources are just as

The FTA also encompasses several security exceptions. The FTA allows either party to take measures which that it deems necessary for the protection of its "essential security interests". In a post September 11, 2001 world trade, the U.S. may wish to invoke the security exceptions of the FTA such as by imposing export/import control programs. The U.S may consider such restrictive measures necessary for the protection of its essential security interest when they are taken in a "time of war" or during an "emergency in international relations".[858] The U.S. may also restrict exports, through the use of million

---

finite as petroleum. The Appellate Body states that "the words of article XX (g) were actually drafted more than 50 years ago". It supported it conclusion by citing the preamble of the WTO Charter which incorporates the concept of "sustainable development" while GATT 1994 does not incorporate such a term. Therefore, the generic term "natural resources" is not static in its content or reference but is rather by definition "revolutionary". See Report of the Appellate Body on United States-Import Prohibition, *supra* n. 138, at 127-130.

[858] The U.S. Department of Homeland Security has issued approximately 150 "no load" orders prohibiting shippers from loading oceangoing cargo bound for the U.S. due to inadequate manifest information, under a new rule requiring 24-hour advance cargo notification before lading. The department is planning to apply the same rule with shipping companies for the air, rail and trucking industries. Under the Trade Act of 2002, the 24-hour rule requires that sea carriers and non-vessel operating common carriers provide complete cargo manifests 24 hours prior to loading the cargo in a foreign port through an approved electronic data interchange system. The U.S. adopted several measures to insure food security against agro-terrorism. See Christopher S. Rugaber, *DHS Official Defends 24-Hour Rule, Cites 150 Orders Barring Cargo Unloading*, 20 Intl. Trade Rep. (BNA) 13 (Mar. 27, 2003). See also Daniel Pruzin, *U.S. Trading Partners Concerned With Rules for Food Registration Under the Bioterrorism Act*, 20 Intl. Trade Rep. (BNA) 1158 (July 10, 2003) (A regulation has been established under the Bioterrorism Act of 2002 that would require foreign food-handling facilities that manufacture, process, pack, or hold food destined for animal or human consumption to register with the U.S. Food and Drug Administration by Dec. 2003. The registration would allow the Food and Drug Administration to act quickly in responding to a threatened or actual terrorist attack on U.S. food supply by giving the Administration information about all facilities handling U.S.-bound food products. Additionally, the rules require each facility to employ an agent in the U.S. to serve as link between the firm and the FDA. The rules require each facility to notify the FDA of the manufacturer, the grower, the country of origin, the estimated quantity, and the shipping country. Each facility will receive a confidential facility number. The cost of hiring an agent will be on average $ 1,000). The Food and Drug Administration requires record-keeping system and prior notice electronically of food imports 8 hours before arrival by sea. Additionally, the U.S. developed the Container Security Initiative (CSI) which requires the Customs service to pre-screen sea cargo containers bound for the U.S. at certain large ports such as port of Naples. CSI is a reciprocal program giving participating countries the option of sending their customs officers to countries seaports to pre-screen cargo containers bound for their countries. In 2004, Dubai Ports became the first Middle Eastern port to participate in the CSI. To improve sea container security, the U.S. created a pilot program, Operation Safe Commerce, which would develop a technology to follow the movement of container through the supply chain. It also developed Customs-Trade Partnership Against Terrorism (C-TPAT) program. It is a voluntary government industry partnership, with some 7,000 members, designed to beef up the security of the U.S. supply chain industry from factory to loading docks. Certified companies under C-TPAT program receive reduced number of inspections at the border. They can also benefit from expedited customs processing programs such as Free and Secure Trade Program (FAST) in which goods are being processed quickly at select border sites in designated traffic lanes. The U.S. is adopting "one face at the border" initiative which includes hiring new officers that will have the combined duties of immigration, customs inspectors, and agricultural inspectors. Under the Maritime Transportation Security Act, port facilities must receive Coast Guard approval letters for security plans otherwise risking partial or total shutdown. The U.S. is also codifying the "known shippers" program, as part of securing air cargo, thus inspecting some 3 percent of the U.S. air cargo. For Jordanian producers, these rules, which are designed to intercept terrorists and weapons, might be costly, burdensome, complex, and might divert scarce resources for production to meeting these requirements. For example, Jordan may

theoretical operations per second (MTOP) thresholds, which relate to high-performance computers used for weather services, software design, and microprocessor technology to Jordan because such technology could be used for military purposes, missile-related equipment and technology. The U.S. may also wish to restrict thiodiglycol chemicals, which are used in the production of textiles and if combined with other acids could form mustard gas or kidney machine triggers that can be used to trigger nuclear bombs.

L. Miscellaneous Articles of the US-JO FTA

One of the difficult questions regarding the FTA is how to define its relationship with other international agreements.[859] The FTA does not explicitly stipulate that it prevails over other agreements in case of conflicts.[860] The U.S. and Jordan could have agreed on a clear conflict clause, similar to article 104 of NAFTA. The lack of a conflict clause may be interpreted to mean that the FTA negotiators were occupied with the substantive provisions of the agreement rather than what could had been deemed a superficial issue.

The FTA covers economic cooperation and technical assistance between the U.S. and Jordan.[861] The language on economic cooperation was drafted broadly. It does not carry any specific methods on how to foster economic cooperation between the U.S. and Jordan. Even more, the provision does not carry any legal obligation and has no timeline within which this cooperation must be implemented. It is vague and exhortatory as it does not list specific and detailed means by which the U.S. will help Jordan through the provision of economic technical assistance.[862] Moreover, the only assistance potentially

---

need to purchase or borrow X-rays machines to screen the interior of containers without impeding the flow of trade. It seems that these rules are intended to create "fortress" America.

[859] Article 1 of the FTA provides that the Parties reaffirm their respective rights and obligations with respect to each other under existing bilateral and multilateral agreements to which both Parties are party, including the *Marrakesh Agreement Establishing the World Trade Organization* (WTO Agreement)". See United States (U.S.)-Jordan: Agreement Between The United States of America and the Hashemite Kingdom of Jordan on The Establishment of a Free Trade Area, *supra* n. 695, art. 1.2.

[860] This is contrary to the US-Israel FTA which provides, under article 3, that its language shall govern in the case of any inconsistency with other agreements, such as the GATT, though the parties reaffirmed their respective rights and obligations under the GATT, which would govern any issue not addressed by the FTA. See US-Israel FTA, *supra* note 701, art.3. Article 103.2 of NAFTA states that in case of inconsistency between NAFTA and other agreements, NAFTA will prevail to the extent of inconsistency. As such, NAFTA prevails in case of inconsistency with other agreements including GATT.

[861] The FTA states, in part, that to realize the objectives of the FTA and contribute to the implementation of its provisions "the parties declare their readiness to foster economic cooperation". The FTA also states that "in view of Jordan's developing status, and the size of its economy and resources, the United States shall strive to furnish Jordan with economic technical assistance, as appropriate". See United States (U.S.)-Jordan: Agreement Between The United States of America and the Hashemite Kingdom of Jordan on The Establishment of a Free Trade Area, *supra* n. 695, art. 13.

[862] Clearly, one may argue that leaving paragraph 13.b without specificity would work better rather than being *ceteris paribus*. It ought to be vague to remain flexible and useful because it could be adapted to necessary changes. However, lack of specificity in paragraph 13.b lends itself to uncertainty and insecurity. The reason for this uncertainty is the lack of test that would guide the parties leading to discretionary interpretation.

offered by the U.S. under this provision is "economic technical assistance". Any economic technical assistance offered by the U.S. is qualified by the term "as appropriate".

The FTA considers annexes and schedules as an integral part of the FTA. However, the FTA also has many side decisions and understandings.[863] These understandings and decisions raise questions about how to define their relationship with the main text of the FTA and how to resolve any conflict with the main provisons of the agreement. Taking into consideration the language of the FTA, which makes only annexes and schedules as part of the FTA, these side understandings and decisions have an ambiguous legal value because it does not seem that they are integral of the main document. These side understandings may be political documents and not legal texts. The advantage of such side understandings may be that they can easily be amended when circumstances change.

All references to GATT 1994 in the FTA refer to GATT 1994, which was in effect on the date of entry into force of the FTA.[864] The US-JO FTA does not take into account any further clarifications or modifications to GATT 1994, which would come as a result of concluding further trade negotiation rounds under the auspices of the WTO. Therefore, the parties have limited the scope of the FTA to the existing rights and obligations of GATT 1994. Further, the FTA operates indefinitely. However, the FTA does have a contract-out provision, which provides for the right of each party to terminate the FTA after giving a six-month notice.[865] The FTA does not specify whether either party can partially or totally terminate the agreement. The FTA does not impose any requirements that must be included in the written notice to justify the termination of the FTA.

III. Implementations and Expectations

This section will attempt to quantify some of the costs and benefits associated with the implementation of the US-JO FTA. Before the conclusion the US-JO FTA, Jordan was designated as eligible beneficiary country under the U.S. GSP program.[866] However,

---

[863] The US-JO FTA has 7 side understandings and decisions. See Memorandum of Understanding on Issues Related to the Protection of Intellectual Property Rights, Memorandum of Understanding on Transparency in Dispute Settlement, Joint Statement on WTO Issues, Joint Statement on Technical Environmental Cooperation, Side Letters on Marketing Approval of Pharmaceutical Products, Side Letter on GATS article 5, and Letters Designating Entry Into Force Date, at <http://www.ustr.gov/regions/eu-med/middleeast/US-JordanFTA.shtml>. Many of these side decisions and joint statements declare some aspiration. The Side Letters on Marketing Approval of Pharmaceutical Products and the Side Letter on GATS Article 5 are notable exceptions. These letter provide that the understanding concerning marketing approval of pharmaceutical products and the understanding on GATS article 5 be treated as an integral part of the FTA. See USTR, *Side Letter on Marketing Approval of Pharmaceutical Products*, http://www.ustr.gov/regions/eu-med/middleeast/IPRcb.pdf (accessed Mar. 30, 2004). As such, based on the suggestion of the U.S., marketing approval of pharmaceutical products is given priority over the Joint Statement on Technical Environmental Cooperation and other side letters.
[864] See United States (U.S.)-Jordan: Agreement Between The United States of America and the Hashemite Kingdom of Jordan on The Establishment of a Free Trade Area, *supra* n. 695, art. 18.4.
[865] Article 2205 of NAFTA also provides the right of each party to withdraw from the agreement upon six months notice.

the GSP program is authorized only for a specific time, but is subject to renewal by legislation. The range of products under the GSP is also limited. Moreover, the GSP has a competitive need limits, which means that the GSP stops after the value of goods shipped to the U.S. from a country reaches a certain limit, which changes annually, unless a country-specific waiver has been granted. On the other hand, the US-JO FTA is a permanent arrangement that has wide coverage. Therefore, between the GSP program and the US-JO FTA, Jordan has now two tracks for presumably preferential treatment. However, the US-JO FTA is the most viable track, and Jordan's GSP status may ultimately become irrelevant. The FTA would provide certainty that may attract more investors and better develop markets. Moreover, the FTA may provide the U.S. with a reciprocal market access in Jordan.

As Jordan opens its market as a result of the FTA, it has become an export and import destination vis-à-vis the U.S. goods. At the time the US-JO FTA entered into force in 2001, Jordan had a trade deficit with the U.S. As of 2004, Jordan ran trade surplus with the U.S. This drastic shift in trade balance with the U.S. has been in mainly in the textiles and apparel sector, a traditional labor-intensive industry (manufacturing processes are sewing and tailoring) with limited capital and technology (technology is a sewing machine).[867]

Although it is too early to read much from time-series data, the trade surplus with the U.S. reveals certain characteristics. The trade surplus with the U.S. is modest in dollar value ($8 million in 2002, $181 million in 2003, and $541 million in 2004). U.S. exports to Jordan also have been relatively constant. In 1993, total U.S. exports were $360.6 million, in 1995 were $335.3 million, in 2001 were $339 million, and exports reached a peak of $552.1 million in 2004.[868] This may reflect the fact that U.S. exporters do not have much interest in Jordan's market because it is not a large import market with high profitability. Another interpretation for the constant U.S. exports to Jordan is the fact that, currently, Jordan has a high unemployment rate ranging between 15-20 percent. Further, 17-30 percent of population is below the poverty line, measured as the amount of income needed to purchase basic necessities. Jordan's GDP is a fraction of that of the U.S. Simply put, a Jordanian with an income lowest in the Middle East may not be in a position to buy U.S. products.[869] However, as Jordan increases its exports to the U.S., its economy may expand and its people may gain purchasing power for U.S. goods.

---

[866] Jordan is still an eligible beneficiary country under the U.S. GSP program even after the conclusion of the US-JO FTA. See note 4 of the U.S. HTS (2003). This is contrary to Mexico which lost its GSP status after the conclusion of NAFTA. However, it is unclear if Jordan would still be eligible for GSP scheme once the FTA phases in completely in 2010.

[867] See Table 9 in appendix 1, page 222. Trade balance statistics are regularly published by the Bureau of Census, U.S. Department of Commerce. For example, the U.S. knows on a monthly basis whether it has a favorable or unfavorable trade balance with Jordan.

[868] If one would compute retained U.S. imports into Jordan (imports minus re-exports), U.S. exports could be lower in volume. At any rate, the increase in Jordan's imports from the U.S. in 2004 is likely the result of tariff reduction under the FTA. It remains to be documented whether increase of Jordan's import from the U.S. was due to high domestic demand or substitution of domestically produced products.

[869] See Economist Intelligence Unit, Country Profile: Jordan 20, 27 (2003).

Moreover, once Jordan fully implements its commitments under the FTA, one may see a rise in U.S. exports to Jordan.

The major sector in which Jordan has its trade surplus with the U.S. is in apparel products. Top apparel exports to the U.S. include some basic higher-volume apparel articles such as men's shirts, women's trousers, sweaters, ladies' outfits and blouses, and sportswear.[870] There are a few high value-added apparel articles such as men's wool suits and jackets. To improve this sector, however, Jordan must create a structure to help manufacturers focus on higher-end products.

Jordan's exports to the U.S. are mainly within the woven or knit apparel orbit and do not advance into other non-traditional export sectors, including light manufacturing industries, cultural industries, ethnic food industries, or olive oil production. In 2004, knit or crochet apparel articles and accessories captured 60.60 percent of total U.S. imports from Jordan.[871] This may mean that unless Jordan moves to other sectors, it might be displaced by more efficient, vertically-integrated producers of textiles and apparel products from India, Pakistan, and China.[872] In several major garment categories, including men's or boy's cotton knit shirts, shirts, and trousers, China currently has only a small share of the U.S. market because of tight quota constraints. However, once these constraints are lifted, China is likely to capture a larger portion of the U.S. garment import market, which is worth more than $70 billion annually.

The main U.S. exports to Jordan are capital goods and farm products. These exports cannot be produced in Jordan, and they have to be imported because they are necessary for the industrial structure of Jordan. The top exports in 2004 list are: cereals, which capture a 16.68 percent share; vehicles, except those used for railway or tramways, which are 12.10 percent of exports; nuclear reactors, boilers, and machinery, which amount to 11.99 percent of exports; electric machinery, sound equip., and TV equip., which capture a 8.70 percent share; and aircraft, spacecraft, and parts thereof, which capture a 6.68 percent share.[873] The other major export item is cereals (e.g. wheat, meslin, rice, corn, buck wheat, millet, canary seed, and grain sorghum), which could fall under U.S. food aid programs (donation, food for peace, and food for progress) or export credits and intermediate export credit programs, such as General Service Manager programs "GSM-1, GSM-2". These programs seem to be tailored for Jordan because it experiences a shortage of foreign exchange earnings and difficulty meeting its food needs through normal commercial channels. Other U.S. high-value added exports are aircraft parts, which are likely to be purchases from the Chicago-based Boeing company.

---

[870] See Table 10 in appendix 1, page 223.
[871] This is followed by not knit apparel articles and accessories which captured 26.87 percent of total U.S. imports from Jordan and of precious metal and stones which had 8.35 percent share (on file with author).
[872] See William Armbruster, *China Syndrome*, J. Com. 38, 39 (Nov. 18, 2002) (China is likely to suck up the apparel business. The Philippines, Malaysia, Thailand, Indonesia, Korea and Taiwan can kiss their apparel and textile exports good-bye. U.S. importers [such as J.C. Penney Co., Liz Claiborne Inc., and Polo Ralph Lauren Corp.] may shift all their sourcing to China since dealing with few vendors is easier for product quality control, on-time delivery, and compliance with security regulations. China's reputation for quality, price competitiveness, and efficient supply chains make it attractive supplier).
[873] For the years 2001-2002 cereals were the top U.S. export product to Jordan (on file with author).

In 1996, among 225 countries, Jordan ranked 132 on the list of U.S. imports from its trading partners.[874] By 2004, it scaled up to rank 69 capturing 0.07 of total U.S. import market.[875] On the export side, in 1996, Jordan ranked 72 as a destination for U.S. exports.[876] By 2004, it scaled up to rank 70 capturing 0.07 of total U.S. exports worldwide.[877] Although, these statistics are impressive, one certainly would not say that the results are "unbelievable".

The majority of merchandise trade between the U.S. and Jordan is seaborne trade, transported by vessel (sea) rather than air. Of all of the U.S. imports from Jordan in 2001, which amounted to $228,970,856, $187,587,984 worth of goods were imported by vessel while $35,581,880 worth of goods were transported by air.[878] This means that goods take a longer time to be transported over the 6,000 mile journey across the Atlantic. Estimates indicate that the average shipping time between New York City, N.Y. and Aqaba, Jordan is three to four weeks. Among all the 361 U.S. ports that receive approximately seven million containers a year, more goods pass through the New York City, N.Y customs port area than any other customs district of entry in the U.S., including the Port of L.A, which is the largest U.S. container complex. In 2003, of the $673,466,552 in total U.S. imports from Jordan, $406,776,222 passed through the New York City, N.Y customs port.[879] This is followed by Charleston, SC, Los Angeles, CA, and Savannah, GA. The need may arise to diversify the routing of Jordan's cargo.

Statistical data shows that trade in merchandise, in the on whole, more important for Jordan than for the U.S. It also shows that the U.S. is a high technology and agricultural exporting country. In contrast, Jordan's economy may be characterized by its abundant cheap labor. As noted earlier, Jordan's main exports to the U.S. are textile and apparel products. Comparative advantage proves that Jordan is better at exporting textiles and apparel products, while the U.S. is better at exporting machinery and agricultural products. Data is not available regarding the trade in services between the U.S. and Jordan under the FTA, though it is an important sector. The positive trade balance for merchandise under the FTA may actually be in stark contrast to the service trade balance. Additionally, there are no data on the costs and benefits of the intellectual property provisions of the FTA.

---

[874] In 1997, Jordan ranked 138. In 1998, it went down the list to rank 146. The following five years Jordan enhanced its rank. In 1999, it ranked 131, 2000 ranked 123, in 2001 ranked 95, in 2002 ranked 73, and in 2003 it ranked 72. (on file with author).

[875] In an ascending order, Canada, China, Mexico, and Japan captured more than 50 percent of U.S. market. Israel, in the 2004 list, ranked 20 with 0.99 market share. *Id.*

[876] In 1997, Jordan ranked 72, 1998 ranked 75, 1999 ranked 81, 2000 ranked 75, 2001 ranked 74, 2002 ranked 73, and in 2003 it ranked 66. Israel, in the 2004 list, ranked 19 with 1.12 share of total U.S. exports. *Id.*

[877] In ascending order, Canada, Mexico, Japan, U.K, and China ranked the top destinations for U.S. exports capturing about 50 percent of total U.S. exports. *Id.* This shows that Canada and Mexico are naturally born trading partners.

[878] In 2002, of $ 412,234,634 total U.S. imports from Jordan $ 323,497,772 were imported by vessel while $ 83,059,067 were imported by air. In 2003, of 673,466,552 total U.S. imports from Jordan $ 519,734,996 were imported by vessel while $ 149,942,601 imported by air. Statistics are delivered from Trade Data Services, The U.S. Census Bureau (on file with author).

[879] *Id.*

Data alone, however does not provide a parameter to grade the US-JO FTA. The data may not take into account political and economic factors, such as the political turmoil in the Middle East or the full-fledged implementation of Jordan's commitments under the WTO. It may be difficult to distinguish the economic effects of the FTA from those of other economic and political forces that evolved around the same time as when the FTA came into force. Moreover, the currently available data, which reflects only partial implementation of the US-JO FTA, already shows the relative positive impact of the FTA. It is impossible to determine whether the FTA alone has produced the increase in trade between the parties and and lead to certain other improvements in Jordan's economy.[880] Also, it is difficult to estimate the full impact of FTA in absolute numbers. The FTA is part of a dynamic trade integration process whose fruits are to ripen over decades. Some economic indicators, however, already show limited gains, more prospects for expanding markets for both countries, and increases in foreign investments.

There are other non-quantifiable benefits for the US-JO FTA that may not be directly related to it. In 2002 the U.S. imposed high tariffs of up to 30 percent on steel imports. Israel, Canada, Mexico, and Jordan were excluded from this tariff measure. They are the only countries that have FTAs with the U.S.[881] On the other hand, during 1981-1985, imports of steels increased forty fold from newly exporting countries. These imports, which came from Jordan, consisted of black plate and galvanized sheet and strip.[882] At that time, Jordan could had been the subject of voluntary export restraint agreement. In that case, the US-JO FTA would have provided an economic shelter for Jordan in the future that otherwise would have not been available.

One should not lose sight concerning of the contribution of other special U.S. programs, such as GSP and Qualifying Industrial Zones (QIZs) programs, to the growth of exports to Jordan.[883] This data is important to determine the success of the FTA. One

---

[880] For example, it would be an interesting to determine whether Jordan's exchange rate has been the primary factor for trade performance since Jordan's Dinar is pigged to the U.S. dollar. At times, when U.S. dollar is depreciating (cheap) exports become more competitive and imports become expensive. Thus, Jordan is likely to benefit from cheap U.S. dollar.

[881] The US-JO FTA states in article 10.8 that, in global safeguards, a party, the U.S. in the steel case at hand, may exclude imports originating in the other party [Jordan] from safeguard measures, if such imports are not a substantial cause of serious injury or threat thereof. The USITC recommended the exclusion of Jordan from its application of the safeguard remedy on steel imports. Hence, the U.S. president, in a presidential proclamation, excluded Jordan in addition to Israel, Mexico, and Canada. All have a free trade agreement with the U.S. In rebuttal of the complainants' arguments regarding the issue of parallelism, the U.S. stated that there is "virtually no imports of steel" from Jordan. The panel in the steel case decided that the U.S. acted inconsistently with its obligations by including all steel imports in its safeguard investigation but excluding imports from Israel, Jordan, Mexico, and Canada in applying the safeguard measure. Appellate Body Report, *United States-Definitive Safeguard Measures on Imports of Certain Steel Products*, WT/DS248/AB/R (Nov. 10, 2003). The WTO Appellate Body supported the panel's finding on parallelism. See Daniel Pruzin, *WTO Appellate Body Upholds Findings against U.S. Safeguard Tariffs on Steel*, 20 Intl. Trade Rep. (BNA) 1863 (Nov. 13, 2003) (the safeguard measure did not meet the parallel treatment for FTA partners).

[882] See USITC Publication 1942, Monthly Reports on the State of the Steel Industry (Jan. 1987).

[883] QIZs is a trade arrangement between the U.S., Israel, and Jordan whereby products manufactured in Jordan with certain percentage of input from Israel can enter the U.S. duty-free.

could try to assert, following China's Deng Xiaoping's dictum, that "it does not matter whether the cat is black or white, as long as it catches the mouse," which means that the data whether from the FTA, GSP, or QIZs, is not important so long as there is increase in trade. However, the data reveals something more than simply impressive statistics.

Singling out the effects of the GSP and QIZs may lead to different conclusions. The combined value of shipments under all special/non-special U.S. programs from Jordan was $412,234,634 in 2002. Of this total, no exports were reported under the agreement on trade in pharmaceutical products, $5,977,246 worth of goods from the GSP scheme, $12,600,834 worth of goods from the US-JO FTA, and $369,455,485 worth of goods from the QIZs program.[884] In 2003, the combined value of shipments under all special/non-special U.S. programs from Jordan increased to $673,466,552. Of this total, $42,892 resulted from the agreement on trade in pharmaceutical products, $35,010,918 resulted from the GSP scheme, $27,919,294 from the US-JO FTA, and $563,928,229 from the QIZs program.[885] This expansive increase in exports from 2002 to 2003 was due mainly to QIZs. QIZs gross exports account for over 80 percent of Jordan's total exports to the U.S.

The US-JO FTA did not benefit all sectors of the Jordanian economy. Few companies actually benefit from the FTA. Other companies may be ill-prepared to benefit from the FTA due to lack of marketing and support skills in the international market. The number of Jordanians who benefit from the FTA is small. Pro-FTA camp focuses on export growth and FDI, while others focus on growth in wage and per capita GDP growth. Conversely, if the economic situation remains unchanged or even worsens, as the case maybe, the FTA may not be seen as a success.

---

[884] See *supra* n. 878.

[885] The local pharmaceutical industry seems to be in a promising position. Exports quadrupled from none in 2002 to $ 42,892 in 2003. These exports are likely to be chemical additives or substances used for medicine.

Conclusion

The US-Jordan FTA was designed both to spur Jordan's economic development and to cement strategic ties between the U.S. and Jordan for geopolitical reasons. The US-JO FTA was concluded swiftly while other trade agreements such as the US-Israel FTA and NAFTA took more time to conclude. The US-JO FTA is much shorter than other agreements. NAFTA is more than a two thousand pages long and contain two thousand articles, whereas the US-JO FTA contains twenty pages of typewritten text, twenty-two pages of annexes, understandings, joint statement, and side letters (excluding schedules of commitments in services and goods).

The apparent assumption is that the US-JO FTA is not an agreement between equals, politically or economically. Jordan entered into the deal with a heavyweight trade player (or better called a hegemon), the U.S., with the former's eyes open on the lucrative U.S. market. Jordan tried to secure as much assurance as possible that its interests will be dealt with fairly. In practice, however, how Jordan is treated depends on the goodwill and the strength of the heavyweight trade player. The U.S. in the FTA did not tak the interests of Jordan into account. Although the FTA in many parts refers to "the Parties" or "each Party," the reference is mostly directed to Jordan; if laws get changed as a result of the US-JO FTA, it is most likely to be those of Jordan.

In many parts, the US-JO FTA reflects the laws and views of the U.S. For example, the rules of origin for textiles and apparels, the definition of a substantial cause for purposes of safeguard measures, anti-circumvention of technological products designed to protect intellectual property rights, e-commerce, visa commitments, *amicus curiae* briefs, and living and non-living resources for the purpose of natural resource definition, come from pre-existing U.S. laws and regulations. The approach adopted in drafting the US-JO FTA is a "cut and paste" approach in which U.S. laws were incorporated into the agreement with few changes. To adopt a contract law language, the entire US-JO FTA was a contract of adhesion or an unconscionable contract, which was submitted by the U.S. as a *fait accompli*. Trade negotiations require political will and administrative efforts and skills, which are finite resources for Jordan. The US-JO FTA was negotiated with a major power that obviously had its own objectives, while Jordan played the role of demandeur. Jordan must be a "rule-maker", rather than a "rule-taker".

The US-JO FTA is a WTO-Plus agreement. The parties entered into asymmetrical commitments. The two clearest examples of this are provisions relating to the service sector and intellectual property. In the service sector, Jordan liberalized certain sectors that previously had been restricted. Moreover, Jordan made further obligations with respect to intellectual property that went beyond those made under the TRIPs Agreement. These two sectors represent deeper integration, harmonization, or Americanization of Jordan's intellectual property regime of domestic policies.

The US-JO FTA does not include an accession provision for other Middle Eastern countries.[886] As such, the U.S. would have to negotiate with every Arab country for a separate FTA. The experience and lessons learned from the US-JO FTA must serve as a base for a new approach for negotiating the proposed US-Middle East FTA. Due to the economic and political disparities between many of the Middle East countries and disparity in the degree of liberalization achieved by those countries, the US-JO FTA may not be the best template for a regional trade agreement. The US-JO FTA is not a "one-size-fits-all" agreement. The U.S. proposed agreements with some Arab countries may require variations that take into consideration the different level of development in each country. The question then would be how to qualify these different FTAs if, for example, they exclude certain sectors from coverage, adopt different coverage approaches, such as what occurred with the coverage of agriculture under the US-Morocco FTA, or tailor the margin of preference.[887] Arab countries may feel motivated by economic pressure created by the formation of the FTA to join or form new FTAs.[888]

---

[886] On the other hand, NAFTA sets the possibility that other countries may join it. Article 2204 states that "any country or group of countries" may accede to NAFTA. Thus, NAFTA's accession provision is not geographically confined. As a matter of fact Argentina, would-be independent Quebec of Canada, Chile, Turkey, and Britain at one point showed an interest in joining NAFTA.

[887] See *U.S., Morocco Fail to Wrap up FTA Negotiations, To Resume Early Next Year*, Inside U.S. Trade (Inside Wash. Publishers) 7 (Dec. 12, 2003) (The U.S. and Morocco differ on market access in agriculture in which Morocco has a half million small wheat farmers. Morocco negotiators refused to accept substantial market access of wheat, red meat, chicken parts and legumes. The U.S. industry opposes the exclusion of these products). The U.S. demands for greater market in agricultural products to level the playing field with the EC that has played larger role in the Moroccan market. As a result of agricultural concessions under the US-Morocco FTA, poor displaced Moroccan farmers may want to replace their crops with hashish and other soft drugs so as to reclaim Morocco's old title as the largest exporter of hashish to meet the EC's lucrative market. Alternatively, displaced Moroccan farmers can work as extras for the domestic and foreign film industry especially that the FTA allows Morocco to continue subsidizing its film industry. The US-Bahrain FTA would eliminate virtually all trade restrictions between the two parties as soon as it takes effect. Under the agreements, all bilateral trade in consumer and industrial products will become duty free immediately after it enters into force. Bahrain will provide immediate duty free access for 98 percent of U.S. agricultural products such as meats, fruits, cereals. It would phase out tariffs on the remaining products such as alcohol and tobacco in 10 years. The U.S. in return will provide immediate duty free access for all of Bahrain's current exports of consumer, industrial, and agricultural products. In the US-Bahrain FTA of 2004, Bahrain agreed to open its service market wider than other FTAs using the negative approach. It also permits immediate duty-free trade in textiles and apparel products immediately provided that these products contain either U.S. or Bahraini yarn or fabric. It also permits temporary transitional allowance for textiles and apparel products that do not meet this requirement.

[888] See Grary G. Yerkey and Christopher S. Rugaber, *supra* n. 316 (quoting Boutros-Gali, Egypt's [former] foreign trade minister, saying that Egypt wants to begin the [US FTA] negotiations "tomorrow"). Although Egypt has made some progress in certain areas such as tariff reduction, customs administration, and tax reform, there are still some problem areas that need to be resolved before FTA talks start. See Rossella Brevetti, *Egypt's Trade Minister Calls for QIZ, Free Trade Accord with United States*, 21 Intl. Trade Rep. (BNA) 1883 (Nov. 18, 2004) (quoting Rashid Mohamed Rashid, Egypt's [new] Foreign Trade and Industry minister, before the Institute for International Economics, that he hoped that FTA talks with the United States could begin in 2005. He also hoped that agreement on "Qualifying Industrial Zones" (QIZs) could be reached soon with the U.S. as a first step toward the free trade agreement. However, USTR spokesman declined to comment on a possible time line for FTA talks saying that the USTR is interested in reviewing bilaterally some of the problems U.S. companies face in the Egyptian market [such as investment disputes, Egypt's authorization of copycat versions of U.S. pharmaceuticals, suspension of U.S. beef imports without scientific basis, ban on imports of chicken, and restrictions on imports of turkey]). The US-Bahrain FTA could function as a feeder to gain preferential market access in the customs union of the Gulf Cooperation

IV. The Social Clause of the U.S.-Jordan Free Trade Agreement

This section addresses the environmental and labor provisions of the US-JO FTA.[889] The environment and labor provisions of the FTA gives the agreement a human face because they address issues other than traditional trade matters, such as tariffs and quotas. The preamble of the FTA includes statements relating to sustainable development, the environment, and labor.[890] The FTA covers environment and labor in articles 5 and 6 respectively.

Negotiations to incorporate non-trade related environment and labor provisions into the FTA were undertaken to meet the demands of the U.S. administration.[891] For the first

---

Council. For example, U.S. exporters could use the US-Bahrain FTA to gain duty-free access to other Persian Gulf markets such as Saudi Arabia taking advantage of the common external tariff of 5% and the elimination of tariffs on intra-Gulf trade starting 2003. This ultimately would break up the customs union among countries members of the Gulf Cooperation Council. See Gary G. Yerkey, *U.S. Will Continue to Support GCC While Negotiating Bilateral Free Trade Pacts*, 22 Intl. Trade Rep. (BNA) 197 (Feb. 3, 2005) (Catherine A. Novelli, assistant US. trade representative for Europe and the Mediterranean, stated that the United States will continue to support the existence of the GCC even as it negotiates FTAs with individual GCC members. The United States wants the GCC to succeed and has no intention in breaking it up).

[889] See Jagdish Bhagwati, *The Boundaries of the WTO: The Question of Linkage*, 96 Am. J. Int'l L. 126, 127 (2002) (the use of the social clause terminology is traced back to former USTR Carla Hills. This is not just a question of semantics. Underlying the determined efforts of these to-date mainly northern lobbies to work their agendas into trade institutions and treaties is a public relations machine that rationalizes the campaigns by arguing that there is an intrinsic, hence legitimate need to bring these agendas onto the trade scene).

[890] The FTA preamble states: [the U.S. and Jordan] Recognizing the objective of sustainable development, and seeking both to protect and preserve the environment and to enhance the means for doing so in a manner consistent with their respective needs and concerns at different level of economic development". The FTA preamble also states: [the U.S. and Jordan] Desiring to promote higher labor standards by building on their respective international commitments and strengthening their cooperation on labor matters". See United States (U.S.)-Jordan: Agreement Between The United States of America and the Hashemite Kingdom of Jordan on The Establishment of a Free Trade Area, *supra* n. 695, preamble. Sustainable development is a concept that contemplates the use of natural resources to meet the needs of the current generation, without jeopardizing the resources for future generations. It embraces two concepts; the concepts of rational development (or wise use) and some elements of eco-development. Therefore, it is an inter-generational concept. It was enunciated in this format by the Brundtland Report, Our Common Future, of World of the Commission on Environment and Development of 1987. It is unclear if the needs of every individual must be met in the current generation or the needs of current generation on the whole. For criticism of the concept of sustainable development see Michael McCloskey, *The Emperor Has No Clothes: The Conundrum of Sustainable Development*, 9 Duke Envtl. L. & Policy Forum 153, 155 (1999).

[891] See also Richard H. Steinberg, *Trade-Environment Negotiations in the E.U, NAFTA, and WTO: Regional Trajectories of Rule Development*, 91 Am. J. Intl. L. 231, 232, 235 (1997) (the trade-environment agenda is driven by wealthy states with relatively stringent environmental regulations which suggests that richer countries will produce less pollution per unit of output than poorer countries-not that richer countries produce less total pollution than poorer countries. Richer countries tend to be more powerful in trade negotiations than poorer countries since, in the international trade context, "power" may be seen as a function of relative market size. When powerful countries engage in an integration-deepening exercise, they require enhanced trade-environment solutions as part of the package they bring home for domestic ratification. For example, in the context of the EC, analyses show that German market power-the most extensive in Europe-has dominated the process and the outcomes of the environment-trade debate. However, in the WTO, the power of richer, greener countries' markets to bring about trade-environment solutions is at its lowest).

time in U.S. trade history, a trade agreement included provisions that address environment and labor in the main text of the agreement.[892] The inclusion of the social clause in the FTA was determined more by economic and political needs that existed in the U.S. than by pressures exerted by Jordanian trade unions and environmental groups.

A. Environmental Protection and the US-JO FTA

While the US-JO FTA includes specific references to environment in various different articles, article 5 is the main environmental provision.[893] The US-JO FTA was the first trade agreement to include environmental provisions in its main text. On the other hand, NAFTA contains environmental protection provisions in a side agreement, known as the North American Agreement on Environmental Cooperation (NAAEC).[894]

The US-JO FTA considers lower environmental protection to be unfair trade.[895] Accordingly, the U.S. and Jordan "shall strive" not to waive or derogate from environmental laws as an encouragement of trade with each other.[896] However, the FTA language is non-binding because it uses mostly hortatory language.

---

[892] See Howard Mann, *NAFTA and the Environment: Lessons for the Future*, 13 Tul. Envt. L.J. 387, 409 (2000) (suggesting that the impact of trade agreements on sustainable development requires that the environment be treated as an issue that is "over here", inside the agreement, not "over there" in another agreement). See Jerome Levinson, *Certifying International Worker Rights: A Practical Alternative*, 20 Comp. Lab. L. & Policy 401, 405 (1999) (arguing that incorporating worker rights into the main body of multilateral agreements has reached a dead end. The only path to progress now is unilateral actions on the part of the U.S. The more effective way is to resort to aggressive unilateral action).

[893] For example, the U.S. and Jordan may exclude from patentability certain inventions to avoid prejudice to the environment. Additionally, the FTA incorporates by reference article XX of GATT 1994 including environmental measures necessary to protect human, animal or plant life or health and measures relating to the conservation of "living and non-living" exhaustible natural resources. See United States (U.S.)-Jordan: Agreement Between The United States of America and the Hashemite Kingdom of Jordan on The Establishment of a Free Trade Area, *supra* n. 695, arst. 4.18 & 12.1.

[894] See North American Agreement in Environmental Cooperation, Sept. 14, 1993, 32 I.L.M 1480.

[895] See United States (U.S.)-Jordan: Agreement Between The United States of America and the Hashemite Kingdom of Jordan on The Establishment of a Free Trade Area, *supra* n. 695, art. 5.1.

[896] The purpose of the FTA is to prevent race to the bottom The term "race-to-the-bottom" refers to a progressive relaxation of state environmental standards, spurred by interstate competition to attract industry, that also occasions a reduction in social welfare below the levels that would exist in the absence of such competition. The widely accepted theoretical model for the race-to-the-bottom is non-cooperative game theory, of which the classic Prisoner's Dilemma (John von Neumann (a mathematician) and Oskar Morgenstern (an economist) wrote Theory of Games and Economic Behavior, the publication of which is generally considered to have given birth to modern game theory. Melvin Dresher and Merrill Flood at the RAND Corporation first used the name "Prisoner's Dilemma" in 1950. When presenting the basic game to a seminar at Stanford University, Albert W. Tucker created the prosecutor-prisoner story to go with the game, which gave it the name of Prisoner's Dilemma. The Prisoner's Dilemma was applied to the generation of public goods as early as 1965 by Mancur Olson and applied specifically to environmental problems in 1968 by Garrett Hardin in the Tragedy of the Commons) is perhaps the most well known example. According to this model, although all states would be better off if they each cooperated with each other by collectively maintaining optimally stringent environmental standards, the incentives are such that each state will instead relax its standards in an ultimately unsuccessful bid to attract industry. On the other hand, revisionist critics contend that the effects of state competition upon state environmental standard-setting are welfare-enhancing, rather than welfare-reducing. Revisionists argue that race-to-the-bottom does

The FTA permits each country to determine its own substantive environmental laws, but requires that those laws provide high levels of environmental protection.[897] The FTA neither requires harmonization of environmental laws nor sets minimum environmental standards. Therefore, the FTA does not override current Jordan or U.S. environmental laws.[898]

The FTA requires that the parties "effectively enforce" their environmental laws.[899] However, the FTA does not determine how each party will enforce its environmental laws. The FTA leaves to each party the choice of measure of enforcement. The FTA speaks of "effective enforcement," which excludes actions by the U.S. Congress or Jordanian National Assembly. In other words, the FTA applies only to the executive actions and does not apply to actions by the legislature.

To measure whether either party of the FTA has failed to "effectively enforce" its environmental laws, the agreement provides a two-prong test. This test requires a "sustained or recurring" course of action or inaction in a manner affecting trade between the parties. The FTA does not define the terms "sustained or recurring." Although "sustained or recurring" implies something that happens more than one time, the definition may not be settled so easily. For example, "sustained or recurring" may be defined as a failure to act twice every year, ten times in one month, or a failure to act every two years. The second-prong of the test requires that the sustained action/inaction be in a manner that affects trade. This prong determines what violation is actionable or non-actionable. Only sustained action or inaction that "affects" trade is actionable. Therefore, environmental obligations are linked to trade in a manner that would otherwise be considered an intrusion into the domestic arena of the FTA parties. The second-prong of the test does not determine if the FTA covers only trade under the agreement only or extends to other trade arrangements such as the QIZs program.

The US-JO FTA reserves to each party the right to exercise discretion in the investigation, prosecution, regulation, and compliance with environmental matters.[900] The

---

not exist. For more on which theory is right see Kirsten H. Engel, *State Environmental Standard-Setting: Is There a "Race" and is it "to the Bottom,"* 48 Hastings L.J. 271, 297 (1997).

[897] "Recognizing the right of each Party to establish its own levels of domestic environmental protection and environmental development policies, and to adopt or modify accordingly its environmental laws, each party shall strive to ensure that its laws provide for high levels of environmental protection and shall strive to continue improve those laws". United States (U.S.)-Jordan: Agreement Between The United States of America and the Hashemite Kingdom of Jordan on The Establishment of a Free Trade Area, *supra* n. 695, art. 5.2.

[898] The environmental statutes of the U.S. have been recognized as some of the most rigorous in the world. See Michael J. Kelly, *Environmental Implications of North American Free Trade Agreement,* 3 Ind. Intl. & Comp. L. Rev. 361, 368 (1993). U.S. environmental statutes include: *Clean Air Act of 1967,* 42 U.S.C. § 7401 (2000) *Clean Water Act of 1972,* 33 U.S.C. §1251 (2000), *The Comprehensive Environmental Response, Compensation, and Liability Act of 1980,* 42 U.S.C. § 9601 (2000), *The Resource Conservation and Recovery Act of 1976,* 42 U.S.C. § 6901 (2000), *The National Environmental Policy Act of 1969,* 42 U.S.C. § 4332 (2000), and *The Endangered Species Act of 1973,* 16 U.S.C. § 1531 (2000).

[899] See United States (U.S.)-Jordan: Agreement Between The United States of America and the Hashemite Kingdom of Jordan on The Establishment of a Free Trade Area, *supra* n. 695, art. 5.3 (a).

[900] *Id.* art. 5.3.

FTA considers a party not in violation of its obligation to "effectively enforce" its environmental laws if that party exercises reasonable discretion or makes a *bona fide* decision as to how allocate resources. This language may be used to avoid the stringent obligation of effective enforcement of environmental laws.

Environmental laws in the US-JO FTA are defined as statutes, regulations, or provisions with the primary purpose of the protection of environment or prevention of a danger to human, animal, or plant life or health.[901] These environmental laws or regulations include: those related to the prevention, abatement or control of the release, discharge, or emission of pollutants or environmental contaminants, those related to the control of environmentally hazardous or toxic chemicals, and those related to the protection of wild flora and fauna and their habitat. Under the FTA, environmental laws are defined narrowly to those laws and regulations "primarily" aimed at protecting the environment or preventing a danger to human, animal, or plant life or health. Under the FTA definition of environmental laws, agricultural law or mining law, for example, may be excluded from coverage. The FTA does not determine the scope of what laws qualify as environmental law.

The US-JO FTA fails to address the distinction between standards regulating a final product and standards regulating the process of production of that product.[902] The failure to make the distinction will restrict the ability of the U.S. to exclude Jordanian products produced in a manner that is damaging to the environment.[903] In addition, the FTA does not set forth the relationship between the FTA and international environmental agreements that use international trade measures as enforcement mechanisms.[904] The

---

[901] *Id.* art. 5.4. The definition of environmental laws in article 5 of the FTA is wider in scope than that of article 45.2 of the NAAEC. Environmental law in the NAAEC is defined as any statute or regulation the primary purpose is to protect the environment, or to prevent a danger to human life or health. Thus, article 5 of the FTA includes the prevention of danger to animal or plant life or health.

[902] The standards regulating the process of production of a product are known as process and production methods (PPMs). PPMs specify criteria for how a product is manufactured, harvested, or taken. Terms such as "made with", "produced by", and "harvested by" signify a PPMs standard. All PPM standards apply to the production stage, for example before a product is placed on the market for sale. These standards specify criteria for how a product is produced or processed. However, the PPM standard may address the environmental effects of a product all during its life-cycle, for example effects which may emerge when the product is produced, transported, consumed or used, and disposed of. For more on PPMs see Steve Charnovitz, *The Law of Environmental "PPMs" in the WTO: Debunking the Myth of Illegality*, 27 Yale J. Int'l L. 59, 65 (2002) (the subject of PPMs is one of the knotty controversies in the debate over trade and environment. The term "processes and production methods" originated in the GATT agreement of 1979 on Technical Barriers to Trade and referred to product standards focused on the production method rather than product characteristics).

[903] In GATT Tuna/Dolphin II case, a case based on article XX exception of GATT 1994 which is incorporated by reference in the FTA, the panel ruled that import restrictions may not be imposed on products solely because they were made or obtained in an environmentally unsound manner outside the jurisdiction of the importing country. The panel reasoned that measures designed to make other countries change their policies, and that are effective only if such changes occur, are not considered justifiable under Article XX (g). See GATT Dispute Panel Report, United States-Restrictions on Imports of Tuna, 33 I.L.M 839 (1994), para. 5.39.

[904] See United States (U.S.)-Jordan: Agreement Between The United States of America and the Hashemite Kingdom of Jordan on The Establishment of a Free Trade Area, *supra* n. 695, art. 1.2. NAFTA in article 104 provides that in the event of an inconsistency between NAFTA and the trade provisions of the listed

absence of a definitive relationship between the US-JO FTA and these international agreements may be seen as a major setback for those seeking to use trade as a vehicle for environmental protection. Finally, the US-JO FTA does not force Jordan to use wealth generated from trade resulting from the FTA for environmental protection.

The US-JO FTA was the second trade agreement to include environmental provisions. NAFTA was negotiated with a side agreement concerning the environment.[905] The NAAEC and article 5 of the US-JO FTA both protect the environment and share some substantive norms. For example, like the US-JO FTA, the NAAEC permits each country to determine its own substantive environmental laws.[906]

There are several important differences between article 5 of the US-JO FTA and the NAAEC. The NAAEC relies on moral persuasion, publicity, and dialogue to ensure compliance. For example, the NAAEC requires each party to prepare and periodically publish a report on the state of environment in its territory.[907] On the other hand, the US-JO FTA does not contain a similar provision requiring periodic reports on the state of environment. Moreover, the US-JO FTA does not address some of the provisions that were addressed in NAAEC. Under NAAEC, any non-governmental organization or individual person may assert a claim to the NAAEC Secretariat that a party is failing to effectively enforce its environmental laws.[908] Because of this provision, many private petitions have been filed that sought to challenge the enforcement of environmental regulations in the U.S., Canada, and Mexico.[909]

---

international environmental agreements, the obligation of a party to use a trade measure under the international environmental agreements "shall prevail to the extent of the inconsistency, provided that where a party has a choice among equally effective and reasonably available means of complying with such obligations, the party chooses the alternative that is the least inconsistent with the other provisions of NAFTA.

[905] Originally, NAFTA was negotiated without an agreement concerning the environment and labor. However, then president Clinton has indicated, when he took over presidency, that he would not submit NAFTA to Congress until negotiations have been completed on several side agreements regarding the environment, labor, and import surges. See Gustavo Vega-Canovas, *NAFTA and the Environment*, 30 Denv. J. Intl. L. & Policy 55, 56 (2001). The NAAEC was implemented to alleviate the concerns of many NAFTA critics who feared that NAFTA would prompt economic growth at the expense of the environment. See Edmund W. Sim, *Derailing the Fast-Track for International Trade Agreements*, 5 Fla. J. Intl. L. 471, 482 (1990) (citing criticism that came also from agriculture, consumer, human rights, and religious groups). See also Beatriz Bugeda, *Is NAFTA Up to Its Green Expectations? Effective Law Enforcement Under the North American Agreement on Environmental Cooperation*, 32 U. Rich. L. Rev. 1591, 1591 (1999).
[906] See North American Agreement in Environmental Cooperation, *supra* n. 894, art. 3.
[907] *Id.* art. 2.1.
[908] NAAEC requires any submission to identify the organization making the submission and aim at promoting enforcement and not to harass an industry. The submission must merit requesting a response from the party in question. The Secretariat determines that a factual record is warranted, it shall do so upon approval by the council of the Commission on Environmental Cooperation. The council can make the factual record public upon two-thirds vote. *Id.* art. 14.1.
[909] Between 1995 and 2000, twenty-eight citizens' submissions on enforcement matters were registered: nine regarding Canadian enforcement, eleven regarding Mexican enforcement and eight regarding U.S. enforcement. Two factual records have been published to date. See. See Vega-Canovas, *supra* note 905, at 61. The first factual record was "The Cozumel Factual Record" of 1997 concerning port terminal project in Playa Paraíso, Cozumel, Quintana Roo in Mexico. The second factual record was "The BC Hydro factual

The NAAEC also establishes a state-to-state dispute settlement process for the failure to enforce environmental laws.[910] Thus, the NAAEC creates a two-tiered system: chapter twenty dispute settlement mechanism for any dispute arising under NAFTA and the separate NAAEC dispute settlement process. The NAAEC permits a dispute panel to impose monetary fines against a country found to have engaged in a persistent pattern of ineffective environmental law enforcement.[911] The U.S.-JO FTA establishes a single dispute settlement mechanism for all disputes under the agreement. While the NAAEC imposes monetary fines, the U.S.-JO FTA imposes trade sanctions for failure to enforce environmental protection. Trade sanctions under the US-JO FTA include tariff increases, import bans, reductions in financial aid, or other financial penalties. The FTA does not determine how to measure or quantify trade sanctions that would be commensurate with a violation of an environmental provision of the FTA.

To ease concerns regarding imposing trade sanctions for environmental violations, the U.S. and Jordan exchange side letters, whereby both parties expressed their intention not to exercise trade sanctions for these violations.[912] These letters were requested by the U.S. and not Jordan. They were the U.S. idea.[913] Although the letters exchanged between the U.S. and Jordan allay fears that trade sanctions will be invoked to enforce the environmental provisions of the FTA, the validity of these letters is in question. Based on the experience of the NAFTA sugar side letter, the U.S. and Jordan should have included the language of the letters into the main text of the FTA so as to form a binding, legal commitment.[914]

B. Labor Protection and the US-JO FTA

The US-JO FTA was the first trade agreement to include labor protection provisions in its main text. The agreement requires the U.S. and Jordan to "strive" to ensure that internationally recognized labor rights are recognized and protected within domestic law.[915] In addition, the U.S. and Jordan reaffirmed their obligations as members of the

---

record" of 1997 concerning hydroelectric dams in British Columbia, Canada. The third factual record was "The Metales y Derivados Factual Record" of 1998 concerning lead smelter in Tijuana, Mexico. For more on these factual records see Mark R. Goldschmidt, *The Role of Transparency and Public Participation in International Environmental Agreements: The North American Agreement on Environmental Cooperation*, 29 B.C Envtl. Aff. L. Rev. 343, 376-383 (2002).

[910] See North American Agreement in Environmental Cooperation, *supra* n. 894, art. 22.

[911] *Id.* art. 34.4.b.

[912] On July 23, 2001, The letters were exchanged between former USTR Robert Zoellick and Jordan's ambassador to the U.S.

[913] See Grary G. Yerkey, *USTR Says Bush Administration Supports U.S.-Jordan Free Trade Agreement "as it is,"* 18 Intl. Trade Rep. (BNA) 1013 (June 28, 2001) (Sen. Grassley suggested attaching "side letters" to the agreement in which the United States and Jordan promise not to use sanctions to enforce labor and environmental provisions of the accord). See also Nancy Ognanovich, *Bush Tells Abdullah He Will Push Hill To Adopt Jordan Free-Trade Agreement*, 18 Intl. Trade Rep. (BNA) 632 (Apr. 19, 2001) (Jordanians indicated that they are going to leave that [specifics of environmental and labor provisions] to the [U.S.] administration to work with Congress directly).

[914] During the NAFTA debate, the U.S. and Mexico agreed to a sugar deal that was attached as a side letter to the text of NAFTA. However, the U.S. and Mexico are still litigating the validity of the letter.

[915] See United States (U.S.)-Jordan: Agreement Between The United States of America and the Hashemite Kingdom of Jordan on The Establishment of a Free Trade Area, *supra* n. 695, art. 6.1.

International Labor Organization (ILO).[916] Jordan has ratified all of the ILO fundamental conventions, of which there are eight.[917] In contrast, the U.S. has ratified only two of the conventions: the convention concerning abolition of forced labor and the convention eliminating worst forms of child labor.[918] The language of the FTA not only indicates trade inconsistency but it also indicates trade hypocrisy on the part of the U.S.

The FTA ensures that each party does not waive or derogate from its domestic labor laws.[919] The U.S. and Jordan, separately, have a right to set their own domestic labor standards. The FTA does not require the harmonization of labor norms. The FTA requires each party to effectively enforce its labor laws. Thus, the FTA adopts the "enforce its labor laws" standard, which is an indication that Jordanian labor laws comply with ILO standards. The U.S. and Jordan may exercise discretion in allocating resources in the enforcement of their labor laws.

The US-JO FTA recognizes cooperation as a mean for enhanced opportunities to improve labor standards.[920] The FTA defines labor laws as those statutes and regulations that are directly related to internationally recognized labor rights.[921] The FTA excludes from its coverage of labor rights the right to strike and the right of non-discrimination in employment.[922] If gender equality was incorporated in the FTA, it may have generated great criticism in Jordan due to cultural or religious concerns. International labor rights are not culture-neutral but rather are culture-laden. Labor laws in Jordan reflect a balance between religious and social forces.

While the US-JO FTA includes labor provisions within its main text, NAFTA contains labor protection provisions in a side agreement. NAFTA originally was negotiated without addressing labor issues. However, this sparked tremendous concern on the part of unions.[923] U.S. companies would potentially move to Mexico because of lower

---

[916] NAALC is absent any linkage between ILO conventions and internationally recognized labor rights. Reference to the ILO in NAALC is limited to article 24.1 which mandates that the ECE chairman be selected from a roster of experts in consultation with the ILO.
[917] See Organization for Economic Cooperation and Development, *International Trade and core Labor Standards* 24 (2000).
[918] *Id.* at 25. The U.S. have not ratified conventions on freedom of association, right to organize and bargain collectively, equal payment, non-discrimination, and minimum age.
[919] See United States (U.S.)-Jordan: Agreement Between The United States of America and the Hashemite Kingdom of Jordan on The Establishment of a Free Trade Area, *supra* n. 695, art. 6.2.
[920] *Id.* art. 6.5.
[921] These internationally recognized labor rights are: right of association, right to organize and bargain collectively, prohibition on the use of any form of forced or compulsory labor, minimum age for the employment of children, and acceptable conditions of work with respect to minimum wages, hours of work, and occupational safety and health. *Id.* art. 6.6.
[922] See Thomas Signals Support forU.S.-Oman FTA After Middle East Visit, INSIDE US TRADE (Nov. 26, 2004) (there are serious labor rights problems in Oman and the United Arab Emirates, where there are severe restrictions on workers' rights to organize and problems related to discrimination against women. This is in contrast to Jordan, Morocco and Bahrain, which have "pretty decent" labor rights in the context of the Middle East. NAALC includes laws against employment discrimination. See Reka S. Koerner, *Pregnancy Discrimination in Mexico: Has Mexico Complied with the North American Agreement on Labor Cooperation?* 4 Tex. F. C.L. & C.R. 235, 236-241 (1999).

labor and wage standards.[924] The North American Agreement on Labor Cooperation (NAALC) came into existence to address these concerns.

The NAALC aims at improving working conditions and living standards.[925] It acknowledges the right of each party to establish its own domestic labor standards. However, the NAALC requires each party to ensure that its labor laws and regulations provide high labor standards consistent with high quality and productivity in workplaces. The NAALC provides an illustrative list of government actions that each party may take to effectively enforce its labor laws.[926]

The NAALC created a Commission for Labor Cooperation to facilitate its objectives in a cooperative and consultative manner.[927] The organizational structure of the NAALC also includes a national component, the National Administrative Offices (NOAs). The NAO is a unique institution that takes up labor rights issues outside the national territory.[928] Unlike the US-JO FTA, any government, non-governmental organization, or individual may submit complaints regarding labor issues involving other NAALC countries to the NAO of their own country. The main advancements in the NAALC evolution were made through the NAO public complaints review.[929] Since the NAALC's entry into force, a total of twenty-three labor submissions have been filed.[930]

---

[923] Matthew J. Griffin, *The North American Agreement on Labor Cooperation: A Flawed Attempt at Promoting Continental Labor Standards*, 21 Suffolk Transnatl. L. Rev. 113, 115 (1997) (noting American Federation of Labor and Congress of Industrial Organizations (AFL-CIO) was major opponent of NAFTA and importance of labor to Clinton's campaign and explaining that U.S. unions claim NAALC created to obtain votes. U.S. labor unions objected to the lack of penalties within NAALC for violations of industrial relations law and the cumbersome nature of NAALC process).

[924] Then presidential candidate Ross Perot described Mexico as "great sucking sound". See Marley Weiss, *The North American Agreement on Labor Cooperation (NAALC): Accelerating Development (s)?* SE27 ALI-ABA 909, 911 (1999).

[925] See North American Agreement on Labor Cooperation, Sept. 8, 1993, 32 I.L.M. 1499 (entered into force Jan. 1, 1994) art. 1.

[926] *Id.* art. 3.

[927] *Id.* art. 8.

[928] See Lance A. Compa, *The First NAFTA Labor Cases: A New International Labor Rights Regime Takes Shape*, 3 U.S.-Mex. L.J. 159, 163 (1995) (a critical function of NAO is to review labor law matters in one or both of the other NAALC parties, not domestic matters. In this sense, the thrust of the NAO's function runs counter to the otherwise firm preservation of sovereignty under NAALC).

[929] See Emmanuelle Mazuyer, *Labor Regulation in the North American Free Trade Area: A Study on the North American Agreement on Labor Cooperation*, 22 Comp. Lab. L. & Policy J. 239, 244 (2001).

[930] One of the well known submissions concerning labor law matter under NAALC public submission procedure was the International Brotherhood of Teamsters (IBT), a U.S. labor union, submission. That submission involved workers at a Honeywell electronics factory in Chihuahua, Mexico who were fired after expressing an interest in joining an independent Mexican labor organization. In a report released in Oct. 1994, the U.S. NAO found that the former Honeywell employees accepted severance pay from the company and, thereby, had preempted an investigation by Mexican officials into their dismissals. On that basis, the NAO declared that it could not conclude that Mexico failed to enforce its labor laws and that it could not recommend that the dispute proceed to ministerial consultations. See David Lopez, *Dispute Resolution under NAFTA: Lessons from the Early Experience*, 32 Tex. Intl. L.J. 163, 196 (1997).

The NAALC created a dispute settlement mechanism to resolve disputes over any matter that could affect the operation of the NAALC.[931] However, the NAALC dispute settlement mechanism applies only to occupational safety and health standards, child labor issues, or minimum wage right that are trade-related and mutually recognized by labor laws of each party.[932] Other labor principles such as forced labor, right of association, right to organize and bargain collectively, and hours of work are not covered.[933] Therefore, the basis for actionable violations is wider in scope under the US-JO FTA than under the NAALC. The NAALC was criticized for its failure to include sanctions for basic labor-relations violations. In the history of the NAALC, no ni single case has reached the arbitration process. The dispute resolution procedures established by the NAALC are bureaucratic, byzantine, cumbersome, and protracted, all of which would hamper timely settlements.[934]

The U.S., in the FTA with Jordan, assumes that labor standards in Jordan are not adequately protected. The U.S. overlooks the fact it should itself begin protecting worker rights by extending labor protection to agricultural workers. Otherwise, it seems hypocritical on the part of the U.S. The U.S. labor laws favor employers over employees.[935] Moreover, the U.S. is a country where May 1st, the International Workers' Day, is not considered a Federal holiday or even celebrated.[936]

---

[931] NAALC created four-step dispute settlement process that consists of: 1) initial consultations between NAOs regarding the other party's labor law, its administration, or labor market conditions in its territory 2) ministerial consultations regarding any matter within the scope of NAALC 3) expert evaluations regarding patterns of non-enforcement of domestic labor law in each party country and 4) further consultations whether there has been a persistent pattern of failure by a party to effectively enforce occupational safety and health, child labor or minimum wage technical labor standards that may lead to non-binding arbitration. See North American Agreement on Labor Cooperation, *supra* n. 925, art. 20.

[932] *Id.* art. 29.1.

[933] Labor principles under NAALC are subject to different treatment. Right of association, right to organize and bargain, and right to strike are subject only to review and consultation. Eight technical labor principles concerned with forced labor, child labor, minimum wage and hour standards, employment discrimination, equal pay for men and women, job health and safety, workers' compensation for occupational injuries and illnesses and protection of migrant workers are subject to evaluation and recommendations by an ECE. Only violations of child labor, health and safety, and minimum wage and hour standards can go forward to dispute resolution with the possibility of sanctions. In case of an alleged persistent of failure to enforce occupational safety and health, child labor or minimum wages technical labor standards, the last venue is the dispute resolution by an arbitral panel, which may develop an action plan for effective enforcement of national labor law. Failure to implement this plan may result in fines or trade sanctions.

[934] See Mazuyer, *supra* n. 929, 248.

[935] See Andrew K. Stutzman, *Our Eroding Industrial Base: U.S. Labor Laws Compared With Labor Laws of Less Developed Nations in Light of the Global Economy*, 12 Dick. J. Intl. L. 135, 142 (1993) (the U.S. judiciary is reluctant to protect employee rights and that it construes worker projections narrowly in favor of employers. Furthermore, the U.S. Constitution does not explicitly protect worker' rights).

[936] The May 1st, International Worker's Day, dates back to the eight-hour working day movement. See Scott D. Miller, *Revitalizing the FLASA*, 19 Hofstra Lab. & Empl. L.J. 1, 13 (2001) (the eight-hour movement of the nineteenth century is based on a vision of working less, living more. It embraces workers' desire for personal time from industrial order, and freedom for home life and cultural matters outside wage and job concerns. (8 hours for work, 8 hours for sleep, and 8 hours for what we will).The movement started. In 1886, Sameul Gompers, the leader of the Federation of Organized Trades and Labor Unions, called for a nationwide strike by all workers on May 1st to achieve shorter working hours. This strike became the first general strike in the history of the international labor movement. The U.S. Army and riot-trained police surpassed the strike by use of force).

In Jordan, the only existing union federation is heavily dependent on government financial support.[937] The government subsidizes the union federation, which is considered a restriction on the right to establish a free union. Even the U.S. AFL-CIO cannot escape such criticism.[938] In the U.S. today only about one out of every seven workers belongs to a labor union. The principal causes for the decline of U.S. organized labor are its overuse of the work stoppage, tolerance for criminal infiltration or corruption, its philosophical underpinnings, and its tolerance for the entrenchment of internal power.[939]

---

[937] See Organization for Economic Cooperation and Development , *supra* n. 917, at 94.

[938] Organized labor is embodied in the U.S. umbrella confederation, the American Federation of Labor-Congress of Industrial Organizations (AFL-CIO). The key forces behind the creation of the Congress of Industrial Organizations had roots in socialism with events during and just after World War I effectively purged organized labor of its radical elements. The AFL is composed mainly of the craft unions and the CIO by contrast organized workers in the mass industrial sector, the basic industries. The American Federation of Labor and Congress of Industrial Organizations often quarreled over direction and philosophy. The AFL had a horizontal structure-all electricians were in the electrician's union regardless of their employer, and the CIO was organized vertically-all auto workers belonged to the auto workers union, regardless of their job description-and these competing structures generated jurisdictional infighting. The typical craft union member was also different from the typical industrial worker. The latter was more likely to be a relatively recent Eastern European immigrant who brought some Marxist ideology along or a worker from the ranks of the underprivileged social classes in America such as the southern Black workers who had migrated northward and into the factories and manufacturing plants after World War I. See Fredrick Englehart, *Withered Giants: Mexican and U.S. Organized Labor and the North American Agreement on Labor Cooperation*, 29 Case W. Res. J. Intl. L. 321 (1997).

[939] The Laborers International Union of North America was one of four major unions singled out as corrupt by a presidential commission in 1985. *Id.*

Conclusion

The FTA can be subdivided into two packages: the less controversial package of tariff reductions and the more controversial relating to environmental and labor issues. The US-JO FTA would have been of little value if it did not include environment and labor provisions within the text of the FTA. The U.S. demanded that these provisions be included within the text of the FTA.

The environmental and labor provisions of the FTA may be described as "not unexpected, symbolic but dangerous, and material step but falling short". Applying all of these terms can help form judgments about the significance of these provisions. The social clause of the US-JO FTA may be described as "not unexpected" because it was negotiated by the Clinton administration and its constituencies who advocate for the protection of the environment and worker rights. The exchange of side letters between the U.S. and Jordan was not expected by the Bush administration. The environment and labor provisions, along with the side letter, reflect U.S. political party lines. The environmental and labor provisions of the FTA are symbolic but dangerous. Considering the purpose of FTA to cement the bonds of friendship and economic relations between the parties, the possibility of invoking trade sanctions for violations of the social clause is remote but still a threat. The FTA contains loopholes that may be exploited by interest groups in the U.S. who would advance their own agendas.

Articles 5 (environment) and 6 (labor) of the FTA represent material steps towards advancing an environmental and labor agenda by linking the FTA with non-trade provisions. However, these articles fall short of expectations. For example, the U.S. and Jordan have recognized in the FTA that it is inappropriate to encourage trade by relaxing domestic environmental and labor laws, but the FTA does not prohibit the parties from doing so. The FTA does not define the relationship between the FTA and the multilateral environmental agreements. Moreover, the FTA does not define terms such as "sustained action/inaction". The social clause of the FTA was structured in a way that would avoid the language of standards. The FTA contains a scapegoat clause that allows each party to exercise discretion in allocating resources to enforce its environment or labor laws. The FTA does not permit non-governmental organization to submit claims that either party is failing to enforce its environmental or labor laws effectively. It will be several years before analysis can determine the real effectiveness of the environmental and labor provisions of the US-JO FTA.

ASSESSMENTS AND RECOMMENDATIONS

In this book I have argued that membership in the WTO should offer Jordan, in collaboration with other developing countries, a better chance of securing and advancing its interests rather than entering into bilateral trade deals with economic hegemonies such as the U.S. where exists great inequality in bargaining power. In current bilateral trade agreements, economic hegemonies such as the U.S. can dictate the rules and weave them to their own advantage. Jordan and other Arab countries can maximize their bargaining position at the WTO by collaborating closely with each other and forming regional trading bloc. Specifically, Arab countries should consider that the free trade ideology has links in Islam.

Islamic law is inclined toward free trade. Islamic law condemns imposing tariffs on trade with other states. Even when tariffs are imposed, they are imposed on the basis of reciprocity. Islamic law also advocates fair and moral trade by prohibiting trade in illegitimate goods, such as pork, alcohol, and *riba*. Enough resources exist in Islamic jurisprudence than can help Arab countries integrate into the modern multilateral trading system while abiding by Islamic teachings.

The method in which the WTO, as an institution, conducts its business may not be perfect. The WTO must accelerate the accession of Arab countries into the organization. Political issues must not lead to the application of different rules for Arab countries than are applicable towards other countries. The accessions of Syria and Saudi Arabia have been blocked by the U.S. and other Western countries based on Syria and Saudi Arabia's positions on human rights, religious freedom, democracy, and the trade boycotts on Israel. The WTO Secretariat should hire more staff from Arab countries and include Arabic as a working language in the trade body.

The WTO dispute settlement mechanism requires preparing commercial data, conducting studies, making economic modeling, and providing substantial documentation. These activities are all very costly. Arab countries must share the legal and financial burdens of engaging in such proceedings at the WTO. Spreading the cost of litigating among Arab countries would make the process more affordable for the Arab countries to be involved.

The agreements covered by the WTO and its judicial decisions are voluminous. Deep understanding of the WTO texts and the effects of these agreements on Arab countries and industries is of extreme importance to determine what their benefits and challenges are. An Inter-Arab Academy for International Trade Law is needed to fill in the gap left by the WTO technical assistance. The purpose of such an academy would be to send candidates to be trained in international trade at different institutions. These candidates can include officials, academia, or representatives from the private sector nominated by their countries based on qualifications and not on political affiliations.

To improve the competitive position of the region, Arab countries would have to be creative, generating alternative ideas and new solutions. The model for future regional

Arab free trade agreements must be grounded in economics and not politics. Future trade agreements should cover agriculture, transportation, financial services, business facilitation, and specific-sector initiatives. The model should move beyond classic tariff reductions to cover unnecessary impediments that compromise trade flows between Arab countries. For example, Arab countries must engage in regulatory harmonization for different testing requirements, controls, and inspections. Arab countries should increase labor mobility by lifting visa requirements for certain nationals of these countries.

Jordan's accession to the WTO was a lengthy and costly process. Jordan agreed to reduce tariffs, open its service market, reform its intellectual property regime, and accede to the ITA. Jordan enjoyed special and differential treatment in few areas, such as tariff reductions. The Jordanian government must introduce policies aimed at cushioning its most vulnerable citizens from the effects of trade liberalization. These policies include re-employment projects, diversified education programs, and funds to offset the extreme adverse effects of trade liberalization.

Jordan's accession to the WTO has been seen as an end unto itself. Permanent industry and non-industry trade advisory committees must be established to solicit the opinions of all Jordanian stakeholders in the work of the WTO and ensure that their views are considered when WTO-related decisions are made. Trade officials and parliamentarians must be involved in WTO negotiations on a regular basis and should be consistently updated as to negotiating positions. There is also a need for an economic impact assessment of trade negotiations. This assessment would analyze the effects of trade negotiations on consumers, industry, competition, and employment.

The US-Jordan FTA was designed both to spur Jordan's economic development and to cement strategic ties between the U.S. and Jordan for geopolitical reasons. The U.S. in the FTA did not adequately take the interests of Jordan into account. Although the FTA in many parts refers to "the Parties" or "each Party," the reference is directed towards Jordan. If laws must be changed as a result of the US-JO FTA, they are most likely to be those of Jordan. In many parts, the US-JO FTA reflects the laws and views of the U.S. For example, provisions relating to rules of origin for textiles, definition of substantial cause for purposes of safeguard measures, anti-circumvention of technological products designed to protect intellectual property rights, e-commerce, visa commitments, *amicus curiae* briefs, and living and non-living resources for the purpose of a natural resource definition reflect U.S. laws and regulations. The US-JO FTA may be seen as a WTO-Plus agreement. The FTA parties entered into asymmetrical commitments. The U.S. acted as demander for including labor and environment within the FTA. In the FTA, Jordan played the role of demandeur. Jordan should not be the "obedient guy" on the other corner of the bargaining table. Jordan must be a "rule-maker" rather than a "rule-taker".

The experience and lessons learned from the US-JO FTA must serve as a basis for the proposed US-Middle East FTA. The US-JO FTA may not be the best template. The formation of the US-JO FTA may encourage other Arab countries, who are motivated by economic pressure, to join or form new FTAs. In concluding, I argue that the WTO system has shortcomings. However, the WTO system, when compared with bilateral trade deals such as the US-JO FTA, can offer Arab countries a better chance in advancing their economic interests.

Table 1. Multilateral Trade Negotiations Rounds

Number	Year	Round Name/Place	Number of Participating Countries	Round Subject
1	1947	Geneva/Switzerland	23	Tariff Concessions
2	1949	Annecy/France	13	Tariff Concessions
3	1950-1951	Torquay/England	38	Tariff Concessions
4	1952-1956	Geneva/Switzerland	26	Tariff Concessions
5	1960-1961	Dillon/Switzerland	26	Tariff Concessions
6	1964-1967	Kennedy/Switzerland	62	Tariff Concessions, Antidumping Code
7	1973-1979	Tokyo/Japan (Nixon before)	102	Tariff Concessions, Non-tariff barriers
8	1986-1993	Uruguay	123	Tariff Concessions, Non-Tariff Barriers, Agriculture, Services, Intellectual Property, Dispute Settlement, the establishment of the WTO

Source: www.wto.org/wto/english/thewto_e/tif_e/fact4_e.htm (last visited Sept. 15, 2002).

Table 2. Total Arab Countries Exports and Imports as of 1999

Product	Exports (%)	Imports (%)
Food and Beverages	3.9	14.9
Raw Materials	2.4	6
Petroleum Products	68.2	4.1
Chemical Products	5.3	8.1
Machinery	3.7	34.2
Manufactured Products	15.8	30.5
Unclassified Products	0.6	2.2
Total	100	100

Source: United Nations Economic and Social Commission for Western Asia, From GATT to the WTO, at 18, U.N. Doc. E/ESCWA/CAB/2001/1 (2001) (Arabic version).

Table 3. Trade Patterns of Arab Countries as of 1999

Trading Partner	Exports (%)	Imports (%)
Arab Countries	9.8	9.6
The European Union	26.2	39.2
The United States	9.6	12.7
Japan	7.7	7.6
Southeast Asia	12.4	5.7
The Rest	25.2	25.2
Total	100	100

Source: United Nations Economic and Social Commission for Western Asia, From GATT to the WTO, at 18, U.N. Doc. E/ESCWA/CAB/2001/1 (2001) (Arabic version).

Table 4. Sectoral Contribution in Gross Domestic Production

Sectors	1995 (%)	1996 (%)	1997 (%)	1998 (%)	1999 (%)	2000 (%)
Agriculture	4.9	5.0	4.4	4.8	3.7	3.8
Manufacturing	14.8	13.2	14.3	15.1	15.6	15.8
Mining	2.9	2.9	3.1	3.1	3.1	2.9
Construction	7.4	7.0	5.9	4.6	4.6	4.5
Services:	67.5	68.9	69.7	69.8	71.4	71.4
Tourism	5.9	6.3	6.0	5.8	6.0	5.1
Communication Transportation	13.9	14.8	14.6	16.8	18.0	17.8
Other Services*	47.7	47.8	49.1	47.2	46.4	48.5

Source: Central Bank of Jordan, *Annual Statistical Issue of Jordan Central Bank* (2000).
* Banks, hotels, and restaurants.

Table 5. Budget Balance (in millions of JD)

Fiscal Year	Revenue	Expenditure	Balance
1998	1700	2055	-355
1999	1784	2007	-223
2000	1801	2005	-204
2001	2067	2300	-233

Source: Central Bank of Jordan, *Statistical Issues of the Central Bank of Jordan* (1998-2001).

Table 6. Trade Balance (in millions of JD)

Item	1991	1994	1996	1998	1999	2000
Exports	599	794	1005	1046	1051	1080
Imports	1711	2590	3044	2714	2635	3259
Re-exports	172	237	248	232	247	266
Total Deficit	-940	-1559	-1791	-1436	-1337	-1913

Source: Statistical Issue of the Central Bank of Jordan (2000).

Table 7. Foreign Aid (in millions of JD)

Country	1996	1997	1998	1999	2000	Total
Arab countries	145.3	141.3	148	117.1	170	721.7
Japan	28.5	28.5	34.5	39.2	46.2	176.9
U.S.	11.1	41.4	35.4	91.9	35.7	215.5
E.U	54.8	32.6	None	None	25.5	112.9
Total	239.7	243.8	217.9	248.2	277.4	1227

Source: Monthly Statistical Issue of the Central Bank of Jordan (July 2001).

Table 8. Jordan Harmonized Tariff Schedule (2004)

H.S. Code	Description	Collection Unit	Duty Rate
8527.00000	Reception apparatus for radio-telephony, radio-telegraphy or radio-broadcasting, whether or not combined, in the same housing, with sound recording or reproducing apparatus or a clock		
8527.10000	Other radio-broadcast receivers, including apparatus capable of receiving also radio-telephony or radio-telegraphy		
8527.12000	Pocket-size radio cassette-players	Value	30%
8527.13000	Other apparatus combined with sound recording or reproducing apparatus	Value	30%
8527.19000	Other	Value	30%
8527.20000	Radio-broadcast receivers not capable of operating without an external source of power, of a kind used in motor vehicles, including apparatus capable of receiving also radio-telephony or radio-telegraphy:		

Table 9. Trade with Jordan in 2003 (in millions of U.S. dollars)

Month	Exports	Imports	Balance
January 2003	35.0	43.5	-8.5
February 2003	20.7	40.5	-19.8
March 2003	91.0	48.6	42.4
April 2003	18.5	47.0	-28.5
May 2003	37.2	41.0	-3.8
June 2003	25.9	45.3	-19.4
July 2003	36.7	64.2	-27.5
August 2003	32.8	69.8	-37.0
September 2003	47.8	82.7	-34.9
October 2003	50.5	66.8	-16.3
November 2003	39.9	57.1	-17.2
December 2003	55.9	66.9	-11.0
TOTAL	**491.9**	**673.4**	**-181.5**

Source: The U.S. Census Bureau

Table 10. Value of The Leading 6 U.S. imports from Jordan under Different Trade
Programs

Value of The Leading 6 U.S. imports from Jordan in 2003 Where no Special Programs
Claimed

HS Description	Value (dollars)
980100 Imports of Articles Exported & Returned, No Change[940]	25,506,828
611020 Sweaters, Pullovers Etc, Knit Etc, Cotton	2,484,690
999995 Estimated Imports of Low Valued Transactions	1,565,604
611212 Track & Warm-Up Suits Etc, Knit Etc, Synth Fibers	1,480,708
490199 Printed Books, Brochures, Etc., Nesoi	1,062,652
611030 Sweaters, Pullovers Etc, Knit Etc, Manmade Fibers	1,020,125

---

[940] USHTS tariff item 980100 covers U.S. goods exported and subsequently re-imported duty-free if the returned goods have not been increased in value or improved in conditions by any process of manufacture or other means while abroad (Jordan in this case). However, if U.S. goods exported and re-imported after alteration or repair in a foreign country, the value added by the foreign country is dutiable. Returned U.S. goods exported and re-imported without increase in value or improve in condition are considered goods of U.S. origin. See Border Brokerage Co. v. U.S., 314 F. Supp. 788, 790 (Cust. Ct. 1970) (the case involved tomatoes grown in Florida and then exported to Canada where they were unloaded, unpacked, sorted, graded by color and size, and repacked. After which they were sold to Safeway Stores of Bellevue, Washington. These tomatoes of U.S. origin were entitled to free entry as returned U.S. products upon importation from Canada, though the tomatoes, while in Canada, had been unpacked, sorted and graded by color and size in their natural condition, and repacked in smaller cartons since the treatment given to them in Canada did not advance their value or improve their condition as tomatoes). As such, U.S. courts apply as a rule of origin for 980100 items whether a product of U.S. origin has itself (apart from its container) been advanced in value or improved in condition while abroad.

Value of The Leading 6 U.S. imports from Jordan in 2003 under the GSP

HS Description	Value (dollars)

711319 Jewelry and Parts Thereof, Of Oth Precious Metal.......................30,903,485

841582 Air Conditioning Mach Etc Incorp Refrig Unit Nesoi.......................966,230

711311 Jewelry and Parts Thereof, Of Silver.......................750,388

291890 Carboxylic Acids with Added Oxygen Func Etc Nesoi.......................414,596

870899 Parts and Accessories of Motor Vehicles, Nesoi 400,875

210410 Soups and Broths and Preparations Therefor.......................203,500

Source: Statistics are delivered from Trade Data Services, The U.S. Census Bureau (on file with author).

Value of The Leading 6 U.S. imports from Jordan in 2003 under QIZs

HS Description   Value (dollars)

611020 Sweaters, Pullovers Etc, Knit Etc, Cotton 133,463,126

620462 Women's Or Girls' Trousers Etc Not knit, Cotton.....................115,187,864

611030 Sweaters, Pullovers Etc, Knit Etc, Manmade Fibers...................48,451,781

610510 Men's Or Boys' Shirts of Cotton, Knitted or Crochet...................40,103,367

610462 W/G Trousers Overalls Breeches Shorts Cotton, Knit 40,054,845

610610 Women's Or Girls' Blouses and Shirts Cotton, Knit 26,901,764

Source: Statistics are delivered from Trade Data Services, The U.S. Census Bureau (on file with author).

Value of The Leading 6 U.S. imports from Jordan in 2003 under US-JO FTA

HS Description   Value (dollars)

711319 Jewelry and Parts Thereof, Of Oth Precious Metal 16,529,704

620462 Women's Or Girls' Trousers Etc Not knit, Cotton......................1,422,775

620341 M/B Trousers Overalls Breeches Shorts Wool, NT Knit............... 1,295,974

711311 Jewelry and Parts Thereof, Of Silver 839,330

620331 M/B Suit-Type Jacket and Blazers of Wool , NT Knit 684,637

610230 W/G Overcoats Carcoats & Similar Art MMF, Knit 640,982

Source: Statistics are delivered from Trade Data Services, The U.S. Census Bureau (on file with author).

WORKS CITED

BOOKS IN ENGLISH

Ballantyne, William M. & Stovall, Howard L. *Arab Commercial Law: Principles and Perspectives* (ABA 2002).

Bhagwati, Jagdish. *Political Economy and International Economics* (MIT Press 1991).

--------. *A Stream of Windows: Unsettling Reflections on Trade, Immigration, and Democracy* (MIT Press 1998).

--------, and Hudec, Robert E. *Fair Trade and Harmonization: Prerequisites for Free Trade* (MIT Press 1996).

Bhala, Raj. *International Trade Law: Cases and Materials* (Michie 1996).

Brown, Nathan J. *Constitutions in a Nonconstitutional World* (St. U. N. Y. Press 2002).

--------. *The Rule of Law in the Arab World: Courts in Egypt and the Gulf* (Cambridge U. Press 1997).

Cameron, Rondo. *A Concise Economic History of the World* (3rd ed., Oxford U. Press 1997).

Carranza, Mario Esteban. *South American Free Trade Area or Free Trade Area of the Americas? Open Regionalism and the Future of Regional Economic Integration in South America* (Ashgate 2000).

Carl, Beverly M. *Trade and the Developing World in the 21ST Century* (Transnatl. Publishers 2001).

Chapra, M.Umer. *Islam and the Economic Challenge* (Islamic Found. 1992).

Conant, Michael. *The Constitution and the Economy: Objective Theory and Critical Commentary* (U. Okla. Press 1991).

Crone, Patricia. *Meccan Trade and the Rise of Islam* (Princeton U. Press 1987).

Demaret, Paul et al., *Regionalism and Multilateralism after the Uruguay Round: Convergence, Divergence and Interaction* (European Interu. Press 1997).

Destler, I.M, *Renewing Fast-Track Legislation* (Inst. Intl. Econ. 1997).

227

Fatemi, Khosrow. *International Trade in the 21st Century* (Elsevier Sci. 1997).

Fawzy, Samiha. *Globalization and Firm Competitivenes in the Middle East and North African Region* (The World Bank 2002).

Finn, Daniel Rush. *Just Trading: On the Ethics and Economics of International Trade* (Abingdon Press 1996).

General Agreement on Tariffs and Trade, Aanlytical Index: Guide to GATT Law and Practice (6th ed., Contracting Parties to the General Agreement on Tariffs and Trade 1994).

Geravis, Daniel. *The TRIPS Agreement: Drafting History and Analysis* (2d ed., Sweet & Maxwell 2003).

Ghazali, Muhammad. *Understanding the Life of the Prophet Mohammad* (Intl. Islamic Fedn. Student Org. 1997).

Gibb, H.A.R & Kramers, J.H. *Concise Encyclopedia of Islam* (4th ed., Brill Academic Publishers 2001).

Gubser, Peter. *Historical Dictionary of the Hashemite Kingdom of Jordan* (Scarecrow Press 1991).

Gwartney, James & Lawson, Robert. *Economic Freedom of the World: Annual Report (2004)* (The Fraser Inst. 2004).

Hasan, Ahmad. *Sunan Abu Dawud* (Sh. M. Ashraf 1984).

Hasanuz Zaman, S. M. *Economic Functions of an Islamic State: The Early Experience* (2n ed., The Islamic Found. 1991).

Hoekman, Bernard & Mersserlin, Patrick. *Harnessing Trade for Development and Growth in the Middle East* (Brookings Instn. Press 2002).

--------. and Kheir-El-Din, Hanaa. *Trade Policy Developments in the Middle East and North Africa* (World Bank Publications 2000).

--------. and Zarrouk, Jamal. *Catching up with Competition: Trade Opportunities and Challenges for Arab Countries* (U. Mich. Press 2000).

The International Bureau of the Permanent Court of Arbitration. *Strengthening Relations with Arab and Islamic Countries through International Law: E-Commerce, WTO Dispute Settlement Mechanism, and Foreign Investment* (Kluwer L. Intl. 2002).

--------. *Resolution of Cultural Property Disputes* (Aspen Publishers 2004).

Issawi, Charles. *An Economic History of the Middle East and North Africa* (Columbia U. Press 1982).

Jackson, John H. et al. *Legal Problems of International Economic Relations: Cases, Materials, and Text on the National and International Regulation of Transnational Economic Relations* (3rd ed., W. Publg. Co 1995).

Jawara, Fatoumata & Kwa, Aileen. *Behind the Scenes at the WTO: The Real World of International Trade Negotiations* (Zed Books 2003).

Lanjouw, G.J. *International Trade Institutions* (Open U. Netherlands 1995).

Looney, J.W. et al. *Agricultural Law: A Lawyer's Guide to Representing Farm Clients* (ABA 1990).

Mann, Catherine L. et al. *Global Electronic Commerce: A Policy Primer* (Inst. Intl. Econ. 2000).

Marrison, Andrew. *Free Trade and its Reception 1815-1960* (Routledge 1998).

Masud, Muhammad Khalid, Messick, Brinkley & Powers, David S. *Islamic Legal Interpretation: Muftis and their Fatwas* (Harvard U. Press 1996).

McCarthy, J. Thomas. *McCarthy's Desk Encyclopedia of Intellectual Property* (2d ed., Bureau Natl. Affairs 1995).

Merges, Robert P. et al. *Intellectual Property In the New Technology Age* (3rd ed., Aspen Publishers 2003).

Mikesell, Raymond F. *The Bretton Woods Debates: A Memoir* (Princeton U. 1994).

Moore, Mike. *Doha and Beyond: The Future of the Multilateral Trading System* (Cambridge U. Press 2004).

Moore, Pete W. *Doing Business in the Middle East: Politics and Economic Crisis in Jordan and Kuwait* (Cambridge U. Press 2004).

Piro, Timothy J. *The Political Economy of Market Reform in Jordan* (Rowman & Littlefield Publishers 1998).

Reuvid, Jonathan. *A Handbook of World Trade: A Strategic Guide to Trading Internaionally* (Kogan Page 2001).

Richard, Yann. *Shi'ite Islam: polity, ideology, and creed* (Blackwell 1995).

Rosenthal, Franz. *Ibn Khaldun, The Muqaddimah: An Introduction to History* (Princeton U. Press 1958).

Safadi, Raed. *Opening Doors to the World: A New Trade Agenda for the Middle East.* (Intl. Dev. Research Ctr. 1998).

Samet, Andrew James & Goldberg, Moshe. *The U.S.-Israel Free Trade Area Agreement* (Bus. L. 1989).

Sharer, Robert. *Trade Liberalization in IMF-Supported Programs* (IMF 1998).

Schonhardt-Bailey, Cheryl. *Free Trade: The Repeal of the Corn Laws* (Thoemmes Press 1996).

Shoult, Anthony. *Doing Business with Saudi Arabia* (2d ed., Kogan Page 2002).

Schumann, Michael S. et al. *Food Safety Law* (Van Nostrand Reinhold 1997).

Al-Suwaidi, Ahmed A.M.S. *Finance of International Trade in the Gulf* (Graham & Trotman 1994).

Terterov, Marat. *Doing Business with Egypt* (Kogan Page 2001).

Tiefer, Charles. *Congressional Practice: A Reference, Research, and Legislative Guide* (Greenwood Press 1989).

Wheelan, Charles. *Naked Economics: Undressing the Dismal Science* (Norton & Company, 2002)

Winham, Gilbert R. *The Evolution of International Trade Agreements* (U. Toronto Press 1992).

Weiss, Edith Brown & Jackson, John H. *Reconciling Environment and Trade* (Transnatl. Publishers 2001).

Wiseman, Alan E. *The Internet Economy: Access, Taxes, and Market Structure* (Brookings Instn. Press 2000).

Wydick, Richard C. *Plain English for Lawyers* (4th ed., Academic Press 1998).

BOOKS IN ARABIC

`Abd al-Sal¯am, Muhammad & Khayr Han¯i. *Ahk¯am Al-Dust¯ur Wa Al-Swa¯biq Al-Barlama¯niah [Rules of the Constitution and Parliamentary Precedents]* 1971.

Al-Shirb⁻in⁻I, Ahmad. T⁻ar⁻ikh al-tij⁻arah al-Misr⁻iyah f⁻i `asr al-hurr⁻iyah al-iqtis⁻ad⁻iyah, 1840-1914 [History of Egyptian Trade in the Age of Free Trade, 1840-1914] (Al-Hay'ah al-Misr⁻iyah al-`⁻Ammah lil-Kitab 1995).

Ibn Khaldun, Muqaddimat Ibn Khaldun [Introduction of Ibn Khaldun], Mahhada Lah⁻a Wa-Nashar Al-Fus⁻ul Wa-Al-Faqar⁻at Al-N⁻aqisah Min Tab`⁻atih⁻a, Wa-Haqqaqah⁻A Wa-Dabat Kalim⁻atah⁻a Wa-Sharahah⁻a Wa-`Allaqa `Alayh⁻a Wa-`Amilafah⁻arisah⁻A `Al⁻i `Abd Al-W⁻ahid W⁻af⁻I (Lajnat al-Bay⁻an al-`Arab⁻i 1957).

Khan, Muhammad Muhsin. Sah⁻ih Al-Bukh⁻ar⁻I (4th ed., D⁻ar al-`Arab⁻iyat li-i-Tib⁻a'at wa al-Nashr wa al-Tawz⁻ir 1985).

Al-Majalah (Matba'at al-jwa⁻ib 1879).

Al-Manhaj al-iqtis⁻ad⁻i f⁻i al-Isl⁻am : bayna al-fikr wa-al-tatb⁻iq / al-Mu'tamar al-Ilm⁻ al-Sanaw⁻i al-Th⁻alith, al-Q⁻ahirah 9-12 Ibr⁻il 1983. [The Islamic Economic System between Theory and Practice] (J⁻ami`at al- Mans⁻urah, Kull⁻iyat al-Tij⁻arah, 1983)

Maududi, Sayyid Abu 'l-A'la. Towards Understanding the Qur'⁻an (Islamic Found. 1988).

Al-Misry, Abd Assamii. Al-Masrif Al-isl⁻Am⁻i `llm⁻iyan Wa-`Amal⁻iyan [Islamic Bank in Theory and Practice] (Maktabat Wahbah 1988).

Munazzmat Al-Mu'tamar Al-Isl⁻ami, Isl⁻am Wa Al-Niz⁻am Al-Iqtis⁻adi Al-Dawli Al-Jad⁻id [Islam and the New International Economic System] (D⁻ar Sir⁻as li-i-Nashr 1982).

Ubayd, Ahmad. Al-Khal⁻ifah Al-`⁻adil 'Umar Ibn 'Abd Al-'Az⁻iz, Kh⁻amis Al-Khulaf⁻a' Al-R⁻ashid⁻in [The Fifth Rightly-Guided Caliph 'Umar Ibn 'Abd Al-\ 'Az⁻iz] (D⁻ar al-Fad⁻ilah 1994).

PERIODICALS

A. SCHOLARLY ARTICLES

Abdul Rahman, Hasbullah Haji. The Origin and Development of Ijtihad to Solve Modern Complex Legal Problems, Vol. 43 The Islamic Q. 73 (No. 2, 1999).

Akinsanya, Adeoye & Davies, Arthur. Third World Quest for a New International Economic Order: An Overview, 33 Intl & Comp. L. Q. 208 (1984).

Ala'i, Padideh. Judicial Lobbying At the WTO: The Debate over the Use of Amicus

Curiae Briefs and the U.S. Experience, 24 Fordham Intl. L.J. 62 (2000).

--------. *Free Trade or Sustainable Development? An Analysis of the WTO Appellate Body's Shift to a More Balanced Approach to Trade Liberalization*, 14 Am. U. Intl. L. Rev. 1129 (1999).

Alatas, Syed Farid. *Introduction to the Political Economy of Ibn Khaldun*, Vol. 45 The Islamic Q. 307 (No. 4, 2001).

Ali, Reema I. and Loubna W. Haddad. *WTO Membership and Compliance in the Middle East countries*, Vol. 22 Middle E. Exec. Rep. Newsltr.11 (Sep. 1999).

Andrews, Lori B. *The Gene Patent Dilemma: Balancing Commercial Incentives with health Needs*, 2 Hous. J. Health L. & Policy 65 (2002).

The Arab Boycott: The Antitrust Challenge of United States v. Bechtel in Light of the Export Administration Amendments of 1977, 93 Harv. L. Rev. 1440 (1979).

Asakura, Hironori. *The Harmonized System and Rules of Origin*, 27 J.W.T. 5 (1993).

Avakian, Serge G. *Global Unfair Competition in the Online Commerce Era*, 46 UCLA L. Rev. 905 (1999).

Badr, Gamal M. *Islamic Law: Its Reaction to Other Legal Systems*, 26 Am. J. Comp. L. 187 (1978).

Baker, Stewart A. et al., *E-Products and the WTO*, 35 Intl. L. 5 (2001).

Balassa, Bela. *The Tokyo Round and the Developing Countries*. 14 J.W.T. 98 (1980).

Bhagwati, Jagdish. *The Boundaries of the WTO: The Question of Linkage*, 96 Am. J. Intl. L. 126 (2002).

Bhala, Raj. *Theological Categories for Special and Differential Treatment*, 50 U. Kan. L. Rev. 635 (2002).

--------. *Challenges of Poverty and Islam Facing American Trade Law*, 17 St. John's J. Leg. Comment. 471 (2003).

--------. *The Myth about Stare Decisis and International Trade Law*, 14 Am. U. Intl. L. Rev. 845 (1999).

--------. *Enter the Dragon: An Essay on China's WTO Accession Saga*, 15 Am. U. Intl. L. Rev. 1469 (2000).

Bassiouni, M. Cherif, & Badr, Gamal M. *The Shari'ah: Sources, Interpretation, and*

232

Rule-Making, 1 UCLA J. Islamic & Near E. L. 135 (2002).

Behdad, Sohrab. *Islamization of Economics in Iran Universities*, 27 Intl. J. Middle E. Stud. 193 (1995)

Benos, William J. *The Movement of Professionals, Technicians, and other Workers across NAFTA Borders*, 8 US-Mexico L.J. 25 (2000).

Bernardi, Peter. *The Great Escape*, 7 D.C.L. J. Intl. L. & Prac. 69 (1998).

Bergemann, Kristi L. *A Digital Free Trade Zone and Necessarily-Regulated Self-Governance for Electronic Commerce: The World Trade Organization, International Law, and Classical Liberalism in Cyberspace*, 20 Marshall J. Computer & Info. L. 595 (2002).

Billah, Mohd. Masum. *Life Insurance? An Islamic View*, 8 Arab L. Q. 315 (1993).

Bjornskov, Christian & Lind, Kim Martin. *Where Do Developing Countries Go After Doha? An Analysis of WTO Positions and Potential Alliances*, 36 J.W.T. 556 (2002).

Blecker, Robert A. *The "Unnatural and Retrograde Order": Adam Smith' Theories of Trade and Development Reconsidered*, 64 Economica 527 (1997).

Bonderman, David. *Modernization and Changing Perception of Islamic Law*, 81 Harv. L. Rev. 1169 (1968).

Borght, Kim Van der. *The Advisory Center on WTO Law: Advancing Fairness and Equality*, 2 J. Intl. Econ. L. 723 (1999).

Botchway, Francis N. *International Trade Regime and Energy Trade*, 28 Syracuse J. Intl. L. & Com. 1 (2001).

Brainard, Lael. *Ready for Launch? The Prospects for Global Trade Negotiations*, 19 Brookings Rev. 14 (2001).

Broadman, Harry G. *International Trade and Investment in Services: A Comparative Analysis of NAFTA*, 27 Intl. L. 623 (1993).

Bronckers, Marco C.E.J. *The Impact of TRIPS: Intellectual Property Protection in Developing Countries*, 31 CM. L. Rev. 1245 (1994).

Bronz, George. *An International Trade Organization: The Second Attempt*, 69 Harv. L. Rev. 440 (1956).

Broude, Tomer. *Accession to the WTO: Current Issues in the Arab World*, 32 J.W.T. 147 (1998).

Bugeda, Beatriz. *Is NAFTA up to its Green Expectations? Effective Law Enforcement under the North American Agreement on Environmental Cooperation*, 32 U. Rich. L. Rev. 1591 (1999).

Carroll, John. *Intellectual Property Rights in the Middle East: A Cultural Perspective*, 11 Fordham Intell. Prop. Media & Ent. L.J. 555 (2001).

Cass, Ronald A. *The Optimal Pace of Privatization*, 13 B.U. Intl. L.J. 413 (1995)

Charnovitz, Steve. *The Law of Environmental "PPMs" in the WTO: Debunking the Myth of Illegality*, 27 Yale J. Intl. L. 59 (2002).

Compa, Lance A. *The First NAFTA Labor Cases: A New International Labor Rights Regime Takes Shape*, 3 U.S.-Mex. L.J. 159 (1995).

Das, Dilip K. *Debacle at Seattle; The Way the Cookie Crumbled*, 34.5 J.W.T. 181 (2000).

Day, James M. *Petroleum Prices*, 1 Am. U. Bus. L. Br. 52 (2004).

Dehousse, Franklin et al. *The EU-USA Dispute Concerning the New American Rules of Origin for Textile Products*, 36.1 J.W.T. 69 (2002).

Demart, Paul. *The Metamorphoses of the GATT: From the Havana Charter to the World Trade Organization*, 34 Colum. J. Transnatl. L. 123 (1995).

Desta, Melaku Geboye. *Food Security and International Trade Law: An Appraisal of the World Trade Organization*, 35 J.W.T. 450 (2001).

Developing Countries and the Multilateral Trade Agreements: Law and the promise of Development, 108 Harv. L. Rev. 1715 (1995).

Dhaouadi, Mahmoud. *An Interpretation of the Implications of Human Nature for Ibn Khaldun's Thinking*, Vol. 32 The Islamic Q. 10 (No. 1, 1988).

Champ, Paul & Attaran, Amir. *Patent Rights and Local Working under the WTO TRIPS Agreement: An Analysis of the U.S-Brazil Patent Dispute*, 27 Yale J. Intl. L. 365 (2002).

Diamond, Robert A. *U.S. Antiboycott Law and Regulations*, 830 P.L.I./COMM. 721 (2001).

Dillon, Thomas J. *The World Trade Organization: A New Legal Order for World Trade?* 16 Mich. J. Intl. L. 349 (1995).

Eckersley, Robyn. *The Big Chill: The WTO and Multilateral Environmental Agreements,* 4 Global Envtl. Pol. 24 (May 2004).

Engel, Kirsten H. *State Environmental Standard-Setting: Is There a "Race" and is it "to the Bottom,"* 48 Hastings L.J. 271 (1997).

Englehart, Fredrick. *Withered Giants: Mexican and U.S. Organized Labor and the North American Agreement on Labor Cooperation,* 29 Case W. Res. J. Intl. L. 321 (1997).

Escoto, Joshua A. *Technical Barriers to Trade under NAFTA: Harmonizing Textile Labeling,* 7 Ann. Surv. Intl. & Comp. L. 63 (2001).

Ezrahi, Ariel M. *Opting Out of Opt-Out Clauses: Removing Obstacles to International Trade and International Peace,* 31 L & Policy Intl. Bus. 123 (1999).

St. Fort, Marie Kately. *A Comparison of the Rules of Origin in the United States Under The U.S.-Canada Free Trade Agreement (CFTA), and under the North American Free Trade Agreement (NAFTA),* 13 Wis. Intl. L.J. 183 (1994).

Foster, Kent S. & Alexander, Dean C. *Opportunities for Mexico, Canada, and the United States: A summary of Intellectual Property Rights under the North American Free Trade Agreement,* 20 Rutgers Computer & Tech. L.J. 67 (1994).

Gantz, David A. *Implementing the NAFTA Rules of Origin: Are the Parties Helping or Hurting Free Trade?* 12 Ariz. J. Intl. & Comp. L. 367 (1995).

--------. *A Post-Uruguay Round Introduction to International Trade Law in the United States,* 12 Ariz. J. Intl. & Comp. L. 7 (1995).

Gardner, Patterson & Patterson, Eliza. *The Road from GATT to the MTO,* 3 Minn. J. Global Trade 35 (1994).

Garduno, Eric & Pietrucha, frank J. *Intellectual Property Rights in the Arab World,* 4 Geo. J. Intl. Aff. 60 (No. 1, 2003).

Al-Ghadyan, Ahmad A. *Insurance: The Islamic Perspective and its Development in Saudi Arabia,* Arab L. Q. 332 (1999).

Ginzburg, Ezra. *An Analysis of Article XIX: The Safeguard Problem after the Uruguay Round,* 17 Neb. L. Rev. 566 (1992)

Goldberg, Stacy D. *Who Will Raise the White Flag? The Battle between the United States and the European Union over the Protection of Geographical Indications*, 22 U. Pa. J. Intl. Econ. L. 107 (2001).

Goldschmidt, Mark R. *The Role of Transparency and Public Participation in International Environmental Agreements: The North American Agreement on Environmental Cooperation*, 29 B.C Envtl. Aff. L. Rev. 343 (2002).

Gordon, Richard I. *Facilitating the Exchange of Scientific Information: Institut Pasteur v. United States*, 6 B.U. Intl. L.J. 179 (1988).

Glossary of Islamic Religious, Banking & Financial Terms, 6 J. Islamic L. & Culture 135 (2001).

Greene Jr., Preston L. *The Arab Economic Boycott of Israel: The International Law Perspective*, 11 Vand. J. Transnatl. L. 77 (1978).

Griffin, Matthew J. *The North American Agreement on Labor Cooperation: A Flawed Attempt at Promoting Continental Labor Standards*, 21 Suffolk Transnatl. L. Rev. 113 (1997).

Halabi, Roni N. *Stability in the Middle East through Economic Development: An Analysis of the Peace Process, Increased Agricultural Trade, Joint Ventures, and Free Trade Agreements*, 2 Drake J. Agric. L. 275 (1997).

Harris, May L. *TRIPS: Historical Overview and Basic Principles*, 12 J. Contemp. Legal Issues 454 (2001).

Hope, Judith Richards and Edward N. Griffin. *The New Iraq: Revising Iraq's Commercial Law is a Necessity for Foreign Direct Investment and the Reconstruction of Iraq's Decimated Economy*, 11 Cardozo J. of Intl. & Comp. L. 875 (2004).

Jackson, John H. *The Birth of the GATT-MTN System: A Constitutional Appraisal*, 12 Law & Policy Intl. Bus.21 (1980).

Jamar, Steven D. *The Protection of Intellectual Property under Islamic Law*, 21 Cap. U. L. Rev. 1079 (1992).

Jasimuddin, Sajjad M. *The Stock Exchange and Islamic Finance: Some Thoughts for a Reconsideration*, Vol. 14 The Islamic Q. 105 (No. 2, 2001).

Jordan Cleared to Join WTO: Removed from Watch List, Vol. 22 Middle E. Exec. Rep. Newsltr. 8 (July 1999).

Karasik, David R. *Securing the Peace Dividend in the Middle East: Amending GATT Article XXIV to Allow Sectoral Preferences in Free Trade Areas*, 18 Mich. J. Intl. L. 527 (1997).

Katyal, Neal Kumar. *Digital Architecture as Crime Control*, 112 Yale L.J. 2261 (2003).

Kelly, Michael J. *Environmental Implications of North American Free Trade Agreement*, 3 Ind. Intl. & Comp. L. Rev. 361 (1993).

Kennedy, Kevin C. *The GATT-WTO System at Fifty*, 16 Wis. Intl. L.J. 421 (1998).

Khan, Ali. *Islam as Intellectual Property "My Lord! Increase me in Knowledge,"* 31 Cumb. L. Rev. 631 (2001)

Khan, Muhammad Akram. *Public Finance in Islam*, 40 Islamic Stud. 227 (No. 2, 2001).

Khadduri, Majid. *The Arab League as a Regional Arrangement*, 40 Am. J. Intl. L. 756 (1946).

Klosek, Jacqueline. *The Euro-Mediterranean Partnership*, 8 Intl. Leg. Persp. 173 (1996).

Kofele-Kale, Ndiva. *The Principle of Preferential Treatment in the Law of GATT: Toward Achieving the Objective of an Equitable World Trading System*, 18 Cal. W. Intl. L.J. 302 (1987/88).

Kostecki, M. M & Tymowski, M. J. *Customs Duties versus other Import Charges in the Developing Countries*, 19 J.W.T. 269 (1985).

Khoury, Amir H. *Ancient and Islamic Sources of Intellectual Property Protection in the Middle East: A Focus on Trademarks*, 43 IDEA 151 (2003).

--------. *The development of Modern Trademark Legislation and Protection in Arab Countries of the Middle East*, 16 Transnatl. L. 249 (2003).

Koerner, Reka S. *Pregnancy Discrimination in Mexico: Has Mexico Complied with the North American Agreement on Labor Cooperation?* 4 Tex. F. C.L. & C.R. 235 (1999).

Koh, Harold H. *The Legal Markets of International Trade: A Perspective on the Proposed Canada-United States Free Trade Agreement*, 12 Yale J. Intl. L. 193 (1987).

Kontorovich, Eugene. *The Arab League Boycott and WTO Accession: Can Foreign Policy Excuse Discriminatory Sanctions?* 4 Chi. J. Intl. L. 283 (2003).

Kuran, Timur. *The Discontents of Islamic Economic Morality*, 86 Am. Econ. Rev. 438 (1996).

Ladouceur, Nicole. *Calibrating the Electronic Scale: Tipping the Balance in Favor of Vigorous and Competitive Electronic Market for Consumers*, 25 Can.-U.S. L. Rev. 295 (1999).

Lanoszka, Anna. *The World Trade Organization Accession Process, Negotiating Participation in a Globalizing Economy*, 35 J.W.T. 575 (2001).

Legierski, Renee T. *Out in the Cold: The Combined Effects of NAFTA and the MFA on the Caribbean Basin Textile Industry*, 2 Minn. J. Global Trade 305 (1993).

Levinson, Jerome. *Certifying International Worker Rights: A Practical Alternative*, 20 Comp. Lab. L. & Policy 401 (1999).

Looney, Barbara. *Should Gene be patented? The Gene Patenting Controversy: Legal, Ethical, and Policy Foundations of an International Agreement*, 26 Law & Policy Intl. Bus. 231 (1994).

Lopez, David. *Dispute Resolution under NAFTA: Lessons from the Early Experience*, 32 Tex. Intl. L.J. 163 (1997).

Mazuyer, Emmanuelle. *Labor Regulation in the North American Free Trade Area: A Study on the North American Agreement on Labor Cooperation*, 22 Comp. Lab. L. & Policy J. 239 (2001).

McCloskey, Michael. *The Emperor Has No Clothes: The Conundrum of Sustainable Development*, 9 Duke Envtl. L. & Policy Forum 153 (1999).

McFarlane, Amy. *In the Business of Development: Development Policy in the First Two Years of the Bush Administration*, 21 Berkeley J. Intl. L. 521 (2003).

Mallat, Chibli. *Commercial Law in the Middle East: Between Classical Transactions and Modern Business*, 48 Am. J. Comp. L. 81 (2000).

Mann, Howard. *NAFTA and the Environment: Lessons for the Future*, 13 Tul. Envt. L.J. 387 (2000).

Mankabady, Samir. *Insurance and Islamic Law: The Islamic Insurance Company*, 4 Arab Law Q. 199 (1989).

Maskus, Keith E. *Parallel Import*, 23 World Econ. 1269 (2000).

--------. *Regulatory Standards in the WTO: Comparing Intellectual Rights with Competition Policy, Environmental Protection, and Core Labor Standards*, 1 World Trade Rev. 135 (2002).

Mersky, Roy M. & Richmond, Michael L. *Legal Implications of the Arab Economic Boycott of the State of Israel: A Research Guide*, 71 L. Libr. J. 68 (1978)

Miller, Scott D. *Revitalizing the FLASA*, 19 Hofstra Lab. & Empl. L.J. 1 (2001).

Mora, Miquel Montanai. *A GATT with teeth: Law Wins over Politics in the Resolution of International Trade Disputes*, 31 Colum. J. Transnatl. L. 103 (1993).

Mort, Susan A. *The WTO, WIPO & the Internet: Confounding the Borders of Copyright and Neighboring Rights*, 8 Fordham Intell. Prop. Media & Ent. L.J. 173 (1997).

Mota, Sue Ann. *Internet Business Method Patents-The Federal Circuit Vacates the Preliminary Injunction in Amazon.com v. Barnesandnoble.com*, 19 John Marshall J. Computer & Info. L. 523 (2001).

Onyejekwe, Kele. *International Law of Trade Preferences: Emanations from the European Union and the United States*, 26 St. Mary's L.J. 447 (1995)

Phipps, Jim & Johnson, Christopher H. *Foreign Law in Review: 2001*, 36 Intl. L. 901 (2002).

Price, David. *The U.S.-Bahrain Free Trade Agreement and Intellectual Property Protection*, 7 J.W. Intell. Prop. 829 (No. 6, 2004).

Radon, Jenik. *Sovereignty: A Political Emotion, Not a Concept*, 40 Stan. J. Intl. L. 195 (2004).

Ray, Edward John. *The Political Economy of International Trade Law and Policy: Changing Patterns of Protectionism: The Fall in Tariffs and the Rise in Non-Tariffs Barriers*, 8 Nw. J. Intl. L. & Bus. 285 (1987).

Reidenberg, Joel R. *Electronic Communications and Legal Challenge: Rules of the Road for Global Electronic Highways: Merging the Trade and Technical Paradigms*, 6 Harv. J.L. & Tech. 287 (1993).

--------. *Restoring Americans' Privacy in Electronic Commerce*, 14 Berkeley Tech. L.J. 771 (1999).

Reiter, Yitzhak. *The Palestinian-Transjordanian Rift: Economic Might and Political Power in Jordan*, 58 The Middle E. J. 72 (2004).

--------. *Higher Education and Sociopolitical Transformation in Jordan*, 29 British J. Middle E. Stud. 137 (2002).

Renaud, John R. *Can't Get There from Here: How NAFTA and GATT Have Reduced Protection for Geographical Trademarks*, 26 Brook. J. Intl. L. 1097 (2001).

Reuter, Paul. *Operational and Normative Aspects of Treaties*, 20 Israel L. Rev. 123 (1985).

Reumann, Meyer. *The Endeavours of Gulf Countries to Meet WTO Requirements*, 16 Arab L. Q. 49 (2001).

Glenn E. Robinson. *Defensive Democratization in Jordan*, 30 Intl. J. Middle E. Stud. 387 (1998).

Rosenthal, Paul C. and Robin H. Gilbert. *The 1988 Amendments to Section 201: It is not Just for Import Relief Anymore*, 20 Law & Policy Intl. Bus. 403 (1989).

Schaefer, Matthew. *Twenty-First Century Trade Negotiations, The US Constitution and the Elimination of US State-Level Protectionism*, 2 J. Intl. Econ. L. 71 (1999).

Seniawski, Barbara L. *Riba Today: Social Equity, the Economy, and Doing Business under Islamic Law*, 39 Colum. J. Transnatl. L. 701 (2001).

Seznec, Jean-François. *Ethics, Islamic Banking and the Global Financial Market*, 23-SPG Fletcher World Aff. 161 (1999).

Shell, Richerd G. *Trade Legalism and International Relations Theory: An Analysis of the World Trade Organization*, 44 Duke L.J 829 (1995).

Sheinblatt, Julie S. *The WIPO Copyright Treaty*, 13 Berkeley Tech. L.J. 535 (1998).

Scheinfeld, Robert C. and Jeffrey D. Sullivan. *Internet-Related Patents: Are they Paying Off?* N.Y. L.J. (Dec. 10, 2002).

Sherry, Suzanna. *Haste Makes Waste: Congress and the Common Law in Cyberspace*, 55 Vand. L. Rev. 309 (2002).

Schultz, Kenneth A. *The North American Free Trade Agreement: The Provisions for the Temporary Entry of Canadian and Mexican Business Persons into the United States*, 15 SPG Intl. L. Practicum 50 (2002).

Shuval, Hillel I. *Approaches to Resolving the Water Conflicts between Israel and her Neighbors: A Regional Water-for-Peace Plan*, 17 Water Intl. 133 (1992).

Sim, Edmund W. *Derailing the Fast-Track for International Trade Agreements*, 5 Fla. J. Intl. L. 471 (1990).

Soofi, Abdol. *Economics of Ibn Khaldun Revisited*, 27:2 Hist. Pol. Econ. 387 (1995)

Spanogle, Jr., John A. *Can Helms-Burton be Challenged Under WTO?* 27 Stetson L. Rev. 1313 (1998).

Steinberg, Richard H. *Trade-Environment Negotiations in the E.U, NAFTA, and WTO: Regional Trajectories of Rule Development*, 91 Am. J. Intl. L. 231 (1997).

Stutzman, Andrew K. *Our Eroding Industrial Base: U.S. Labor Laws Compared With Labor Laws of Less Developed Nations in Light of the Global Economy*, 12 Dick. J. Intl. L.135 (1993).

Tarullo, David K. *Logic, Myth and International Economic Order*, 26 Harv. Intl. L.J. 533 (1985).

Toman, Michael A. *International Oil Security: Problems and Policies*, 20 Brookings Rev. 20 (2002).

Thomas, Chantal. *Balance-of-Payment Crises in the Developing World: Balancing Trade, Finance and Development in the New Economic Order*, 15 Am. U. Intl. L. Rev. 1249 (2000).

Thomas, Cottier. *The Impact of New Technologies on Multilateral Trade Regulation and Governance*, 72 Chi.-Kent L. Rev. 415 (1996).

Uslaner, Eric M. *The Democratic Party and Free Trade: An Old Romance Restored*, 6 NAFTA: L. & Bus. Rev. Am. 347 (2000).

Vega-Canovas, Gustavo. *NAFTA and the Environment*, 30 Denv. J. Intl. L. & Policy 55 (2001).

Verrill, Jr. Charles Owen, Peter S. Jordan, and Timothy C. Brightbill. *International Trade*, 32 Intl. L. 319 (1998).

Walbridge, John. *Logic in the Islamic Intellectual Tradition: The Recent Centuries*, Vol. 39 Islamic Stud. 55 (No. 1, 2000).

Weiss, Marley. *The North American Agreement on Labor Cooperation (NAALC): Accelerating Development (s)?* SE27 ALI-ABA 909 (1999).

Willingham, Barrett J. *Electronic Commerce and the Free Trade of the Americas*, 6 NAFTA: L. & Bus. Rev. Am. 483 (2000).

Wittes, Tamara Cofman. *The Promise of Arab Liberalism*, Policy Rev. 61 (July 2004).

Yamani, Ahmed Zaki. *The Eternal Shari'a*, 12 N.Y.U. J. Intl. L. & Pol. 205 (1979).

Young, Michael K. *Dispute Resolution in the Uruguay Round: Lawyers Triumph Over Diplomats*, 29 Intl. L. 389 (1995).

Yusef, Abdulqawi A. *Differential and More Favorable Treatment: The GATT Enabling Clause*, 14 J.W.T. 488 (1980).

Zhang, Xin. *Implementation of the WTO Agreements: Framework and Reform*, 23 Nw. J. Intl. L. & Bus. 383 (2003)

Zedalis, Rex J. *A. Theory of the GATT "Like Product" Common Language Cases*, 27 Vand. J. Transnatl. L. 33 (1994).

B. LOOSELEAF SERVICES

Brevetti, Rossella. *DeFazio Asks for WTO Case against OPEC Production Cuts*, 21 Intl. Trade Rep. (BNA) 565 (Apr. 1, 2004).

--------. *Egypt's Trade Minister Calls for QIZ, Free Trade Accord with United States*, 21 Intl. Trade Rep. (BNA) 1883 (Nov. 18, 2004).

IMF Extends Credits to Jordan, 13 Intl. Trade Rep. (BNA) 305 (Feb. 21, 1996).

Ognanovich, Nancy. *Bush Tells Abdullah He Will Push Hill to Adopt Jordan Free-Trade Agreement*, 18 Intl. Trade Rep. (BNA) 632 (Apr. 19, 2001).

Pruzin, Daniel. *U.S. Blocks Iranian WTO Application; Syria Prevented from Placement on Agenda*, 19 Intl. Trade Rep. (BNA) 36 (Jan. 3, 2002).

--------. *U.S., EU Push Saudis to Improve Market Access Offers for WTO Entry*, 17 Intl. Trade Rep. (BNA) 1654 (Oct. 26, 2000).

--------. *WTO Approves Accession of Jordan to Trade Body*, 17 Intl. Trade Rep. 29 (BNA) (Jan. 6, 2000).

--------. *Chile, Qatar Signal to WTO Interest in Hosting Ministerial Meeting Next Year*, 17 Intl. Trade Rep. (BNA) 1888 (Dec. 14, 2000).

--------. *Palestinian Authority Prepares to Pursue WTO membership; Observer Status First Step*, 18 Intl. Trade Rep. (BNA) 869 (May 31, 2001).

--------. *Staff Action to Push Pay Raise Interrupts Several WTO Meetings*, 19 Intl. Trade Rep. (BNA) 1985 (Nov. 21, 2002).

-------. *U.S. Trading Partners Concerned With Rules for Food Registration Under the Bioterrorism Act*, 20 Intl. Trade Rep. (BNA) 1158 (July 10, 2003)

--------. *Progress Cited in Saudi Accession but Partners Still Waiting For Details*, 20 Intl. Trade Rep. (BNA) 1324 (July 31, 2003).

--------. *WIPO Members Agree to New Filing Fees under Treaty, Reduced Electronic Filer Fees*, 20 Intl. Trade Rep. (BNA) 1649 (Oct. 9, 2003).

--------. *WTO Appellate Body Upholds Findings against U.S. Safeguard Tariffs on Steel*, 20 Intl. Trade Rep. (BNA) 1863 (Nov. 13, 2003).

--------. *WTO Members Discuss Accession of Algeria, Lebanon, Iraq Explores Membership Process*, 20 Intl. Trade Rep. (BNA) 2079 (Dec. 18, 2003).

--------. *In Push to Finalize WTO Accession Deal in 2004, Saudis May Hold Talks Past Dec. 19*, 20 Intl. Trade Rep. (BNA) 2077 (Dec. 18, 2003).

--------. *Saudi Flexible on Easing Investment Curbs during WTO Accession Talks, Report States*, 21 Intl. Trade Rep. (BNA) 288 (Feb. 12, 2004).

PTO Issues Rules, Amendments to Implement Madrid Protocol Act, 20 Intl. Trade Rep. (BNA) 1647 (Oct. 9, 2003).

Rugaber, Christopher S. *DHS Official Defends 24-Hour Rule, Cites 150 Orders Barring Cargo Unloading*, 20 Intl. Trade Rep. (BNA) 13 (Mar. 27, 2003).

Syria Sanctions Bill Passes Senate with Lugar Amendment, Inside U.S. Trade (Inside Wash. Publishers) 13 (Nov. 14, 2003).

Thomas Signals Support for U.S.-Oman FTA after Middle East Visit, Inside U.S. Trade (Inside Wash. Publishers) (Nov. 26, 2004).

Trademark Law Amendment Enacted, Published, 14.3 World Intell. Prop. Rep. (BNA) (Mar. 15, 2000).

U.S., Morocco Fail to Wrap up FTA Negotiations, to Resume Early Next Year, Inside U.S. Trade (Inside Wash. Publishers) 7 (Dec. 12, 2003).

USTR Argues Iraq Contract Exclusion Fall within WTO Rules, Inside U.S. Trade (Inside Wash. Publishers) (Dec. 12, 2003).

WTO Agrees to Begin Accession Talks with Iran, Taps Lamy as Next DG, Inside U.S. Trade (Inside Wash. Publishers) (May 27, 2005).

Yerkey, Grary G. *U.S., Jordan Sign Framework for Trade and Investment Pact*, 16 Intl. Trade Rep. (BNA) 468 (Mar. 17, 1999).

--------. *U.S., Jordan Make "Substantial" Progress in Talks on Free Trade Agreement, USTR Says*, 17 Intl. Trade Rep. (BNA) 1224 (Aug. 3, 2000).

--------. *USTR Says Bush Administration Supports U.S.-Jordan Free Trade Agreement "as it is,"* 18 Intl. Trade Rep. (BNA) 1013 (June 28, 2001).

--------. *U.S. and Saudi Arabia Sign Agreement that Could Lead to Free Trade Negotiations*, 20 Intl. Trade Rep. (BNA) 1353 (Aug. 7, 2003).

--------. *U.S Trade Policy Overlooks Middle East Region, Could Hurt War on Terrorism, PPI Study Says*, 20 Intl. Trade Rep. (BNA) 323 (Feb. 13, 2003).

--------. *President Bush Lays Out Broad Plan for Regional FTA with Middle East by 2013*, 20 Intl. Trade Rep. (BNA) 856 (May 15, 2003).

--------. *U.S May Soon Lift Ban on Travel to Libya, Bowing to Pressure from Business, Congress*, 21 Intl. Trade Rep. (BNA) 289 (Feb. 12, 2004).

--------. *U.S. Will Continue to Support GCC While Negotiating Bilateral Free Trade Pacts*, 22 Intl. Trade Rep. (BNA) 197 (Feb. 3, 2005).

-------- & Rugaber, Christopher S. *U.S. and Egypt Beginning to See "Eye-to-Eye" on Need for FTA but No Talks Scheduled yet*, 20 Intl. Trade Rep. (BNA) 1145 (July 3, 2003).

C. NEWSPAPERS

Mike Allen & DeYoung, Karen. *Bush Calls Trade Key to Mideast; President Launches Plan for U.S. Pact in Region*, Wash. Post A01 (May 10, 2003).

Brussels Resists Demand for Iraq WTO Seat, Fin. Times 4 (Jan. 26, 2004).

Cha, Ariana Eunjung. *Iraqis Face Tough Transition to Market-based Agriculture*, Wash. Post A10 (Jan. 22, 2004).

The Committee for Industrial Credits. *Israel's Present Position in Relation to G.A.T.T.*, 2 Econ. News 75 (No. 2, Dec. 1949).

Copyright Infringements Referred to Courts, Jordan Times 5 (Nov. 14, 2003).

Down the Aisle Again, Jordan Times 11 (Jan. 12, 2003).

Draft Law on Arbitration of 2001, Ad-Dustour 5 (June 23, 2001).

Draft Law implementing the Free Trade Agreement between Jordan and the U.S., Al-Rai, 27 (Feb. 28, 2001).

Ghani, Ashraf. *Afghanistan Craves for Investment*, Wall St. J. A10 (Dec. 1, 2004).

Hattar, Saad G. *Economic Council Sets Deadlines for State Institutions to Present Reform Plans*, Jordan Times 1 (Dec. 22, 1999).

Iraq Takes First Step to Join WTO, Fin. Times 14 (Feb. 12, 2004).

Jordan Police Intensify Action against Piracy, Jordan Times 18 (May 15, 2001).

JMP and Al Razi Mark Jordan's First Merger in the Pharmaceutical Sector, Jordan Times 11 (Nov. 27, 2002).

Ma'ayeh, Suha. *Improved IPR Enforcement Gets Mixed Reviews*, Jordan Times 10 (May 10, 2001).

Merger Announcement Applauded by Bankers but Urge Incentives, Jordan Times 11 (Feb. 24, 2003).

Turner, Mark. *Iraq and the U.N.*, Fin. Times 3 (Mar. 26, 2004).

D. MAGAZINES AND OTHER PERIODICALS

Armbruster, William. *China Syndrome*, J. Com. 38 (Nov. 18, 2002).

Business in Qatar, Economist 64, 70 (Mar. 26, 2004).

The Dating Game, Consumer Rep. 9 (Mar. 2004).

Debt-Swap Agreement Signed with France, 36 Econ. Rev. Arab World 7 (May 2002).

Economist Intelligence Unit, Country Profile: Jordan (2003).

E-Commerce Takes Off, Economist 3, 20 (May 15, 2004).

Field, Alan M. *Can Trade Bridge the Gap?* J. Com. 18 (July 21, 2003).

Morocco: Down in the Dumps, Economist 48 (Mar. 4, 2000).

Nail-Biting: Jordan's Fairly Fair Election, Economist 38 (June 21, 2003).

Oil: A Burning Question, Economist 71 (Mar. 27, 2004).

Patents and the Poor, Economist 22 (June 23, 2001).

Ann Saccomano, *Free but with a Price*, J. Com. 13, 14 (Dec. 9, 2002).

Simpson, John. *Reforming Rules of Origin*, J. Com. 12A (Oct. 4, 1988).

Special Report: Self-doomed to Failure-Arab Development, Economist 24 (July 6, 2002).

Special Report: Telecoms, 48 Middle East Econ. Dig, 26 (No. 15, Apr. 9, 2004).

Saudi Arabia on the Dole, Economist 47 (Apr. 22, 2000).

Useem, Jerry. *Will the Real WTO Please Stand Up?* 145 Fortune 34 (Jan. 21, 2002).

DOCUMENTS OF INTERNATIONAL ORGANIZATIONS

A. U.N. DOCUMENTS

El-Naggar, Said. *The Effects of the WTO on Arab Countries*, U.N. Economic and Social Commission for Western Asia, at 2, U.N. Doc E/ESCWA/CAB/2001/6 (2001) (Arabic version).

Implications of WTO/TRIPS for Technology Transfer in the Pharmaceutical Industry, U.N Economic and Social Commission for Western Asia, at 31, U.N Doc. E/ESCWA/TECH/1997/7 (1997).

The Role of the State in the Globalized Economy, with Egypt and Jordan as Case Studies, U.N. Economic and Social Commission for Western Asia, at 54, U.N. Doc. E/ESCWA/ED/2000/2/ Add.1 (2000).

Trade Facilitation and E-Commerce in the ESCWA Region, U.N. Economic and Social Commission for Western Asia, at 5, U.N Doc. E/ESCWA/ED/2001/2 (2001).

Declaration on the Establishment of a New International Economic Order, G.A. Res. 3201, U.N. GAOR, 28th Sess., Supp. No. 1, at 3, U.N. Doc. A/9559 (1974).

Marrakesh Agreement Establishing the World Trade Organization, Final Act, Annexes and Protocols (Apr. 14, 1994), 1867 U.N.T.S. 3.

International Convention on the Harmonized Commodity Description and Coding System (June 14, 1983), 1035 U.N.T.S. 3.

Notification of Withdrawal of the Government of Lebanon from the General Agreement on Tariffs and Trade (Dec. 27, 1950), 77 U.N.T.S. 367.

Notification of Withdrawal of the Government of Syria from the General Agreement on Tariffs and Trade (June 7, 1951), 90 U.N.T.S. 324.

Vienna Convention on the Law of Treaties (May 23, 1969), 1155 U.N.T.S. 331.

B. LEAGUE OF NATIONS DOCUMENTS

Terms of the British Mandate for Palestine Confirmed by the Council of the League of Nations, 3 LEAGUE OF NATIONS O.J. 1007 (1922).

C. OECD DOCUMENTS

Organization for Economic Cooperation and Development. *International Trade and Core Labor Standards* (2000).

D. WTO DOCUMENTS

PANEL REPORTS

Appellate Body Report, *Argentina-Measures Affecting Imports of Footwear, Textiles, Apparel and other Items*, WT/DS56/AB/R (Mar. 27, 1998).

Appellate Body Report, *Australia-Measures Affecting Importation of Salmon*, WT/DS18/AB/R (Oct. 20, 1998).

Panel Report, *Brazil-Measures Affecting Desiccated Coconut*, WT/DS22/R (Oct. 17, 1996).

Appellate Body Report, *Brazil-Measures Affecting Desiccated Coconut*, WT/DS22/AB/R (Feb. 12, 1997).

Appellate Body Report, *Brazil-Export Financing Program for Aircraft*, WT/DS46/AB/R (Aug. 2, 1999).

Panel Report, *Canada- Measures Affecting the Export of Civilian Aircraft*, WT/DS70/R (Apr. 14, 1999).

Panel Report, *Canada- Measures Affecting the Export of Civilian Aircraft*, WT/DS70/RW (May 9, 2000).

Appellate Body Report, *Canada-Measures Affecting the Importation of Milk and the Exportation of Dairy Products*, WT/DS103/AB/RW (Dec. 3, 2001).

Appellate Body Report, *Chile-Price Band System and Safeguard Measures Relating to Certain Agricultural Products*, WT/DS207/AB/R (Sep. 23, 2002).

Panel Report, *Egypt-Definitive Anti-Dumping Measures on Steel Rebar from Turkey*, WT/DS211/R (Aug. 8, 2002).

Request for Consultation by Thailand, *Egypt-Import Prohibition on Canned Tuna with Soybean Oil*, WT/DS205/1 (Sept. 20, 2000).

Appellate Body Report, *European Communities-Regime for the Importation, Sale, and Distribution of Banana*, WT/DS27/AB/R (Sep. 9, 1997).

Appellate Body Report, *European Communities-Measures Affecting the Importation of Certain Poultry Products*, WT/DS69/AB/R (July 13, 1998).

Panel Report, *European Communities-Measures Affecting the Importation of Certain Poultry Products*, WT/DS69/R (Mar. 12, 1998).

Panel Report, *European Communities-Anti-Dumping Duties on Imports of Cotton-Type Bed Linen from India*, WT/DS141/R (Oct. 30, 2000).

Appellate Body Report, *European Communities-Anti-Dumping Duties on Imports of Cotton-Type Bed Linen from India*, WT/DS141/AB/R (Mar. 1, 2001).

Appellate Body Report, *European Communities-Trade Description of Sardines*, WT/DS231/AB/R (Sep. 26, 2002).

Appellate Body Report, *European Communities-Anti-Dumping Duties on Imports of Cotton-Type Bed Linen from India*, WT/DS141/AB/RW (Apr. 3, 2003).

Panel Report, *European Communities-Anti-Dumping Duties on Malleable Cast Iron Tube or Pipe Fittings from Brazil*, WT/DS219/R (Mar. 7, 2003).

Appellate Body Report, *European Communities-Conditions for the Granting of Tariffs Preferences to Developing Countries*, WT/DS246/AB/R (Apr. 7, 2004).

GATT Panel Report, *United States- Restriction on Imports on Tuna*, Sep. 3, 1991, GATT B.I.S.D. (39th Supp.) 155 (1991).

Appellate Body, *Guatemala-Anti-Dumping Investigation Regarding Portland Cement from Mexico*, WT/DS60/AB/R (Nov. 2, 1998).

Appellate Body Report, *India-Quantitative Restrictions on Imports of Agricultural, Textile and Industrial Products*, WT/DS90/AB/R (Aug. 23, 1999).

Appellate Body, *Japan-Taxes on Alcoholic Beverages*, WT/DS8/AB/R (Oct. 4, 1996).

Appellate Body Report, *Korea-Definitive Safeguard Measure on Imports of Certain Dairy Products*, WT/DS98/AB/R (Dec. 14, 1999).

Appellate Body Report, *Korea-Measures Affecting Imports of Fresh , Chilled and Frozen Beef*, WT/DS161/AB/R (Dec. 11, 2000).

Appellate Body Report, *Mexico-Anti-Dumping Investigation of High Fructose Corn Syrup (HFCS) from the United States*, WT/DS132/AB/RW (Oct. 22, 2001).

Panel Report, *Mexico-Measures Affecting Telecommunications Services*, WT/DS204/R (Apr. 2, 2004).

GATT Panel Report, *Thailand-Restrictions on Importation of and Internal Taxes on Cigarettes*, Nov. 7, 1990, GATT B.I.S.D. (37th Supp.) at 200 (1990).

Appellate Body Report, *Turkey-Restrictions on Imports of Textile and Clothing Products*, WT/DS34/AB/R (Oct. 22, 1999).

Appellate Body Report, *United States-Imposition of Countervailing Duties on Certain Hot-Rolled Lead and Bismuth Carbon Steel Products Originating in the United Kingdom*, WT/DS138/AB/R (May 10, 2000).

GATT Panel Report, *United States- Restrictions on the Importation of Sugar and Sugar-Containing Products Applied Under the 1955 Waiver and Under the Headnote to the Schedule of Tariff Concessions*, Nov. 7, 1990, GATT B.I.S.D. (37th Supp.) at 228 (1990).

Appellate Body Report, *United States-Standards for Reformulated and Conventional Gasoline*, WT/DS2/AB/R (Apr. 29, 1996).

Appellate Body Report, *United States-Import Prohibition of Certain Shrimp and Shrimp Products*, WT/DS58/AB/R (Oct. 12, 1996).

Appellate Body Report, *United States-Definitive Safeguard Measures on Imports of Wheat Gluten from the European Countries*, WT/DS166/AB/R (Dec. 22, 2000).

Panel Report, *United States-Definitive Safeguard Measures on Imports of Wheat Gluten from the European Communities*, WT/DS166/R (July 31, 2000).

Appellate Body Report, *United States-Transitional Safeguard Measure on Combed Cotton Yard from Pakistan*, WT/DS192/AB/R (Oct. 8, 2001).

Appellate Body Report, *United States-Definitive Safeguard Measures on Imports of Circular Welded Carbon Quality Line Pipe from Korea*, WT/DS202/AB/R (Feb. 15, 2002).

Panel Report, *United States-Continued Dumping and Subsidy Offset Act of 2000*, WT/DS217/R (Sep. 16, 2002).

Appellate Body Report, *United States-Safeguard Measures on Imports of Fresh, Chilled or Frozen Lamb Meat from New Zealand and Australia*, WT/DS177/AB/R (May 1, 2001).

Appellate Body Report, *United States-Countervailing Measures Concerning Certain Products from the European Countries*, WT/DS212/AB/R (Dec. 9, 2002).

Appellate Body Report, *United States-Sunset Review of Anti-Dumping Duties on Corrosion-Resistant Carbon Steel Flat Products from Japan*, WT/DS244/AB/R (Dec. 15, 2002).

WTO Secretariat, *United States - Subsidies on Upland Cotton- Constitution of the Panel Established at the Request of Brazil*, WT/DS267/15 (May 23, 2003).

Panel Report, *United States-Definitive Safeguard Measures on Imports of Certain Steel Products*, WT/DS248/R (July 11, 2003).

Appellate Body Report, *United States-Definitive Safeguard Measures on Imports of Certain Steel Products*, WT/DS248/AB/R (Nov. 10, 2003).

Panel Report, *United States-Measures Affecting the Cross-border Supply of Gambling and Betting Services*, WT/DS285/R (Nov. 10, 2004).

Arbitrator Decision, *United States-Continued Dumping and Subsidy Offset Act of 200-Original Complaint by the European Communities-Recourse to Arbitration by the United States under Article 22.6 of the DSU*, WT/DS217/ARB/EEC (Aug. 31, 2004).

WTO REPORTS

Appellate Body, *Annual Report for 2003*, WT/AB/1 (May 7, 2004).

Application from Jordan, *Application for Accession to the Agreement on Government Procurement*, GPA/38 (July 19, 2000).

Committee on Subsidies and Countervailing Measures, *Semi-Annual Reports under Article 25.11 of the Agreement*, G/SCM/N/52/Add.1/Rev.5 (Oct. 18, 2002).

Committee on Trade and Development, *Technical Assistance and Training Plan 2004*, WT/COMTD/W/119/Rev.3 (Feb. 18, 2004).

Communication from the United States, *Preparation for the 1999 Ministerial Conference*, WT/GC/W/115 (Nov. 19, 1999).

Decision on China's Accession, *Accession of the People's Republic of China*, WT/L/432 (Nov. 23, 2001).

Dispute Settlement Body, *Overview of State of Play of WTO Disputes*, WT/DSB/W/209/Add.1 (Nov. 18, 2002).

Doha Ministerial Conference, Declaration on the TRIPS Agreement and Public Health, WT/MIN(01)/DEC/2 (Nov. 14, 2001).

Doha Ministerial Conference, Doha Ministerial Declaration, WT/MIN(01)/DEC/1 (Nov. 14, 2001).

Notification from Jordan, Committee on Anti-Dumping Practices-Committee on Subsidies *and Countervailing Measures-Notification of Laws and Regulations under Articles 18.5 and 32.6 of the Agreements*, G/ADP/N/1/JOR/2/Corr.1 (June 8, 2004).

Notification from Jordan, *Domestic Support of Jordan*, G/AG/N/JOR/1 (Sep. 17, 2002).

Notification from Jordan, *Implementations of Transparency Obligations*, G/SPS/27/Rev.7 (Nov. 1, 2000).

Proposal by Jordan, *WTO Negotiations on Agriculture*, G/AG/NG/W/140 (Mar. 22, 2001).

Working Party on the Accession of Jordan, *Introduction to Jordan's Agriculture Sector and Agricultural Policies*, WT/ACC/JOR/14 (July 1, 1998).

WTO Director-General, *Protocol of Accession of Jordan: Notification of Acceptance and Entry into Force*, WT/Let/333 (Mar. 14, 2000).

Working Party on the Accession of Jordan, *Report of the Working Party on the Accession of Jordan*, WT/ACC/JOR/33 (Dec. 3, 1999).

Working Party on the Accession of Jordan, *Membership and Terms of Reference*, WT/ACC/JOR/5 (Nov. 1, 1996)

Working Party Report on the Accession of Jordan, *Part II-Schedule of Specific Commitments on Services*, WT/ACC/JOR/33/Add.2.

Working Party on the Accession of Lithuania, *Membership and Terms of Reference*, WT/ACC/LTU/1/Rev.1 (June 14, 2000).

WTO and UNEP Secretariats, *Committee on Trade and Environment-Compliance and Dispute Settlement Provisions in the WTO and in Multilateral Environmental Agreements*, WT/CTE/W/191 (June 6, 2001).

WTO Secretariat, *Development Implications of Electronic Commerce*, WT/COMTD/w/51 (Nov. 23, 1998).

Committee on Agriculture, *WTO List of Net Food-Importing Developing Countries*, G/AG/5/Rev.5 (Mar. 26, 2002).

WTO Secretariat, *International Trade Statistics for 2003* (2003).

WTO Secretariat, *Goods Schedule of Jordan: Staging Annex*, WT/ACC/JOR/33/Add.1 (Dec. 3, 1999).

PRESS RELEASES

Press Release, Non-Governmental Organizations Facilities Provided During the WTO Ministerial Conference in Singapore, PRESS/TE 012 (Aug. 26, 1996).

Press Release, WTO Announces Appointments to Appellate Body, PRESS/32 (Nov. 29, 1995).

Press Release, WTO Completes Appointment of Appellate Body Members, PRESS/179 (May 22, 2000).

Press Release, WTO Chairpersons for 2004, PRESS/371 (Feb. 11, 2004).

Press Release, WTO Secretariat Reports Significant Decline in Anti-Dumping Investigations, PRESS/374 (Apr. 20, 2004).

UNITED STATES GOVERNMENT DOCUMENTS

A. LAWS

An Act to Implement the Free Trade Area Agreement between the United States and Israel of 1985, 19 U.S.C. § 2112 n. (2000).

Appropriations Act of 1990, 16 U.S.C. § 1537 (2000).

Balanced Budget and Emergency Deficit Control Act of 1985, 2 U.S.C. § 904 (2000).

Clean Air Act of 1967, 42 U.S.C. § 7401 (2000).

Clean Water Act of 1972, 33 U.S.C. §1251 (2000).

Comprehensive Environmental Response, Compensation, and Liability Act of 1980, 42 U.S.C. § 9601 (2000).

The Endangered Species Act of 1973, 16 U.S.C. § 1531 (2000).

Farm Security and Rural Investment Act of 2002, 7 U.S.C.A. §§ 7901-7918 (West Supp. 2005).

Foreign Relations Authorization Act of 2002, Pub. L. No. 107-228, § 604, 116 Stat. 1350, 1395 (2002).

Internet Tax Freedom Act of 1998, 47 U.S.C. §151 (2000).

Iran and Libya Sanctions Act of 1996, 50 U.S.C. § 1701 (2000).

The National Environmental Policy Act of 1969, 42 U.S.C. § 4332 (2000).

North American Free Trade Agreement Implementation Act of 1993, 19 U.S.C. § 3312 (2000).

The Resource Conservation and Recovery Act of 1976, 42 U.S.C. § 6901 (2000).

Trade and Development Act of 2000, 19 U.S.C. § 3721 (2000).

Trade Agreements Act of 1979, 19 U.S.C. § 2513 (2000).

Trade Act of 1974, 19 U.S.C. § 2436 (2000).

Tariff Act of 1930, 19 U.S.C. § 1202 (2000).

The Trade Sanctions Reform and Export Enhancement Act of 2000, 22 U.S.C. § 7210 (2000).

U.S. Const. art.1, § 2.

United States-Jordan Free Trade Agreement Implementation Act of 2001, 19 U.S.C. § 2112 n. (2000).

U.S. Digital Millennium Copyright Act of 1998, 17 U.S.C. §§ 512, 1201 (2000).

B. REGULATIONS

Amendment to the Generalized System of Preferences, 60 Fed. Reg. 25266 (Mar. 17, 1995).

Iranian Transactions Regulations, 31 C.F.R § 560 (1996).

List of Countries Requiring Cooperation with an International Boycott, 59 Fed. Reg. 65, 572 (Dec. 20, 1994).

List of Countries Requiring Cooperation with an International Boycott, 69 Fed. Reg. 75,
  604-01 (Dec. 17, 2004).

Major Drug Transit or Major Illicit Drug Producing Countries for FY05, 69 Fed. Reg.
  57809 (Sep. 28, 2004).

*Restore Nondiscriminatory Trade Treatment (Normal Trade Relations Treatment) to the
  Products of Afghanistan*, 67 Fed. Reg. 30535 (May 7, 2002).

*Special Information Sharing Procedures to Deter Money Laundering and Terrorist
  Activity*, 67 Fed. Reg. 9889 (Mar. 4, 2002).

Textiles and Textile Products, 19 C.F.R. § 12.130 (2005).

Treaty Trader, Treaty Investor, or Treaty Alien in a Specialty Occupation, 22 C.F.R. §
  41.51 (2005).

C. CONGRESSIONAL HEARINGS AND OTHER MATERIALS

H.R. Subcomm. on International Law, Immigration, and Refugees of the House Judiciary
  Comm., *Hearing on Immigration-Related Issues in the North American Free Trade
  Agreement*, 103d Cong. 1st Sess. 134 (Nov. 3, 1993).

H.R. Subcomm. on International Economic Policy and Trade of the Comm. on
  International Relations, *Hearing on Interfering with U.S. National Security Interests:
  The World Trade Organization and the European Union Challenge to the Helms-
  Burton Law*, 105th Cong. 1st Sess. 2-3 (Mar. 19, 1997).

Embassy of the United States in Jordan, *Rules of Origin Manual*, http://www.usembassy-
  amman.org.jo/FTA/Rulso.pdf (Aug. 2001).

Ltr. from Cher Young, Consular Assoc., U.S. Embassy in Amman, Jordan, to Bashar H.
  Malkawi, Student, Am. L. Sch., *Number of Visas Issued under the U.S.-Jordan
  Free Trade Agreement* (Aug. 5, 2003) (on file with author).

Sen. Comm. on Finance, *Hearing on Jordan Free Trade Agreement*, 107th Cong. 1st
  Sess. (Mar. 20, 2001).

USTR, *National Trade Estimate Report on Foreign Trade Barriers 2004*,
  http://www.ustr.gov/reports/nte/2004/arableague.pdf (accessed July 15, 2004).

USTR, *Memorandum of Understanding on Transparency in Dispute Settlement Under
  the Agreement Between the United States and Jordan on the Establishment of a Free
  Trade Area*, http://www.ustr.gov/regions/eu-med/middleeast/memodis.pdf (accessed
  Apr. 29, 2003).

USTR, *Memorandum of Understanding on Issues Related to the Protection of Intellectual Property Rights*, http://www.ustr.gov/regions/eu-med/middleeast/memopro.pdf (accessed Mar. 15, 2003).

USTR, *Side Letter on Marketing Approval of Pharmaceutical Products*, http://www.ustr.gov/regions/eu-med/middleeast/IPRcb.pdf (accessed Mar. 30, 2004).

D. UNITED STATES INTERNATIONAL TRADE COMMISSION MATERIALS

United States International Trade Commission, *Economic Impact on the United States of a U.S-Jordan Free Trade Agreement* (U.S. Govt. Printing Off. 2000).

United States International Trade Commission, *Processed Foods and Beverages: A Description of Tariff and Non-Tariff Barriers for Major products and Their Impact on Trade* (U.S. Govt. Printing Off. 2001).

United States International Trade Commission, *Monthly Reports on the State of the Steel Industry* (U.S. Govt. Printing Off. 1987).

United States International Trade Commission, *Effects of the Arab League Boycott of Israel on U.S. Businesses*, (U.S. Govt. Printing Off. 1994).

United States International Trade Commission, *Annual Report* (U.S. Govt. Printing Off. 1983).

E. CASES

Anheuser-Busch Brewing Assn. v. U.S., 207 U.S. 556 (1908).

Venez. Cement v. U.S., 372 F.3d 1284 (11th Cir. 2004).

Diamond v. Chakrabarty, 447 U.S. 303 (1980).

Georgetown Steel Corp. v. U.S., 810 F.Supp. 318 (Ct. Intl. Trade 1992).

Israel Aircraft Indus. Ltd., v. Sanwa Bus. Credit Corp., 16 F.3d 198 (7th Cir. 1994).

In re Nantucket, Inc., 677 F.2d 95 (C.C.P.A.1982).

Lung v. Freeman, 92 U.S. 275 (1875).

Mast Indus., Inc. v. U.S., 882 F. 2d. 1069 (Fed. Cir.1987)

Juice Prod. Assn. V. U.S., 628 F. Supp. 978 (Ct. Intl. Trade 1986).

Save Dom. Oil, Inc. v. U.S., 240 F. Supp. 2d 1342 (Ct. Intl. Trade 2002).

Save Dom. Oil v. U.S., 357 F.3d 1278 (Fed. Cir. 2004).

St. St. Bank v. Signature Fin. Group, Inc., 149 F.3d 1368 (Fed. Cir. 1998).

U.S. V. Guy Capps Inc., 204 F.2d 655 (4th Cir. 1953).

U.S. V. Murray, 621 F.2d 1163 (1st Cir. 1980).

E. U.S GOVERNMENT PUBLICATIONS

U.S. Dept. State, *Havana Charter for an International Trade Organization* (Off. Pub. Affairs 1948).

U.S. Dept. Com. *Somalia: A Country Study* (Lib. of Cong. 1993).

F. TREATIES

General Agreement on Tariffs and Trade, opened for signature Oct. 30, 1947, 61 Stat. T.I.A.S. No. 1700, 55 U.N.T.S. 187.

Protocol of Provisional Application to the General Agreement on Tariffs and Trade, signed Oct. 30, 1947, 61 Stat. A2051, 55 U.N.T.S. 308.

FOREIGN GOVERNMENT DOCUMENTS

Central Bank of Jordan, *Statistical Issues of the Central Bank of Jordan* (1998-2001).

Commercial Agency Law No. 28 of 2001, al Jaridah al Rasmiyah No. 4496 (Official Gazette) (July 16, 2001).

Customs Law No. 20 of 1998, al Jaridah al Rasmiyah No. 4305 (Official Gazette) (Oct. 1, 1998) as amended by Law No. 27 of 2000, al Jaridah al Rasmiyah No. 4443 (Official Gazette) (July 2, 2000).

Electoral Districts Regulation No. 42 of 2001, al Jaridah al Rasmiyah No. 4498 (Official Gazette) (July 23, 2001).

Internal Regulation of the Chamber of Deputies of 1996, al Jaridah al Rasmiyah No. 4106 (Official Gazette) (Mar. 16, 1996).

DUSTOUR Al-URDUN [Constitution] art. 26 (Jordan).

Jordan Department of Statistics, *Size of Population*, Jordan in Figures 2001 (No. 4, 2002).

Jordan Customs Department, *Selectivity in the ASYCUDA System*, http://www.customs.gov.jo/ publication.asp (accessed Mar. 4, 2005).

Jordan Customs Department, *How can you make a Self-Assessment of Duties and Taxes Payable on your car*, http://www.customs.gov.jo/ viewins.asp?id=222&title=Instructions (last updated Jan. 26, 2005).

Law Sanctioning Jordan's Accession to the World Trade Organization No. 4 of 2000, al Jaridah al Rasmiyah No. 4415 (Official Gazette) (Feb. 24, 2000).

Law of the Agricultural Marketing Organization No. 40 of 1988, al Jaridah al Rasmiyah (Official Gazette No. not avail.) (1988).

Provisional Law on Food Control No. 79 of 2001, al Jaridah al Rasmiyah No. 4522 (Official Gazette) (Dec. 13, 2001).

Provisional Copyright Law No. 52 of 2001, al Jaridah al Rasmiyah No. 4508 (Official Gazette) (Oct. 1, 2001).

Provisional Law on National Production Protection No. 50 of 2002, al Jaridah al Rasmiyah No. 4560 (Official Gazette) (Aug. 15, 2002).

Provisional Law on the Cancellation of the Agricultural Marketing Organization No. 22 of 2002 al Jaridah al Rasmiyah (Official Gazette No. not avail.) (May 16, 2002).

Provisional Law on Agriculture No. 44 of 2002, al Jaridah al Rasmiyah No. 4558 (Official Gazette) (Aug. 1, 2002).

Provisional Anti-Dumping and Subsidies Regulation No. 26 of 2003, al Jaridah al Rasmiyah No. 4587 (Official Gazette) (Mar. 2, 2003).

Regulation on Safeguard of National Production No. 55 of 2000, al Jaridah al Rasmiyah No. 4465 (Official Gazette) (Nov. 16, 2000).

Provisional Patents Law No. 71 of 2001, al Jaridah al Rasmiyah No. 4520 Official Gazette (Dec. 2, 2001).
Trademarks Law No. 34 of 1999, al Jaridah al Rasmiyah No. 4389 (Official Gazette) (Nov. 1, 1999).

DECISIONS OF THE JORDANIAN BAR ASSOCIATION

Decision No. 55/27, Journal of the Jordanian Bar Association (No. 11 1955).

Decision No. 57/24, Journal of the Jordanian Bar Association (No. 3 1957).

Decision No. 89/669, Journal of the Jordanian Bar Association (No. 6, 7 & 8 1991).

Decision No. 90/1104, Journal of the Jordanian Bar Association (No. 12 1991).

Decision No. 95/1554, Journal of the Jordanian Bar Association (No. 6 1996).

Decision No. 95/1418, Journal of the Jordanian Bar Association (No. 6 1996).

Decision No. 95/1067, Journal of the Jordanian Bar Association (No. 1, 2 & 3 1996).

NON-U.S. CASES

Case C-49/88, Al-Jubail Fertilizer Co. & others v. Council, 1991 E.C.R. I-03187 (1991).

"Sindicato Nacional de Controladores de de Trafico Aéreo," LXXVII/99 Semanario 46 (9a época 1999).

EUROPEAN UNION DOCUMENTS

The European Commission, *Internet Chat with E.U Commissioner Pascal Lamy and Egyptian Trade Minister Youssef Boutros-Ghali, New WTO Round. Talking Trade-What's Going on?* http://europa.eu.int/comm/chat/lamy9/index_en.htm (Nov. 21, 2002).

PRESENTATIONS AND ADDRESSES

Abulgasem, Mustafa Abdalla. Presentation, *The Arab-Mediterranean Countries between the Conditions of the Barcelona Process and the WTO: A Comparative Study* (Conference on Arab Countries and the World Trade Organization, Inst. Arab & Islamic Stud., U. Exeter, U.K, Sep. 23, 2002) (copy in file with author).

Hassouna, Hussein. Ambassador of the League of Arab States to the U.S., Address, *The League of Arab States and International Law* (Am. U. Sch. L., Apr. 21, 2004) (copy on file with author).

INTERVIEWS

Telephone Interview with Maha Ali, Director of Foreign Trade Policy Department, Ministry of Industry and Trade (May 18, 2004).

Telephone Interview with Fakhry Hazimeh, Counselor of Economic Affairs, Permanent Mission of Jordan to the WTO and U.N. (July 9, 2004).

Interview with Edmund R. Saums II, Director for Middle East Affairs, Office of the United States Trade Representative, in Washington, D.C (Oct. 27, 2004).

Printed in Great Britain
by Amazon.co.uk, Ltd.,
Marston Gate.